History and Myth

History and Myth

Arthur Lower
and the Making of
Canadian Nationalism

Edited by
WELF H. HEICK

University of British Columbia Press

Canadian Shared Cataloguing in Publication Data

Lower, Arthur Reginald Marsden, 1889 —
    History and Myth: Arthur Lower and the
    making of Canadian nationalism / [selected
    essays by Arthur Lower]; edited by
    Welf H. Heick.

    1. Canada — Addresses, essays, lectures.
2. Nationalism — Canada — Addresses, essays,
lectures. I. Heick, Welf Henry, 1930- ed.
II. Title. III. Title: Arthur Lower and the
making of Canadian nationalism.
FC   971'.008
[LC: F1026.L]
[UBC: F5012,L69]
ISBN 0-7748-0035-6

International Standard Book Number 0-7748-0035-6.

Printed in Canada.

This book has been published with the help of a gift to scholarly publishing made in honour of Dr. Harold S. Foley for his distinguished services to the University of British Columbia.

Contents

Acknowledgements

The articles in this book were published originally in other books and journals. The author, editor, and publisher are grateful to the following publishers for permission to reprint the material cited.

Canada Month: for "The Forest, Heart of a Nation," *Canada Month,* November 1963, pp. 21-23.

The Canadian Banker: for "The Massey Report," *Canadian Banker* 59 (Winter 1952): 22-32.

Canadian Forum: for "Bonnie Chairlie's Gone Awa,'" *Canadian Forum* 19 (May 1939): 44-46.

Canadian Historical Association: for "The Origins of Democracy in Canada," C.H.A. *Report* (1930): 65-70 and "Two Ways of Life: The Primary Antithesis of Canadian History," C.H.A. *Report* (1943): 15-28.

Culture: for "Two Nations or Two Nationalities," *Culture* 4 (December 1943): 470-81.

Dalhousie Review: for "Foreign Policy and Canadian Nationalism," *Dalhousie Review* 15 (April 1935): 29-36.

Duke University Press: for "Metropolis and Hinterland," *South Atlantic Quarterly* 70 (Summer 1971): 386-403.

History: for "The Evolution of the Sentimental Idea of Empire," *History* n.s. 11 (January 1927): 289-303.

Information Canada: for "Brief to the Committee of the Senate on Human Rights," In Canada, Parliament, Senate, *Proceedings of the Special Committee on Human Rights and Fundamental Freedoms* (Ottawa: King's Printer, 1950), pp. 311-25.

The Institute of Public Affairs, Dalhousie University: for "The Maritimes as a Strategic Point in North America," *Public Affairs* 4 (December 1940): 57-60.

Journal of Canadian Studies: for "That humble fellow, the historian: Some reflections on writing history," *Journal of Canadian Studies* 7 (February 1972): 45-50.

Maclean's: for "Our Shoddy Ideals," 1 November 1937, pp. 24, 39-40; "If We Joined the U.S.A.," 15 June 1948, pp. 7-8, 71-74; "What This Country Needs Is Ten New Provinces," 15 October 1948, pp. 7, 77-79; "I Came Back and I Am Content," 1 July 1951, pp. 2, 47-48; "Is the RCMP a Threat to Our Liberty?" 6 July 1957, pp. 8, 57-58, and "Would Canada Be Better Off without Quebec?" 14 December 1964, pp. 27, 51-52.

Ontario Educational Association: for "Canada and a Free Society: Liberalism, Its Nature and Prospects," *Annual Report* (1948): 68-75.

Queen's Quarterly: for "The Case Against Immigration," *Queen's Quarterly* 37 (Summer 1930): 557-74 and for permission to include a revised version of "Time, Myth and Fact: The Historian's Commodities," *Queen's Quarterly* 63 (Summer 1957): 241-49.

The Royal Society of Canada: for "The Canadian University," *Proceedings and Transactions,* 3rd Series, 47 (1953): section 2, 1-16 and "Speaking to Each Other," *Proceedings and Transactions,* 3rd series, 56 (1962): 69-80.

Saturday Night: for "Is Distrust of Ability Formula for Success?" 23 April 1955, pp. 7-8.

University of Manitoba: for "National Policy ... Revised Version," *Manitoba Arts Review* 3 (Spring 1943): 5-14 and "A Bright Future for a Dull Subject," *Manitoba Arts Review* 3 (Fall 1943): 10-21.

University of Texas Press: for "Professor Webb and 'The Great Frontier' Thesis," in *The New World Looks at Its History,* eds. A. R. Lewis and T. F. McGann (Austin: University of Texas Press, 1963), pp. 142-54.

University of Toronto Press: for "The Social Sciences in the Post-War World," *Canadian Historical Review* 22 (March 1941): 1-13 and "Religion and Religious Institutions," in *Canada,* ed. George W. Brown (Toronto: University of Toronto Press, 1950), pp. 457-83.

Foreword

The questions that any man must ask of himself when he looks back over his life are: What have I been doing? What does it all amount to? What is it worth? These questions concern the whole range of life, and the answers to them must, in many facets, be personal, too personal for answering in the public place of the printed word. But one of the largest facets of an individual's life is presented by his professional career, and this is a public matter and may be publicly discussed. This is especially true for anyone whose public career has made use of public language. It may not apply with direct force to the mathematician or to the scientist. But to those who have put themselves down in words, whether written or spoken, its application is direct. They need not justify their work, but they must not shrink from examining and assessing it.

The historian is no more under this necessity than his close colleagues, such as those who devote themselves to the practice and theory of government or to the public phases of philosophy or to the economy. Neither is he under it less. And since he is a writing man, it is natural for him to continue his writing in summary and explanation.

These words may stand as the *Apologia pro vita mea*. I have worked at history and the teaching of history more or less all my life. I can vouch many good men to warranty that as a teacher I have been successful. Whether as an historian I have added up to a great deal, I do not know. There would be two judgments: those of others and my own. Reviews of my books have invariably been kindly and often eulogistic. My own internal reviews of what I have done are another matter, and it is hard to know whether I have been a just judge: in their own cause, few men are.

It would be tedious merely to examine a succession of books and articles in some attempt to explain their meaning and purpose: they are there, and they can speak for themselves. On the other hand, it may not be without point to try and describe what has lain behind the innumerable words I have put on paper. In television broadcasts, now published,[1] Ramsay Cook asked me how I came to be an historian. I answered him, partly in fun, that "I was called of God to be an historian." Ramsay said he did not believe me. There was, however, a grain of truth in what I said.

---

[1] Eleanor Cook, ed., *The Craft of History* (Toronto: Canadian Broadcasting Corporation, 1973).

There has not been a time in my life, from earliest childhood on, when I have not been attracted by the mystic quality that hangs over time past. It is the same quality that hangs over far places. These things still possess that same quality, unchanged and just about as forceful. "I have never rolled to Rio," says the man in the song, "and I suppose I never will." Well, I have rolled to Rio and it does not seem nearly as far away as it once did. But there are plenty of places to which I shall never roll, just as there are plenty of books I shall never read. That I regret.

That is point number one, the sheer attraction of far-off things that excites the imagination. There is no theological sense in which this could be deemed being "called of God," but it indicates something deep within my nature, a kind of predestination, and perhaps that has a little of what is meant by the old phrase "called of God."

Point number two would have to be pleasure in self-expression, delight in words. If one does not have something of this about him, I do not see how he can write, except in a mechanical, lifeless way. Recall how, in the scene with the players in *Hamlet,* the principal actor was carried away by his passion over Hecuba. "What's he to Hecuba or Hecuba to him?" asks Hamlet in the soliloquy that follows the play scene. The query is more directly applicable to the actor than it is to others, but even to the historian it is applicable in part: that is, he must be caught up in what he is doing, and so see further into the murk of the past than he otherwise would.

Nine times out of ten, he will do this best if he is writing about a subject that is near (and dear) to him. In most cases that means a topic set in his own society. In my case, that means, further, about Canadian history. I have done an occasional article on an English topic and some which discuss the relations of Canada and the United States. As a result of an extensive trip some years ago, I wrote a great deal on the countries of the southern hemisphere, either in, or formerly in, the Commonwealth. My publishers apparently thought few in Canada would be interested and refused to publish it. Yet all these subjects were not entirely removed from my own concerns. For example, the parallels between Canada and South Africa are close. Such matters give one *concern,* I think, to be more than a mere fact-gatherer. A person must have concern and preserve his objectivity as best he can.

The connections between this absorption in one's concern and its expression in words no doubt are not direct and they are extremely subtle, but they do exist. For one thing, the individual who has had something of this inner experience wants to tell others something about it. The connection between historical writing and literature is close: history is a branch of literature (among other things), and while good, conscientious work can be done by those who have no literary gifts, their work will be a bird without wings. To rise to heights, in historical writing as in any other kind of writing, men must be touched, if ever so lightly, with a spark of the divine fire. That few of us historians have these gifts is evidenced by the reluctance with which students of literature admit us into the circle of the élite. The very greatest, the Thucydides and the Gibbons, may be given a polite seat somewhere towards the back of that audience, but to the lesser lights the door is usually shut. They have to find their compensation in other directions; in consequence, many of them attempt to turn themselves into "scientists" and thus to preserve their *amour propre*.

I have never been able to convince myself that I am to be taken very seriously as a "scientist." I gave this path a serious try and spent many a month compiling price indexes, tables of imports and exports, and the like. As these were all historical, they had, and have, their value. I could claim no epoch-making significance for them. They were *useful*. They were also the extreme of aridity. Luckily I moved away from them into pleasanter surroundings, and just as useful. One of my books is a half-way house on this road, the *North American Assault on the Canadian Forest*. It is as "scientific" as my capacity permits: that is, it has no *parti pris*, except a certain sympathy for the destroyed forests; it is objective, statistical, based mostly on original material. It is useful in the sense that snow shovels or cars are useful.

It is no sin to be *useful*. In fact — and this may merely reflect my puritan youth — usefulness seems to me, in one way or another, to be the ultimate test. What is useful is a hard question to answer. Saints' prayers were once deemed highly useful: they would be little valued today. The snare to our feet in this word *useful* is the adverb *directly*. To most men, the pursuit of the will-o'-the-wisp of poetic excellence is "useless." Yet poetry has its place in life; some would argue a great place. Historians are always tempted to retreat behind the shield of "usefulness." That is all right, providing they do not attach too narrow a meaning to the term. At their best, they are probably as useful as the epic poet, celebrators of great deeds in a great way, inspirers of their people. And so they may find themselves in the presence of the indubitably great, the Homers and the Virgils.[2]

The idea of usefulness may be explored still farther. To be useful necessarily means to have quality, to be trained, in other words, to be something more than an amateur bungler. This brings in the idea of professionalism. Years ago, the Canadian historian had little feeling of professionalism about him. He may not have been a bungler (though sometimes

[2]For the relationships between history and epic, see E. M. W. Tillyard, *The English Epic and Its Background* (London: Chatto and Windus, 1954), especially Part I, Chapter III and Part IV, Chapters V and XI.

he was), but he need not be a professional. Special training was not given a high place. Neither was scholarship, or in more old-fashioned terms, "learning." History was often left to the journalist, to the politician, active or retired, to clergymen — to anyone who wished to try his hand at it. There were some good features about this. After all, while prior to the nineteenth century there was no professional training for historians, there were many great historians. A good intelligence, a wide experience and some education would carry a man far. Over the years, that has almost ceased to be the situation.

Today we have the elaborate apparatus of professionalism surrounding the cult of history — vast archives and libraries, historical journals, graduate schools, publishing houses — all the formidable apparatus provided by a society which approves of professional expertise. There is little doubt that as a result the writing of history has moved forward. The past has become much clearer than it was: there are fewer misinterpretations, myths have been disintegrated, truth has come to prevail over wider areas. Those who write history today, and for a good many years past, know how to observe the great canons (the first of which is no falsification), how to do their research, how to tuck their footnotes neatly in, how to dot all the "i's" and cross the "t's." They may not write brilliantly, but in general they write well. "Give me ain spark of nature's fire, that's all the learning I desire," shouted Bobby Burns. Do our modern historians have that spark? The only answer I could give is that some of them do and some of them do not. There is always a temptation to assert that the old hand-made product was superior to the modern machine-made article. It would not be "scientific" to come down on either side. We come to individuals and as individuals they must be assessed, not as members of an age.

As for myself, all I can say is that I have always tried to write well, that I had a good training in English, both at school and college, and that I have enjoyed shaping words. For the more mechanical aspect of the craft, I have been as careful as I could, and while I may not have mounted very high, I do not think I have floundered dismayingly. I agree, however, that there is danger in over-professionalism. If a man comes to be an expert, he is in peril. He may cease to be much else. I hope that our Canadian school of history will not bog down in mere professionalism, mere expertise, but that it will retain the creative spark of life.

When I became assistant to the late Adam Shortt at the Board of Historical Publications, Ottawa, I consciously set out to make myself an "expert" in Canadian history. It seemed the logical thing to do. I learned a good deal about the *craft* of history there, if on a narrow plane. When I went to Harvard, the gates opened wide: the utmost professionalism was joined to a humane and philosophical approach. I think Harvard carried professionalism too far, as Americans in general do. It was hardly respectable to stop and chat about this and that: the fresh water that may come out of a spring of apparently aimless conversation was not highly regarded. Idleness was not for the Harvard intellectual. *Non dulce erat in loco desipere.* I defy anyone to submit to the rigorous Harvard training and not come out with a deep sense of the importance of that which he had set his hand to do.

There were other matters conjoined to the high calling whereunto Harvard (God-like, if not quite God) had called me. First of all I was by nature serious-minded. Secondly, as I have already said, I had always been fascinated by the mystery of the past. Thirdly, my nature also bent me strongly in the direction of the "public thing," the *res publica,* the life of the community to which I belonged; that is, to some form of politics. I had often thought of a political career, but luckily I came to understand I would not do for that, even had opportunity presented itself. But I was always concerned with the human condition, especially in my own part of the world, and this was heavily reinforced by the dominant place that evangelistic religion then held in Canadian life. And I had grown up in an expanding and optimistic Canada, much taken up with the great task of the occupation of the West. Being also strongly attached to the local gods, loving my surroundings, I was bent in the direction, among fields of history, of Canadian history. I may have also been influenced by having been brought up, if not exactly in, yet on the edges of Huronia, familiar with the stirring tales that clustered round that term. Further, for some reason or another that I cannot explain, I had from my boyhood a strongly marked sense of the group. This could have stopped at the simple level of "the team," but it went on to interest me, greatly bolstered by my reading, in the historic "team," that is to say, the state. At first for me this was the British state, but gradually it changed into my own, the Canadian. As time went on, it naturally became more complex and I came to see a little way into its nature. This interest has lasted me the rest of my life.

When I first went to Harvard, I framed for myself a definite field of study. I wanted to see how the civilization of Europe came to be transferred to America and how the transfer affected it. At that time I had never heard the name of Frederick Jackson Turner or of anyone else who had given special attention to that kind of history. I had, however, read Parkman, all of him, and Parkman had certainly not turned my imagination aside from the topic, far from that. I selected my Harvard courses as well as might be in relation to the central subject. I suppose that it is what I have been examining ever since: how does a civilization get transferred from one environment to another, and what are the effects of the transfer on it? This involves looking at the civilization before the transfer and at what happens to it after it is made. I already had a fair knowledge of the English way of life, from my undergraduate training, my parents, my war service, and my general reading. To that, I now joined American colonial history, a formative course on "The Frontier" (the heritage of Turner) and other courses in American history. For them I here pay my respects to Professors Samuel Eliot Morison and Frederick Merk, as to the others who are no longer with us. Of Canadian history, Harvard was then as innocent as, until quite lately, it has remained. The omission at least increased my sense of proportion: as a fellow student frankly told me: "Canada was only a cultural hinterland of the United States." Secretly I hoped that it could become something more and that I could aid in making it more. I could take no narrow view; anything that concerned Canada must concern me.

I returned to Canada in that spirit. The great days of occupying and settling the land had already passed, but Canada was still in its beginnings: it may have been formed geographically and constitutionally, but it had a long weary road to travel until its inhabitants came together in anything like a genuine community. They seem little nearer that point today than when I began to become curious about it. I have found in this tension between faith and doubt, faith in one's country and doubt as to whether it can ever amount to anything, or indeed, continue to exist, a stimulus to thought and conduct. "Make it amount to something," a voice has always kept saying to me. That voice explains my peripheral activities (some of which are reflected in various articles in this volume), activities some of which may not be strictly historical and some of which may be looked at askance by younger men schooled in strict professionalism, but all of which fit into my central core, good citizenship.

Of such activities, I have often spoken. One of them, the wilderness, has directly inspired a considerable share of what I have written. One of the books I most enjoyed writing was *Unconventional Voyages.* It gives a sufficient idea of what untamed nature has always meant to me. That interest has grown of late years into concern for our physical environment. As I see the horrors of the "developer" pushing us out of first this place and then that, watch the trees fall, the fields disappear, and the steel cells rise, I become more and more concerned with the way in which "civilization" is turning this country (and others) into a prison. Oh, for an atom bomb, I sometimes call out in my despair. We once had the freedom of nature and some of its simplicity. Today we are crowded closer and closer, with the ills that crowding produces. An atom bomb would be stringent, it is true, but it's the equivalent of atom bombs or slowing down breeding that alone can in the long run save this old earth. Horrible prospect and one that if Canadians have wisdom, they can avoid. Can they?

Of another topic, politics, I have already spoken. I quickly realized that I could be no party man, but it was not until I was in my thirties that I saw clearly that the old Conservatism of my family was not for me. That brought me into the middle of the road, and it is there that I have walked ever since. I have always been attracted to the moderate left, which involves humanitarian sympathy for the unfortunate (this came easily from a son of the old Methodist church), but I have had little patience with the doctrinaires of that left who would prescribe a panacea for our ills. A society is too complex for panaceas. And is not compromise of the essence in a country like this? How could Canada exist without a willingness to compromise between Catholic and Protestant, French and English, East and West, town and country, low tariff and high tariff? A rigid attitude in all such matters would simply blow the country to pieces.

This lesson I found it hard to learn. I suppose I am not by nature a tolerant person. At any rate, to accept modes of life very different from my own was hard for me. Part of that was simply the ignorance of youth, the inability to see what the other lot were really like. My days in the north country did much for me in that respect, for I got to know and to like many different kinds of people — French, English, Indian, and the innumerable foreign stocks of the average "camp." I did not get nearly as far in that knowledge as opportunity afforded, and that I regret. Eventually, joined to my long residence in Ottawa and to the study of Canadian history, it at least brought me out to full acceptance of "the French fact." Years ago, I used to proclaim to my students that Canada could only continue to exist if it could succeed in becoming a completely bi-cultural (not necessarily bilingual) country. I still proclaim it and I still find the idea raises many hackles. It will be for the future to smooth those hackles.

This urgency for tolerance and understanding between French and English is reflected, I hope, in both of my more considerable books, *Colony to Nation* and *Canadians in the Making,* as also in the piece called "Two Ways of Life."

In an introduction to such a book as this I must touch on one more of my peripheral activities, my interest in civil liberties. Like the others, this comes directly out of my own nature, but the place of history in it has also been large. I suppose I have always been something of a rebel, which has meant being "agin' the government." I have found it hard to submit to formal discipline. I read Macaulay when I was about eighteen. He answered to something deep within me. I sum it up in one word: Freedom. Who that acquainted himself with seventeenth-century England could take another line? Not for me the "sainted martyr," Charles the First! No, indeed, I was with Cromwell and *his* "Saints." Or, preferably, with John Hampden, withstanding the petty tyrant of the fields. To the history of seventeenth-century England, I owe my deep appreciation of the blessings of English constitutionalism and the majestic institutional framework with which it endowed us. Several of my articles reflect this concern.

In concluding, I must ask myself the serious question (and leave it to others to answer) whether with these interests and many others distracting my attention and sullying the purity of my research, I am an historian at all. Perhaps a mere publicist, a kind of magnified journalist, a propagandist. In going through life, everyone wants a compass, except of course, the completely objective, unprejudiced observer, the Platonic ideal of the "researcher" sitting up in the moon observing foolish mortals, the observer whose sole concern is "truth." Pilate's jesting question has not yet got answered. I am quite sure that no amount of historical research will answer it. Historical research will clear away much rubbish and perhaps allow the dim outlines of an answer to be discerned. Luckily I have not been handicapped by being a pure researcher, a blank page to be written on by an invisible hand. I have just tried to be as fair and impartial within my lights and knowledge as I could be. And something which no pure researcher should ever be, I have always been *concerned.* And I have never tried to pose as something other than I am: a citizen of no mean country, devoted to its well-being, and beyond that, to trying to build the wall of civilization a little higher and of more desirable material.

All such matters stray into the pages of *My First Seventy-five Years.*

Here I stop. I am an old man, but I find the panorama of the past, a certain stretch of which is now spread out in my memory, as enticing as ever it was. I cannot discern it simply. I cannot see clear evidence of the hand of God in history, as Ranke thought he could. I am a child of my times, with all their uncertainties and their scepticisms. If there is some inscrutable destiny or deity behind all this vast process of history, it is too remote for me to bother about. I am a child of the here and now. A horrible confession for a man pretending to be an historian. But an historian is not merely one "interested in the past": primarily he is interested in humanity and in all that lights its way, past and present. *Pax vobiscum.*

Arthur R. M. Lower
August 5, 1974

Introduction

In Canada's centennial year Arthur Lower wrote in the preface to his autobiography *My First Seventy-five Years*: "Any academic worth his salt should be able to play the kind of role I have played, provided he does not get himself idiosyncratically out of line with the forces that actuate the country's life." Throughout his adult life, from World War I on, he did concern himself with the forces that actuated Canada's life: the domestic changes that were transforming his country from an agriculture-based colony to an urban, industrial nation and the external pressures that were shifting the focus of power within the North Atlantic triangle from Great Britain to the United States. His purpose was to cultivate a mature Canadian nation and to educate his fellow Canadians concerning their role in the operation of these forces.

As historian and involved citizen, Arthur Lower has been one of the most important intellectual figures in twentieth-century Canada. In writing his autobiography he performed a function unique in Canadian academic circles. Modestly stating that he would "describe a more or less typical Canadian career that has touched life at a certain number of points," he really wrote a brilliant picture of his generation. This volume presents a set of his essays: read together with his autobiography, they produce the powerful image of a Canadian vitally involved in the life of his country.

During his career Lower wrote — one should say "has written" for even in retirement a new manuscript has constantly been in some stage of preparation — twelve book-length monographs, slightly over three hundred essays, and well over one hundred book reviews.[1] The essays chosen for this volume represent his positions upon the great variety of topics, historical and contemporary, that caught his eclectic attention. To a remarkable degree, they also reflect the urgent issues of the past half-century in Canada and of the present scene. The choice of essays is basically my own, but I have consulted frequently with Arthur Lower. With one exception, Essay #1, they are presented as they were originally published, the only changes being of an editorial nature.

One of the major questions Canadians have faced in the twentieth century has been the definition of Canadian nationalism. It was to this task that Lower addressed himself as historian, as educator, and as publicist.

[1]See pp. 317-33.

As historian he has given leadership to and challenged other Canadian historians. As educator and publicist he also stands in the first rank, for he used history as a base for comment, criticism, and prophecy. It is here that the strength of his personality and of his passionate concern that the historian be involved, as his own Foreword makes clear, show through.

Late in his career he moved into the speculative field of the philosophy of history in order to argue the case for his own approach. The historian, if he is first rate, is an artist, and it is his task to combine fact and myth to create a story which has meaning and significance for the generation which will read this history and to give the people the knowledge and strength to carry on the task of nation building. The problem with most "professional" historians is that they have remained too much like ostriches, buried in the sand of facts, unable to look up to the heights of myth.

In the formative years of his professional career he sought out the factual data from which could be deduced the key to a Canadian national identity. The first position he adopted as a frame of reference and a basis of explanation was Frederick Jackson Turner's "frontier thesis." This approach dominated his doctoral dissertation, his early published essays, and the four of his monographs published before World War II. During this period his chief interest was in economic history, specifically currency developments and forest industries. The latter subject shows the timeliness of his works; as he decried the spoilage of natural resources, he forecast the ecological concerns of Canadians four decades later.

The quality of the work he did within the frontier thesis made Lower the best of Canadian frontier historians. However, this thesis proved too parochial and economic history too lifeless to satisfy him. His great concern for the country led him to participate actively in the great debate of the 1930's and the Second World War. Out of this concern rose his fundamental belief that the nature of the Canadian nation could be understood only in terms of two dialectics: between the two ways of life of the French and the English and between colony and mother country. The fact of "two ways of life" is the primary antithesis which gives Canadian nationhood its distinctiveness. Canadians' success or failure in grappling with this fact will determine the fate of the nation. The secondary antithesis resides in the desire of Canadians to achieve a maturity and freedom, psychological even more than political, from the imperial British connection. In 1946 he combined these two dialectics and added the evidence from a wide range of areas of Canadian history to write *Colony to Nation*. His commitment, literary flair, and imagination make this book his greatest piece of historical writing.

His shift away from the frontier thesis to the two great antitheses had a subsidiary effect. A son of the frontier, he recognized, albeit reluctantly, the powerful influence of the metropolitan centre and began to apply the "metropolitan thesis" in his work.

In Arthur Lower's recognition that history is a study relating to man, his hopes, his fears, and his intellectual curiosity, the subject is clearly classified among the humanities. However he also sees history as one of the social sciences — a tool whereby the citizen comes to understand the past, appreciate the present, and plan for the future. He understood history in this latter sense in his roles as educator and publicist. On the campus he used the classroom to instil in his students a deep appreciation of their country and a desire to shape future events. Through essays in both professional and popular journals he sought to teach all levels of society what was required of them before they would meet the high standard of values necessary to a genuine Canadian nationhood. Like the historian, so the average Canadian was called, not to be a mere passenger on the ship of state but to take "his watch on the bridge."[2]

As publicist Arthur Lower has written on a wide range of topics germane to the task of fostering the development of the Canadian nation: how a culture matures, the standards that culture needs to meet, the problems facing Canadians in the area of national life and how to resolve them. More specifically his prime interests have been in the areas of civil liberties, immigration, education, and external relations. His position on these matters is based on a well thought-out conservative liberalism. The tenets of this liberalism were most fully developed in *This Most Famous Stream.*

Style was constantly near the forefront of his thought while he wrote — and in his criticism of his students' work. Fact and myth had to be presented with commitment and flair! An inherent literary bent had been strengthened by an academic training which stressed the literary as much as the historical and by life-long personal cultivation. The result was a powerful, precise, charming style that has been used as a bench mark by fellow historians and samples of which have found their way into literary anthologies.

Over a decade ago Hugh MacLennan, Lower's contemporary in the search for the Canadian national identity, wrote:

> For a long time, it seems to me, we Canadians have been willing to admit that ours is a deeply neurotic society. If talking about troubles and frustrations were all that is needed for a mature literature, we would have had a huge literature already, for we have been talking about them most volubly for several generations.
>
> But a neurotic who merely talks about himself is not only a bore to others; he is a nuisance to his own family and a burden to himself.

[2]See p.114.

If there is one thing an art can never afford to be, it is boring. The causes of the neuroses must be faced, admitted and described, they must be lifted out of the dark of the mind and made visible. Within a society, it is the function and duty of the artists to do this, and as we look back on history, we find that most great art has emerged from the agony of this self-healing process ....

Being myself so deeply involved in the excitement of building my own little section of the bridge, I am perhaps a poor witness in the matter. But I think — indeed to me it is now self-evident — that the familiar process of the maturing of a colony into a nation, though not by any means complete, is at least well under way.[3]

To Arthur Lower, historian, educator, publicist, citizen, must be given a great deal of the credit for the distance that the maturation process has moved forward. Present day Canadians must look at his work in order to learn what needs to be done to complete the process. Future generations will need to refer to his work to understand how Canada came to be an aware, mature nation.

W. H. H.

[3]Hugh MacLennan, "After 300 Years, Our Neurosis is Relevant," in *Canada: A Guide to the Peaceable Kingdom,* ed., William Kilbourn (Toronto: Macmillan, 1970), pp. 8-9.

In these days and in this malleable society of ours, the citizen cannot be a mere spectator, a mere dissector of society: he must also be a formative agent in society. He cannot, if he would, be a mere passenger on board ship. He must stand his watch on the bridge and help with the navigation—help lay out the course, which means that he must know where he wants to go. That task is laid on him: it is laid both on his pen and on his voice. He will have to perform it as his conscience directs but he will refuse it at his peril.

I.

Historical Essays: Speculative.

Philosophy of history is a relatively fresh area for Canadian historians. Reflecting in the twilight of his career, Arthur Lower crystallized the position fundamental to his role as a builder of the Canadian nation. In "History and Myth" (Essay #1), a recent recasting of "Time, Myth and Fact," he argues that in order for history to transmit to its people the vitality necessary for cultural awareness and nation building, it needs to be a mixture of fact and myth. In "That humble fellow, the historian" (Essay #2) he sets forth his belief that the historian must be committed to something beyond history to rise above the second rate and achieve greatness. In his own case that something was "the act of faith" that creating Canada has been.

1 | *History and Myth*[1]

History begins in myth.[2] It usually begins with some kind of "origins" myth, of which the creation myth is a familiar example. Virgil began Rome's history for it by obligingly inventing a creation myth. The Homeric myths do not have much to say about creation: they are "beginnings" myths, myths of the early days, "when there were giants in the land." *Paradise Lost,* like the *Aeneid,* is a synthetic myth. So powerful were both of these that for millions of mankind they actually constituted a version of history. Milton's epic probably comes closer to supplying the accepted account of the Christian creation myth than does the original, though the original, in view of its widespread dispersion and great tenacity, may be regarded

[1]"History and Myth" was written in 1974 and is published for the first time here. It is an expansion of the basic points first set forth in "Time, Myth and Fact: The Historian's Commodities," *Queen's Quarterly* 54 (Summer 1957): 241-49.
[2]The common meaning for myth carries a suggestion of untruth. Myth is equated to an imaginary nothing. The dictionary meaning is "a traditional story of unknown authorship, ostensibly with an historical basis, but serving to explain some phenomenon of nature (such as) the origin of man or the customs, institutions, religious rites of people" (Webster's *New World Dictionary,* 1962). I use the term here to mean "account accepted," "that which is generally believed to be true." This is not far from the formal dictionary meaning.

as the second most powerful of the myths of our Western world.

The most powerful of all myths is that of the founding stories of Christianity, the crucifixion and the resurrection. Here is a version of what actually happened, accepted over many generations in minute detail and of infinite influence over the lives and affairs of men. What its relationship is to what actually happened no one knows.

The myth, as the illustrations indicate, acquires all the hardness of actual fact: all the verisimilitude, all the picturesque and local detail, the minute detail, of what might be assumed to have actually happened. It supplies words for speakers and works them out in logical relationship to their circumstances. The imaginative mind of man allows no detail to escape. The result is the fusion, or if you like, the confusion of myth and fact, the perfect artistic fusion. The great myths give birth to the great epics and "scriptures," while the epics and "scriptures" re-establish and affirm and extend the myth.

The myth becomes so fortified in this process that it is capable of withstanding the heaviest assaults; one of its main bastions, adding to its accepted authenticity, is its emotional colouring. It becomes impiety to doubt the myth. Those who question are disloyal, heretical, outcast. Again, the Christian myth supplies the clearest example. Only as other factors begin to weaken the myth is criticism able to come in, and this entrance of criticism is delayed by a thousand inhibitions: in my youth, for example, among simple people dropping the Holy Scriptures to the floor, if done on purpose, was a grievous offence. And yet how far a cry from that to the intellectual processes by which the Scriptures have been eroded! The intellectual assault is generated out of the myth, conditioned by the myth, and in its development gives rise to great quantities of learning, to the most astute textual observation, to the study of languages, regions, and cultures which may eventually substantially destroy the myth but in so doing create vast new masses of fact and a new sense of time.

Again the Christian myth offers the best example. It is a direct step from "searching the Scriptures" to the spade of the archeologist and its revolutionary effects. A minor example will illustrate the patient learning that is in itself a pious exercise upon the myth and yet, in its sum, may be destructive of it. A colleague, a New Testament scholar, told me quite excitedly one day that he had found a new translation for one of the words in the familiar "Consider the lilies of the field: they toil not, neither do they spin!" The evident intention, to suggest that the lilies were good for no practical purpose, would be brought out much more clearly and would be more faithful to the original if a term from the flax industry were substituted for "toil." The passage would then read: "they scutch not, neither do they spin." That is, "they cannot be dressed by beating out, nor can they be spun." The translation puts meaning into a rather obscure passage.

It represents years of work — just one word clarified.

The myth provides an account of the origins of the group, makes this account acceptable as actual fact, and buttresses it with piety. The account, or myth, lasts indefinitely, but is eventually eroded by intellectual processes arising from the erstwhile guardians of the myth — the priesthood and their off-shoots. Its erosion results in vast extensions of knowledge of fact and of time.

The myth gives colouring and force to the group's conception of its own destiny. A myth of this sort may arise at any moment in history; "Rule Britannia!" for example. The group's conception of its own destiny is expanded by its consciousness of itself and by its experience. Consciousness of self and experience we call history: the group's history may be known, or it may be fancied: for it, the record, however it may stand, is its history, a satisfactory account of itself. In French Canada, for example, which has a "sopoforic" combination of myth and fact as its history, *la survivance* is the key word — it explains all, and in satisfactory — and satisfying — fashion. The word is itself the myth.

Myth, plus consciousness of destiny, plus satisfactory account of the group's experience, gives, in certain striking major cases (though minor ones fit in, as, again, the example of French Canada), the world view, the plan of time, and an attempted reconciliation of the eternal clash between good and evil, right and wrong, "God" and "the devil." The age-old bargain between God and the devil gets many a classical representation. God becomes stirred out of his complacency into fresh acts of creativeness simply from the necessity of beating the devil, whom He cannot allow to win, but whom He cannot defeat by some piece of divine super-magic. The thread runs through the Hebrew creation myths, the Book of Job, the Aeschylean portrayal of the struggle between Zeus and Prometheus. It is conspicuous in the Faust legend, and Goethe builds up his great poem around it.

For myth as "world view," "a plan of time," the Christian religion itself provides the most familiar of illustration. The original myth-foundation is simple and huge: it colours imaginations and awakens sympathies. It is buttressed by every known experience, aesthetic, emotional, intellectual, mystical, political. In each of these fields of experience are solid masses of achievement. The myth takes on rainbow hues of every sort for every man. It has provided for many generations of men satisfactory explanations of all major issues and a satisfactory scheme of the order of things. It has provided a chart through time.

The myth establishes the accepted outline of fact. Did St. Peter go to Rome and was he there martyred? I have heard simple men argue passionately in support of this view of the history of St. Peter. How did they know? What did that matter? They believed! A similar myth of great

force is that involving the life of St. Francis of Assisi. Less than half a
century after the saint's death, his followers were sharply divided between
those who wished to stick to his ideals of poverty in their rigour and those
who wished to conform to the standards of the ecclesiastical world about
them. In the year 1260 the official "legend," as it was called, of the saint
was commissioned by the order. Three years later it was completed and
in 1266, a general chapter of the order held at Paris under the presidency
of Bonaventura, the man who had written the "legend," made arrangements
for the collection and destruction of all the other material relating to St.
Francis. The official "legend" of the saint remained intact until late in
the nineteenth-century.[3] For *legend* read *myth*; the authorized version of
events, forced on everyone and accepted by everyone. The fate of the
"history" of St. Francis is common: pious and artful men keep conspiring
to make the facts accord with the myth. These pious men are the guardians
of the myth: they are its priests — and they supply the individuals who
eventually damage or destroy the myth, or possibly, re-create it in new
and more effective form.

The myth establishes its own version of history, partly by the colouring
of fact, partly by deliberate suppression of unwelcome facts. All revolutions
seem to proceed in this way, colouring or discolouring history for centuries,
perhaps forever. Examples abound. The Nazis burned the books. The
Russians seem to be engaged in a non-stop performance of rewriting their
history to suit the occasion, whatever it may be. The English disturbances
of the mid-seventeenth century ended up in the restoration of Charles II
and the hanging of poor Cromwell's corpse in chains. For nearly two
centuries, Cromwell remained the stock figure of the tyrant — until the
reviving puritanism of the nineteenth century gave him a new reputation.
On this puritan continent, he became a hero, but in many pious Anglican
hearts "the martyred king" still reigns. The English revolutionary century
was unfortunate in its myth-making processes, in that neither side succeeded
in making a clean sweep of the other's myths. The result is that there
are still two sets of myths, two versions of the revolutionary events, still
Roundheads and Cavaliers, Whigs and Tories.

Americans, erudite Americans as well as ordinary men, react emotionally to the myth of the American Revolution. The words "The British"
still form a stereotype which colours the thought and action of even the
most detached. Possibly it was an image of this stereotype somewhere at
the back of Franklin Roosevelt's brain which caused him to take his pro-
Russian, anti-British line at Yalta.

Take those most potent myths, the religious prejudices and preconcep-

---

[3]David S. Muzzey, *The Spiritual Franciscans* (New York: American Historical Association,
1907), p. 4ff.

tions generated by the Reformation. They have been colouring the fact ever since. They are little closer to allowing it to be seen in its "true colours," whatever they may be, than they were 400 years ago. Take the myth of Christianity itself. Christianity brought about the first and the greatest of the revolutions. It so completely obliterated the old pagan world that not a patch of it remains, except in unconscious folk-ways. There is no one left now to plead its cause, to put its values as he feels they should be felt, to challenge the positions and beliefs of the victors. If this were not a revolution what was? If we had effective accounts "from the other side," as we have for the Reformation, how different our attitudes might be! Christianity dyed all subsequent history with its own colours. How can the historian recover the native hue of the material? To understand classical paganism intellectually is far from being a pagan by birth and up-bringing, with pagan values intuitively held. We are all creatures of our myths.

At any given moment in the last nineteen centuries, who was to say what was myth and what was fact? Was the feeding of the five thousand myth or fact? The inference of the narrative is fact. The Crusades were fact in their occurrence, but they never would have occurred but for the myth. Did Luther say he would go to Worms though forty thousand devils stood in the way? Did he throw his ink bottle at one of these devils? These were for long enough accepted as "facts." Wolfe's repetition of Gray's "Elegy" on his way to climb the Heights of Abraham, was it myth or fact? Every generation, every year of history, sees its own new myths generated. They buttress the general edifice in some way. To the serious historian, you may say, they do not matter. Yet it may take him generations to cut through the thicket into which they grow. George Washington's little hatchet laid low the cherry tree far faster than the historians could hack away the myth which the deed attributed to him originated. At every point in the human story, big and little, grave and gay, the fact is coloured by the myth. And the completely detached mind has never existed.

Examine your own experience. How do you divorce your *amour propre* from "what actually happened" — in a car accident, say, or a quarrel? Transfer your own unregenerate person to the personality of a people or a period and see if you can leave yourself out!

See, indeed, if you can make the transfer. One knows his own society but does he know any other? That is, really know, from the inside, as it were, not merely by intellectual *tours de force*. Over many years I have done my best to understand French Canada, but I am very much aware that I cannot see life through the eyes of a French Canadian. I can in the large, as it were, but not in the small. I can put myself imaginatively into the position of a conquered people, but I cannot think the thoughts that they think. For that matter, Canadians cannot put themselves into the positions of Americans, well as they may think they know American life. They are not citizens of a great power themselves, and they cannot think like citizens of a great power, that is, like Americans. The farther one goes from his own culture, the less likely he is to be able to penetrate the culture that he studies. In the history and culture of a country as close as France, there are countless little points of circumstance which to a Frenchman must have been familiar from childhood, but which to outsiders are either unknown or carry no emotional colouring with them. What echo for example, does the phrase "Day of Dupes" awake in English ears?

There are of course, exceptions to every rule — for example, the penetrating and sympathetic studies of English life made by Élie Halévy[4] — but in general, I imagine that the history of a country or a culture or a religion written by an outsider, compared with equally competent studies done by the insider is much like what the English dons' Latin verses are to Latin verses.

History is the joint product of myth and fact, soul and body. The historian is closely related to the epic poet. But the historian writes in prose and is much more strictly bound by the fact than is the poet: the unpardonable sin for the historian is perversion of the evidence in an attempt to create a myth, whereas creation of myth, with no concern for evidence, is the measure of the epic poet's success. Fact without myth — the dry-as-dust historian — is dead: myth without fact is not history. The historian must be something to his Hecuba and she to him.

The myth with which the historian deals is not quite as universal as the life and death myths of the great tragic dramas. It is concerned, rather, with a people's conception of itself, on whatever plane. A good example may be drawn from English history: a myth, or rather, two myths, which have been highly formative in the whole range of Anglo-Saxon civilization and the exported versions of one of which have twice helped to bring down the world in bloody war.

The first of these myths is to be found in *The History of the Kings of Britain* by Geoffrey of Monmouth. In modern times this book has come in for fresh examination from several authorities.[5] It appeared about the

---

[4]Elie Halévy, *A History of the English People in the Nineteenth Century*, 2nd revised edition (London: E. Benn, 1949-68, c 1949-1962).

[5]Clement Acton Griscom, *The Historia Regum Britanniae of Geoffrey of Monmouth, with Contributions to the Study of Its Place in Early British History*, (London and New York: Longmans, Green, 1929). Griscom is inclined to believe that Geoffrey was rather more than an inventor and romancer: a gatherer-up of folk tales, at least, and that perhaps he did have access to books of some authenticity on early Britain which have since perished. This edition contains the first carefully collated text of the *Historia*. T. D. Kendrick, *British Antiquity* (London: Methuen, 1950) traces the influence of Geoffrey down to its decline. J. S. P. Tatlock, *The Legendary History of Britain: Geoffrey of Monmouth's Historia Regum Britanniae and Its Early Vernacular Versions* (Berkeley: University of California Press, for Medieval Academy of America, 1950). This book examines the *Historia* in microscopic detail and succeeds in

year 1138. Geoffrey was a second-generation Norman, born in Monmouth-shire. He appears to have been thoroughly Welsh by assimilation with no love for the conquered Saxons. His book is virtually a celebration of the glorious resistance of the Britons to all their various foes, Romans, Picts, and Saxons. We may well believe that a Welsh-born Norman, writing a short two generations after the conquest, seeing about him the triumphs of his own Norman French baronage (his book is dedicated to one of them) and with the lilt of the Welsh tongue on his lips, could look out upon the world and find it good — especially since he was enjoying an expanding career within the church. His own traditions must have been mixed: Welsh, Norman French, and the Church universal, all on the edges of conquered England. What more likely than a celebration of the glorious past of a people who had long ago been conquered by the Saxons but who now, in the persons of such individuals as Geoffrey himself, might be regarded as rising again? A lustre would be reflected from the ancient kings of Britain, and a justification for lording it over conquered Saxons.

The *History of the Kings of Britain* takes us back to the famous Arthur and some of his knights, to Vortigern, Hengist, Horsa and a long succession of more or less recognizable Romans to an almost unrecognizable Julius Caesar. It then plunges boldly into "B.C." and confronts us with such celebrities as King Cole and King Lear. Finally, it winds up in the inevitable birthplace of all respectability, Troy. It is as a result of the fall of Troy, and the flight of Aeneas and his companions that Albion receives her first king. He is one Brutus and from him comes the name of his island, Britain. It would not be a long step from such a genealogy to the circumstances of the writer's day: the Britanno-Normans and the Normans generally could easily feel themselves descended not from rough Teutonic barbarians but from the flower of the ancient civilized world. The book became popular at once.

Until the end of the Middle Ages, its popularity scarcely declined, nor was its authenticity seriously challenged. As the memory of the Norman conquest receded, the people of the island came to think of themselves as "Britons" and thence "Trojans" of the noblest descent. Though Arthur had had a certain vague existence before it appeared,[6] Geoffrey's book

---

finding where Geoffrey got most of his material. It decides that he is to a large extent a romancer and that there was no Arthur cycle before him. A casual reading of the ancient British chroniclers Gildas (sixth century) and Nennius (c. ninth century) at once gives the sources of much of his material. It is quite possible that he had opportunity to gather up various other bits of Welsh folk lore, and also that written materials to which he had access have since perished. The tremendous and detailed elaboration of the Arthurian romances must have come in later days. Christopher Brooke, *The Twelfth Century Renaissance* (London: Thames and Hudson, 1969), pp. 1-3, 163, 166-167. A good bit of detective work on one phase of the myths is Flavia Anderson, *The Ancient Secret: In Search of the Holy Grail* (London: Gollancz, 1953).

[6]See Brooke, *Twelfth Century Renaissance,* pp. 166-81.

became the parent of virtually the whole Arthurian body of romance. Sir Thomas Mallory's stories of King Arthur and his Round Table are only an amplification of the *History of the Kings of Britain.* In our day, Geoffrey lived once more in Tennyson's *Idylls.*

During the entire period down to the sixteenth century, the *History of the Kings of Britain* constituted the orthodox version of British-English history. No one doubted, or if they did, they got put into their place as semi-heretics. It was only in the sixteenth century itself, with the intellectual quickening which forms the English Renaissance, that queries arose. By the end of that century prominent Elizabethan antiquaries, such as Camden, Stowe, and Leland (the "antiquary" was the predecessor of the modern historian) had abandoned credence: their antiquarian researches may not have been very deep, but they had been deep enough to make them see through the *History of the Kings of Britain.* In particular, and perhaps thanks in great measure to the discovery of America, they had begun to give up belief in a stylish past and to see that if you got far enough back into the past, you came, not to glorious kings, but to savages. This, which seems so apparent to us, was a major step forward on the road to the modern sciences of man.

The most important step forward, however, was taken in the seventeenth century and arose out of the conflict with the Stuarts. The long period of personal rule, 1629-1640, was studded with law cases involving the basic principles of the constitution. Of these Hampden's celebrated ship-money case, 1638, was only the most famous. Each case involved historical research. Sir Edward Coke had already resurrected Magna Carta and furbished it up, and now lawyer-antiquarians such as Sir Henry Spelman and Sir John Selden were to do the same for many other nooks and crannies of the Middle Ages. Long before the fighting broke out in 1642, historical controversies had been sharpening and clarifying the issues. History at first was merely a weapon in the cause, but eventually the result of the appeal to history, made by both sides, was a much more orderly knowledge of the English past.

To many among the Roundheads, the facts of history seemed to correspond with the facts of the situation. The one side was led by a king whose father had been an alien, whose mother a Catholic. This king had a French Catholic wife and an archbishop who seemed to stand for everything "Romish" and arbitrary. Ranged round their monarch were the majority of the feudal dignitaries. Opposed was the great bulk of the rising classes of the nation, the solid gentlemen and prosperous merchants. The class division was not completely symmetrical, naturally, but "Cavalier" and "Roundhead" nevertheless were good terms.

When the fighting began, it was inevitable that sooner or later numbers of men should come to identify Charles with the cause of the few and

Parliament with that of the many. The plain man, not the simple fellow on the bottom of the heap but the plain man who felt his virtue rising, must have had no difficulty in regarding himself as "the real Englishman." It would be easy for him to associate his traditional "betters" with French absolutism, foreign falseness lurking under the guise of good manners, Popishness and all the evils that came from across the Channel. The parliamentary party would be pushed back to nativism and to the simple "rebellion of plain people against tyrants" conception of civil war.

Now there was in the distant English past, a foreign foe with whom tyrannous rulers could easily be associated. Not only was the hereditary enemy French, not only was the deceptive Charles's wife French, but Frenchmen from Normandy had once conquered England. In the year in which the Civil War ended, 1646, this event was already 580 years in the past, but what are five or six hundred years in the life of a people, and its folk memory? Were not the Norman oppressors still everywhere visible, in the shape of the feudal classes and in the tyrannical laws? This was the interpretation of English history made by the left-wing groups in the Civil War, the Levellers and Diggers. In the words of the chief of the Diggers, Gerrard Winstanley:

> For what are all those Binding and Restraining laws that have been made from one Age to another since that Conquest, and are still upheld by Furie over the people? I say, what are they? but the Cords, Bands, Manacles and Yokes that the enslaved English like Newgate Prisoners, wear upon their hands and legs as they walk the streets: by which those Norman oppressors, and these their Successors from Age to Age have enslaved the poor People by ...." "That Norman yoke, and Babylonish power ... yet you still lift up that Norman yoke, and slavish tyranny, and hold the people as much in bondage, as the Bastard Conqueror himself ....[7]
>
> When William, Duke of Normandy had conquered England, he took possession of the earth for his freedom, and disposed of our English ground to his friends as he pleased, and made the conquered English his servants, to plant the earth for him and his friends. And all kings, from his time to King Charles, were successors of that conquest: and all laws were made to confirm that conquest. ...[8]

In civil warfare with its accompaniment of class warfare, another foundation myth was born: the myth of Saxonism, destined to perish and

---

[7]Gerrard Winstanley, *The True Leveller's Standard Advanced* (1649), in the *Works of Gerrard Winstanley,* ed. George H. Sabine (Ithaca: Cornell University Press, 1941).

[8]*The Law of Freedom in a Platform,* or *True Magistracy Restored,* ibid., p. 521.

be merged with the Gothic myth and thus to form the mighty myth of Germanism, powerful, creative, destructive, down to our own day. Understanding of our world is surely impossible without some prior understanding of this myth. Admittedly since the defeat of Germany in two world wars, the submergence of doctrines of white racialism and the emergence of non-white, we are in another world, a world in which the old myth no longer operates and those who were its children have degenerated into mere survivals — "Wasps," as the clever ones will have them — "White, Anglo-Saxon Protestants." Yet the Germanic myth made much of the nineteenth century. It made the Gothic revival in architecture. It made Victorian literature and nineteenth-century German literature. It made a large part of the politics of the English-speaking world. Above all, it sustained and partly made nineteenth-century Protestantism and puritanism with the vastnesses these drew in their train. It was believed in by profoundly serious-minded, intelligent, devout people. It created that world that is just over the hill. Not to understand something of it is to shut out comprehension of that splendidly creative segment of our past — of ourselves.

It is possible to trace the Gothic myth back to its dim source in German mythology. The memory of the *Völkerwanderung* has never died in Germany: it was renewed in Lutheranism and renewed again with the defeat of Napoleon: here, on both occasions, was "that true north, strong and free" sweeping aside the effete, the tyrannical, the Romish south. The first political application of consequence comes at the time of the English Civil War: it is the struggle against the Stuarts which brings the "Gothic" myth to life as Saxonism and shoulders aside the "British."

The "Saxons" of seventeenth-century parliamentary England, looking back into the past, were not slow to discover that they were not Britons at all; Geoffrey of Monmouth's fall from his mighty place was to be completed by the parliamentary victories, and our ancient Norman Welsh monk was to go underground, leading an obscure and untraced life there, until his unexpected resurrection in the nineteenth century. This resurrection, or better, exhumation, only constitutes one of the curiosities of history, but it is in itself testimony to the power and longevity of the myth. Geoffrey and his myths came to life again riding on the tail end of the Romantic Movement. Romanticism, as Tennyson and Wagner evidence, reached back through the Middle Ages into dim antiquity. As a result, *Morte d'Arthur* makes another appearance in literature, if not in history, along with the stories of Odin, Siegfried, Brunhild, the Grail, Parsifal, and others such, which take us back by a Germanic route to about the same periods as those "described" by Geoffrey.

Once Geoffrey and his ilk were rediscovered, again there began to be heard talk of the high, mysterious lineage of the kings of Britain. This time all authorities united in judgment of his work in its earlier passages as sheer romance. Yet I once saw a whole page advertisement in the London *Times* which consisted in a genealogy of George V, tracing that monarch back through inconsiderable figures like Egbert, King of Wessex, and Clovis of the Franks, through Julius Caesar to Tarquinius Superbus and thence to Aeneas. Arrived at Aeneas the genealogist found the rest of the going easy and reached his eventual goal — David, son of Jesse. On his way, he threw out a link to a distinguished descendant of David who lived in Palestine at the period when B.C. was changing into A.D. The idea of the king as the descendant of the god is not yet dead: it revived, emphatically if momentarily at the coronation of George VI in 1937.

Those who paid for the advertisement described themselves as "British Israelites." In "British Israelitism," at the distance of eight centuries, Geoffrey of Monmouth and his confrères lived again. And as witness of what lively corpses they were, I cite a press controversy which took place in the pages of the Toronto *Globe and Mail* as recently as 1952. A clipping gives the atmosphere:

> As to roads, if credit be given to the ancient laws of Cambria, these were begun by King Molmutius and completed by his son Bellinus, 400 B.C. On their completion a law was enacted throwing open these roads to all nations and foreigners.

This is pure Geoffreyana: its exact pages could be indicated. The writer of the letter expresses himself well and knowingly alludes to "authorities of weight" — "the researches of M. Thierry, Thomas Nicholas, Prof. Sayle, Sir F. Palgrave, Thomas Huxley, Prof. Freeman," "and a host of others"[9] all long since dead. These men were all reputable nineteenth-century intellectuals, some of them of wide reputations. They would probably be startled at being called as witnesses in a sham battle over a fictitious past. The myth would, however, appear to be proof against the assaults of intellectualism.

To return to the seventeenth century, the "Saxons," having cut off the head of their "Norman" king, and thereby temporarily buried Geoffrey, a new process of myth-making began.[10] "Goth," a term which began to make a frequent appearance in writing after 1660, is the equivalent of our modern "Germanic" or "Teutonic." The Saxons were Germans: Hengist and Horsa were there to prove it, and they were kings, too. The Gothic Saxons had swept out of the island great loads of derelict Roman lumber. They had gone on to establish folk moots, witenagemots, trial by jury and the parliamentary system. Stalwart Saxons (well-disguised as Norman

[9] *Globe and Mail,* September 27, 1952.
[10] See Samuel Kliger, *The Goths in England* (Cambridge: Harvard University Press, 1952).

French barons) had wrenched Magna Carta, the people's charter, from a reluctant Norman tyrant. Saxons had knocked the stuffing out of degenerate Frenchmen at Agincourt, 1415: they had defeated the Armada, 1588, the fleet of another lot of Latins, who had also had the bad judgment to remain Catholics. Last but not least, they had pulled down Stuart absolutism, and established that perfect government which came in with Dutch William in 1688.

In the eighteenth century, the interest in things "Gothic" widened. People began to look at the "Gothic" cathedrals, the "Gothic" castles and the mysterious ruins of the past. Horace Walpole built synthetic "ruins" on his estates. Great men built "grottoes" and advertised for "hermits" to occupy them. Poets turned away from the formal Augustan verse form, Latin and Catholic in its associations, and of the intellect only, towards something less regular, less symmetrical, with more feeling in it, more "natural." This was the route by which Romanticism came into English culture.

Romanticism, from one point of view, may be regarded as a footnote to the Protestant Reformation and the renewal of confidence in itself by northern, German, "backwoods" Europe.

Towards the end of the eighteenth century, those "one hundred per cent Goths" who had come out to America on the *Mayflower,* were engaged in booting out still another "Norman" tyrant in the shape of the insufficiently Saxonized George III.

> The Goths hold that government springs from the people, is instituted for their behoof, and is limited to the particular objects for which it was originally established.... The Roman views the government as an institution imposed from without, and independent of the people.... That the mind of New England is plainly distinguished from that of the mother country, is due chiefly to the fact that our forefathers belonged to that grand era in British history, when the English mind, under the impulse of the Reformation, was striving to recover its Gothic tendencies, by the elimination of the Roman element.[11]

Most interesting of all would be to trace the evolution of "Gothicism" in Germany, for here was the country in which the myth was to be carried to its most intense point. The German lyric poetry of the early nineteenth century is crammed with this romantic nostalgia for a day gone by, a good

[11]Ibid., pp. 108, 109, quoting George Perkins Marsh, *The Goths in New England* (Middlebury, Vermont: J. Cobb, 1843), pp. 11, 16.

old German day of warriors, heroic sentiments, fair maidens, lonely mountains, ruined castles:

> Hast du das Schlosz gesehen
> Das hohe Schlosz am Meer?
> Golden und rosig wehen
> Die Wölken darüber her.
>
> Wohl habe ich es gesehen,
> Das hohe Schlosz am Meer
> Und den Mond darüber stehen
> Und Nebel weit umher.
>
> Der Wind und des Meeres Wellen
> Geben sie frischen Klang?
> Vernamhst du aus hohen Hallen
> Saiten und Festgesang?
>
> Sahest du oben gehen
> Den Konig und sein Gemahl?
> Der roten Mantel Wehen
> Der goldnen Kronen Strahl?[12]

Eventually the Germanic, or Gothic, myth was to be elaborated into the ferrago of the nineteenth century's racial myths and the crimes of the Nazis.

There are close connections between the development of the Gothic myth in Germany and in England and at least two open channels of intercommunication. The first channel was Thomas Carlyle, a man full of German philosophy, some of the choice passages of which he has been accused of appropriating without acknowledgement. Carlyle's hero worship,

---

[12] The Castle by the Sea, Ludwig Uhland;
> Hast thou the castle seen,
> The high castle by the sea?
> Golden and rosy-hued clouds
> Around it and over it floating?
> Indeed have I seen it,
> That high castle by the sea
> And the moon far above it standing
> And the mist spread far out around it.
> The wind and the waves of the sea
> Gave they their echoes clear?
> Heardst thou from out lofty halls
> Music and festal song?
> Sawest thou high up there going
> The King and his beauteous spouse?
> Their scarlet robes all fluttering,
> The beams from their golden crowns?

his "great man" theory of history, his contempt for "niggers" and members of parliament, all mark him as a true son of heroic "Gothic" forbears. It was only a step from Carlylean nonsense to Wagnerian heroics and Nietzchean lunacy.

Another open channel was embodied in Houston Stewart Chamberlain, son of a British admiral. He went to Germany, became Germanized, more German than the Germans, and wrote a book[13] that is regarded as influential in accentuating the racial myth: a foundation stone in the house that Hitler was to build.

Particularly interesting to the historian must be the way in which the Gothic myth conditioned and inspired so much of the history-writing in England down nearly to the end of the nineteenth century. Men well known in their day and of considerable reputation, such as Turner,[14] Hallam, [15] Kemble,[16] in their works on the Anglo-Saxons return to the ancestral sources — the birth days of the race, those days of primitive virtue. John Richard Green (1837-1883), in the course of the first few pages of his *Short History of the English People,* resoundingly declares that the basis of the society of the English "folk" was the freeman. The great bishop Stubbs in the opening chapters of his *Constitutional History,* lauds the Germanic barbarians, who swept out the stale remains of degenerate Romanism. Everywhere in Europe, he says, where new life budded, life which was to form and inform the Middle Ages, it was Germanic life. From Spain to the Vistula, the creative power which was raising the New Europe was Germanism.[17]

Freeman is even more emphatic: he becomes lyrical. "The Norman Conquest brought with it a most extensive foreign infusion which affected our blood, our language, our laws, our arts.... still it was only an infusion...." It represented "the temporary over-throw of our institutions." "In a few generations, we led captive our conquerors.... Under John, the old English liberties are won back in another form."[18] Such passages as the following indicated the atmosphere in which Freeman wrote: "Time

[13] Houston Stewart Chamberlain, *The Foundations of the Nineteenth Century,* 2 vols. (London: John Lane, 1909).

[14] Sharon Turner (1768-1847), *The History of the Anglo-Saxons, from their first appearance above the Elbe...,* 4 vols. (London: T. Cadell and W. Davies, 1799-1805).

[15] Henry Hallam (1777-1839), *The Constitutional History of England,* 6 vols. (London and Paris, 1827).

[16] John Mitchell Kemble (1807-1857), *The Saxons in England,* 2 vols. (London, 1849). Considered the best authority until William Stubbs (1825-1901), *The Constitutional History of England in Its Origin and Development,* 3 vols. (Oxford: Clarendon Press, 1866).

[17] With all this Victorian emphasis on Germanism, A. J. Toynbee is in emphatic disagreement. The Germans were mere barbarians, with nothing to contribute. European civilization came out of the Christian church.

[18] Edward Freeman, *The History of the Norman Conquest of England,* 6 vols. (Oxford: Clarendon Press, 1867-1879). Extracts taken from Vol. I, pp. 1-6.

was when supporters and opponents of Parliamentary Reform thought to strengthen their several positions by opposite theories as to the constitution of the Witenagemot. To this day a popular orator will sometimes think that he adds point to a declamation by bringing in Saxon Aelfred as the author of trial by jury.... Every notion of this kind must be wholly cast away...." While it is true, he continues, that there will not be found in the Anglo-Saxon period a representative assembly, ministers responsible to it, judges independent of king and people, jurors, etc., yet the mere fact that he finds it necessary to say this indicates the strength of the myth. And "he will find the first principles from which all of these were derived!" "...Our parliament is the true and lawful representative, by true and lawful succession, of the ancient meeting of the Wise...."[19] "We Saxons were conquered," Freeman says, in so many words, "it is true, but we absorbed our conquerors: the island became Saxon again."

Sir Charles Dilke, in his *Greater Britain,*[20] a survey of overseas Englishry of the 1860's, lauds the "Saxon race," wherever he finds it. It is the fount of creativeness. In Dilke's pages it is evident that "Saxon" had become a term of convenience for putting the same label over English-speaking people wherever found. The "Gothic" myth was shifting into the "Saxon myth." In Canada, "Saxonism" contrasted with what Dilke saw as the sloth, the superstition, and the slovenliness of French and Catholics. Good Queen Victoria in 1864, deplored the policies of "those two wicked old men," Palmerston and Russell, who were opposing the plans of the German Bismarck. In 1870 and 1871, the "English race" throughout the world prayed for the success of German arms. Here was manly strength, as opposed to the unmanly feminine French; Christian morality, as opposed to the cult of sex; northernism as opposed to southernism, and strong, decent Protestantism as opposed to the superstitions of popery. When Bismarck occupied Paris, the Almighty, always on the side of The Right, was in English eyes, visibly declaring himself.

My own youth was spent in the delayed Canadian autumn of the Gothic myth. In Canada and the other English-speaking lands of the Empire, "Gothicism" demanded too much acquaintance with historical tradition to make it important save to the few. What the many grasped naturally was the concept of "the motherland." The Gothic myth was transmuted into *Britishism* and in that form, it had a deep hold on people, much of which it retains. In the late nineteenth century, on the walls of most Canadian parlours, there hung Nelson dying on the *Victory,* or Napoleon, a captive on the deck of the *Bellerophon.* On such walls Wellington

---

[19] Ibid., p. 71 ff.
[20] C. W. Dilke, *Greater Britain. A Record of Travel in the English Speaking Countries during 1866 and 1867,* 2 vols. (London: Macmillan, 1868).

shook Blücher by the hand after Waterloo. "Oh, for night or Blücher!" It had been Blücher! "A damned nice thing, Creevey," had exclaimed the Duke, "the nearest run thing you ever saw." The few discordant notes sounded by Kaiser Wilhelm II had hardly yet been heard in the depths of Ontario. It took more than five years for speeches like "Germany's future must be on the sea" really to register on eardrums attuned to quite a different kind of world.

For the English-speaking world, along that route lay the deflation of the Germanic myth, and of its variant, *Britishism,* too. Its course may be easily traced: from the high levels of Carlyle, Freeman, and Froude, down to the jingoism of the 1870's, the movement for imperial federation of the 1880's, the spectacular jubilees of Queen Victoria, 1887 and especially 1897, the poet Kipling, Cecil Rhodes, and the sobering experiences of the conflict with the Boers. After that came the grim realities as the two branches of the myth raced down to collision in war.

Among scholars, by the end of the nineteenth century, new intellects were dulling the colours of medievalism. Foremost among them was Frederick William Maitland (1850-1906), most brilliant of legal historical minds, brilliant too, as stylist. He was first among many equals: Edward Jenks described the "Myth of Magna Carta" and at his heels came T. F. Tout and the Manchester school of medievalists. All these men spent their lives disinterring the real "Gothic" past, as their pre-occupation with the eleventh, twelfth and thirteenth centuries shows. These "scientific" historians were not merely destructive, and if the early hero myths dissolve into barbarian savagery, the post-conquest triumphs stand up well, especially the achievement by which the barons wrested Magna Carta from King John.

But the old heartfelt tone was gone. The new approach was cold, objective. Instead of heroes bearding King John in the name of all, establishing the liberty of England forever, it found a selfish baronage grasping what privileges it could for itself and making a mere gesture towards extending them to those below itself. The school of Maitland and his successors looked at the Middle Ages more realistically than had its predecessors, with fewer prepossessions. It found motives mixed and objectives confused. It found the uncertainties and the lack of a sense of direction with which we ourselves are surrounded. It found life and life's tangled skein. And myth was but one factor in life, whose place in the scheme of things could be ticketed, as could other factors.

Nevertheless, the high concentration of English medieval studies on the eleventh, twelfth and thirteenth centuries indicates how deep an impression had been made on good minds by the vast catastrophe in which Norman had replaced Saxon. Only in Germany itself did the Gothic myth continue to have vitality. There, it was to be transmuted into the pseudo-science of *Rassenwissenschaft* (as distinguished from anthropology proper), which would find itself reinforced by Hitlerism and its expounding prophets. Eventually, so potent are men's myths, it was only after many years, and with millions of lives lost in the fires of war, that the Gothic myth, the myth of Germanic supermanism, was swept away.

Since late Victorian days, every imaginable myth, English or not, has been disinterred and dissected. We have been in the full age of analysing, intellectualizing, classifying, depersonalizing, history-writing. Where have we got to, as a result of it all? Myth no longer stands a chance. If there are still a few obscure passages in times past, we at least know now that there was nothing out of the natural course of events to make them obscure. As John Henry Newman put it: a purely intellectual treatment of religion leads to unbelief.[21] To nothingness, he might have added. And when a devil is expelled, do not seven devils, finding the house swept and garnished, take up their dwelling therein?

The myth is elaborated in the creative primitive period, the poetic period, when men are seen larger than life, in the age of heroics and miracles. It endures until, for one reason or another, very frequently because of religious or political controversy, it becomes the subject of intellectual exercise and suffers the pains of dissection. At this point it passes over into history. History becomes more and more the subject of intellectualizing processes which strain out more and more of the myth. At such a juncture we are in the midst of "scientific" history. But then may come a generation which is no longer attracted by mere fact-gathering. It seeks meaning. It seeks to formulate "laws" of history, as Toynbee did, or philosophies of history, as Spengler did. In so doing, it may be, it removes history too far from its roots, makes it too rarefied, and those who write it discover themselves left without readers. The specialist will have found that his particular collection of facts is of interest almost solely to — himself! The next stage might be a return to "popular" history, a return to myth.

I doubt if the "scientific" historian can have an indefinite run: few men can live in the full glare of intellectualism. Man will have his myths. Let us hope that they will do him less harm than certain by-products of the pure intellect which, whether from the study of the eroding critic or the laboratory of the scientist, seem to have as their effect or end, his destruction.

---

[21]John Henry Newman, *Apologia pro vita sua: being a reply to a pamphlet entitled, "What, then, does Dr. Newman mean"?* 4th ed. (New York: Appleton, 1866), p. 269.

2 | *That humble fellow, the historian: Some reflections on writing history**

For some forty years, from 1919 to 1959, I was one of the active and ardent workers in the historical vineyard. I am still a worker, though rather less ardent, and the years of my retirement have given me some detachment. While one can never wholly separate himself from a lifelong occupation, yet if he no longer actively follows it, it is possible that he may recover *himself* from it. Someone or other remarked of another person that "he was born a man but died a grocer." Splendid as is the state of the historian, I myself am more anxious to die as I began, a man, rather than as I became, an historian: as an individual; as simply, for better or for worse, myself.

Nor do I think that the psychology the statement implies, its insistence on personality as primary, will make anyone the worse historian. How are you going to write about human concerns and activities unless you can yourself enter into them with some vigour and understanding? It is hard for me to believe that a pale ghost can write, with much vitality, history or anything else. I do not contend that he cannot write in accurate, scholarly fashion: he can do quite well the sort of thing on which I myself served my apprenticeship — labouriously establishing the number of board feet of white pine timber exported year by year from the port of Quebec, the prices of the same and the varying conditions of the market. If one has some imagination, this kind of work becomes arid, and wider, more living subjects draw one.

At that point, possibly, the writer passes from being merely a scholarly historian to being an historian. He begins to see a little way into the nature of men and things, and if he can go far enough along that road, it may be that the muse will smile upon him and give him at least a microscopic spark of eternal life.

However high a mountain peak he may climb, the historian, nevertheless, may not be able to take his place alongside the giants of the written word. Dr. Johnson, writing at a time when Gibbon's volumes were tumbling forth, is reported to have had this to say:

> Great abilities are not requisite for an historian: for in historical composition all the greatest powers of the human mind are quiescent. He has facts ready to his hand; so there is no exercise of invention. Imagination is not required in any high degree: only about as much

**Journal of Canadian Studies* 7 (February 1972): 45-50.

as in the lower kinds of poetry. Some penetration, accuracy and colouring will fit a man for the task, if he can give the application which is necessary

Dr. Johnson's words, as usual, are sobering. If comparisons in such matters be possible, few would put Gibbon, Thucydides, and the rest on a level with Shakespeare, Milton, and others of the supreme. Many, however, might put them on a level with Dr. Johnson! His proclamation bears looking at in detail. "His facts ready to hand." The doctor must have been referring to the "general historian," rather than to the scholar with dust in his nostrils, and for this latter type of historian, "some penetration, accuracy and colouring will fit him for the task, if he can give the application which is necessary." We can even leave out the "colouring" and can be quite sure that the product of a modern graduate school "can give the necessary application."

"Great abilities are not requisite," "no exercise of invention," "imagination not in any high degree," these are the judgments that hurt. Every year hundreds of volumes in the field of history fall from the world's presses. Some of them are patently mere works of compilation; others are attempts to explain great phases of civilization and the factors which induce change in them. Some are in almost unreadable style; others are of high quality. Are they all to be swept into the Johnsonian dustbin? Are all historians second-rate people? That is a status many among them seem ready to accept, a status ranking historians with sociologists, economists, and such like, but one which forever prevents them from passing through the pearly gates.

Is it necessary to eat humble pie and accept this second-rate status? One well-known historian, Macaulay, was in his day also a poet, and perhaps Johnson would have said at once that he exemplified the dictum and had only about as much imagination as needed for the lower kinds of poetry. Are all doors, then, closed?

Genius, so the saying goes, consists in an infinite capacity for taking pains. If so, there must be scores of men at present writing history who rate as geniuses, for the number of books which represent years of patient, accurate toil is almost unlimited. "An infinite capacity for taking pains" will open only the outer gates.

It is hard for me to upset Dr. Johnson's verdict, and perhaps, awful thought, because he was right! It would be easy to set down a score of good, solid credentials for the historian — the annual presidential addresses of the various historical societies and associations are full of them — but would all of these put together bring down the divine fire to the altar? Would not the novelist (of sufficient calibre), the dramatist, and, above all, the poet (modern poets definitely excluded) continue to scorn the historian as essentially pedestrian, as cut to Dr. Johnson's cloth?

On the other hand, would not a Gibbon who could depict the sweep of the *Decline and Fall of the Roman Empire,* a crowded canvas of humanity extended over vast distances of space and time, depict it arrestingly, and impress coherence upon it, would would not such a man deserve to rank at least with the great artists, if not with the great poets?

The historical craft guild has not contained many Gibbons, it is true. And yet Gibbon, in a sense, can be reckoned among the rest of the mere professionals. Many of the great names among the brethren have been writers who have drawn, for the most part, upon their own personal experiences, who in a sense have been writing autobiography. One thinks at once of Herodotus and Thucydides among the ancients, of Clarendon, and of Churchill. Among the "greats" there have been few men of research in the modern sense, for to "the greats" this modern notion of research would probably not have been welcome, simply because of its pedestrianism. Bede, who is a "great" if only because a solitary figure, may be an exception; Polybius, another. Far from collecting original material, Tacitus, upon whom scholars lean for knowledge of our Germanic forbears, is said to have been a retailer of stories about them, who used his material mainly to make jibes against his own unpleasant society, a sort of Roman Rousseau contrasting noble savages with civilized degenerates. When at the end of the seventeenth century, Madox produced his valuable book on the Exchequer, a veritable product of original research, he was at pains to apologize to his readers for the "low" subject into which he had been putting his efforts: he had not been occupied with the resounding deeds of princes recorded in style to match, but with humdrum details of administration. Madox takes his place as one of the founders of our modern schools of "research historians," a useful man to whom the Johnsonian dicta clearly apply.

It is probably the "research historian" against whom Dr. Johnson's animadversions were directed. Yet it is the "research historian" who has swelled out in numbers, volume, and, possibly, quality, to give us the modern profession. In the process he surely has mounted up to considerable heights. The great Ranke may have been a plodder, but any man who could write his way through his unending rows of volumes must have surely had qualities well beyond the ordinary. And then, confining ourselves to those who have written in English, what are we to make of the Macaulays, the Parkmans, the Stubbses, the Maitlands? Though Richardson and Sayles have begun demolishing Stubbs and our own Eccles chiselling bits off Parkman, the structures built by these nineteenth-century "greats" still stand there, some of them more or less venerable ruins, some of them divided up into apartments, and some of them down at heel, but some pretty well intact. Yet they stand there, and we gaze on their vastness with respect, perhaps jealous that we cannot equal it.

Such writers raise the question, which may be the nub of the discussion, as to what is a classic, whether in history or other art form. Definitions come easily — "a generally accepted work of outstanding quality," "a work that has stood the test of time," and so on. By whatever form of words a "classic" is defined, many pieces of historical writing probably will pass the test. But do any of the historical classics produced by men such as those just named get promoted into the status of general literature? A second- or third-rate historian such as Carlyle is sure of his place in the pantheon, as is Macaulay for his essays but not for his *History*. Why? Is it merely style that makes a classic? Or is there something more worthy about Carlylean fascism than about Stubbs's sober Englishism? To my mind the most formative historical — or sociological — work that has appeared in English, one combining a revealing thesis with a short and elegant exposition, is Turner's essay, *The Frontier in American History*.[1] It has many inadequacies but what other short bit of writing has been so seminal? It surely is a classic. But it is no "Ode on a Grecian Urn." It is a classic in the sense that, shall we say, Boyle's law on the properties of gases is a classic (but one hardly of the magnitude of Newton's law of gravity!). Such classics do not need to join to intellectual penetration a high range of aesthetic and imaginative appeal. We come back to Dr. Johnson. But they surely deserve as secure a place in the canon of "Eng. Lit." as do its long lists of novelists, essayists, and poets.

It is not the distinction between amateur and professional that is to be sought, for in most of the creative arts a man is either a professional or he is nothing. Can we think of anyone without lifelong training, whatever his native genius, just sitting down and writing out another Beethoven symphony or carving a figure of high quality out of a block of marble? Or, despite Max Beerbohm's Duke in *Zuleika Dobson,* dashing off just *one* inimitable sonnet? The questions answer themselves. And since lifelong application means accomplishment, classical works rise out of larger bodies of work, like the higher peaks of a mountain range, like Wordsworth's best poetry above the large mass of his writing. It must be so with historians; the great historian will usually be found to have produced a large bulk of work.

It is to the deceptive nature of prose writing that we owe the notion of the amateur and his prowess. Granted you cannot carve a statue, yet being able to speak and wield a pen, of course you can write! You cannot write poetry, you probably cannot write a novel, but if you can write a letter to a friend, why can you not write history? The serried rows of unread books on many a library shelf suggest that it is easier said than done. Writing — even a letter — means training; writing history means a great deal of training. Historians, as a rule, are not jealous enough of their professional skill. They are almost alone among the social scientists in not

[1] F. J. Turner, *The Frontier in American History* (New York: Henry Holt and Co., 1920).

having fenced themselves in behind a jargon of their own. (I hope they never will!)

Like other forms of training, before results of consequence follow, training must be joined to *flair:* historians are born, not made. I myself was personally acquainted with an historian who began his studies in physics. But, as he himself put it, "I could not keep away from those books." That is, in the old religious sense of the term, he found a vocation for himself. Every worth-while professional man has found a vocation for himself. A vocation ensures devotion: it ensures integrity, industry, and many other fine qualities but it does not ensure *flair.* Of itself, it does not put a man on the heights. To have a vocation is not very different from being, in the modern sense, "engaged," that is, "caught up in," "devoted to," "committed to." Most historians are committed to their craft. Most are committed to something more than their craft. "The pure historian," if such exists, no doubt can turn with equal facility and objectivity from doing a history of Bulgaria to one on Peru. At least, he can "write up" such histories. What he writes may well be a useful, objective record of factual material suitable for an encyclopedia, but will it be anything more?

It would seem as if the historian must be committed to something more than history. Even the great canvas on which Gibbon painted was intended to depict "the triumph of barbarism and religion," and that was depicted with fervour. Emotion — very polite eighteenth-century emotion — drove the great man's pen, and there is never any doubt on which side he stood. He was therefore not objective. How many historians have been? Is there any doubt as to which side of the Reformation the Catholic historian Lingard stood on, or whether Bishop Stubbs, who saw everywhere in Europe the creative heritage of the Germanic invaders, was or was not a Teutonist? Until our own days with their growth of vast scholastic resources, writers in English have never, indeed, whether intentionally or not, left their readers in any doubt as to which side they stood on: whatever their subject they were all national historians — even Lingard, the Catholic. The non-English English have first been national in their local sense and then in the broader racial sense, too. The major commitment of the historian, it would seem, has been to his national group — or if we wish to widen it, let us say to his cultural or linguistic group. Since he belongs to that group, that is something he probably cannot avoid.

So to *flair* must be joined commitment. But *flair* is the word, natural gift, aptitude: a something not to be measured, to be judged only by its manifestations. Being "called of God" will not lift the historian out of Dr. Johnson's black pit.

Can we go further?

It is to be doubted if we can. Men, historians included, will get out of the ranks of the second-rate only if they are not second-raters. Within the crowd most of its members must be second-raters. Second-raters have to bear their fate: it is not a dishonourable one.

"Imagination," the doctor declares, "is not required in any high degree." Let the historian accept the dictum. But might it not be better to rephrase its words: "Imagination is required but only to a moderate degree"? Even so, it would not be necessary to believe that imagination in a high degree is forbidden! Can any good historical writing, in fact, be done which does not have a considerable imaginative faculty behind it? Evidence must not be *imagined,* that is, manufactured, but how far will one get in reconstructing a past situation if he cannot put himself to some degree in other men's shoes, see through other men's eyes, look into motives, discern the logic of events and circumstances? It is dull history that merely proceeds rigorously from footnote to footnote; useful history, no doubt, in a pedestrian way, but "missing so much and so much."

That is another way of saying that between the writer and his material a creative act must take place. I may illustrate what I have in mind from one of the other arts, music. A piano stands in a room. When a small child goes to it, he bangs at the keys and makes a noise. When a pianist sits before the piano, he looks at the strange script of black dots and other marks before him, puts his fingers on the keys, and there comes forth something ordered and measured. If it is a simple song, persons present may easily learn to hum it, whistle it, sing it. More complex music takes more reproducing, but what has come forth seems to have an independent existence of its own. Something has occurred between the mechanical contraption, the piano, and the player. Something hanging there between them in the air, as it were, independent of both of them once it has been made — a new "fact" (*factum:* something made, created). It will be said that something came out of the musician's mind or brain. Something did. Something also came out of his fingers, out of the notes of the music, and out of the piano. Between this complex whole, whose complexities I have only suggested, something has been *made* or, if you like, *created.* I will not push the figure back farther to the original composer of the music, for that is not necessary, though the composer might perhaps come into the analogy as God, the Creator, whose original act is being perceived and fulfilled by the secondary figures of musician and piano. The figure I present, the player and the piano, is adequate: it gives a good illustration of the situation of the historian and his material. Out of the complex, in this case historian and documents, as with the pianist and the music, there comes a creative act, a new thing under the sun, the historical work. It is no doubt the same in all creative acts.

Then there is constantly presenting itself to the historian that topic which of all topics fires the imagination, time. The historian is bound up with time; life is bound up with time. The years inexorably roll on: the historian must be able to feel their motion. He can draw on his own lifespan, and note how its perspectives change as the years pass by. He can measure his own lifetime against the passage of the generations. Through family memories he may reach back a century or two. And then he has to walk without a stick. How measure the centuries against one's own life, however long, or one's person-to-person memories, however far they stretch? How recapture the "atmosphere" of the long ago? Whatever the external aids — documents, pictures, monuments — one finds himself trying to dream into it, that is, to imagine it. For the ordinary person the past is past, what's over is over, and that's that. Of this the historian finds it hard to convince himself. Must all that busy, pulsing life be gone? May it not go on somehow as does the life of a city he has left? Silly, of course, but is the dead past dead? Never quite to one whose business it is to bring it to life.

One day a few years ago I sat looking out over the Straits of Dover, out over the course that Roman ships followed in the long-ago. It is supposed that a few triremes may have been maintained against the Saxon pirates in a near-by harbour long since destroyed by the sea. I closed my eyes and tried to imagine what I might have seen eighteen hundred years ago. Opening them, far out at sea, I saw the sun glance on a patch of white. Roman trireme? Of course not: just the upper works of a tanker. So triremes and all that they imply had to be imagined. But what would one give for a "snatch" of incidental conversation among those Roman sailors, a "snatch" such as the novelist can hear on every street corner? No tape-recorders in those days, alas! It may be that such mechanical devices will make historians-to-come less imaginative, not more. Will they be better historians?

The relentless march of time forces on one more than imaginative day-dreaming. Historian, archaeologist, anthropologist, geologist, physicist, astronomer, all stand in a great chain, all exploring the unexplorable, so to speak, all pushing back the bounds of knowledge — of life! So the scholar or scientist who is not also a philosopher, whether formally so called or not, can never be in the front rank. Historian and philosopher, dealing with humanity and life, cannot be far apart. And does not contemplation of time lead into contemplation of time's nature, to the eternal verities, indeed? Is there not a direct chain between the here and the now and the origins of it all long ago (if it had origins!)?

Whatever we may think of Dr. Johnson's dictum, however closely it may seem to hit the mark, it may at least be conceded that it does not prevent the historian from having qualities in addition to those that for most aspects of his calling are essential. Just because a man is an historian, he is not necessarily earth-bound. It seems to me that the more of the higher range of creative qualities he has, the higher he is likely to mount. Historians as such may never be Homers, but Homers may occasionally condescend to be historians.

II.

Historical Papers: Professional

As a professional historian, Arthur Lower did seminal work in several areas. In "The Origins of Democracy in Canada" (Essay #3), he set down his first major position, adapting Frederick Jackson Turner's frontier thesis. Having come upon Turner's concept in Frederick Merk's class at Harvard, Lower related it to experiences he had had in Barrie, Ontario, then a community only recently removed from the frontier, as a child and later as part-time forest ranger. However, he went beyond the mere political implications of the thesis to ask why there had been a less thorough expression of democracy in Canadian national life than in American. He could not accept the environmental determinism implicit in Turner's argument without juxtaposing to it his understanding of the special contribution of tradition to the Canadian experience. He continued to use the frontier thesis, but for reasons given in "Professor Webb and 'The Great Frontier' Thesis" (Essay #4), he could not accept it as his exclusive historical concept.

While the frontier thesis was primary in his work up to World War II, economic history dominated his subject matter. His four major works produced during that time all related to economic matters, especially to man's use of the forest. This interest in the forest emanated from a lifelong contact. His research into the timber industry was reflected by such professional papers as "The Trade in Square Timber,"[1] which remained the definitive work on the subject for forty years — until Lower published *Great Britain's Woodyard* in 1973. His love of the forest is represented in this volume by "The Forest: Heart of a Nation." (Essay #20).

During the war years, his interest in the human element in history and in the historical factors that shape a culture, specifically the Canadian culture, was re-activated. This next stage of his historical thought was hastened by his concern for the fate of Canada during the crisis. He presented the essence of his position in his presidential address to the Canadian Historical Association in 1943 — "Two Ways of Life: The Primary Antithesis of Canadian History," (Essay #5).

The metropolitan thesis is the converse of the frontier thesis. Having rejected the latter as the exclusive agent of Canadian history, he began

---

[1]Presented at a meeting of the Royal Canadian Institute in February 1932 and published by the Institute in 1932.

to explore the validity of the metropolitan concept. In "Metropolis and Hinterland" (Essay #6), which pertains to the broad sweep of world history, he reached the pessimistic conclusion that, should the pattern of the ever-expanding metropolis continue, the unhappy fate of an "ecumenopolis" with everything under cement was inevitable. As a son of the forest and the water, Lower viewed such a future negatively.

The essay "Religion and Religious Institutions" (Essay #7) illustrates his eclectic interests. In analysing the political, social, and cultural implications of the religious situation in Canada, he asked his questions from a Canadian, rather than a foreign, viewpoint. Although his interest in religious history was a subsidiary one, other historians of the subject still recognize that he accomplished more to restructure the Canadian approach to the topic than anyone else.

3 | *The Origins of Democracy in Canada*

The history of a country seems to consist in a complex of social loyalties and individual interests projected against a background of environment. The three factors compose, to borrow a mathematical term, a triangle of forces, and the historian's task lies in solving the equations representing it.

In this country, as in every other, social groupings have from the beginning had an important place. As a rule they have had their political reflections, taking their place as important elements in the party system. As time has passed they have undergone interesting evolutions, usually in the direction of increasing adaptation to the conditions of the new country. In the early days, people naturally found themselves bound together by sentiments and prejudices that had their origin elsewhere than on Canadian soil. While these early bonds of society are not all dead, many of them are dying, and their place is being taken by loyalties more nearly indigenous. But even today, the country is a sort of museum of all the movements and passions, imported or native, which have swept over it in the past.

An apt illustration of the thesis is afforded by the Orange Order in Canada. Before the large Irish immigration of the twenties and thirties of the last century, nothing was more remarkable than that, amid the unceasing political and racial strife of the English and French, there should

---

*Delivered at a meeting of the Canadian Historical Association at Montreal on May 23, 1930 and published in the C.H.A. *Report* (1930): 65-70.

have been rarely broken religious peace. When the Irish, Protestant and Catholic, came, they brought with them the loves and hates of their own country, and ever since religion has taken its place along with race as one of the elements of discord and of political strife in this country. As time has gone on, the first fine frenzies of the devotees of either faith have subsided. Twelfth of July celebration is no longer, as a rule, the occasion of a pitched battle. Even for Orangeism, a second transplantation has been rather too much, and consequently in the newer parts of the country it does not flourish as it does in Ontario. The old loyalty has been sloughed off, apparently not adapted to local conditions, but a new one, the Ku Klux Klan, another alien importation but one more directly related to the problems of the day, has taken its place.

It is difficult to disentangle the elements of sentiment and emotion in an individual's social alignment from the element of reason, but the confusion between the two accounts for most of the inconsistencies in men's political behaviour. In Canada politics will never be understood until the conscious motive is separated from the unconscious. A right assessment of the two would give a very clear image of Canadian development. In such an assessment a balance would have to be struck with the second force in the triangle, self-interest, hydra-headed in the variety of its expression but too often completely anti-social.

The third factor, the physical background, has not as yet been intensively studied by the Canadian historian, but the triangle cannot be solved until such a study has been undertaken. Certain of its more immediate effects are sufficiently obvious. Thus the political situations arising out of our limited amount of arable land and consequent small population, the remoteness of one habitable section from another, the climatic difficulties confronting labour, navigation, and internal communication, are sufficiently patent. The more remote and intangible effects have not yet been rendered patent.

The historical deductions from geography have been worked out in some detail for the United States by American historians of the school of F. J. Turner, and they have shown very well how the frontier has conditioned the whole social setting, manner of thought and political reactions of the people of their nation. Turner's thesis has not yet been thoroughly applied to Canadian history, and, indeed, there are factors present in the development of each country which are inconspicuous or absent in that of the other. It must therefore be a modified or adapted version of the thesis which can be fitted to Canada.[1]

---

[1]Two articles mainly concerned with the physical parallels between the two countries in their frontier development are W. N. Sage, "Some Aspects of the Frontier in Canadian History," C.H.A. *Report* (1928): 62-72 and J. L. McDougall, "The Frontier School and Canadian History," C.H.A. *Report* (1929): 121-26.

Probably the most striking and important aspect of the thesis is that one which dwells on the connection between the frontier and democracy. There can be little question but that American democracy had a forest birth, and there also can be little doubt of the validity of the larger thesis that the frontier environment, or life lived on the margins of civilization, tends to bring about an equality of which the political expression is democracy. But it may be doubted whether social equality could work out into political democracy unless the society possessing it had not possessed certain theoretical positions as to its nature before it was projected into its frontier surroundings. The French Canadian and the American before 1763 both were faced with the same frontier conditions, and within limits both made the same response to them. Both had much social equality, much rude good comradeship, the virtues of pioneer hospitality, adaptiveness, and initiative in meeting the demands of forest life. Both were restive under control, making good scouts but poor regulars. There was infinitely more independence and assertiveness in French Canada, infinitely less readiness to do the will of a superior, than in old France;[2] but it may be safely assumed that once the conditions which made for this independence had passed, the age-old controls of French life, the clergy and the nobility, and the pressure of authority which was in the very air of the *ancien régime* would have made themselves felt,[3] and the independent Canadian would have had to bow the knee in the same manner as his ancestors.

Not so the American. He had all the independence of the coureur de bois and something more: he had behind him the consciousness that he was a free man, that his ancestors had been free men, and that his whole society stood for the rights and privileges of the individual. Thus when pioneer conditions had passed, the attitude toward life which they had induced remained as a conscious philosophy or creed, something to be fought for. It is only with the fading of the memory of the frontier and the elevation of descendants of frontiersmen into a sort of aristocracy, at least a plutocracy, over an immigrant and alien bottom layer that the old framework of American society tends to loosen. It has not loosened much yet, but it is doubtful if the political ideals of the original population, reinforced as they were by a most intense frontier experience, can be indefinitely passed on to a citizenry much of which has little of them in

---

[2] Note how quickly seigneurial control disappeared after 1763. In 1775 Carleton found authority of church, seigneur, and government powerless to coerce the habitants. They had seized the opportunity which the English Conquest afforded of throwing off the controls which had long been irksome to them. See on this subject Chester Martin, *Empire and Commonwealth* (Oxford: Clarendon Press, 1929), p. 179.

[3] As in part they did after the Quebec Act had begun to make its pressure felt; a new set of controls, the clergy and the popular tribunes, took the place of the old, and to this day the French Canadian is much more amenable to discipline than is the English.

its heredity and much of which is slowly becoming a lower class.

In Canada, democracy has been even more of a condition and less of a theory than it has been in the United States. Our political ideas have been British, not American, and in British political idealism democracy, until a recent date, had no place. In it freedom, it is true, had a large place, but a careful distinction must be made between the old English notion of freedom and the concept suggested by the word democracy. For three-quarters of a century after the Loyalists came, lip service was paid to freedom, but "democracy" was discreditable, at least among the people who "mattered." It was something that caused French Revolutions or which was associated with the American tobacco chewers discovered by Martin Chuzzlewit. The whole weight of officialdom and its connections in British North America was thrown against it, and only very slowly after the securing of responsible government was the disreputable personage admitted into the drawing-rooms of respectable society. Yet today it is the name that is above every name. Here is an interesting historical development which has not yet been traced out as completely as it might be.

The Loyalists brought with them to Canada a bitter experience of popular action. Haldimand said, perhaps truly enough, that they had had all they wanted of assemblies. Their chief men were aristocrats. Yet in half a century their settlements were being agitated by cries for responsible government. In so far as they supported this agitation and in so far as it did not obtain its chief support from the later comers, the frontier had done its work.

But it is probably necessary to distinguish between responsible government and democratic government. So far as the writer knows, Baldwin, Papineau, and Lafontaine were not enthusiasts for democracy. Mackenzie probably was, and he more than any other prominent figure represents the frontier at that period. Yet in Canada, the frontier, that is, roughly, the countryside as opposed to the little governmental and mercantile centres of power and influence, never scored the ringing victory of Andrew Jackson and his frontiersmen in the United States.

It is curious to reflect how little support Mackenzie received. Logically most of the province should have supported him, for most of the province must have been affected by the grievances for which the ruling class was responsible, the conditions obtaining as to land and land grants, the Clergy Reserves, the Anglican attempts at an established church, the tyranny of the semi-official Bank of Upper Canada. Similar conditions in the United States, both before and after the Revolution, had caused serious outbreaks. Bacon's Rebellion, the Alemance fight, Shay's Rebellion, and the Pennsylvania Whiskey Rebellion are familiar examples. A similar inspiration, if not actual grievances, had been at the bottom of the triumph of the frontier in the elections of 1828. Yet here was Upper Canada and, to a lesser degree,

New Brunswick and Nova Scotia, suffering under more severe oppression that these others had been and to a remarkable extent taking it "lying down."[4]

The explanation is twofold. The character of the population differed from that of the western states. The democratic spirit in its political expression was a post-revolutionary development in which the Loyalist migrants had not shared. Later immigrants were not completely emancipated from Old World modes of life and thought. The pioneer in his day-to-day life manifested all the characteristics of his American brother [5] except the fierce desire of the latter to control the political situation. Mackenzie, a pioneer only by courtesy, a pioneer born in Scotland and seeing the frontier from the windows of a York printing house, was not an Andrew Jackson. Again, the provincial unit was small and control in various forms was easily exerted.

Both of these factors come together and are nicely illustrated in the case of Egerton Ryerson and the Methodists. Methodism was essentially a religion of the frontier, a fact which accounts for its rapid spread through an originally non-Methodist population, and if they had been left to themselves, its adherents, many of them of Loyalist origin, would almost certainly have gravitated into the rebel camp. But it happened to have Ryerson at its head, and he also was Loyalist, but a Loyalist and Methodist of a more sophisticated type than the simple pioneer. Consequently, old sentiments and the old allegiance triumphed in his person, and, grievances or no grievances, Strachan or no Strachan, he retained the loyalty of frontiersmen and Methodists.

The events of the rebellion period are not particularly creditable to a proud people. It should logically have been a great popular movement against undoubted grievances. Instead of that, its inherited social alignments, from which much of the meaning had evaporated, took all the fire out of it.

Though, partially as a result of the rebellion, self-government came, democracy did not prevail, and as late as 1867 Sir John Macdonald could vigorously and without condemnation champion a property suffrage. Property and privilege is written into the British North America Act to a much greater extent than it is written into the American Constitution, itself a document far from democratic.

---

[4]Lower Canada cannot be included in the comparison, for although the same grievances were present and were powerfully at work, the element of race cuts across them all, and it would be difficult to say how far the rebellion was racial and how far social and economic.

[5]As for instance in the emotional nature of the religion he demanded. The Bay of Quinte Loyalists became Methodist within a few years after their arrival, and elsewhere in the country the "old time religion" was hot, strong, and violent in its displays, just as it was in the frontier districts of the United States. "Camp-meetings" sometimes came near to being veritable emotional orgies.

By 1867, the frontier of settlement in Canada had practically ceased its advance, and pioneer spirits were trekking westward to the prairie states. In the Hudson Bay territories the energetic and unruly agitation of Dr. Schultz against vested interest was typifying the frontier spirit. There were also recurring in the West interesting repetitions of the democratic phenomena of many another frontier. One of the most illuminating of these was the so-called republic of Assiniboia set up in the sixties by one Spence[6] Nothing of the sort seems ever to have occurred before on what is now Canadian soil, but it is in the direct line of descent from the Mayflower Compact and the Watauga association. It is in the West, too, that, more recently the phenomena associated with the frontier type of democracy have been most frequently in evidence. Undoubtedly influenced by similar legislation of the western states, Manitoba in 1916 attempted to set up a law for the initiative and referendum.[7] The farmers of the West have displayed a hostility to the chartered banks, reminiscent in milder tones of the outcry of the thirties against the Bank of the United States. It is on the prairies that the most successful revolt against the old political parties has occurred.

Despite the continuance in the West down to the present of democratic phenomena such as the foregoing, the present democratic tone of our institutions cannot be looked upon as having been an inevitable political evolution. In 1867 there was no body of opinion in favour of democracy. In fact, as has been said, opinion was in the other direction. Yet today our governments are responsive to the slightest breath of the air of public opinion and sometimes in their efforts to anticipate it, move ahead of it. Providing it be vocal enough, there is no class in the community that cannot force government's hand. This would not have been true sixty years ago. The problem is to account for the change.

Democracy both as a theory and a condition made great headway in Great Britain after 1867, but it is impossible to believe that British political practice had any important influence on Canadian. There was no echo in Canada of John Bright's famous campaign preceding the Second Reform Bill and no echo of the bill itself. Our democratic evolution must have come from elsewhere.

Robert Gourlay in his day made excellent fun of the provision in the Constitutional Act for a hereditary nobility in Canada and pictured the Marquis of Erie as a petty lawyer in a small country town or the Duke of Ontario observed by some passer-by in the act of getting in his

---

[6]Joseph James Hargrave, *Red River* (Montreal: Lovell, 1871), p. 428 ff.
[7]The statute was declared *ultra vires* of the Manitoba legislature by the Judicial Committee of the Privy Council. See W. B. Munro, *American Influences on Canadian Government* (Toronto: Macmillan, 1929), p. 95n.

own hay.[8] Descriptions exist of the unconventionality of the Canadian legislatures of the early days and of the illiteracy (and worse) of their members.[9] In the state of society reflected in matters such as these surely lies the key to the problem. You cannot make a silk purse out of a sow's ear, and you cannot make class distinction of any permanence in a country where there is not much wealth and where everybody has started in the race for its accumulation from approximately the same point and started very recently. In other words, society in a new country is almost necessarily equalitarian and democratic, and therefore sooner or later politics must become so. If they do not, it is because the long arm of an old polity is felt stretching out toward the new. France stretched out such an arm towards Canada before 1763 and kept the new country mildly feudal. But even in feudal New France, the seigneurs had little to distinguish them from the habitants except their pride and poverty. England stretched out such an arm after 1763 and for many years kept the institutions of the new country mildly aristocratic. But when self-government came, the régime of privilege rapidly evaporated in the sun of economic equality.

It need not necessarily have been so. In a small and isolated community, where opportunity was narrow, privilege might easily have maintained itself. Probably eastern Canada alone was large enough to have avoided this, certainly the Dominion as at present constituted is, but in any case the influence of the outside world would have prevented it. With our traditions of political freedom working in the modern world, we must have come out somewhere near the point at which we have in fact arrived. Moreover, we lay close to a country in which during the nineteenth century democracy was, so to speak, being continuously re-manufactured, re-created anew with every belt of new country opened up. In the tone of society, as in every other particular, we were influenced by the United States, and there is no doubt that the march of democracy in the United States influenced its march in Canada. The backwash of western democracy forced political equality in all the eastern states, and by the forties the last property qualifications and the last established church had disappeared from New England. Its effect on Canada must have been similar, for while the boundary tends to retard the spread of ideas northward, it does not stop it. It may be concluded that our own pioneering era plus the influence of American pioneer life brought about political democracy in Canada.

There were minor factors, of course. Thus in the session of 1885, Sir John Macdonald alleged as one of the reasons for his attempt to put the

---

[8] Robert Gourlay, *Statistical Account of Upper Canada,* 2 vols. (London: Simpkin and Marshall, 1822), 2: 296.
[9] See *inter alia* Sir Edmund Hornby, *Sir Edmund Hornby, An Autobiography* (Boston and New York: Houghton-Mifflin Co., 1928), p. 62.

control of the suffrage into the hands of the dominion Parliament that certain provinces were widening the franchise for the simple purpose of giving votes to persons who would vote against the Tories.[10] Again, party government tends to an ever-widening franchise because one party bids against the other for the favour of the electorate. This remark would apply with some force to the English Second Reform Bill.

Despite American influence, there are observable differences between our democracy and that of the United States. We have never erected democracy into a creed in Canada, and consequently we endure without even feeling their inconsistency, let alone injustice, such undemocratic remainders as the property suffrage in municipal politics and property qualifications for the Senate. We endure, or did endure until recently, distinctions of rank that have never been tolerated in the United States. We like to think that our democracy does not shout as loud as does that of America. These differences, for the most part small, probably proceed from three causes. The first is that our frontier experience, owing to differences in habitable area, has not been as intense and prolonged as has that of the United States. We have not all been ground up quite as fine by it as the Americans. Sir John Beverley Robinson was able to keep his coach and four and to pose as grand seigneur in "Muddy York," but it is unlikely that he could have done so in contemporary Cincinnati. The second cause is that Old World sentiment has been much stronger in Canada and the Old World connection much more recent than in the United States. And the third lies in our monarchical form of government; in the old days we were governed, and we have never quite got accustomed to governing ourselves. Government to many of us still seems a thing apart, not quite our own concern. The perpetuation of monarchical forms, even though the life has long since gone out of them, doubtless tends to act as a curb to the fullest expression of democracy. At any rate, the differences just mentioned between our democracy and that of the United States consist in a general way in this, that democracy in Canada has not had quite as thoroughgoing an expression as it has had amongst our neighbours.

[10]John Lewis, "Canada under Macdonald," in *Canada and Its Provinces,* Adam Shortt and Arthur Doughty, general eds., 23 vols. (Toronto: Brook and Co., 1914), 6:98.

4. │ *Professor Webb and "The Great Frontier" Thesis**

It is not given to many historians to become the centre of a cult. For one at least that honour, however, has been reserved — for the man whose spirit may be assumed to hover over the gatherings of his disciples, Frederick Jackson Turner. He being dead, yet speaketh. Nor does he lack a priesthood to expound his message.

Turner had the good luck to put into a few words ideas that had been latent right from the days of the discoveries. Like a lesser Darwin, he reduced the innumerable descriptions and observations made before him to a few simple sentences. A short, precise essay gave him the reward of the man who hits upon a synthesis — not only a place among historians but a place in history. It is not the object of the present paper merely to fill another prescription to the original formula, but, in so far as the insight of its writer permits, to raise some basic questions and in particular to look at the latest set of variations upon the original theme, that of Professor Webb in his *Great Frontier.*[1]

In the dim past, as an undergraduate in a not undistinguished Canadian school of history, the present writer never heard of Turner. It was not until he got to the Harvard Graduate School that the name of the god began to beat upon his ears. Not everyone there was a worshipper at the shrine, then some thirty years old. But there was little hostility, nor did I hear any fundamental criticism. Some years later, at a meeting of the American Historical Association, a session was devoted to the elucidation of Turnerism. Again I can recall no basic criticism. Since those days Mr. Webb has become the leading exponent of the Turner thesis, and now in his *Great Frontier* he tries for a new and greater synthesis, which shall carry forward and complete the work of the master.

How successful has he been? How successful, for that matter, was his master? I can only give my personal reflections. They may be useful as coming from a Canadian, a being who is at once within and without the American scene; far enough in to understand it pretty well and far enough out to be cold-blooded in his evaluation of it. I remember distinctly my first reaction to Turner. "How interesting this is!" I thought, "what a light it casts over our own historical experience as well as that of the United

---

**The New World Looks at Its History,* eds. A. R. Lewis and T. F. McGann (Austin: University of Texas Press, 1963).
[1]Walter Prescott Webb, *The Great Frontier* (Boston: Houghton Mifflin, 1952).

States. How much it tells me about myself, especially about myself in the presence of those twin magnificences. Oxonians and Harvard men." As a humble product of the frontier, I was complimented by Turner on my excellence, and in my turn I complimented him upon his.

Turner's limitations, however, soon began to make themselves apparent. I framed a topic for debate in our graduate history club: "Social inheritance or physiographical environment, which shall we rate the more powerful?" I thought then and I still think that the question goes to the root of the matter. I put my views in an article published in the Canadian Historical Association's *Annual Report,*[2] and based my thesis upon a comparison of English and French Canada. I claimed, and I would still claim, that the severest indictment of Turner is that he never worked his position out into some such general terms. He apparently was a man who saw clearly but saw narrowly. He did not get beyond the American frontier. He never made of his synthesis a grand, sociological doctrine such as Darwin made out of his data for biology. Professor Webb, his disciple, now essays to supply the missing elements and to frame them all into one intellectual concept, Metropolis (Europe) and Frontier (New World). Is his work sound? What criticisms shall we offer of it? Are there alternatives? (That is, can the writer of this paper do any better?)

Like Professor Webb, I knew the frontier at first hand, a very different frontier from his, however, that of the northern Canadian forest. I did not grow up in it, but I spent several formative seasons there. And I did grow up in an environment not far removed from the forest frontier. Moreover, as a Canadian, I was familiar through politics, books, and accumulating personal experience with another pioneer people as different from mine as well could be, my French-speaking fellow citizens. I therefore may have had certain advantages over many American students of the frontier.

Turner, it seems to me, under an exterior of objectivity, had a good deal of the romantic about him: he was romantic, or nostalgic, for the familiar environment which he had left forever and which had left him forever. In consequence, did he not overplay his hand? Or, rather, as dealer did he not throw all the best cards to his favourite – the new land as compared with the old? Here, on the edge, in the bush, is simple honesty and manly vigour; here is native courtesy and a native sense of equality: here, in short, are all the rude and commendable qualities of the Forest of Arden. Here is Thomas Jefferson in the shape of Jaques, and here is Rousseau masquerading as – who else could it be – Touchstone!

Virtually the whole of Turner's thesis, and much of Webb's, can be

[2]See essay #3: "The Origins of Democracy in Canada," pp. 26-33.

put in two words: geographic determinism. Put Frenchmen and Germans down alongside each other in the same habitat for long enough and they become the same people. Well, they have been alongside each other for a great many centuries in various parts of the Rhine valley, and are they the same people? French-speaking Canadians and English-speaking New Englanders have been alongside each other in similar habitats for three and a half centuries. Are they the same people? English-speaking Canadians and English-speaking Americans have been alongside of each other and mixed up with each other for several generations. Are the two peoples identical? Remarkably similar, I grant, but rather owing to similar traditions than to a similar habitat.

It is my invidious duty, in this place and on this occasion, to pour some critical acid on Professor Webb's work. It is not my task here, I take it, to criticize his book, but his thesis. Nevertheless, since the two cannot be completely separated, I feel compelled to observe that I detect in the book the same ground swell of nostalgic romanticism which seems to me present in Turner. More seriously, I detect limitations of interest and limitations of knowledge. Webb speaks of *The Frontier* in the abstract, but his leading illustrations are drawn from the United States and most of them from a book with which historians have been familiar for some years, to wit, *The Great Plains*[3] — whatever may be the point of departure for his study, it tends to end up in western Texas. I must use, as I would use for Turner, the harsh words *parochial*. If this paper could be of ample enough length, I would cite examples. I must say, also harshly, that to me his acquaintance with the history of the rest of the world seems limited and cold. There are a dozen references to the medieval world which seem to indicate lack of sympathy, lack of knowledge, and lack of insight. Every reference he makes to my own country, Canada, is either smudged or else downright wrong. These are not good qualifications for a man who presents a thesis which he tells us may well revolutionize the art of writing modern history.

I come now to the thesis itself. As stated many times in the text, it is (unless my stupidity is hiding something from me) simply that the great discoveries were collectively the most important event in human history and that they have greatly affected the Europe from which the discoverers set out. Well, if there is any reputable historian alive in the Western world who will contest the general truth of such a thesis, he must be a queer specimen. Mr. Webb quotes Adam Smith in support of his thesis. Rather he should quote himself in support of Adam Smith's thesis, for it is hard to see how he has done more with it than dotted a few "i's": he has given some lively and readable descriptions of episodes or developments that

[3] Walter Prescott Webb, *The Great Plains* (Boston: Ginn, 1931).

have not perhaps before been put into consecutive sequence. His description, for example, of the eighteenth-century "Bubbles" is perhaps one of these, but it cannot claim originality. Similarly, his chapter on "The Parabola of Individualism" is useful, but the subject has been discussed a dozen times. Laski attempted to make the same point in *The Rise of European Liberalism* (which it is evident he would have preferred to call *The Fall of European Liberalism).* George Soule, I think it was, during the Depression talked about American liberty as consisting of two centuries of hardwood lands and one century of open plain. Barbara Ward appears to see these centuries since the Reformation as temporary aberrations on the part of the children of Mother Church, who sits patiently waiting for their return to the fold. Aldous Huxley in his *Brave New World* and George Orwell in *1984* have imaginatively pictured the fate that awaits the sons of liberty when free lands are no more. Professor Webb tells us about it once again, in the language of the scholar but with more than a shade of the accent of Karl Marx on the one hand and of Mother Church on the other. We Westerners are to be scourged with a lash having many thongs.

It may be that now, with the free lands of the world occupied, individualism and freedom will disappear and the ant-heap society replace them. The assumption, both in Webb's book and in various others, seems to be that man broke out of some such society at the end of the Middle Ages, kept out of it for a few centuries while floating along on the "boom" which accompanied the successful conquest and occupation by western Europe of the outlying world, and is now lapsing back into it because migration, that is, the availability of new land, has to come to an end or, in other words, because there is no more frontier. It is a large assumption. From status to contract back to status. But were there any individuals among the Crusaders? Was there any freedom in an England that forced out of the various kings the great monuments of our parliamentary and legal institutions?

If a society is "closed," it may well be that the effect is to make people fight all the more vigorously for their rights. Someone has characterized the frontier as a region marked by "the philosophy of retreat." If you don't like it here, you get out and try somewhere else. If the wrong kind of people begin buying up houses on your street, you sell yours and move. You don't stand and fight. Some Puritans left England because conditions were not to their liking. Others stayed behind and fought it out, incidentally laying many courses in the wall of English liberties. The thesis could be argued that the frontier, for the English-speaking peoples, stifled as much freedom as it created.

"Democracy," which is supposed to be the major product of the frontier, especially of the American frontier, is a large and loose term. The American conception of it lays more emphasis upon social equality than does the

British, and rather more than does the Canadian. By "democracy," the British seem to mean little more than parliamentary government and the rule of law; they still accept a hierarchical society without much demur. We in Canada do not accept such a society, though we do accept the monarchy. Undoubtedly the New World has made for social equality. But there is a very important point here, the one I made years ago in the ancient article to which I have referred, and that is that every new country, whatever the shape of the society of its motherland, makes for a degree of social equality and a corresponding sense of freedom. Every difficult environment, old or new, does the same thing:

> Two voices are there; one is of the sea,
> One of the mountains; each a mighty Voice!
> In both from age to age thou didst rejoice,
> They were thy chosen music, Liberty!

In French Canada, daughter of absolutism in church and state, the new free environment of the forest turned French feudalism right round and made it work in favour of the habitant; all the French writers of the eighteenth century agreed that the Canadian peasantry was without sense of social distinction and far too independent for the liking of superior persons like themselves. But there was nothing more likely than that the twin absolutisms brought across the water would have regained their hold as society became more fixed: year by year, as escape to the bush became more difficult, their bonds would have tightened until New France approximated to Old. What saved the political freedom of the new world French was the English Conquest: they were conquered into the freedom of English political institutions. Their religious freedom was not saved — the church did reassert itself, and for freedom from it, a French Canadian would either have had to oppose himself to his own society or return to the post-revolutionary mother country. For New France an infinite frontier of free land would not have eventually meant either freedom or democracy.

I yield to no one in my estimate of the place in human history of the addition of a new world to an old. Of course it was the most important thing that could have happened to man! How could it possibly be otherwise? But does not this constitute a basic criticism of *The Great Frontier?* Is it not one prolonged labouring of the obvious?

Dropping down a level, I cannot accept the author's low view of western Europe at the end of the fifteenth century, nor does it seem necessary to his thesis. Of course man secured a new world, a second chance, a free field, but that hardly means that he had his back to the wall. I doubt if a Renaissance Italian, if he could return, would feel that he owed much to the New World. More probably he would feel that the New World owed a good deal to him.

The preceding sentence brings us to the second term in the Webb thesis, metropolitanism. This term has intriguued me for years and I have elsewhere written a good deal about it.[4] I can find little similarity in my views on the subject and those of Mr. Webb.

It does not seem to me that the concept of the metropolis can properly be applied to an area as large and varied and amorphous as Europe. But the frontier concept can be applied to much of that area. Baltic forests for some centuries had been contributing those same "wind-falls" of capital, to use Professor Webb's happy term, that the forests of the outer world were later — mainly in the nineteenth and twentieth centuries — to augment. There are many other examples — Baltic and North Sea herring and, at a later date, for the indirect harvests, that northern staple wheat: wheat, so important to metropolitan Great Britain in the nineteenth century, whether it came from Prussia, Romania, Kansas, or the Ukraine.

Incidentally, his discussion of windfalls may entangle Professor Webb, as windfalls should. In *The Great Frontier,* to show enormous gains easily reached, he quotes the experience of the Hudson's Bay Company from 1670 to 1720.[5] A share of stock, he states, purchased at Ł100 in 1670, brought its owner in the following fifty years declared dividends of 343 per cent and in addition an undivided profit of Ł800, a total of 1143 per cent on the original investment, slightly less than 23 per cent annually. Now the interest tables inform us that one dollar, or one pound, or one anything, compounded semi-annually at 6 per cent will in fifty years become 19.22 dollars, pounds, etc. Six per cent does not seem an unreasonably high rate for the period 1670-1720. At 7 per cent, one dollar becomes $31.19. Webb's $11.43 for both reserves and dividends represents slightly less than 5 per cent, a very low return, it would seem to me, for the times and the risks. Windfalls probably seldom were as lucrative as Webb's simple arithmetic works them out to be. The so-called "Great Frontier" was a good deal harder nut to crack than a person otherwise uninformed would gain from this book. It has remained a hard nut to crack, not only in dollars but in blood.

The frontier, that is, the outer world, always will be a hard nut for any metropolitan centre, or power, to crack, simply because before the cracking has gone to its logical limits internal resistance to it sets in. The North American Indians constitute almost the only example of a native people easily swept aside. The Africans and Arabs cannot be swept aside. The East Indians, both of the peninsula and of the islands, were not swept away, though for generations their countries were greater souces of wealth than was North America. The Chinese, towards whom gestures of sweeping

---

[4]See essay #6: "Metropolis and Hinterland," pp. 61-74.
[5]p. 184.

were made, may end up by sweeping us away: their historians could then write about the trans-Pacific frontier, as I suppose Gothic, Mongolian, and Turkish historians, had they existed, would have written about "the South West" and as Arab historians actually did write about "The West" — the Moghreb.

The idea of the new land, "the land out there," new frontiers, is surely as old as man. How many Naples — Newtowns — have been founded since man set out on his upward road! Naples, Neapolis, Neuvilles, Neu-stadts, Novgorads, Nijni-Nofgorads — they must exist all over the world. A history of the idea "frontier" would be a history of civilization itself and a sound sociology of the same.

Evidently, the idea of the frontier, as originally announced and often since assumed, needs vast enlargement.

In like manner, the idea of the metropolis, which is antecedent to that of frontier, or hinterland, requires exploration on many fronts. It must include not only conquest, colonization, imperialism, but also all the count-less factors that make for growth. And these are not only outward and physical but inward and cultural. What made some cities into metropolitan centres with almost limitless powers of growth? What is the role of politics, what of the staple trade, of geography? It does not help elucidation of the idea "metropolis" merely to equate it to "Europe," a large enough term in itself.

The historian may well ask himself how much of this tremendous burden legitimately rests on his shoulders.

The so-called metropolis "Europe" has contained both metropolis and frontier. With or without the New World, it is apparent that for a couple of thousand years or so now it has had considerable powers of growth. The Middle Ages, far from being ages of stagnation, as *The Great Frontier* seems to regard them, were themselves witnesses of development in many directions. There was the *Drang nach Osten,* carried out, as the late J. W. Thompson showed, in much the same spirit and with much the same results, if on a smaller scale, as the later conquest of the outer world. The fourteenth-century German newspaper editor, if he had existed, could well have said to the rising generation, "Go east, young man, go east." "There," he could have continued, "you can get free lands and cheap labour, merely for the taking. The lesser beings from whom you take them you can sell in the markets of the west as [what Europe soon came to call them] Slavs, or slaves. With the Slavs or slaves you retain, you can work your land and rise to baronial rank."

The idea has never died in Germany: it was revived forcefully under Hitler. Hitler had promised, according to one writer, that warriors who had attained certain honours "would be given estates in conquered coun-tries." One of the Nazi air aces, Von Werra, "thought he would see what

Poland had to offer in the way of estates." He took his bride there on their honeymoon. She writes: "...we drove around but could not make up our minds whether we wanted to breed cattle or fish. I wanted a lake and streams with fish, and also a house that had a tower. He wanted land and facilities for breeding horses."[6] That sounds very much like the men who believed they had a right to singe the king of Spain's beard or their successors who acted on the maxim that the only good Indian was a dead Indian. No one would deny that the scale was vastly enlarged when the outer world was opened, but the psychology was much the same, and probably the unsettling effects on institutions not dissimilar.

It is ridiculous to believe, and surely no serious historian does believe, that without the New World Europe would have lain stagnant. The old continent had already built a brilliant civilization and made many of the fundamental inventions (one need only mention the clock and printing), and no doubt would have gone on to make many more, New World or no New World. It got a powerful "assist" from the new resources made available by the discoveries (especially the physical resources), and possibly this is all that Professor Webb is claiming.

At any rate, European metropolitanism had risen to considerable heights well before the discoveries. Venice, Genoa, the Hanse cities, Antwerp — these and others could properly be considered metropolitan. To explain their growth would be to write their history. Pirenne tells us that Italian metropolitanism germinated from the reopening of the trade routes to Constantinople after they had been cut by the Arab thrust west. He says that free trade made Antwerp after the older Flemish cities such as Bruges and Ghent had wound themselves up in the restrictions of the various guilds. But these are merely large, impressionistic strokes. What is germane to our purpose here is that in the prediscovery period a large, though naturally not a world, scale of growth was evident.

I agree — who would not? — that we can probably give the largest share of the credit — or discredit — for what has happened since to the opening of the outer world. Might I dare to be personal and say that for years I have taught that the Industrial Revolution was "made in America," proceeding from the seller's market set up by colonization, a market which for many reasons impinged with greatest force upon England? To "made in America," I should add "made in India." I am sure, however, that the complex structure we call "growth" cannot be explained on the basis of any one factor, however impressive. "When we begin to search for the causes of the economic growth of a country...our embarrassment is not of poverty but of riches. We are swamped by explanations," says

[6]Kendall Burt and James Leason, *The One That Got Away* (London: Collins, 1856), p. 218.

J. K. Galbraith.[7] Mr. Galbraith goes on to examine a number of the more prominent explanations of growth, such as population increase, capital formation, natural resources, and various others. He comes to the conclusion that, while all are significant, they operate with varying intensity at various times and places, and no one of them is dominant. He thinks growth can go on today, if I understand him, without what have always been regarded as its prime necessities, new resources. His argument is probably too abstract to suit most historians, but if historians persist in searching for causes, they would do well to be familiar with lines of thought that are evidently not far from commonplace to the economists.

It seems to me that "the frontier" in the hard terms of economic development (which possibly drags in in its wake political and cultural development) must consist in usable resources. The frontier as a way of life is another matter: I love a lodge in some vast wilderness or a life on the ocean wave as well as any man, but that is another story. So the hard-headed economists probably must have their way, for they are at least logical, and "frontier" must be equated to "usable resources."

When we avail ourselves of what is a mile down under earth and sea, the additional resources result in growth just as surely as additional land. Oil a mile underground may create a community on top of it which will go through all the stages of social growth and manifest most of the frontier phenomena in the process. If it is American or Canadian oil, with a sense of self-government in its molecules, there will be easy informality among the new arrivals in the field, meetings will be held and committees formed. Later on, if the field holds out, the familiar signs of class differentiation will become visible — and just as much on the basis of oil as of land. If it is Arab oil, with polygamy in its chemistry, then, of course, the social evolution which slides along on it will be different.

But, again, one must always be careful to add that no one would deny the overwhelming scale of the land frontier experience of North America and the consequent interest and conspicuous nature of the social phenomena based on it.

Americans have rejoiced in their new society, and, until yesterday, most of them were glad to believe that they had turned their backs on the Old World. Their Revolution has influenced their thinking on this matter of the frontier, as on all others. Canadians did not make the same sharp break with the past; as a result, they have been ready to give weight, perhaps undue weight, to tradition. While Americans with names like Smith and Brown have been busy proving to themselves that they have long since ceased to be Englishmen, Canadians with names like Brown and

---

[7]John Kenneth Galbraith, "The Causes of Economic Growth," *Queen's Quarterly* 65 (Summer 1958): 169.

Smith have been apt to congratulate themselves on how English — or, rather, how British — they still were. Both may have gone too far. To me, an English Canadian, my American friends seem to have just as many English traits as I have, and in some directions more. If new societies are to get clear views of themselves, they will have to try to give true weight to both tradition and environment.

American students of the frontier have been apt to stress how much the new environment changed their institutions. Canadians have been apt to emphasize the continuity of theirs. As in all historic situations, "there is much to be said on both sides." The great institutions which the English-speaking world shares, such as representative government and the common law, were not worked out after the American Revolution but before it. They were not worked out in the modern period but in the medieval. If the New World had never been discovered, the English presumably would have gone on developing their free institutions nevertheless. We owe much of our freedom today to medieval Englishmen, and that is what I was taught as a boy in a little town close to the edge of settlement when we had to memorize the thirty-ninth section of Magna Carta. We in Canada have no bill of rights of our own, and we have never made a declaration of independence. But we believe pretty generally, I think, that "no freeman should be captured or imprisoned or disseised or outlawed or exiled or in any way destroyed ... except by the lawful judgment of his peers or by the law of the land."

Yet nothing is clearer than that a new environment changes institutions in detail. Professor Webb thinks that some of them are too big and hard to go through the frontier sieve: he instances the Catholic Church. I agree, except in that I imagine the Catholic Church itself has also been changed in detail by new environments: I doubt if Chinese Catholicism is quite the same as the Catholicism of French Canada. The latter, for example, is kept in fighting trim by the Protestant world around it. Would this be true of Catholicism in, say, Bolivia? There is a field here for much further work.

I wish that to Catholicism, as more or less frontier-proof, Professor Webb would add English parliamentary government. I also wish that students of the frontier would exercise their skill in attempting to refine the word democracy. A glance at non-English frontiers would be enlightening to them in this respect, for, as I have already said, every frontier brings forth the same phenomena of adaptability, energy, and a rough kind of equalitarianism.

As opposed to the loose social democracy of the frontier, which is transient unless supported with well-established institutions, I put weight on the medieval inheritance. But the medieval inheritance was badly disrupted during the earlier phases of colonization, and as a result a gulf

was flung across Europe and the Western world which has never closed
— the gulf of the Reformation. The Reformation cannot be well understood
unless it is viewed as a revolution — the first of the great revolutions that
have made the modern world. It was a revolution which touched every
nook and cranny of life. If we must have a single explanation for things,
and I hope we must not, I would prefer the Reformation to the frontier.
It goes wider and it goes deeper. It is not a matter of mere economic
determination. It changes the nature of man.

If one makes a journey from Ottawa to London, to Melbourne and
Auckland, and thence to San Francisco, Washington, and back to Ottawa,
he will have gone round the world, a long way. If, however, he walks
a few hundred feet from west to east along Sherbrooke Street in Montreal,
he will have gone further in fifteen minutes than he did on his journey
round the world. If he walks ten yards or so across the Mexican border
from California, as I did recently, he will have gone further still. If you
go round the world on the route I have mentioned, you remain within
the encompassing mantle of English speech and English institutions. You
note many local differences in detail, but they are small as compared with
the similarities. Then you take your walk along Sherbrooke Street or across
the border at Tijuana, and immediately — you are in another world! You
have crossed cultural frontiers that are of greater dimensions than land
frontiers and infinitely more stubborn. The approximate coincidence of
these frontiers with the success or failure of the Reformation is sufficiently
obvious.

The occupation of the lands now forming the United States was a
vast and mighty episode in human history, and no one will belittle the
bulk of it, its colour, and the innumerable consequences that have flowed
from it. But it was not the whole story of man's dispersal throughout the
world. And its characteristics did not arise solely from the process of
expansion. They were not by any means all made on the spot.

Coming from a country that still has a frontier and that, in the unconquerable north, must always have one, I am just far enough outside American frontier studies to feel that, while they have given rise to admirable
new historical insights, they have also been marked by a certain parochialism
and some of the lack of objectivity that goes with romanticism. I would
hope that as they go on, they will gain that catholicity of knowledge and
outlook which is a distinguishing and distinguished aspect of the general
edifice of American historiography.

5 | Two Ways of Life: The Primary Antithesis of Canadian History*

The schoolboy, with unerring judgment, picks out as the dullest subject of his acquaintance, Canadian History. Given the way it is usually presented to him, the schoolboy is right. But need he be? Does his judgment arise from the intrinsic nature of the material? I do not think so. On the contrary, the historian of Canada has at his command exciting and diversified resources, if he have but the skill to make them diversified and exciting.

Foremost among them, surely, are the glaring contrasts upon which this country rests — its sharp antagonisms, the diversity of the groups within it, its unbelievable geography, the ringing clashes everywhere upon all the great fundamentals. The human scene in Canada, both in time and space, is as full of bold colours as a typical Canadian landscape. The painter has used these effects: if the historian cannot, but puts everything into dull grey, it is his fault if people pass him by.

Of all our clashes, who will deny that the deep division between French and English is the greatest, the most arresting, the most difficult? Here is the most resounding note in our history, the juxtaposition of two civilizations, two philosophies, two contradictory views of the fundamental nature of man. For the historian, to neglect it is to leave the battle line. I propose therefore to devote this paper, with what skill I can command, to a short exploration of this primary antithesis of Canadian history. Since it is nothing less than two historic ways of life that I am going to look at, it is especially necessary to keep in mind the warning against "the dilettante who believes in the unity of the group mind and the possibility of reducing it to a single formula."[1] Whatever I have to say will, I hope, be taken by members of both races in the same spirit in which it is uttered, with a wish to understand but no desire to wound. While I shall be as objective as I can, I am well aware that to one of the divergent groups I myself belong.

A paper of this sort, attempting to look at a few of the fundamentals upon which this country is built, with a view to securing some of that release of tension so necessary to our national well-being, should logically begin with medieval Catholicism and St. Thomas Aquinas, for no one who wishes to understand Canada will get very far until he has studied the

---

*Delivered at a meeting of the Canadian Historical Association at Hamilton on May 25, 1943 and published in the C.H.A. *Report* (1943): 15-28.
[1]Max Weber, quoted in R. H. Tawney, *Religion and the Rise of Capitalism* (West Drayton, Eng.: [1948]), p. 283n.

medieval structure which a section of this country preserves with singular integrity. Failing the possibility of so comprehensive an approach, the movement which stands at the threshold of our present era, the Reformation, may serve as a point of departure. To that revolt against ecclesiastical metropolitanism, the medieval church, which had been rapidly disintegrating in the liberal world of the Renaissance, owed the renewal of vitality that expressed itself in the Counter or Catholic Reformation. In France, the first of our mother countries, the historical process was delayed for three-quarters of a century by civil strife. This gave to the religious problem a solution not in terms of compromise, as in England, but in those of the new Catholicism. The French Reformation, when in the first quarter of the seventeenth century it at last began to formulate itself, soon showed that it was not merely an imitation of that of Spain or Italy. It was French and northern. It was not particularly intellectual or artistic — no earnest religious movement can be — it had little either of the subtlety or the cruelty of the true Latins beyond the mountains. It was enthusiastic, serious, moral, evangelical. There was about it none of the fireside comfort of Anglicanism, little of the cold selfishness of Calvinism. It was a warm, human faith, full of visions and harmless miracles, strict in the standards of conduct it enjoined on its adherents. For those whose roots lie in nineteenth-century Protestantism, it diffused a religious atmosphere which, save for its ritualistic and sacramental basis, is not difficult to understand: it was a kind of nineteenth-century Methodism in a seventeenth-century Catholic setting. It was above all things missionary, and the missionaries it was to give the New World, the Brébeufs and Lalemants, were to become in the manner of their deaths strong pillars of France in America. Their shadows have loomed the larger as they have receded, and today the proud memory of the martyrs gives to French-speaking Canadians a centre of loyalties and a support which their English-speaking fellow countrymen have nothing to match.

It was in the man who was to be the first bishop of Quebec and in the nature of the church he established that the French Catholic Reformation was most deeply to affect Canada. François de Laval was strong-willed, haughty, eager for power, a puritan in morals, ultramontane — as was perhaps natural in a man whose younger days were passed among the confusions of the Fronde, with its tarnishing of royal power — jealous of the privileges of the church as opposed to the state, jealous of his rights as bishop, jealous of his personal dignity in the presence of the governor. Such traits have many times been repeated among his successors.

The ecclesiastical system whose foundations he laid was never to falter in proper loyalty to the king, but within the orbit of that loyalty it was to become as strong as the state itself. Education was in its hands from the first — as was inevitable in a period where education was universally a department of religion. The priesthood under him was formed into a disciplined body of men who were not allowed to become incumbents of "livings," but remained missionaries — fighting troops to be moved about from station to station at the discretion of their commander. The system still holds. The instrument Laval fashioned has proved its strength and its worth.

After Laval's time, Canadian-born became more and more common among the priesthood. This had its advantages and disadvantages. The Canadian priests were at one with their people; they were the natural shepherds of their flocks. On the other hand, they were provincials, with little experience except in their own small world. Their culture contrasted unfavourably with that of highly trained Jesuits and Sulpicians from France, but this lag in culture in the period following the original immigration is a familiar story in all new countries, a stage that must be worked through as a new society forms itself. It was as nothing compared with the asset of the curé's closeness to his people. When the evil days came, he had been fitted to become their natural leader, their salvation in tribulation. He retains his place to this day. A moment's glance at history should be sufficient to take all meaning out of that charge so often levelled by bigoted people that the French Canadians are "priest ridden." [2]

Laval built on natural foundations, for Catholicism of this popular, even democratic, northern type reflected the genius of the French people who came to Canada, the peasantry of Normandy and its neighbourhood, just as its close relation, Anglicanism, has suited the neighbouring peasantry of southern England, and as paternalistic and sacramental religions suit any peasantry. The life of the peasant is a series of ritual occasions — planting and harvesting, being born, coming of age, begetting, dying. The land has always been there and it always will be. Man's occupancy is transient, and the individual is only one in a long chain from forefathers to descendants. All are one family, interrelated if not in this generation, in the last or the next. All give unquestioned obedience to the great mother goddess, the earth-mother, who can easily be made to wear a Christian dress. The restless strivings, the desire for change, "improvement," "progress," "opportunity," which we today take as the normal condition of life, are absent. Man is subject to nature and to nature's moods: he learns to acquiesce in the drought and the flood, the good years and the bad. As his animals and plants grow and come to harvest, so he grows and comes to harvest. His religion is among the simplest and oldest of all creeds, Catholic almost by accident.

---

[2] It is well known that after the conquest the habitants were very glad to escape from the obligation of the tithe, but that indicates no general dislike of the clergy, simply a healthy independence, which has been demonstrated on more than one subsequent occasion, as, for example, in the elections of 1896.

The business of the peasant — or habitant, as he became in Canadian parlance — was not to make progress but to "make land": to "make land" many hands were necessary. Nature responded, as she always does. Practically all pioneer peoples are prolific; the transplanted French were especially so. There was lack neither of food nor function for every new child. A socially minded people saw no evil in being surrounded with their own and in the swift, steady widening of the family connection. Quite the reverse. They found happiness in life, not in things. A new and finer house meant less to them than sons and daughters growing up in the neighbourhood. If some died, others came: they would all meet hereafter. If some were lame or halt or blind, that was God's will. It was life that He and nature commanded, not the saving of life. This other-worldliness, still so marked in the countryside of Quebec, and not at all divorced from practical wisdom, was reinforced by the immemorial teaching of the church: man's real life begins hereafter. A genuine belief in immortality works profound effects on the manner in which a people lives. Catholicism and the countryside, simple French peasant traditions, as old as agriculture and the French joy in human companionship, came together into a strong complex which to this day shows little sign of giving way.

Yet for decades the countryside of New France was a neglected plant, overshadowed by the adventurous foliage of fur trader and missionary. Old France had men for high tasks but not peasants for export. Nor did the home-loving peasantry of a non-emigrating race wish to leave their native soil. The English separate themselves from home and family with ease — and often with relief: they dislike the cramping atmosphere of small communities. The French cling to the ties of mutual support: they dislike going away from the near and the familiar. They accept and enjoy the life of small communities. It is not surprising that only a few of them came to the new province, less than ten thousand, it is said, but all of them firm in their Catholicism and carefully guarded from taint or touch of heresy! From these all persons of French-Canadian race are descended. The combination of a faith kept free from all possibility of contamination, of a close environment, the banks of the St. Lawrence, and this extraordinary degree of in-breeding, produced a stock whose homogeneity surely can have few parallels. For the rest of us, with our multitudinous descents, this close-knit world is almost impossible of entry. All its members have clouds of common ancestors, all have had identical historical experiences, and all hold the same creed. Even today, amid the complexities of the modern world, the degree of differentiation seems relatively slight. All French Canadians are, as it were, the same French Canadian.

The process of forming a new people began as soon as the first children were born. By the conquest, it was for practical purposes complete. The seventy thousand Canadians of 1760, in a century of wrestling with the wilderness, had created a new society: one resembling the old peasant societies of France but with its own orientation, especially with its own family clans and its own passionate love of the land it had made its own and the soil it had won from the wilderness and the natives; a society entirely cut off from the rest of the world, turned inward upon itself to a degree few people of English speech can grasp; a society unbelievably parochial but in every sense a strong blood-brotherhood. This was the little world that was to crash under the triumph of English arms. The heart of the French nation had never been in empire, and it saw the vision of Champlain fade without regret. But what of the children of France, the Canadians, those who had taken such firm root in the soil that was to pass under the alien flag? What of them, isolated now in the hostile, Protestant, English continent of the conqueror?

It is hard for people of English speech to enter imaginatively into the feelings of those who must pass under the yoke of conquest, for, except in the southern states, there is scarcely a memory of it in all their tradition.[3] Conquest is a type of slavery and of that too we have no memory — except as masters. Conquest, like slavery, probably must be experienced to be understood. But one can intellectually perceive what it means. The whole life structure of the conquered is laid open to their masters. They become second-rate people. Wherever they turn, something meets their eyes to symbolize their subjection: it need not be the foreign military in force, it need not be the sight of the foreign flag, it may be some small matter — a common utensil of unaccustomed size and shape, let us say, taking the place of one familiar. And then there is the alien speech, perhaps not heard very often, but sometimes heard, and sometimes heard arrogantly, from the lips of persons who leave no doubt that the conquered are in their estimation inferior beings. Even the kindness of the superior hurts.

Nor does conquest sit easiest on the humble. The educated may make their peace, learn the foreign language, and find many areas in common, but the humble cannot cross the gulf — they feel pushed aside in their own homes. Hence it is that nationalism will always live longest, even if not blazing up into fierce flame, in the hearts of the people, who will seek to maintain their own ways by the passiveness of their behaviour, and little by little, as opportunity offers, will edge forward into any chance space left vacant by their masters.

Conquest in the forces it sets in motion may be tantamount to a revolution. The conquered are so bludgeoned by fate that they come to find new spiritual springs of life. Something like this did happen in French

---

[3] Yet as late as the nineteenth century an historian like Freeman could draw a line between the Saxon people, with whom he identified himself, and their conquerors, the Normans. In his writings the Saxons were always "we," and the Normans "they." The memory of conquest dies hard.

Canada. French Canadians are strong as a group today not least because they passed through the valley of the shadow a century and three-quarters ago.

No one can suggest that the English Conquest was cruel, as conquests go, or the English government harsh. If the French in Canada had had a choice of conquerors, they could not have selected more happily. But conquerors are conquerors: they may make themselves hated or they may make themselves tolerated. They cannot, unless they abandon their own way of life and quickly assimilate themselves, in which case they cease to be conquerors, make themselves loved. As long as the French are French and the English English, the memory of the conquest and its effect will remain. Not until the great day comes when each, abandoning their respective colonialisms, shall have lost themselves in a common Canadianism, will it be obliterated.

Within the old régime the French-Canadian type was formed: all its history since has been merely a superstructure on the foundation then laid. Anyone understanding the conquered people and gifted with a sufficiently prophetic eye could, in 1760, have foretold the attitude of the French Canadians toward conscription in 1941, or for that matter in 2041. In external affairs, including war, it is, was, and will be simply that of most of the other small Latin and Catholic peoples of the hemisphere who have been cut off from their parent stock and find themselves in a world that has moved far away from the pole about which they swing, they whose metropolitan centre is not London, or Moscow, or New York, but Rome. If we can understand the reactions of Ecuador or Paraguay to this northern world of Anglo-Saxons, Slavs, and Germans in which we live, we shall understand that of Quebec readily enough.

In the 180 years since the conquest, new phases of the basic situation have naturally presented themselves. As numbers and wealth increased and as English parliamentary institutions were introduced, a new class grew up — the intellectuals who spilled over from the too abundant material for the priesthood into the secular professions, especially the law. In French Canada, where everyone likes to talk and to hear good talk, the lawyer, *l'avocat,* has had a field day. His opponent invariably being another lawyer, every election has turned itself into an oratorical contest, and since a superbly convenient whipping boy has always stood ready to hand, it has been inevitable that every contest should involve him — *les sacrés Anglais,* the damned English. Is it therefore too much to suggest that every political fight from 1791 to the present day has had as its fundamental, if unexpressed issue, the English Conquest? If the situation were reversed, the same would be true of us — as it is to some degree true in the southern states. But why does the point need labouring? Does not the municipal government of the capital of our largest and wealthiest province turn on an even more ancient issue than the Plains of Abraham — on that obscure Irish skirmish, the Battle of the Boyne?

The French-Canadian intellectual, whether lawyer, journalist, or priest, has run true to type. He has lived in a world of ideas — or notions — but he has been better at talking, perhaps, than doing. He has had a difficult road, because for him there cannot be that free play of the intellect so naturally assumed by his opposite numbers in the English camp. His education has formed his mind before the world has opened to him, and he has had to do his thinking within a system whose boundaries are rigid. The results have been the weak development of the objective studies, the slam-banging personal tone of French-Canadian journalism (which is also agreeable to the spirit of the French race), its sometimes rather tenuous connection with facts, but above all the shoving-over of discussion and emotion to another concept, that of the race. The intellectual, priest or layman, has been the protagonist of the race. It is a natural, if somewhat unhealthy role. Any virile group cut off from free expansion will necessarily turn inward and console itself with its own virtues. It will at all costs seek survival and an opportunity to break its bonds. This is the motive power behind nazism, fascism, and "Japanese-ism": Germans, Italians, Japanese, all suffer from a species of claustrophobia. So do many French Canadians, marooned in an English continent. Like causes produce like results. The utterances of extreme racialists everywhere, whether in Germany or in Canada, come back to about the same thing. But it has been our good luck, here in Canada so far, that the extremists of neither race have captured control of the state.

Nevertheless, as the outside world has pressed more and more on the French island in America,[4] racialism has become more and more self-conscious and has absorbed into its concepts more and more of life, so that today it is impossible to tell whether the race is the bulwark for the faith or the faith for the race. Possibly the latter. It would appear to the outsider as if the French church today could to some extent stand apart from its own spiritual significance as a manifestation of Christianity and find its function in binding together people of common blood and speech.

We English Canadians have not until recently been very much plagued by intellectuals. Most of them who have not been drained off into practical tasks, we have managed to ship to the United States. The French have not had that easy solution. Their society was completed long ago, and there has not been a great deal for the intellectual to do except watch the English men of business tear it to pieces. The French intellectuals cannot

---

[4]And how heavily it does press! Note how American persuasiveness has at last drawn the "Quints" out of their backwoods French environment and put them on a public platform singing English songs! The reference is to their appearance at Superior, Wisconsin, during May, 1943, to sponsor certain ship launchings.

enter into that world, any more than can our own. They can merely stand at the threshold, their sensitive souls lashed with the thought that they may be regarded by the bustling representatives of the conquering race as second-class citizens. Hence their discontent. Hence much of the explanation for the Papineaus, the Bourassas, the Chaloults, with the rather pathetic cry, repeated from generation to generation, for more "posts," more safe government jobs, free from the rude blasts of English initiative.[5]

But French Canada, even if its people so desired, has not remained frozen in Maria Chapedelaine-ish postures. Things do move. The most conspicuous change is the coming of industrialism and the swing from rural to urban.[6] In 1871, 80 per cent of the French people of Quebec were rural, today only 42 per cent are. One of the most interesting questions that confronts the social scientist is what urbanism and industrialism will do to the Canadians of French speech. Will this unique peasant structure, this strong fortress of the Catholic Reformation, be able to adapt itself to the new kind of life? French Canada today is in the grips of the first revolution its people have ever known, the conquest excepted, the industrial revolution. What will be the outcome of the clash of medievalism and modernism, of the régime of the natural law and the acquisitive ethic? Will Catholicism adapt itself? Can the countryside continue to send out its sons and daughters in such a strong tide that peasant values, the faith and the church, will continue to dominate the cities? Will the race as a binding concept more and more displace the faith under the dissolving forces of urbanism? Will urban values work back into the countryside and give to rural Quebec, as they have already given to rural Ontario, a kind of suburban atmosphere? Will the forces of continentalism triumph over this strong fortress of localism? Will the international unions displace the Catholic? Whatever the future holds, the appointed guardians of race and faith will put up a good struggle.[7] The rural clergy will not be tempted overly much by the English shibboleth of a "high standard of living":

[5]It is in the 92 Resolutions of 1834 and in one of Mr. Chaloult's speeches of May, 1943.

[6]   Rural and Urban French Population of Quebec, 1871-1941

Year	Rural	Urban	Total	Per Cent rural
1871	745,125	184,692	929,817	80.3
1881	806,690	266,860	1,073,820	
1891	No Returns	—	—	—
1901	848,229	473,866	1,322,115	
1911	904,357	702,138	1,606,495	
1921	920,553	968,716	1,889,269	
1931	945,035	1,325,024	2,270,059	41.2
1941	1,107,380	1,587,652	2,695,032	41.7

Table from 1931 census, 1,755, table 35, and 1941, bulletin A-4. The total rural increase in Canada 1931-41 was 310,000 of which the French in Quebec contributed 162,000.

[7]In the last decade the French added to their population almost 70 per cent more people than those of British origin did to theirs, 553,000 as compared with 331,000.

they see the trap that lurks in that. They will not be too much in favour of high wages and only mildly of progressive and social measures, for their people have not yet reached the stage where they feel it necessary to be parsimonious of life. Heaven may not be quite as close as it once was and temporal values may be getting more emphasis than they used to do, but the group is still more than the individual, life still more than the means of livelihood, and the simple standards of the countryside will for a long time carry themselves into the cities.

From this exploration of French Canadianism one figure is absent, the man of business. With very good reason. Except in minor roles, he is an inconspicuous figure. If one takes his *Manual of Canadian Securities* and looks at the serried ranks of Directors listed therein, he will find only a corporal's guard of French names. The explanation is simple. Here is a society founded under a philosophy that admitted only a subordinate place to the man of business and his pursuits, that, even in his luxuriant fur-trading days, managed to keep him more or less in his place, and that by historical accident was rather thoroughly purged of him. It is possible to find Catholic societies in which a degree of capitalism has prevailed, though it is to be suspected that in them Catholicism has been subject to very severe strains. Sometimes, as in nineteenth-century France, it has been shouldered aside. But in such a preserve of the church as French Canada, it would be vain to expect any striking development of native capitalism — except the special form of capitalism represented by ecclesiastical corporative organization. Both historically and today the weight of French-Canadian society is against capitalism. The values it seeks to conserve are quite other. The businessman does not walk among the French as a god. Honours are paid not to the captains of industry but to the political, and especially to the ecclesiastical figures. I can see no end to English-Canadian domination of the machinery of production in Quebec except the abandonment by the French of their attitude to life and their acceptance of ours — either that, which they will not deliberately make, or the invocation of the power of the state to take over English enterprise and thus a slipping back into a more or less efficient paternalistic socialism, in which the intellectuals at last have all the *postes* they want as public factory managers.

No; for this characteristic phenomenon of yesterday, the businessman, we shall have to turn to the other side of the house, where he may be examined in riotous abundance. Our first contact with him is shortly after the conquest when he comes rushing in on the heels of the military. He is in a hurry. He wants to get things done. He has ends to gain, an object in life. That object is one comprehended only remotely by the peasant. From the first the New World has released in men the passion of greed. Greed in itself as a human quality the peasant can understand well enough but not greed erected into a way of life and fortified not only with the majesty of the law but with the sanction of a religion. Yet no other group has so systematically set up acquisition as an object in itself and made it the centre of a cult as have the men of business of the English-speaking world.

In 1760 the new creed had not gone as far as it has since, and there continued to resist it the older elements in English life, feudalism in its eighteenth-century form of aristocracy and certain sections of the Church of England. It was in the fighting and governmental services that these elements found their strongest expression. It was therefore these that were to have the best relations with the conquered Catholics. The weight of the English thrust into the conquered territories was not, however, to consist in officials and the military, but in men representing the new way of life, which had already appropriated for itself a theology by which it could rationalize its conduct. This way of life became dominant in Canada and remains so.

The connection between Protestantism, especially Calvinism, and material achievement has been the subject of much investigation. Wherever Calvinism has prevailed, societies largely committed to the acquisitive way of life have arisen. The coincidence seems logical, for while the spirit of acquisition is as old as man, Calvinism subtly reinforces it. The burning question it presented to its adherents — and in altered terms still presents — was whether God had elected them unto salvation.[8] There was no infallible means of finding out, but God might give a sign. And what more visible sign could the individual receive than that he should be prospered? But the sign would not come if one merely sat and waited for it. So the faithful set about each to his own individual duty, doing, as he believed, God's work. As someone has said, there is no more awesome sight than a churchful of Scotch Presbyterians upon their knees praying God to give them strength to do His will unto their fellow men, and then arising to go forth and do it! Calvinism created strong men, strong in their convictions, strong in their demands for elbow room to carry out their allotted tasks. But not men who were much concerned with their fellows. That was God's business. While the Jesuits were threading the wilderness to bring Christianity to the Indians, the New England Puritans were burning them alive in their own villages. [9]

---

[8] Today this question is put in much terser and secular form: "Can I make good?" Charles A. Beard and Mary R. Beard, *The Rise of American Civilization* (New York: Macmillan, 1930), make the point that since about the mid-nineteenth century, the ethic of success has dominated the older ethics: not "Is it just, is it right?" becomes the question, but "Can I succeed?" To fail in the presence of the group emerges as the unpardonable sin. See their chapter 20, "The Triumph of Business Enterprise."

[9] A century later the bourgeois of the North West Company were zealously supporting the first Presbyterian church in Montreal, but that church showed a conspicuous absence of interest in the activities at the other end of the fur trade.

✗ Lower ignores the Presbyterian concept of "stewardship". The individual is responsible to use his gifts, talent and any resulting wealth for the benefit of others. Such views made these people good colonists.

In countless ways the Calvinistic type of Protestantism accentuated the motives of accomplishment and success. Everywhere it found its most congenial soil in urban areas, among the middle classes. In industry, it became the support of self-made men, men who "did not need the government to help them in *their* business," and in politics, it came to stand for *laissez faire* and the policeman state. Its spirit reigned supreme in Victorian England, the spirit of drive, of providence and thrift, of smug success. How far it all was from the scriptural injunction to take no thought for the morrow!

Nowhere was the acquisitive ethic more at home than in the New World. There the field was open and nature invited exploitation. Hence the strong link between it, the Scotch or New Englanders, the staple trade, and the characteristic expression of the staple trade, the metro-politan-hinterland relationship. Traditions that might have held it in check were weak. Nearly everything sooner or later was bent in the one direction — the contempt of the older ideals and the intolerance that the new and the moving invariably manifests for the old and the static. The goal of material success passed over easily into success in terms of accomplishment or of power and in these forms afforded the driving energy that has mainly made America.

No one would assert that there have been no other aspects of life represented among the English-speaking population of Canada. Among our farmers many of the traits of peasant societies survive, and the antithesis between the country way of life and the urban has been almost as sharp at times as that between French and English.[10] Certain areas of English settlement come close to the French countryside itself in their conformity to older social patterns.[11] In the region of religious or cultural tradition there is the Anglican emphasis on service to the state and on the ideal of the gentleman; or the Scottish ideal of the learned man, the philosopher. Very prominent is humanitarianism, that powerful body of emotions, sentiments, beliefs, and actions, which has penetrated every nook and cranny of our Canadian life. It would be interesting to analyse the complex way in which these all twine around each other. But space does not permit. English-speaking Canada has fallen under these various traditions in about the same way as the United States, though at a retarded rate, for here there have been influences restraining their free play. For example, our continuing connection with Great Britain has provided some shelter for a class structure and a quasi-official church, the Church of England. For the first seventy-five years after the conquest, this older English tradition

[10]It had a large share in the Upper Canadian Rebellion of 1837, the Clear Grit party, and, of course, in the more recent agrarian movements, especially Alberta "Social Credit."
[11]See Enid Charles, "The Trend of Fertility in Prince Edward Island," *Canadian Journal of Economics and Political Science* 8 (May 1942): 213-46.

— the "squire and parson" concept of society — made a strong fight of it with commercialism — as in its modern form it is doing again today, under the special circumstances of the war, with its strengthening of the forces of history. But it too became more or less assimilated to the dominant tone, as witness the business relationships of the Family Compact men, and left the field pretty clear for the exploitive and acquisitive attitudes, which had an almost unchecked run until a decade or two ago. There must be few English Canadians of middle life who were not brought up on the conviction that their business in life was to succeed, "to make good," "to get on," "to get to the top," "to amount to something."

Methodism, whose social gospel also opposed a certain counterweight to acquisition, split under its pressure. The industry and thrift inculcated by the creed brought worldly success to many of its followers, who trailed off into the acquisitive camp, taking with them the phraseology of simpler days and the shell of the old attitudes of brotherhood and often leaving awkward gaps between profession and performance. But the genius of Methodism continued to assert itself in characteristic social movements, temperance, social service, and so on. Eventually it found logical expression in a more or less formal political socialism: much of the drive in Canadian socialism comes out of Canadian Methodism, and as it does battle with Canadian individualism, it carries forward the Christian ethic of support for the weak and the lowly against the strong and the established.

These are the two most significant traditions at work in our English-speaking community today: they represent its sharpest antithesis, and the future will witness a battle over which shall organize it. Neither one is now very firmly attached to its original religious base. The Methodist-humanitarian tradition satisfies itself with a social gospel and a social task: it resorts easily to perfectionism — to utopianism, pacifism, a vague internationalism, and a "planned society." The Calvinist-individualist-success conception of life, stripped of its fine phrases about election unto salvation, initiative, individualism, being nothing more than mere selfishness, was the first to run beyond Christian bounds. Those who live in this area find themselves today confronting life either on the basis of a rather mechanical benevolence and simple good fellowship or face to face with a frank hedonism and a stark paganism.[12]

The dynamics of acquisition have transformed the world, but the societies dominated by them — of which our own is one — despite their brilliance, are hollow at the centre. For deep in the heart of this way of life there seems to be a denial of life. It sets up for itself a goal of goods, of plenty, of a "high standard of living," and here finding common ground

---

[12]The American divorce tradition, which is paganism, is a descendant of the individualism of American Puritanism.

with humanitarianism, surrounds itself with devices designed to smooth out life's ills, to make life easier, to prolong and save life. It secures food and shelter of an excellence never before attained. It increases the span of life, makes individuals healthier, stronger, taller, more alert. It decreases illness, physical disabilities, infant mortality, maternal mortality. And yet, solicitous as it is for the individual's well-being, the societies it has created are slowly withering. Speaking of the disappearance of the English from the Eastern Townships, the authors of a recent book on Quebec say: "A peaceful victory, a grand victory, for today there are 300,000 French there as against less than 50,000 English. Note that the relations between them are excellent because our people have not returned the blows which their ancestors received.... 'The French are right to act in this way: it is better (instead of retaliation) to give the English splendid funerals'. ... The majority of the English have become a population of old people ... who having sold their property to the French, live in retirement in the villages. These villages present as it were 'the foretaste of a cemetery.' "[13]

Many people become indignant because they would say the French are pushing the English out. I cannot see that the French are to blame. They are a virile people who can see no virtue in childlessness. If we have no instinct for group survival and choose the easy way out of comfort and race suicide, we have ourselves to blame.

Our two Canadian ways of life exemplify the antithesis that in general terms might be put somewhat as follows: the nearer what might be called the peasant-spiritual, or rural-natural, the primitive outlook on life, the stronger the hold on life, the greater the survival value of the group, the less considered the individual, the greater the complaisance in taking what life brings, good fortune or bad, good health or bad, sound limbs or crooked. In contrast, the more in the other current, acquisition, materialism, commercialism, urbanism, individualism, Calvinism − call it what you like − the greater the parsimony with life, the more concern for the individual, the more strenuous the efforts to keep him from blemish, to make perfect specimens, to patch up the defective, to prolong life, the less ability to create it. *The "high standard of living" seems to destroy life.* The one complex, in its extreme, leads to mere animalism, the other to extinction. Where is the happy medium and what philosophy will support it?

In Canada, the two outlooks have had marked geographical correlations. The urban-acquisitive complex has deepened in proportion to the longitude west. Prince Edward Island and Nova Scotia have been less affected by it than Ontario, Ontario than Manitoba, and Manitoba than British Columbia. Under the weight of the Depression this tendency is not now so marked. The English in Manitoba and Saskatchewan alike

---

[13]*Notre Milieu: Aperçu général sur la province Québec* (Montreal: Fides, 1948), pp. 97-98.

are decreasing, and in Ontario and British Columbia they are being kept afloat by immigration from other provinces. In Saskatchewan the pattern stands out with especial clearness: in the last ten years, those races close to the soil have held their own despite misfortune — Ukrainians, Germans, Hungarians, etc. But the commercial races — those who do not see life as existence but as opportunity — have gone sharply down in numbers, the English, the Syrians, the Jews, and the Chinese.

There is also a decided religious correlation. Believe it or not, you will have a considerably larger family if you are a Pentecostal than if you are a Presbyterian. The further one moves away from the simple, rural, pietistic groups, such as the Mennonites, among whom there were, in 1931, 159 children under the age of five for every 1,000 persons, into the more sophisticated, urban, middle-class, acquisitive areas, which make large demands on life, the less is the likelihood that his group will replace itself in the next generation. At the extreme stand the Christian Scientists, just where one would expect them, with 45 children under five per 1,000, the perfect embodiment of prosperous middle-class dessication. When its characteristics are analysed, every denomination falls exactly into the anticipated place.[14]

Correlations of group survival value may in fact be made by the bushel. There are positive correlations such as the rural life, pietistic or authoritarian religion, religious dogma, pioneer areas, old static areas, poverty, short life-expectancy, religious communism, communal segregation, lower class, labour in new industries, possibly aristocracy: and negative correlations such as urbanism, size of urban unit, individualism, altitude in the middle class, commercial attitudes, professional occupations, income, divorce, "feminism," the size and newness of automobile, exploitive economies, such as the mining and logging economy of British Columbia, suburbanized rural areas, humanitarianism, possibly agnosticism, intellectualism. In

---

[14]   Children 0-4 Years of Age Per 1,000 of Total

Denomination

Denomination	
Mennonites	159.3
Roman Catholics	125.5
Mormans	123.3
Greek Orthodox	121.7
Pentecostals	103.7
Lutherans	97.8
Baptists	90.5
United Church	87.5
Anglicans	85.5
Presbyterians	80.5
Salvation Army	75.5
Jews	75.0
Christian Science	45.3

Table compiled from 1931 Census, vol. III, p. 310.

general it is the humble who have survival value. It is the meek who shall inherit the earth.

It is an ironic commentary upon history that that group which began with a return to life, with a triumphant affirmation of life, with a *"Welt-Bejahung,"* the Protestant, should now, with minor exceptions, have fallen into a denial of life, a fear of animal "robustiousness," while the other group, which persistently belittled this life and lived in the shadow of immortality, should be exhibiting in our day every evidence of that affirmation which Protestantism once made. Protestantism as a traditional way of life has got too far away from nature. Sophistication has been too much for it. Given our present attitude to life, we are probably fighting our last victorious war. If the test comes again in the future, we shall have too few young men to fend off the races such as the Japanese that ask less return from life but are more able to live. Our people are willing to make every effort to ensure by military means the immediate survival of their group but they seem not to have the slightest interest in what may happen to it a few years into the future. It may therefore be that their fate, too, is to pass under the harrow and from intimate contemplation of the arrogant superior, find for themselves the secret that the humble already know. *Deposuit magnifices de sedibus....*

Does this mean that we shall have to choose between the way of life we have built up and our survival as a group? Shall we have to return to what most of us would feel to be a much poorer kind of civilization? I trust not, though if our civilization is to survive I am certain that some kind of compromise will have to be effected and many aspects of our present way of life greatly modified. Amid much that is good many of them are just idiotic. Everyone can amuse himself by compiling his own list of lunacies, but conspicuous among the major changes that will have to come is a modification of the ethic of acquisition, the *appetitus divitiarum infinitus,* the unbridled indulgence of the acquisitive appetite, as Tawney puts it, and the degenerate indulgence that surely accompanies it.

If our urban civilization were to fall through dry rot, through failure of manpower, hardly less ironical a fate would be in store for the non-acquisitive group, which is, in Canada, the French. Without the initiative of the English Protestant man of business, the present-day mechanical civilization could not have come into existence. Without it, the French would have remained a quiet rural people, probably not more than a quarter as numerous as they are now. If old William Price, or some other, had not opened up the Saguenay a century and a quarter ago, and if his successors had not built on to his achievements, instead of the lumber, the pulpwood, the water-power and the aluminum that now come out of that valley, there would have been a few farms on the shores of Lake St. John, a few small local sawmills, and that would have been all. There would have been that many fewer opportunities for life. The industrial structure of Quebec rests on this initiative, which has provided work for the hundreds of thousands from the countryside who otherwise would have had to stay on the farm as bachelors and spinsters, or divide and subdivide the land in Malthusian misery. The question forces itself, "who has created the French race in America?" I make bold to say that the English industrialist has created about three-quarters of it.[15]

So the fate of the two peoples seems indissolubly linked. At present they complement each other, unhappily and acrimoniously. But may the day not come when understanding will be greater? May the English not learn a little tolerance, the French gain a little breadth? May the English, through suffering, perhaps, lose a little of their arrogance, the French a little of their touchy vanity? May the extreme commercialism of the English not be modified, the more obvious blatancies of their civilization overcome, their acquisitive ethic toned down? May the French not come forward and take their place in running a modern state, finding constructive ideas to contribute, getting a little further away from medievalism, from a philosophy that sacrifices nearly everything to survival value? May the deep fear which afflicts both sides — the fear of the French of losing their identity and the fear of the English of being outnumbered — not be dissipated in a common loyalty to a common country?

That day may come and it may not. Pressure from the outside world may bring it, though of that I am doubtful. The lessening numbers of the English may induce in them more of a live-and-let-live attitude. The penetrative qualities of North American civilization may bring French society closer to the continental norm. Most likely of all, it seems to me, the tensions and troubles of our times, which are not going to end with the peace, will some day burn out the grosser aspects of our English materialism, giving us a truer and deeper insight into life than what we have now, reforming our society in some such way as society was reshaped at the end of the Middle Ages and thereby establishing a new set of values in which both races can share. The two communities will never be one, there can be no question of a blood-brotherhood, but sooner or later they will take up their respective weights, some kind of equilibrium will be reached, of that I am sure. We have not lived together for nearly two centuries merely to see the Canadian experiment fail. It will not fail. This country of high colours and violent contrasts will not fail. One of these days the two races, forgetting lesser allegiances, will unite in mutual loyalty to it, and build it into a structure of which our successors will be proud.

---

[15]Reckoning in the industrial French population of the United States.

6 | *Metropolis and Hinterland**

The present age has witnessed the end of a long period marked by the ascendancy of island or maritime states, which have been succeeded on the world's stage by continental powers. From the fifteenth to the twentieth century it was the peoples, states, and cities situated on the western coast of Europe or on the eastern coasts of America that flourished most in wealth and political importance. Spain, Portugal, France, Holland, England, Belgium, and the United States founded empires. Britannia came to rule the waves. The lights of London were reflected in the sidewalks of New York. The great age of maritime enterprise opened the world to all the littoral powers, even those somewhat remote from the main ocean. Sweden and Denmark both founded colonies. A colony, an unsuccessful one, was sent out by the city of Riga. Late in the game, when the whistle had almost blown, Germany, Italy, and Japan essayed the same adventure. Down to the Peace of Versailles of 1919, perhaps down to the end of the Second World War, the unannexed world was civilized man's oyster, and it was the peoples best situated on the sea-front who had traditionally opened it. There had been a previous age when men kept to the dry land, when Germans tried to colonize the eastern frontiers of Slavdom, and Slavs were pushed still further into the eastern wilderness. But the drive to the east came while techniques of transportation and other agencies of mobility were still primitive, and Europe, unlike nineteenth-century America, did not turn its back on the sea. Nor had Europeans advanced politically and socially to the point where they were capable of organizing great land empires. So the land states of the Middle Ages declined in importance before the rising sea states. Today, the sea states are in retreat before the great new sea and land powers.

The ocean empires naturally concerned themselves with empty sea-coasts, and while they might claim vast stretches of the interior, it was only slowly that they made effective penetration. Most of the cities of Central and South America (Mexico was an exception) were on or near the sea-coast. York, Upper Canada, founded as late as 1792, was the first colonial capital of the British Empire far removed from the guns of a British warship. When modern means of transportation and other technical devices did enable the sea powers to penetrate the interior by settlement, division

**South Atlantic Quarterly* 70 (Summer 1971): 386-403. Copyright 1971 by the Duke University Press.

between them and their colonies began: <u>inland Upper Canada had obtained</u> <u>"responsible government" within little more than half a century of its</u> <u>founding</u>. Continental stretches peopled by settlers striking roots in native soil and distant trans-oceanic control did not go well together. The ocean empire, if it remained an empire, was commercial and military. From it swarms of emigrants could pour out, but its strategic figure was the merchant, the man with a purse who could buy (or seize) something in the new land to send back to the old. Sea empires have mothered colonies of settlement, but in themselves have been urban and commercial.

Yet, one stage further back sea empires rest on the land. They rarely arise except through the power of organized territorial states. The sea empire of Carthage was a possible exception, that of Venice another. The Roman Empire, centered on a city, was not, for Rome was a rural state with a little urban nucleus, a state which expanded territorially until in the Italian peninsula it had base enough to fight Carthage and win. The Hanse cities founded no empires: Hanse merchants came and went on the suffrage of the territorial king. *Per contra,* territorial states of simple, medieval organization did not need the support of commercial cities. Seated in capitals that scarce deserved the name of city, a Charlemagne and a Rotbart could marshal their myriads and rule vast stretches of land. They might not be able to maintain their empires, but their successors, the national kings, learned how to extend their kingdoms, and after they had made feudalism safe for the middle class, the man of business could carry on and begin to talk about the virtues of free enterprise. Once sufficient stability was assured, the edifices of wealth could rise, the controls of ledger and law court could manifest themselves, men could be bound by contract, and urban life, expression of "the free play of economic forces" for those who were free to avail themselves of them after their "play" had been assured by someone else, could grow up.

Although commercial society must as a rule be carried within the womb of the state, it has often taken charge of the destinies of its parent. In England, within a century after baron and priest had been sufficiently knocked about by the Tudor Henries, the commercial state was visibly rising. Within two centuries the men of business, having taken a prominent part in overturning the old monarchy, were bending the laws and institutions of the kingdom to their own purposes. In the nineteenth century they completed their triumph, securing effective political and economic control and so dominating their age that intellectuals shaped a semi-philosophy to explain the virtuous and inevitable nature of the simple desire to grab: "business," resting on the solid foundation of "each for himself and the devil take the hindmost" (the more dignified term is *laissez faire),* was enthroned, and the creed of monetary success came to occupy a commanding position.

"Business" can only be done where men meet: if opportunity offers for much business, many men meet. Thus cities grow: they are in essence groups of men organized, not for living, as is the countryside, but for accomplishment. The farmer expresses himself in his own work, that of his family, and his animals: the man who uses the economic advantages which make a city expresses himself in the co-ordination of the work of men. The life of movement, the dynamic life, in fields other than that of war, finds its natural habitat in the city. Urban life and commercialism are firmly joined. Cities represent economic control. Even quite small collections of men become focal points from which the affairs of larger regions are directed. The advantages of nodal points determine the range of country which such points control. If they grow large, it is because the men in them are able to extend their activities over wider and wider areas. But the larger they grow, the more they lose their character as communities: they become merely places where business is done or pleasure is to be had, and at a certain stage in their growth everyone tries to escape from them, leaving behind only the unfortunates who have little to do with the direction of affairs. The logical culmination is the square mile of "The City" in London, where at night no one lives but the caretakers and the cats. By the time such a stage is reached, the city has become the centre of direction for a region whose extent is limited only by the natural advantages of position and the techniques of transportation. If it is a political capital also, from it the destinies of millions of men of every race and clime may be directed. The importance and complexity of the affairs administered from it bring to it a high concentration of ability. Part of this devotes itself to amusing the rest, creating such characteristic metropolitan art forms as the theatre and opera. Such forms, when thoroughly integrated, elaborated, and intellectualized, take their places among the historic cultures of the world, which have invariably been urban, and usually metropolitan. An independent artistic, musical, and literary culture may be taken as the final stage in metropolitanism: its development marks the completion of the process. By the time it has arrived, the original city has ceased to be in any proper sense an integer: it was not London as an integral political unit which reached out into the Seven Seas, but the people of Great Britain, whose communal business is done in London. A great metropolis is a combination of office and hotel. While much attention has been given to the economic factors in the growth of cities and to the sociological problems cities engender, there has not been the same emphasis on the political and cultural sequences of urbanism.

When over a thousand years ago power moved north of the Alps, it slowly dragged civilization with it. Not until power had forged territorial communities could natural geographic advantages begin to build great cities. The greater the area of order resting on power and the greater the economic and geographic advantages, the greater the city. Paris became great because it stood at the strategical and economic centre of France; and France, the richest countryside of Europe, had been welded into a unit by the French kings, who had their seat at Paris. Paris grew on the political growth of France. Berlin, mere outpost of Germandom until the eighteenth century, grew on the successful wars and diplomacy of its masters, first into the capital of a great nation and then into the focal point for the commerce, industry, culture, and politics of all central Europe. Its fall was even more rapid than its rise. Berlin, stuck off in the northeast corner of Western civilization, seemed a synthetic rather than a natural metropolis.

Normally, cities grow through some favourable geographical factor which is improved upon and exploited by the farseeing. This invariably turns out to be some natural feature of communication which brings the city into profitable relationship with regions of natural resources. Paris represents a ford in the Seine, Moscow a portage route from the Baltic to the Caspian, London the first point up from the sea at which the Thames could be forded, and Shanghai the entrance to the Yangtze Kiang. Great navigable rivers usually give rise to great ports at their mouths. Island cities represent security or command narrow sea entrances. Most great cities have the essentially middleman function of levying toll, under a score of intricate forms, on the goods that pass by, as the term entrepôt, so frequently used to describe them, indicates. Cities founded upon industry may become large and important, but industry historically comes after commerce (as, for example, Constantinople); and while commercial entrepôts frequently also become great centres of industry, the opposite is not usually true: Pittsburgh is not New York.

Toll is taken first in simple forms, such as harbour, wharfage, pilotage, and warehouse charges, but it soon goes on to develop into commissions and profits on goods and cargoes bought and sold and into insurance on goods and ships. When mercantile interests become strong enough, trade associations are formed, both to secure further development of the city's advantages and as pressure groups to obtain favourable legislation or administrative action from government. If such groups are able to make out a good case for their demands, especially by arguing that they are in the interests of the community as a whole, government may base general policies upon them, especially if an entrée into government circles is afforded through personal or family connections. Men of business spoke with fairly loud voices in the councils of the great autocrat Louis XIV. In eighteenth-century England, Whig aristocrats and Nonconformist businessmen arrived at such a close understanding that merchants could always get a Hat Act or an Iron Act (1750) from government, and Whig ministers could get to wife a daughter and heiress from Nonconformist merchants. It is only a step from commercial policy to "high policy," that area of decisions leading up to peace or war. In the eighteenth century, commercial rivalry was among the major causes of the long duel between Great Britain and France which led to the British conquest of Canada and parts of India. No one can read the documents of the time without seeing how close behind the soldiers and the politicians were the businessmen. The merchants had, in effect, succeeded in creating an empire: metropolitan control had arrived at its logical culmination, the domination of great regions of the earth.

The original impulse of development rests, as has been said, upon some geographical advantage, but unless natural resources can be utilized, position alone will not bring about a great concentration of humanity: the perfect harbour of Halifax has not been sufficient in itself to build a great city; it is too far away from utilizable wealth. Most great centres have risen on their close relationship to one or more readily available sources of wealth. In their earlier stages they seem to have been the gates through which this wealth went out to other areas, but in their more developed aspects they have been receivers of wealth from other sources, either for local consumption or further distribution. Southern English ports rose on exports of raw wool to the continent, but they flourish on imports of goods from overseas. In this way older cities often develop secondary centres, and between the two a reciprocal relationship obtains: Montreal has been a Canadian outpost of Liverpool; Toronto is a Canadian outpost of New York. Such relationships rest on the import into the older city of the natural form of wealth for which the newer is a good gathering and shipping point. The characteristic source of wealth upon which great cities have grown (though not necessarily the only one) consists in a commodity for which demand is great and of which there is available a large supply of reliable and fairly uniform quality. The bulk of international trade has invariably been composed of such staple articles. It has been the staple trades of the last four centuries that have shaped colonization, colonial policies, colonial politics, many aspects of international relationships, and the high policy which has so often expressed itself in war.

Staples have represented large stores of rather easily obtained wealth. They have tended to dominate the economy of the areas from which they have been secured. Such areas have invariably had less mature economies than those of the regions which have taken the staple product. They have been areas without complexity of life where land and other natural resources have been more abundant than people. In this sense they might be called "new countries." Medieval England, with its staple trade in wool, compared with the receiving market, Flanders, was "new." It was less thickly populated than Flanders and had less of urban life and its aggregations of skills and sophistication. The gaudy feudalism of Old England, rural and half-barbaric, compares closely with the high-coloured life of the Old South of the United States, based on another textile staple, cotton. It was not until raw-wool export was checked by various mercantilistic devices and woolen manufacture was established that a rural civilization equipped with a few ports of exit began to change into an urban or industrial civilization and ports of exit began to become ports of entry. For England, the transition marked the beginning of the road toward metropolitanism.

Most staples give rise to similar patterns of relationship between the area of supply and the area of demand. The older or more fully developed area lacks certain necessities of its expanding life, either because it has exhausted or exceeded its own supplies or has never had any. It then begins to secure these from "newer" areas which have what it needs, as Flanders secured the wool of medieval England. Its merchants send their agents to the new area of production, and there they establish themselves as buyers or shippers or, to use the time-honoured term, "factors." Since the agents open up new opportunities for the natives, they find themselves in a position of power. Whether they pay in gold or glass beads, they are probably the only avenue by which capital can enter the region, and the persons dealing with them most likely have no alternative market. This enables the factors to put pressure on the natives, for even if factors are fairly numerous, they soon come to agree among themselves on prices and conditions, and in the initial stages of the staple trade, no producer of the commodity in question has the knowledge or connections which would enable him to market his product directly in the import market. Their own internal competition merely carries their apparatus of control a step further, for the stronger among them, in order to make sure of having sufficient supplies for shipment, begin to offer "advances" to the producers on the security of their prospective production. The producers soon find themselves in debt to the export merchants and have to take whatever price they are given. The tobacco planters of pre-revolutionary Virginia, the Washingtons included, were chronically in the debt of the Scottish tobacco factors in Virginian ports: possibly the relationship had something to do with the revolutionary fervour of these magnates.

When an agent has lived long enough in the countries where his "factory" is, he becomes partly naturalized, especially if he has come out young. He may marry a woman of the country. If she is a "native" he may marry her "country style," as did the Hudson's Bay factors: then when his term of service is over, he can provide for her and her offspring and return home. If the woman be a wife, summary solutions are more difficult, and if she is white, impossible. Old fur traders who made the mistake of marrying their squaws had to stay in the country. The Scottish merchants in the Canadian centre of the trade, Montreal, who frequently annexed Canadian seigneuries by marrying the heiresses of the seigneurs, also usually stayed in the country: of these James McGill, who, because childless and not knowing what to do with his money, left his estate to found a university, was an example. Marriages between a factor and a women resident of his own race and creed could present no distinctive pattern: possibly the family all returned "home," or if it remained and was of sufficient status, tried to prevent itself from falling into general colonial society by having the children sent "home" to be educated and by cultivating a strong spirit of colonialism. This latter pattern survives in Canada to this day, and some of the "exiles" in such cities as Montreal and Toronto try to keep themselves apart from ordinary Canadian life many generations after their ancestors first removed to the New World.

The middlemen, if partly naturalized, may come to feel some responsibility for the welfare of the persons engaged in the chain of production they have set going and may manifest towards them a paternalistic attitude. This may include some interest in bettering their mode of life, or more likely, their mode of production: the Hudson's Bay Company, when it became monopolistic, could cease whiskey trading and encourage fur conservation. The end product of this type of interest is acclimatization to the point of territorial conquest and the erection of a government: the East India Company went out to trade and remained to prey, but in its later stages, it had to assume the responsibilities which the governor must display toward the governed. Most frequently, however, the factors simply display irresponsibility. They are strangers in the new land, and they only await their opportunity to leave it. When they have "made their pile," they aim to return home and retire, marriage being one of the few chains that can prevent their doing so. They have no regard for the future of the country in which they are working and exploit its natural wealth without compunction. If there is not much of it, the factor goes home after its exhaustion; the temporary activity of which he has been the activating agent ceases, and the area is poorer than before, like an abandoned mining camp. The destructive effect of the exploitation of a staple natural resource by outsiders who thought of it purely in terms of readily obtainable wealth was never better described than by Peter Fisher in his *History of New Brunswick*. Referring to the square timber trade in that province, he says:

A stranger would naturally suppose that such a trade must produce great riches to the country; and that great and rapid improvements would be made. That large towns would be built, that the fair produce of such a trade would be seen in commodious and elegant houses, extensive stores and mercantile conveniences, in public buildings for ornament and utility, good roads and improved seats in the vicinity of the sea-ports, with Churches, Kirks, Chapels, etc: all these with many other expectations would be but a matter of course. But here he would not only be disappointed, but astonished at the rugged and uncouth appearance of most parts of this extensive country. There is not even a place that can claim the name of a town. The wealth that has come into it has passed as through a thoroughfare to the United States, to pay for labour or for cattle. The persons principally engaged in shipping the timber have been strangers who have taken no interest in the welfare of the country; but have merely occupied a spot to make what they could in the shortest possible time. Some of these have done well, and others have had to quit the trade; but whether they won or lost, the capital of the country has been wasted, and no improvement of any consequence made to compensate for it, or to secure a source of trade to the inhabitants when the lumber shall fail. Instead of seeing towns built, farms improved and the country cleared and stocked with the reasonable returns of so great a trade, the forests are stripped and nothing is left in prospect, but the gloomy apprehension when the timber is gone, of sinking into insignificance and poverty.[1]

That is exactly how the staple trade in square timber left much of New Brunswick, the regions over which it raged most destructively being to this day sunk in "insignificance and poverty."

Except that staple industries which depend on the soil may under reasonable conditions go on forever, the staple industry is very similar in nearly all respects to mining: there are mines of short life and mines of long. In short-lived staples, such as the Pacific sea-otter trade, the commodity disappears and the industry with it, leaving no trace behind. In more capacious staples, such as West Indian sugar, whole communities of apparently permanent nature may be built, only to sink into ruin when the conditions which supported the staple disappear. A staple like wool may apparently go on as long as people need warm clothing. England today probably grows far more wool than it did seven centuries ago, when the medieval staple was at its typical zenith.

If there is enough of the staple commodity to weather the first furious attacks on it, conditions may stabilize, and then the pattern of exploitation will go on unrolling according to its inner logic. Firms will descend from father to son, and this will hasten the naturalization of the factors. At first they often are sons or nephews of the partners at home; in another generation they become cousins or more distant relatives. While friendly relations will be maintained with the original metropolitan establishment, the factors in ports of staple-producing areas will tend to become independent. If the new area is of the same language and cultural group as the old, as are English colonies and England, these firms will merge into the general life of the new community. If it is not, they may remain foreign

---

[1](1825; reprinted, St. John, N.B., New Brunswick Historical Association, 1921), p. 72.

indefinitely, more particularly if there is much difference in the technical levels and general civilization of the two areas: Jardine, Mathieson and Co. were established on the China coast generations ago, and the seizure of the trading post of Hong Kong in the 1840's was inspired by the interests of such firms. With a post under their flag, they felt no need for naturalization and remained as British as when they began. The long struggle of the Hudson's Bay Company (founded 1670) against assimilation into Canadian life also illustrates the point.

If the new area has advantages of its own, it sooner or later takes on aspects of independent life. A community arises and with it new complexities. Men such as settlers and local merchants who have cast in their lot entirely with the new country develop local interests and loyalties. They are not content to remain under the thumb of outside or alien merchants. Even the factors, if financially untrammelled, object to outside control. The community itself comes to realize that possession of the natural resource in question gives it a certain bargaining power, and it invariably tries by communal action to use that power. Medieval England, after a century or two of political effort, managed to stop the export of raw wool. Modern Canada tries to get better prices for its wheat by invoking the power of the state in various types of collective bargaining. In the 1920's rubber planters in Malaya and elsewhere tried to restrict the growth and output of raw rubber, of which the regions concerned had a virtual monopoly. By such devices the producers of the staple may manage to make some headway against the metropolitan importing merchants. Even so, their position seldom ceases to be precarious. A new technique may ruin their staple, as the artificial silk industry ruined the natural silk industry of Japan. The supply may fail: some day the gold mines of the Rand will be exhausted. Metropolitan demand may cease: when Rome declined, North African wheat fields went back to desert. Or it may turn to alternative sources: Canada's bargaining power in the international wheat market is severely limited by Argentinian and Australian production. Choice of producers is the most powerful lever in the hands of the importing community. Being the older and more mature, it usually has the trade connections, the transportation, and the capital to buy wherever supplies offer. It is in a strong position and can often drive hard bargains with its suppliers. That country would appear to be happiest which does not depend mainly on a staple, even though, like Upper Canada, it may at first show slow progress. Such countries are usually colonies of settlement, tending towards the peasant type of agriculture. The colony of New France was one such; the showy fur trade went on over the head of the agricultural colony along the St. Lawrence, which lived an almost self-sufficient life. Its settlers were neither rich nor poor and had above them the tyranny neither of the noble (the seigneur could not be a tyrant) nor of the factor. The parts of North

America, English or French, which are marked by the yeoman type of agriculture, avoiding the depression of the peasant and the excesses of the staple producer, appear, so long as they can escape the pit of industrialism, to offer the maximum combination of progress and content. Sooner or later, however, they may change to demand centres (as several parts of modern Ontario have done), pass over to metropolitanism, and have their simplicity swamped.

Conflicts between metropolitanism and yeoman society invariably ensue. In Canada it was this struggle which precipitated the rebellions of 1837. In modern times the western wheat farmer has been at the mercy of the metropolitan European consumer more often than not. He has fought back with whatever weapons the Canadian state has been able to use. A patent illustration comes from South Africa. The society maintained by the Boers of the Transvaal was patriarchal rather than yeoman, but it had many features in common with yeoman societies. The discovery of diamonds on the boundary in 1869 had resulted in the metropolitan power taking the Griqualand district from the Transvaal, while the discovery of gold on the Rand in the early 1890's brought in a flood of outside miners and set in train the events that led to the Boer War, with the resulting conquest of the country.

The new area may not have many advantages, and then the factor may retain his dominant position indefinitely. The slowness with which any genuine community grew up in Newfoundland and the powerful position of the merchant vis-à-vis the fisherman is an example of the demand-supply relationship that until yesterday had hardly got beyond the stage of the naturalization of the middleman. The merchants of Bristol and other West Country fishing ports succeeded in preventing settlement in the island for some generations, and when at last they failed, their power passed to their local representatives, who gradually gained some independence and passed from the stage of mere agents to semi-independent merchants: it was these men who traditionally ran the colony, and for their own benefit. On the other hand, the supply area may have many advantages, and there may be erected upon it a social structure of impressive proportions. The southern states were able to build up something just short of a nation mainly upon the staple of cotton. Such societies invariably have a kind of ruddy, tubercular flush about them: they appear to be extremely vigorous and vital, whereas in reality they contain within them the seeds of dissolution. They often take on high colours and give rise to a hectic kind of social life. The old plantation society still lives in these terms in the pages of romantic novels. The same kind of high, wide, and handsome existence was built up by the North-West fur barons at Montreal in the late eighteenth and early nineteenth centuries. There is more than a suggestion of it in the lumber circles of Vancouver, B.C. It is a reflection of the cash that successful dealings in a staple put in a man's hands and of the atmosphere of uncertainty that marketing the staple generates.

No matter how large its resources may be, however, or how grandiose the social structure erected upon them, the staple economy may easily come crashing down through events over which the area itself has little control, as did the Canadian wheat structure in 1929. It is essentially a dependent economy, at the mercy of outside demand. Unless it can find sources of life within itself, it remains, whether self-governing or not, in a semi-colonial relationship to that metropolitan area which holds the keys of its life.

Many variations of the simple demand-supply relationship have been known to history. Supplies tapped by an older area in a new have often proved larger than necessary; the modern wheat trade reflects this. The new areas yoked to wheat are like factories with some of the windows boarded up. Often two or more older areas compete for the supplies of one producing area, as happened in the North American fur trade of the seventeenth and eighteenth centuries. In this case the new area was far too weak to take advantage of a seller's market, and what happened was that the quarrels of the rival fur traders were reflected first in the colonial feuds of New France and New York and next in the classical wars between the two metropolitan societies themselves. A new area with something worth-while to export is rarely let alone by the strong powers which want what it has, but invariably reduced to colonial or semi-colonial status. New centres of demand often arise within the new area itself. These build up much the same kind of relationships with the local producers as those of the outside demand centres: after London came New York, after New York, Chicago, and after Chicago, Minneapolis.

The demand centres have invariably sought to preserve their advantages, and these efforts have given rise to complex social and political patterns, to which have been attached terms such as *mercantilism, colonialism, imperialism.* The Flemish wool merchants tried to monopolize English raw wool, but since England was itself a political community of considerable weight and not merely the area of a single staple, they failed. Spain for a long period, thanks to her sea power, monopolized the gold of South America. The French, Dutch, and English empires of the seventeenth century tried to monopolize the products of their colonies. England in doing so built up the hodgepodge of laws, regulations, prohibitions, and bounties that forms the classical example of "the mercantile system." The demand-supply or metropolitan-colonial relationship has, in fact, invariably found political expression. It was powerful in inflating and keeping aloft the great balloon of imperial piety which was the distinguishing mark of the British Empire in its overseas English-speaking area. Metropolitanism would never have been able to do this of itself, for the exploitative process tends to divide men into "sahibs" and "natives," but in the colonies of settlement it has joined with the natural feelings of respect and affection of colonists for their motherland in maintaining political structures for its own benefit. In Canada, the Montreal commercial group form an excellent example of this, constant in their attitudes and interests during more than a century and a half; for them the "British connection," although piously and sincerely regarded, was consciously or unconsciously an instrument in the struggle for political power.

Where the metropolis has had a choice of supply areas, it has sometimes, thanks to competing interest groups at home, thrown away its opportunity of forcing each one down to the lowest level through bargaining. In nineteenth-century Great Britain, the interests maintaining particular supply bases were able, under a system of mercantilism, to dig themselves in so strongly that they managed to force the English consumer to take their wares, regardless of the advantages to him in getting them somewhere else. Until 1846 Great Britain got most of her sugar from the West Indies. French and Spanish islands invariably were able to produce more cheaply than the British (this was especially true after the abolition of slavery in 1833), but the West Indian planters were able by political pressure to keep high duties going against foreign sugar. The same was outstandingly true of British North American wood. In the 1830's a similar producer's interest began to build up about Cape of Good Hope wines, though in that case the tide of free-trade sentiment in Great Britain prevented a major colonial interest from arising.

The modern world exhibits an inversion of the whole demand-supply conception. In days gone by, supplies were invariably limited and human wants were always expanding; there was a perpetual seller's market. Today, in normal times, production and transportation are so easy and substitutes so numerous that much of the world suffers from a chronic glut of almost everything. In the sixteenth century, after the murder of Lord Darnley, husband of Mary, Queen of Scots, his clothes were given to the queen's new favourite, the earl of Bothwell, who had them recut to fit himself. Today, few great men, even in frugal Scotland, would be grateful for a gift of second-hand clothes. Nearly every community, simple or complex, is today a supply area, trying to force its wares on others by every shift that can be devised. There is little need any longer for the agent to go out to the faraway port for his purchases: all he has to do is to sit at home, and the natives will sooner or later come along and compete with each other in forcing their goods on him.

Two of the basic factors in the process by which demand gave way to supply consist in the rise of England as a national economic state and the discovery of the New World, with its subsequent exploitation. Medieval England grew wealthy on its wool trade, building up overseas connections and local industry because of it. At an early period, about the thirteenth century, domestic development put a strain on certain resources, notably timber for ship masts, and caused merchants to look abroad for supplies. These they found across the North Sea, in Scandinavia and the Baltic, natural regions of supply for fir and oak, hemp, flax, tar, and other marine necessities. While other European countries competed for these northern goods, it was England that was most successful in dominating the situation; by the seventeenth century, between England and the north of Europe there was growing up a typical metropolitan-colonial relationship exhibiting all the usual phenomena except direct political control. Northern Europe, from Hamburg to Archangel, from Copenhagen to the Gulf of Finland, had become by the beginning of the nineteenth century an English hinterland, and one part of it, Norway, almost an English colony. It is not so many years ago that the best route from Bergen to Oslo lay across the North Sea to Newcastle and back again. Modern Norway is a land where large numbers of people understand English, where English cigarettes are smoked, and English popular tunes whistled.

The English metropolitan-colonial economy was greatly hastened in its rate of development and extended in space by the results of the discovery of America. Spanish gold, despite prohibitions, poured out for English wool, dislocating English rural life but shoving the country forward a stage in industrialism. The England of 1600, still without colonies, had a more complex economy than had the England of 1500. In the course of the seventeenth and eighteenth centuries, under the stimulus of external demand, foreign and colonial, England entered upon the Industrial Revolution and rapidly became a centre of demand herself for everything conceivable, taking the calico of the eastern tropics and the sugar of the western with equal avidity. Native English industry, under this pressure forced to discover shortcuts to production which took the form of mechanical devices, soon outran native demand and began to force its products upon the original supply areas. Expansion went in a spiral. A combination of good situation, natural resources, and shrewd politics which did not hesitate to give merchants the legislation they wanted or use military force to crush a rival, as in the three wars with the Dutch, eventually made England the centre of all the great historic trades. When Amsterdam and Antwerp gave way to London, the centre of the world's demand seemed to become permanently fixed. Mastering first the supply areas of northern Europe, England went on to secure the tobacco of Virginia, the sugar of the West Indies, the indigo and rice of the Carolinas, the silk of India, the cotton of the south and the timber of the north, the wool of Australia, the gold of California, the wheat of Kansas and of western Canada, the beef of Argentina, the rubber and tin of the East Indies, and a large share of the oil of all the world.

This remarkable historical sequence took English traders, missionaries, and governors across the sea to America and all the way round the edge of Eurasia from Gibraltar to Shanghai, building the nineteenth-century empire and the régime of free trade and internationalism often denominated the Pax Britannica. Whipped up in its pace by one of its by-products, the Industrial Revolution, demand expanded until its very imperiousness called into existence so many ways of production that, as described above, it had to retreat before supply, and the problem became not that of obtaining the good things of the earth but of disposing of them. English demand had laid the world under tribute. By the end of the nineteenth century the entire earth had become a hinterland to Great Britain, and in Great Britain all the controls centred in that perfect embodiment of metropolitanism, London.

Had the evolution gone on to its logical limit, London would have become the capital of the world. As it was, rival economies built up metropolitanisms of their own. Berlin and, especially, New York, became competing centres. Then politics stepped in again in the form of war; and despite two victories in one generation, England, and London with it, began to lose its pre-eminence. This was due as much to the wars as to economic processes. Rather more, for both wars enabled the New World to develop enormously at the expense of the Old. By 1945 power, based on continental area and a continental scope of resources, had shifted across the Atlantic. When the atomic bomb made its appearance, the Old World of the mere businessman was shattered irretrievably. All hope of "free enterprise" in any dominant sense disappeared, and the world lay at the feet of that political entity which possessed the most potent means of destruction. If the essence of the whole process here termed metropolitanism is that power builds controls and tends to centre at a point, whether power be expressed in terms of dollars or of weapons, it would seem that man in the year of grace 1971 had come close to the end of a cycle: he had built his social structures up into larger and larger forms until the point had been brought within sight, though not actually attained, where all the inhabitants of the planet could be controlled by one individual sitting in a small room and pushing the appropriate buttons.

7 | *Religion and Religious Institutions**

Religion is one of the most important factors in the shaping of a culture. In no country is this more evident than in Canada, whose historical experience is conditioned by the uneasy association of two religious opposites, French Roman Catholics and English Protestants. The English cultural group is itself divided into a Protestant majority and a Roman Catholic minority; and Catholics as a whole are divided by linguistic and historical differences among themselves. Add to this delicate balance of creed and culture a pioneer experience which has not yet been concluded and which conserves the spirit of achievement commonly identified with Puritanism, and the result goes far towards explaining the prominence, throughout Canadian history, of religion, formal and informal, organized and unorganized.

Canada is a state founded on one of the deepest of historical experiences, the conquest of one people by another. As a result of the British Conquest of New France in 1763, the country came to be shared by two national-cultural groups with two languages, two prevailing religions, and two ways of life — one, the French, the older and the conquered: the other, the English, the Protestant, the conqueror. While the attitudes which the words imply have lost some of their rigour, Canada remains a country of two peoples, two languages, and two predominant religions.

This situation has deeply affected every aspect of Canadian history: in fact, it is Canadian history. Politically, it has thrust suspicions, jealousy, and mistrust into the forefront of public life, and only with extreme difficulty has the Canadian ship of state weathered some of the storms cradled in the ocean of race and religion. A notable example was the fight over separate Roman Catholic schools in Manitoba, upon which, in large degree, the general election of 1896 turned. Religion has resulted in the federalization of the cabinet, whereby not only must each race have its quota of portfolios, but some of the secondary racio-religious groups must also have theirs. Thus at Confederation in 1867, the necessity arose not only for due quotas of French Roman Catholic and English Protestant ministers, but also for an Irish Catholic minister and a special Protestant representative for the English of the Province of Quebec.[1]

**Canada,* ed. George W. Brown (Toronto: University of Toronto Press, 1950).
[1] In Newfoundland, which in 1948 voted to join Canada, the division of portfolios has been on a generally tripartite basis, with representation for Roman Catholics, the Church of England, and the United Church of Canada (formerly chiefly Methodist). The Salvation Army also has been represented on the Council of Education.

Constitutionally, the racio-religious situation is reflected in three clauses of the country's fundamental instrument of government, the British North America Act of 1867: sections 51-1, 93, and 133. The first of these gave a fixed membership to Quebec in the House of Commons; the second guarded the school rights which religious minorities possessed at the time the Act was passed; and the third provided for the equality of the English and French languages in Parliament, in the courts, and in the legislature of the Province of Quebec. Confederation was achieved only through this understanding between the races on fundamentals, and while it is possible to argue that its terms are limited and that there is a distinction between religion and race, the plain truth is that it never would have been accomplished had not the French minority assumed that it was being given a co-ordinate place with the English and that its religion was being put on an equal footing with that of the English. In Canada, as elsewhere, "Catholic" is a larger term than "French," but so large and homogeneous is the French group that in practice it is difficult to separate the two. Not all Roman Catholics are Frenchmen, but all Frenchmen (or almost all) are Roman Catholics.

The outstanding fact is that, despite the deep divisions of the Canadian people, they have been able to live together with comparatively little armed strife. The only conflict of serious proportions was the Rebellion of 1837, which was disapproved by all but a minority of the French, and was not religious in its causation but rather economic, political, and cultural in the broadest sense. Ten years after the conflict came virtually complete internal self-government for the Province of Canada, with French ministers sharing the responsibilities along with English; and thirty years after, or in 1867, came Confederation, which gave a large measure of autonomy to the provinces and thus relegated the English minority within the Province of Quebec to a position of negligible political power.

At Ottawa, capital of the new Confederation, the two races met on equal terms, and it was not long before the national parties cut completely across racial and religious lines. Canada has had among her prime ministers Conservatives who have been Roman Catholics and Conservatives who have been extreme Protestants, just as she has had Liberals of both religions. The national parties have been successful in preventing the growth of political parties organized along religious lines (there has been nothing in Canada like the old German Centre party); if for no other reason, they deserve the deep gratitude of the country.

Roman Catholicism in Canada has everywhere been confronted with Protestantism. Even the remote countryside of Quebec, where a word of English is seldom heard and few Protestants exist, never loses consciousness of the aggressive Protestant world just over the horizon. The result has been, and still is, a zeal hardly to be found elsewhere in the Roman Catholic world today. Charges of slackness, of lapses from morals, of venality, which are frequently made against the priesthood of countries wholly Catholic, are seldom heard in Canada.

Canadian Catholicism, French or English, does not closely follow the European pattern. In a country like Italy, large numbers in all classes, especially among the intellectuals, have apparently fallen away from the Church. Others give it nominal allegiance: even if the women of the family, as a matter of feminine habit, remain more or less faithful, the men, apart from a few ceremonial occasions, seem to give the Church a wide berth. This pattern seems to extend into most European countries and, beyond Europe, is said to prevail in the urban areas of South America. It has as yet made relatively slight impression upon Canada. Among English-speaking Catholics there is no anticlericalism, and church-going is assiduously practised by men and women alike. In this group there is little suggestion of the superstitious primitivism of the southern Latin countries, and for the obvious reason that English-speaking Catholics are either middle class or steadily passing into the middle class. In French Canada the country people remain as attached to the Church as were their forefathers, and in certain limited respects their attachment is on a rather primitive, peasant level.

In the cities, especially in Montreal, the Latin pattern is beginning to appear. There is a proletariat to whose depths the Church may fail to reach, and there is an élite whose conforming observances are becoming somewhat mechanical and among whom may be found men who no longer conform. They, however, are the exception, and the Catholicism of French Canada, pressed on all sides as it is by English Protestantism, still stands strong and zealous. It is a religion by no means as superstitious or primitive as that of, say, Spain, and it is observably penetrated by the puritan spirit of the English continent.[2]

The Roman Catholic world of Canada, as the reader will have concluded, is no tight unit. The major factor of division within it is language. Of the total population of Canada in 1941, 43.2 per cent were Roman Catholics. Of the latter group, 67.7 per cent were French, with the remainder divided among people of a great variety of racial origins and languages. Among these, the Irish Catholics led, followed by English, Ukrainians, Scottish, Polish, and Italian Catholics, in the order named. Each of these groups, except the English, has something of racial distinctiveness, but all (with slight exceptions among the Italians) assimilate to the English-Canadian, not to the French, way of life. The increasing significance of Roman Catholics of the English pattern was recognized in 1946 by the

---

[2]A dispatch to the Toronto *Globe and Mail,* December 17, 1947, reported Premier Duplessis of Quebec as expressing himself strongly in favour of strict observance of Sunday.

pope when he nominated a second Canadian cardinal in the person of an "English" archbishop (of Highland Scottish descent): at the centre of the faith, the English and the French Catholics of Canada, disproportionate though their numbers are, were thus equated.

In a single essay it is impossible to comment upon the characteristics of the various sub-groups within Roman Catholicism, but it should be pointed out that the rural-urban division or that of native and non-native-born might be more significant than the division into language groups.[3] The average urban Catholic congregation in the non-French areas by this time probably contains some mixture of all the racial strains. In the country, especially in the West, the original settlements retain their religious and linguistic affiliations and hence their own peculiarities. In Canada the most outstanding of these is the rather large percentage of persons whom the census waveringly classifies now as Greek Catholics, now as Roman. This group, mostly Ukrainian in origin, is only loosely affiliated with Rome.

The characteristics of Canadian Roman Catholicism, however, are most plainly displayed in French Canada, which consists in a homogeneous group of nearly four million people, who have been in the country for three centuries and come close to forming a nation within a nation. French-Canadian Catholicism, save for the exceptions noted above, retains many of its medieval aspects. The wayside shrines, the numerous churches and the constant sound of bells, the clergy in habits of brown or white or black, the places of pilgrimage with miraculous powers ascribed to them, all heighten the impression of medievalism. It is further reinforced by the prominence given to the scholastic philosophy in higher education, by the complete clerical control of education, and by the cheerful allegiance given to the Church. Quebec is perhaps unique in the modern world, a virtual theocracy.

Thus it is not surprising that the French-Canadian Catholic Church has been ultramontane from the beginning. François de Laval, first bishop of Quebec (1658-1688), allowed no spark of Gallicanism to enter his province while he reigned there supreme, and under his successors it received no encouragement. New France from the first has been a faithful ward of the papacy, and that allegiance, weakening the emotional attachment to the Crown of France, made the adjustment under the English flag much easier.

Even under such circumstances, however, Quebec has not escaped its anticlericalism, nor, indeed, its free-thinkers. Papineau, the principal figure of the rebellion period of the 1830's, was not a practising Catholic, and

---

[3]In 1941, more than 90 per cent of Canadian Roman Catholics were native-born. About 40 per cent of these were classed as rural. Of non-native, non-French Roman Catholics, about 45 per cent appeared to be rural.

the party that founded itself upon his movement, the *Parti Rouge* (prominent
c. 1850-1870), contained a group that was both anticlerical and sceptical.
The Church was too strong for it; its hour was brief and there were few
who did not soon return to shelter in the fold. Today, under the impact
of urbanism, scepticism on the part of the intellectuals again seems to
be on the increase, but it is not yet conspicuous.

Protestantism in Canada shares the common characteristics of Protestantism everywhere, but it has been influenced by the circumstances of
North American life and by the parent churches, European or American.
In a new country, where men must fight their personal fight against nature,
individualism is naturally strong. Since a new civilization had to be built
up out of the forest, the sense of purpose was equally strong. It is this
sense of objective, transferred to the religious sphere, which men call
puritanism, and a puritan attitude is one which all pioneer countries apparently develop: the Roman Catholicism of seventeenth-century New France
was puritan in its seriousness. It opposed the frivolities, such as dancing
and the theatre, which military officers from France tried to introduce.
The colony of New France had too great a task in hand — winning a
continent for God and for France — to bother with frivolity. Similarly,
in modern Soviet Russia, the sense of immediacy induced by concentration
on an objective has brought a willing acceptance of austerity and some
aspects of the strait-laced morals which are commonly regarded as puritan.

Add to all this, in English Canada, the Calvinistic heritage of most
of its people, and the character of English Canada as a country founded
and rooted in puritanism is easily explained. English Canadians are generally industrious, thrifty, orderly, efficient, self-controlled, and unimaginative.
Idle dalliance they tend to regard as mortal sin, and their characteristic
products are not poets but engineers and businessmen.[4] In the middle of
the twentieth century, this earnest country, emerging from the chrysalis
of pioneering, is finding that there are more things in heaven and earth
than are dreamed of in the puritan philosophy. Modern English-speaking
Canada, vigorously smashing her inherited inhibitions, provides a spectacle
which is sometimes frightening, sometimes ridiculous.

If Protestantism has kept Roman Catholicism on the *qui vive,* the reverse
is also true. In Canada the spirit of the Reformation has never died. In
small social groups, each person is uneasy until he finds out the religion
of the others present, for a chance word might injure amicable relations.
The day has gone by when Catholics and Protestants were constantly "at
daggers drawn," but they still feel self-conscious in one another's presence,
and on either side are organizations the major purpose of which is to keep

---

[4]Their most prominent poet of the day, Professor E. J. Pratt, confines himself almost exclusively
to sober epics of heroic accomplishment with a strong scientific and mechanical flavour.

the ancient fires alight. In Canada, religion can never be, as it is in England, a private affair. "Going over to Rome" cannot be viewed as merely a personal experience: it is also treason to the group.

Other characteristics of Protestantism derive from the North American frontier experience rather than from the Reformation heritage. Religion has not been highly intellectualized in Canada. It has always been possible, especially in larger cities or in educational centres, to hear sound intellectual sermons, but for the most part preaching has been old-fashioned in tone. Yet when the so-called higher criticism began, at the end of the nineteenth century, to penetrate the Canadian Protestant world, it aroused no great opposition among the mass of church-goers: there was nothing comparable to the American fundamentalist movement or the determined stand of whole communities (as in Tennessee) against "subversive" doctrines like evolution.

As Protestantism has worked away from its original fervours, it has introduced ritualism. To the Anglican Church this procession from zeal to formalism is an old story, but to the other denominations it is new. There can now be found in Canada non-Anglican churches in which the position of the baptismal font is considered important; this certainly would not have been true a generation ago. Many people, if they cannot have emotion, demand form, and with form sometimes goes beauty. Neither in architecture nor in service, however, has Canadian Protestantism achieved much on the aesthetic side: most of its buildings are as ugly as the sin they reprobate, and the sudden overlay of ritual in plain nonconformist environment sometimes achieves the same result.

Anglicanism (the Anglican Church is the state church of England on colonial soil), whether Canadian or American, has, in the aesthetics of religion, preserved much of the dignity and beauty of ritual and edifice which are its heritage from the medieval past. But Anglicanism has been affected also by the frontier ideals of homespun simplicity mixed with the warmth of neighbourly fellowship, so that, except in a few localities, it is Low Church in form and often manifests as much evangelical fervour as Methodism — and far more than Presbyterianism.

Protestantism everywhere tends to divide into innumerable sects, for the ultimate logical Protestant denomination consists of one person — the individual face to face with God. In few countries has this been more evident than in Canada. The dominion census of 1941 lists some seventeen different and recognized denominations, then lumps together dozens more under the heading "other." Most of those listed are small, however, and the dispersion of Protestantism is not really so great as the innumerable conventicles of its minor sects would indicate. Thus, in 1941, of the 55.20 per cent of the Canadian population which was Protestant, 90.34 per cent was comprised within five denominations: Anglican, Baptist, Lutheran, Presbyterian, and the United Church of Canada. The two largest Protestant churches — the Anglican and the United — together accounted for 63 per cent of the Protestant total. The innumerable minor sects made up, all told, only 9.66 per cent of the Protestant population.

The importance of this minority should not, however, be minimized. At present the minor sects consist in people who demand a highly emotional, simple religion of sentiment and salvation, people whose educational and economic status is low. Sects take over large churches in downtown areas of the great cities or turn old buildings into meeting-houses. These, in contrast with the failure of the older denominations, they fill. The old Methodist camp-meeting preachers of the early nineteenth century gave their hearers a spiritual diet of hell-fire and damnation, and strong pioneer appetites found it satisfactory sustenance: the modern sects give their urban audiences religious "soap-opera," and our more sentimental and self-pitying age finds it highly congenial. But just as Methodists, with the lapse of time, became prosperous and dignified (so that they now dispute over the position of the baptismal font), so the descendants of present members of the sects, a century from now, will probably have made their emotional services into ritualistic occasions, complete with surpliced choirs. Like nearly all Protestant denominations, the sects are in great part phenomena of race and class.

Protestant denominations in Canada which have their parent churches abroad have come to differ appreciably from them. Canadian Anglicanism has been less majestic and superior than English Anglicanism in its attitude towards Nonconformists. Canadian Methodism has not been so prim as English Methodism. Canadian Presbyterianism was never so dour, intellectual, and stiff as Scottish Presbyterianism. This does not mean that Canadian churches are mere extensions of American churches: they have their own individuality. A semi-state church in early English Canada, the Anglican, set a standard of dignity for all the leading denominations which was absent in the United States. The presence of a large Roman Catholic and French population heightened evangelical consciousness, making against ritualism but for responsibility. In Canada, as contrasted with the United States, experimentalism was much less marked, fission did not go so far, energies were less widely scattered, sobriety and dignity were more conspicuous. So far as the writer knows, no Kentucky snake-cult has appeared in Canada, no Father Divine. But this has not prevented Canada from producing (for export to the United States) certain conspicuous figures in this nether world of Protestantism, notably Aimee Semple McPherson, the picturesque evangelist of the 1930's.

The balance is not all in favour of the more northerly of the two English-speaking countries, however, for the inventiveness, audacity, imagination, and courageous tenacity necessary to create a religion like Mormonism has found little counterpart in Canada. Canadians are preeminently safe and sane people: they are not the people for daring, half-crazy experimentation, and when Mormonism eventually reached Canada, it came as a simple rural religion, the worst vagary of which was not polygamy but soft money.

Pioneer individualism is closely related to pioneer ability to organize: each rests on the strong but adaptive qualities necessary to conquer the wilderness, and individualism, anything but anarchic, supplies the driving-power for the co-operative task. In both Canada and the United States these qualities have been carried up from the pioneer farm to the highest levels of society. No peoples can organize themselves more quickly for war or for peace than can those of North America. In Canada the numbers to be organized have remained small, and the result has been obvious in the tendency for national bodies quickly to appear. The Dominion is itself an example of this. Canadian political parties spread with rapidity to the Pacific coast in the wake of federalism. So did the Canadian Manu-facturers' Association. Banks soon covered the country with their branches. Higher education becomes more and more closely organized — even French Canada finds it hard to resist being drawn in.

The churches have been no exception to this trend. Anglicanism, owing to its origins, has been one creed from the beginning. But both Methodism and Presbyterianism, each so divided in its homeland and in the United States, soon after Confederation came together in Canada into great nation-wide churches — the Methodist Church of Canada and the Presbyterian Church in Canada. In 1925 these churches, along with the Congregational Church, went farther and formed the United Church of Canada. [5] Even those stubborn individualists, the Baptists, have come close to a national organization. As the half-century mark is reached, the only major Protestant denomination that still remains divided — on the racial lines of its European origins — is the Lutheran, and there are now signs that it, too, is becoming Canadian. The nationalization of Protestant bodies has inevitably produced Erastian churches, whose tendency to identify the state with themselves and themselves with the state is not very healthy, but this is a stage that must be worked through. Sooner or later the Protestant conscience asserts itself, whatever the state, and then complete Erastianism ends.

All the foregoing is but another way of saying that Canadian Protes-tantism reflects a strongly middle-class and puritan society.

Religious development in Canada divides into several well-marked periods:

1. The wholly Roman Catholic and French period, before the English Conquest (1763).

---

[5]Owing to their system of voting themselves into or out of the Union by congregations, a privilege not accorded to the Methodists, a considerable minority of the Presbyterians remained outside.

2. French Catholicism, with some Protestant intrusions in the Province of Quebec, and the beginnings of Protestant colonization in other provinces, 1763-1820.

3. The growth of Protestant provinces: Nova Scotia, New Brunswick, Prince Edward Island, and Upper Canada.

4. The period of Protestant ascendancy, 1830 to the present. This long period, in which the major part of Canada's growth occurred, is marked by the following important phenomena: (*a*) the shift of Protestantism from a minority position to a majority — a shift accentuated by Confederation (1867) and by the great immigration of the early twentieth century; (*b*) Catholic recovery in former New France, with French occupation of former English countrysides: (*c*) the possible emergence of equilibrium after 1918.

At the beginning of the French régime, in the early seventeenth century, the French government, under Henry IV, accorded various charters and trading rights to individual Huguenots: these were swept away in the Roman Catholic revival under Louis XIII, and it became the policy of the French government, rigorously adhered to, to allow no Huguenots to enter the colony. During the second half of the seventeenth century the foundations of the French-Canadian Catholic Church of today were firmly laid by Bishop Laval, whose intense anti-Gallicanism was reflected in the ecclesiastical province which he created in his own image. All his priests were "missionaries" who were never allowed to obtain any legal rights in their benefices and who were moved about at his discretion. To Laval more than to any other one man, Canadian Catholicism owes its missionary zeal, its ardour, and its puritan spirit.

Towards the middle of the eighteenth century a cetain relaxation of zeal was observable: this did not go far, but it did admit of the residence of a few Huguenot merchants in the colony and a lessening of austerity in public and private manners.

After the conquest it seemed, for a brief interval, that the Roman Catholic religion might be proscribed. The question was, Would the penal laws of England, which permitted virtually no toleration, be applied in their full rigour? English government in the 1760's was in confusion, however, and the rapidly changing administrations of the day developed no continuity of policy. Local governors used their common sense, and there was no interference with Roman Catholicism as a private creed. Within a few years after the conquest, on the roundabout suggestion of certain officials in London, a French priest went to France and was quietly consecrated bishop of Quebec. Returning to Canada, he received official recognition in the title "Superintendent of the Romish Church." This, however, with the passage of time imperceptibly yielded to "Bishop of Quebec." Eleven years after the conquest the Quebec Act restored to the French church many of the rights (though not all the property) it had possessed under the king of France. The version of Canadian history generally upheld in the Province of Quebec — that the aftermath of conquest was unspeakable oppression and tyranny, combined with religious persecution — is almost completely a myth, and French historians would do a service to their country and their scholarship if they tried to dissipate it. [6]

The English Protestant population of the Province of Quebec remained negligible until the arrival of refugees from the American War of Independence (the United Empire Loyalists). These German, Dutch, Irish, and English Protestants were settled upon the upper St. Lawrence; a few years later, in 1791, they were given a provincial organization of their own, Quebec being divided into Lower and Upper Canada. In the original province the English population remained inconsiderable until the Great Immigration which began soon after 1820 and continued for a generation. This new flood from the British Isles raised the English Protestant population in Lower Canada from a few thousands to a maximum of 30-35 per cent of the total, and Montreal by mid-century had almost become an English city.

Nova Scotia came to the English Crown under the Treaty of Utrecht, in 1713, but it did not receive any English population of importance until during the Seven Years' War, when New Englanders migrated there to take over the lands of the expatriated Acadians. These New Englanders were frontiersmen and Baptists: they stamped their character on the Annapolis Valley and other parts of Nova Scotia. In the 1770's English Methodists from Yorkshire settled in the Isthmus of Chignecto; about the same time, Scottish Highlanders, both Catholic and Presbyterian, occupied Cape Breton and the adjacent mainland coasts. The capital, Halifax, consisted in an upper crust of Tory Anglican officials and merchants and a lower class of Catholic Irish. These migrations gave the religious pattern to Nova Scotia which it has ever since retained. New Brunswick, which was originally settled by United Empire Loyalists — who might have been Anglican or anything else, depending on the "preachers" who did, or did not, visit them — was more affected by later immigrations than its sister province. In the Great Immigration (*c.* 1820-1850), which added in large number to the population of all the provinces except Nova Scotia, many Irish, both Catholic and Protestant, came to New Brunswick. Prince Edward Island from the first was Scottish (Catholic and Presbyterian) and French.

The Loyalists who settled in Upper Canada were either Lutherans (Hessian mercenaries and Dutch), nominal Anglicans, or, more commonly, it would appear, nothing in particular. Methodist missionaries from New

---

[6]As one of their distinguished representatives, the Abbé Arthur Maheux, has done: see *Ton Histoire est une épopée* (Quebec: Charrier et Dugal, ltée., 1941).

England began to preach among them in the 1790's, and by 1812 Methodism was probably the strongest denomination, numerically, in the province. It was, however, far surpassed in influence, wealth, and culture by the Anglican Church, to which nearly all officials belonged. Anglican officialdom soon formed a little provincial aristocracy, which managed to monopolize most of the good things and to provide a classical education for its sons. The group came to be called the "Family Compact," but it was not peculiar to Upper Canada, for there were Anglican "Family Compacts" in all the provinces, just as there had been in many of the American colonies before the Revolution.

In Upper Canada, the heat generated between the Anglicans and the humbler Protestants, chiefly the Methodists, provided the major political dynamic down to the 1840's. Strife centred mainly on the control of education and the disposition of the lands set aside for the use of "a Protestant Clergy," the so-called Clergy Reserves. Anglicans claimed a monopoly of these lands (with a gesture in the direction of the Established Church of Scotland); Methodists took the lead in disputing their claim.

The leaders of the two denominations, Archdeacon Strachan for the Anglicans and Egerton Ryerson for the Methodists, battled vigorously in press and pulpit for several years, and the controversy became an important factor in preparing the ground for the Rebellion of 1837. But Ryerson was of Loyalist parentage, and he soon dissociated himself and his Methodist followers from the extreme group. Even so, the Anglican slur of "republicanism" and "disloyalty" stood ever ready for use.

Under such circumstances, it is good to find men like Chief Justice Robinson carefully distinguishing between the political and the religious rivalries of the two denominations. [7] Robinson was an ardent Anglican, but he fully recognized the service which the Methodists rendered to provincial society in carrying the gospel to the remotest corners of the backwoods, and he was at all times ready to help them in the extension of their religious efforts. Dissension in Upper Canada was due not to religion but to denominationalism.

Just after the middle of the nineteenth century the "Clergy Reserves" issue was settled, and denominational tempers were allayed. Meanwhile, both Methodists and Presbyterians had established their own institutions of higher learning. Throughout the rest of the century the Protestant denominations lived together in reasonable amity. Nothing is more noticeable today than their *rapprochement:* there is even discussion, in a preliminary stage, about a possible union of Anglican and United churches.

The situation in Upper Canada, already rendered bitter by the issues

---

[7]C. W. Robinson, *Life of Sir John Beverly Robinson ... Chief-Justice of Upper Canada* (Toronto: Morang, 1904), p.178.

of republicanism and loyalism, was made still more difficult by the immigration of tens of thousands of new settlers from the North of Ireland. These settlers brought with them all the belligerence accumulated in two centuries of warfare against Irish "papists." They transferred Ireland's historic misfortunes to Canadian soil, but, finding the comparatively few "papists" of Upper Canada foes hardly worthy of their steel, they turned their attention to the French Catholics of Lower Canada. There had been singularly little friction between French Catholic and English Protestant until the Irish came to Canada. Their Orange Order has seen to it that strife never entirely dies down. At the middle of the twentieth century, feelings are not so high as they were between 1837 and 1897, but they are still strong, and there are few months in which some rabid Protestant is not denouncing "priest-ridden" Quebec, with resultant counterblasts from extremists in French Canada. This, to put it mildly, does not make for national unity, and its relation to Christian brotherly love seems obscure. Another interesting effect of Irish immigration was the friction between French-Canadian and Irish Roman Catholics where they came into contact, which often has developed animosities as bitter as those between Protestants and Catholics.

In the Dominion of Canada (1867) the former Province of Canada was divided into the two provinces of Ontario and Quebec. With the addition of Nova Scotia and New Brunswick, in which the Protestants had a majority, the influence of Roman Catholics was reduced. In the Assembly of the Province of Canada, Roman Catholic members, whether English or French, had not found that race or party prevented them from uniting on important religious issues. They had been able, with fair regularity, to get their way: thus in 1863, a non-party, bi-racial majority, made up of members from both halves of the province, secured the passage of an act extending the system of separate (or Catholic) schools in Upper Canada. After Confederation, no Catholic combination, even had it occurred, could have forced its measures through the Parliament of Canada. The generation following Confederation was marked by several legal battles between the two faiths and by two armed outbreaks which, though not primarily religious, had important religious implications. In all these, Catholicism met defeat.

In 1869 the dominion government completed its negotiations for taking over the lands of the Hudson's Bay Company. Within the Territories was a small settlement of *métis,* or half-breeds, at the junction of the Red and Assiniboine rivers. Gross mismanagement by the government of the day gave these people the impression that in coming into the Dominion they would lose their lands. They refused to admit Canadian officials and set up a provisional government under Louis Riel, which executed Thomas Scott, one of its opponents. Scott was an Orangeman, and the act was regarded throughout Ontario as a planned piece of "papist" malevolence.

Ottawa sent an armed expedition to Fort Garry, Riel left the country, the rising evaporated, and fortunately no more blood was spilled. But no one was hanged for Scott's death, and in consequence Ontario Orangemen redoubled the salvoes of hatred which they kept firing at "French papists." Quebec's response was to make a strenuous effort, through immigration and political influence, to gain control over the new Province of Manitoba, which, in 1870, was organized as a result of the Riel episode. All to no avail, for within ten years Protestant immigration had swamped the *métis* and the French language, thus winning the English battle for the West.

When Riel led the Saskatchewan Rebellion in 1885, the religious fight was already lost, for by that time there was no possibility of making the Prairies a French-speaking, Roman Catholic area. The principle of separate schools was, however, incorporated in the arrangements made for Saskatchewan and Alberta when they were created provinces in 1905, with the result that in Catholic districts the public schools have practically become Catholic schools.

Meanwhile, in 1871, the Province of New Brunswick had decided to abolish certain school privileges theretofore possessed by Roman Catholics. Its legislation was upheld by the highest courts, and since then there have been no "separate" schools in New Brunswick, though the "public" schools in Catholic districts tend to be virtually Catholic schools.

On Riel's execution, after the second rebellion, a wave of nationalism swept over Quebec; the result was the return of a provincial government openly devoted to favouring French and Catholic interests. This government decided to award to the Catholic authorities of the province a considerable sum of money in compensation for the Jesuit lands sequestrated after the conquest. Once again the passions of Ontario Orangeism were aroused, and efforts were made to get the federal government to disallow the Act.[8] D'Alton McCarthy, the leader of the movement, failing at Ottawa, turned to the West and succeeded in blowing up again the fires of anti-Catholicism lighted by the rebellions: the school policy of the Manitoba government was the result.

Whatever its proponents might say in its defence, this policy was essentially a bid by a few extremist politicians for electoral popularity among the Ontario Orange elements at the expense of the long-enjoyed school privileges of the French (which, in the main, consisted in the privilege of doing without schools). It was transferred to the dominion stage in 1895, when, after a series of legal struggles, it became necessary for the dominion government to pass legislation in negation of Manitoba's policy. The resulting battle convulsed Parliament and the country and exhibited Canadian politics in their most confusing form. The Conservative government, headed

---

[8] The problem of Dominion-provincial relations was involved.

by a former Grand Master of the Orange Order, attempted to coerce Manitoba by legislation favouring the Roman Catholics: the leader of the Opposition, the French Catholic Wilfrid Laurier, who had been champion-ing provincial rights, refused to be a party to the coercion of a province. In the election which followed, in 1896, he was damned by the French clergy and elected by the French people. With some difficulty he managed to pour enough oil on the waters to quiet the country.

Soon afterwards Ontario Orangeism found its emotions absorbed in the balmy atmosphere of Queen Victoria's Diamond Jubilee (1897) and in the hot currents of the Boer War (1899). This war brought a renewed wave of imperialism to English Canada and of nationalism to French Canada. Both emotions were in reality religious in that they were deeply felt, were unconnected with material interest, represented devotion to a way of life, and lived on the mysticism of racialism.

After the Boer War, English Protestantism found its energies going in new directions. Those were the years when the Canadian prairies were being settled, and thither went tens of thousands of people from Ontario. Material development acted as a lightning-conductor and the country en-joyed a few years' surcease from racial and religious strife. When, in 1903, the Alaska Boundary Award went harshly against Canada, both races, to their surprise, found themselves possessed of common sentiments, each discovering a measure of Canadianism in common antipathy to both English and Americans.

Such a union could not last, and subsequent events put the severest possible strain upon the relations between English Protestants and French Catholics. It is true that they centred on Canada's relationships with the Empire, and that the differences were more racial than religious, but the strong tendency of English-Canadian Protestants to identify the terms "French" and "Catholic" modifies the importance of the qualification.

If the manner in which great issues have been settled leaves any doubt that Roman Catholicism lost weight in the country after Confederation, a statistical test removes it. In 1851 the proportion of Roman Catholics in the Province of Canada (Upper and Lower Canada taken together) was 49.6 per cent. In 1861 it was 48 per cent; in 1871, 46 per cent. In the provinces which came together to form the Confederation (Nova Scotia, New Brunswick, and Canada), the proportions of Roman Catholics in 1851 and in 1861 were 46.1 per cent and 44.2 per cent, respectively. At the first census after Confederation, in 1871, this proportion had fallen to 41.5 per cent. Since then, in the country as a whole, it has fluctuated little, as table 1 indicates.

Further analysis shows that in the period from 1871 to 1901 the numbers of English Catholics in Canada were almost stationary: it was the French who maintained the numerical weight of the religion during

Table 1
Roman Catholics in Canada, 1851-1941
(Percentages)

	1851	1861	1871	1881	1891	1901	1911	1921	1931	1941
Ontario and Quebec	49.6	48.0	46.0	45.0	43.4	45.7	48.4	49.8	49.9	53.0
All Canada	46.1	44.2	41.5	41.2	41.2	41.5	39.3	38.5	38.5	41.7

this period. In the twentieth century the French have continued to show remarkable fertility: despite three decades of heavy Protestant immigration (1900-1930), the proportion of French-speaking Canadians to the total population has not greatly changed. Catholics whose origins go back to the British Isles have added very modestly to their numbers, as may be seen in table 2.

Table 2
Increase in Certain Religious Groups, 1901-1941

	1901	1941	Percentage increase
French Catholics	1,649,000*	3,378,000	104.8
Other Catholics	580,000	1,614,000	178.2
"British" Catholics	473,000*	770,000	62.8
Non-British, non-French Catholics	107,000*	844,000	688.7
Protestants	2,929,000	6,155,000	110.1

*Figures marked with an asterisk are approximate. The Canadian census correlates religion and racial origin only for 1931 and 1941. Before that, other methods of computation must be used. These are, chiefly, the high degree of coincidence between the terms "French" and "Roman Catholic" — 97 or 98 per cent — and the almost completely "British" origins of non-French Catholics before 1901. The approximations are believed to be close.

It is obvious from the table that non-French Catholicism in Canada has, for weight of numbers, depended during the twentieth century on European Catholics of the recent immigration. Among the millions who poured into Canada from 1901 to 1931, many were of Catholic background: table 2 indicates the remarkable addition they have made to Canadian Catholicism. Before 1901 it was divided rather simply into groups of French- and English-speaking communicants. Today it is polyglot. If the returns for 1931 and 1941 are accurate, the newcomers are not quite so faithful to their Church as were the older Catholics. The proportion of Poles who returned themselves as Catholics in 1931 was 84.2 per cent, but in 1941 it was 80.8 per cent. Similarly, Ukrainian Roman Catholics decreased from 67 per cent to 62 per cent. It is apparent that European Catholics will not provide an important balance to French Catholicism in fertility, for they seem to be reducing their rate of increase with extreme rapidity: from 1931 to 1941, a decade of no immigration, it was scarcely more rapid than that of "British" Catholics. If the "British" Roman Catholic group were further subdivided, the statistics would show that the Irish Catholics increased during the decade by only 4.9 per cent — well below the low level of Protestants.

Table 3

Some Rates of Increase, 1931-1941

	French Catholics	"British" Catholics	Other Catholics	Protestants
1931	2,849,000	689,000	747,000	5,720,000
1941	3,378,000	770,000	844,000	6,155,000
Per cent increase	18.9	11.7	14.3	7.6

A statistical examination thus seems to show that, as compared with the middle of the nineteenth century, Roman Catholicism has by the middle of the twentieth century fallen into a somewhat more emphatic minority position and that its English-speaking group has lost appreciably in proportionate weight. Whether this will be compensated by the energy of the newcomers who entered in the twentieth century remains to be seen. Few acute observers would hold that the entire group of non-French Catholics in Canada is as important in the nation's life today as it was two generations ago.

French Catholics, in contrast, have been able by their reproductive powers to maintain their proportionate place, and today, as a century ago, they easily lead all other components of the population in fertility. Not only that, but during the last three-quarters of a century they have won back from English (and mainly Protestant) possession large areas of the countryside. Today the Eastern Townships of Quebec, bordering Vermont and New Hampshire, are once more French: the New Englanders who settled them a century and a half ago have proved easy victims to the French in this struggle for survival. Large sections of the Ontario side of the Ottawa Valley have likewise become French. In New Brunswick the French have increased from 15.72 per cent of the total in 1871 to 35.81 per cent in 1941. In northern Ontario the region from the Quebec border westward to Hearst has within the last generation been colonized by French Canadians. In the West, however, they have not held their own.

Along with this remarkable reversal of the verdict of the conquest of 1763, both in Quebec and outside it, has gone a proportionate increase in influence. French-Canadian Catholicism is homogeneous and apparently self-confident. Less than 3 per cent of the members of the race have failed to remain within the fold. Zeal is strong both at home and abroad, and the foreign missionary effort of the group is said to be among the highest in the world. Curiously enough, zeal does not spill over into attempts to proselytize the neighbouring English: the French attitude seems to be that one's religion is one's own affair, and that, while it is the duty of a good

Catholic to extend its bounds through reproduction, it is not his task to interfere with his neighbours' beliefs.

Intellectually, French-Canadian Catholicism, until recently, has not been remarkable, but, as the sense of inferiority that results from conquest is shaken off, it is finding itself both intellectually and culturally; the contributions of French Canada to literature, painting, and allied arts are far in excess of those of Catholic English Canada. The papacy presumably knows its own business best and probably was well aware of trends when it created an English cardinalate in 1946 in Canada: to the non-Catholic it would nevertheless appear that the Catholic centre of gravity is, and must for an indefinite time remain, in French Canada.

For Canadians, the interests of a historical summary of the positions of the two faiths will most likely be found in the conclusions drawn. How, it will be asked, do the two faiths compare today? Is there any likelihood of a major shift in their relative positions, leading to the dominance of one of them?

The answers may be found in statistical history. For nearly a century the two faiths have been in relative equilibrium and the two races have maintained approximately the same relative positions. Thus, while local shifts have occurred and will occur, it is unlikely that there will be a major change in the balance. Even in New Brunswick, where the rapid increase of French Catholics has often led to the conclusion that the province will soon be wholly French, it is almost mathematically certain that the French will not attain equality of numbers until the year 2000, if then. Every year that passes subjects the two races and faiths to the same environmental, political, and social influences. The utmost which can be accomplished by evangelical zeal in either camp is delay of the rate at which the gap between the two patterns of life is narrowed. In French Canada, language and tradition enable a strong rear-guard action to be fought. In English Canada, this is not possible, and in habits of life, including rate of reproduction, political attitudes, and moral outlook, the two groups steadily approximate.

It is probable that French Canada is undergoing the same process, though at a slower rate. Modern industrialism and urbanism are subtly affecting the former simplicity of the French way of life, driving it gradually into approximation to the English. Moreover, both races and creeds have found much in common. In the last century, Protestantism has moved far from its European origins, and in most of the denominations it has taken on its own Canadian shape.

In finding that they are children of the same soil, with the same political roof over their heads, French and English, Roman Catholics and Protestants, are very slowly discovering their common interests. Nationalism is proving a bridge. A century ago or less, many, perhaps most, Protestants were contemptuous of their French fellow-citizens as poor, downtrodden, "priest-ridden" peasants, and did not try to conceal their contempt. Today such religious and social intolerance is passing. Many Protestants will concede that there may, after all, be something in a way of life which does not consist entirely in "dollar chasing." Catholics will occasionally admit the inadequacy of a merely rural ideal or a way of life which cannot do much to improve the earthly circumstances of the individual. These changes look towards approximation.

There is, moreover, a common fear, shared by all Catholics and by many Protestants, of communism. Protestants emphasize the tyranny that it implies; Catholics, the atheism. To the hurt of Protestantism, which it divides, and more emphatically to the hurt of Protestant liberalism, this fear of the great unknown, the foreign unknown, is driving Canadians together, emphasizing that polarization of the world which is occuring elsewhere.

The present state of religion in Canada (in contradistinction to the present balance between Protestantism and Catholicism) reflects the great world currents of thought and action, but with a time-lag which arises from the immaturity of Canadian society. In neither Protestantism nor Catholicism have trends progressed as far in Canada as they have in the Old World. Canadians are not yet a people of ideas — they are too new, too insecurely combined. Consequently, the ideas of Europe, the creative continent, come to them after a rather long interval of time and are often mediated through Great Britain and the United States. As an example, German Biblical criticism made little impression in Canadian theological schools for two generations after it had reached its height in Germany, and then its chief exponents were from England.

European conditions cannot, therefore, prevail in Canadian religion, either Protestant or Catholic. To the Catholic from France, the French-Canadian church is apt to appear credulous and naive. Intellectually, this charge cannot be made against Protestantism, the major denominations of which are now abreast of good European thinking in theology, the relation of religion and science, and similar matters. But paganism, indifference, and atheism (which can proceed as easily from a Catholic as from a Protestant background) are not yet as characteristic in Canadian life as they are in older and more sophisticated communities. Protestants in Canada seem to show greater interest in the church than do Protestants in older countries. Church attendance in Canada is much larger, proportionately, than it is in either Great Britain or the United States. The Protestant church apparently draws in more young people than in either of the other countries. Most people have some kind of connection, real or nominal, with the church, and those who put themselves down in the census merely as "Protestant" are few; those who return "no religion" are fewer still. In Protestant Canada, anticlericalism is never encountered and, except in extreme circles (as among Communists), while often there is sharp criticism, there is virtually no hostility to the church.

It would be hard to prove Canadian Protestantism to be "the opiate of the people." That function may be left to the moving-picture theatres. Evangelical Protestantism, far from putting a man to sleep, keeps him only too wide awake. Not only does it impose the most tremendous of all burdens on him — his own absolute responsibility for his fate, finite and infinite — but it constantly throws at him the challenge that he is his brother's keeper and makes him feel that the world's safety and salvation depend not on his rulers or his boss or his priest but on him. It is the inability of so many people to measure up to the challenge of Protestantism that constitutes the danger and accounts for the decline in the church, not any weakness in the Protestant principle.

Absence of hostility to the church (accompanied by mere indifference and the loss of the old, simple faith, common to a scientifically educated generation everywhere) has perhaps been purchased by a too-ready acquiescence of the churches in the demands of the state. To every Canadian Protestant church, except some of the minor sects like Doukhobors and Jehovah's Witnesses, the state's command has become almost a rule of conscience, tending to override individual judgment. In the last two wars only a few hardy souls dared to stand out against the decrees of the state and fight for the dictates of their own consciences. It is not hard to explain the attitude: the Protestant churches so far identify themselves with the state — it is *their* state — that divergence is hardly conceivable. Catholicism still stands on its international position, but it has made many retreats and is today far more under the influence of the state than it was centuries ago. Here again, church and state in Quebec are close to being one, and in emergencies the line of cleavage runs, not between church and state, but between the two Canadian divisions of the state — province and Dominion; or between the two peoples — English and French. [9]

Certain psychological attitudes are common to all religions. Of these, mysticism is one. In days gone by, French-Canadian Catholicism produced its share and more than its share of mystics; the annals of the seventeenth century, with its missionaries, martyrs, and devoted founders of nunneries and monasteries, are full of them. Today they are less abundant, and in English Catholicism their absence is conspicuous. Even in French Canada they tend to be outnumbered, if not obscured, by those who proclaim not the mysteries of the faith but those of the race. Mysticism in Protestant circles has run a similar course. In Canada, Protestant mysticism has always been of the frontier variety, consisting in intense religious experiences which

[9]The province was 86.6 per cent Roman Catholic in 1941. Ontario was 76.8 per cent Protestant.

have often caused the recipients to indulge in grotesque emotional displays, such as shouting, "speaking with tongues," or rolling on the ground. Protestant mysticism, usually confined to simple pioneer people, emotionally starved except for the opportunities conveyed by a heady evangelicalism, has tended to exhibit grotesque parallels to the Dionysiac cults of antiquity. The withdrawn philosophic mystic, the Kierkegaard, the Keble, the Barth, is not a common phenomenon on Canadian soil. When the English Canadian gets an education, he leaves emotional religion and mysticism behind and goes in for something "practical" — social service, politics, stockbroking, or bridge-building. The Canadian air is hard on mystics: the winters are too cold and there is too much work to do.

As a result, most denominations, even the Catholic, have a utilitarian atmosphere. They stress good works and the social gospel. The most dynamic creed in Canada has undoubtedly been Methodism, and Methodism began by converting the frontier Loyalists and inducing them to live orderly and more or less sober lives. A century ago it launched the temperance crusade and ever since it has been closely identified with opposition to alcohol. Until the twentieth century it brought up its young people in an atmosphere that did not permit smoking, card-playing, dancing, theatre-going, or attendance upon horse-races. In the early twentieth century it launched a foreign missionary movement the zeal of which was comparable to that of the Counter-Reformation or the Crusades. Its adherents were strong supporters of the League of Nations. Many of them were active in progressive movements in politics, so that today former Methodists constitute perhaps the most important single component in Canada's social-democratic party, the C.C.F. Methodism (since 1925 merged in the United Church of Canada) has always supported every form of good work. It has been essentially a social religion and as such is remarkably well adapted to the Canadian outlook on life. While it remained a separate denomination its character was so clear that it might be singled out for special mention, but what is said of Canadian Methodism applies in greater or less degree to virtually all the Protestant denominations, except that few Anglicans or Presbyterians have considered that conformity to the entire list of Methodist taboos was necessary for Christian conduct.

This essay is concerned with Canadian religion, not with Canadian lack of religion. However, a word must be said on this most common of modern phenomena. Notwithstanding the relatively vigorous state of the Canadian church as compared with those of other lands, paganism has spread into Canada, as everywhere else. During the generation between the two wars, Canadians, like Americans, seemed to be determined to kick their institutions to pieces. They made fun of their politicans; they jeered at their preachers and the faithful who followed them, and mocked their parents' decorous youth. In a hundred ways they attempted to cast off the puritanism in which they and their forbears had been steeped. There was no sophistication about Canadian sin: it was just ugly. How far paganism has gone, no one can tell. The divorce rate mounts steadily. Sex crimes, the immoderate and often illegal consumption of alcohol, "wild" parties, and other excesses, all continue to increase. No doubt Canadians, like others who repent a youth which has been too well spent, will not stop until they have run the gamut, sown their wild oats, and had opportunity to reflect on their course of action.

The present age is a constant whirlwind and it is impossible to predict which of its many aspects will eventually dominate. Paganism must have its day, presumably, but there is little danger of Canada's becoming a pagan country. Paganism is, as it were, skin-deep: it has been present in every age, but not in every age has it been possible to indulge publicly in pagan practices. When release has been obtained, the present fit will wear off and the more permanent characteristics of the people will again manifest themselves. No longer will it be possible for a great church to fulminate against, say, the theatre, and expect much of a hearing — that is just an aspect of growing up, and the days of innocence are passing. But the stern northern climate will continue to impose its own seriousness of purpose, making its people fight hard to establish decent conditions of life; and their inherited tradition of altruism, carried over by the school, the university, the church, and other agencies (not least, the state), will impel them to the type of liberal humanism which their best spirits have always had most at heart.

The future will not be to mysticism: there are few dark corners in our present age of electric light. It will not be to mere ritualism — the Canadian is too practical-minded to become much interested in rites and ceremonies. The future will be to a liberal humanism which keeps in view the old familiar goal, *Mens sana in corpore sano.* This attitude has had its sharp struggles with pure commercialism, and whenever a pitched battle has occurred, it is the free enterprising society of commercialism which has been defeated. Liberal humanitarianism has been moving steadily into politics for many years, and it is rapidly giving us the social-service state. Vigorous objection is always made to each new measure in the programme (such as family allowances), but these measures steadily increase. They are not the mere voting of the money of the rich majority by the poor minority: they reflect Canadian Protestant mentality, and the indications are that Canadian Catholic mentality, if not naturally preoccupied with social humanism, finds it relatively easy to accept it.

Can society live on such conceptions? Liberal humanism provides no patent, doctrinaire blueprint for life: it cannot rival communism in the assuredness of Utopia. But it is far from the "each-for-himself" philosophy that in certain countries has prostituted the good term "liberalism": it has long since left mere individualism far behind and is definitely an idealist philosophy. But it is far more concerned with heaven here below than with heaven hereafter. As such, is it enough? Must Roman Catholicism return to the mysticism of former centuries? Must Protestantism recover for itself, before it becomes respectably entitled to the name religion, the spiritual ecstasies of another age? In short, must supernaturalism reign again?

These are questions which cannot be answered here. Increasing disturbance in the world, increasing danger, may bring greater emphasis on the mystical in religion. But a practical people, still with numerous jobs of construction to complete, placing strong emphasis on the importance of material welfare, retaining a confidence in science and "progress" which has been lost by peoples who have suffered a harsher fate, will find it difficult to reconvert to mysticism and other-worldliness. Canadians feel that there will always be enough mystics to keep their outlook from becoming merely mechanical and purely crass. If the atmosphere which covers the practical Canadian landscape can nourish two generations of people to whom no sacrifice was too great in the cause they conceived to be right and just, then mysticism and its traditional belief may possibly be left to take care of themselves.

Protestant, liberal humanism fits exactly the technological civilization of our day. It is dynamic, adaptable, equalitarian, and optimistic. It does not embrace all Canada, but its spirit is not without influence in those parts of the country which do not know it directly. It has moved far enough away from the old days to meet Catholicism with tolerance and communism with discussion. It is more flexible than either of these world religions, and now that the Second World War and the pressures of the social situation have broken the smugness of its Calvinism and the rigours of its individualism, it may have a long future. No country could be more thoroughly committed to this liberal humanism than is Canada.

III.

Values

In 1929, after four years in the United States studying for his doctorate and teaching, Arthur Lower returned to Canada to teach at Wesley College in Winnipeg. Later, with a quarter-century perspective, in "I Came Back and I Am Content" (Essay #8), he explained that he had made his choice in order to participate in the building of a nation. In "The Social Sciences in the Post-War World" (Essay #9), he set forth as a basic premise that to the degree in which history is a social science and the historian a social scientist, he must be actively engaged, as educator and as planner, in the building of the society in which he lives.

This emphasis fits his view of Canada as a nation whose path through history had been along deliberately planned lines ("The Massey Report" — Essay #10). He has never been a radical democrat; indeed a strong element of élitism runs through his thought. In "Is Distrust of Ability Formula for Success" (Essay #11), he complained of Canadian society's failure to appreciate those persons with intellectual capacity who ought to be the leaders in the task of nation-building. In his presidential address before the Royal Society of Canada ("Speaking to Each Other" — Essay #12), he argued that knowledge and an appreciation that some use needed to be made of it was what united the élite of higher intellect, whatever their discipline.

A major task of this élite was to set standards. One of the threads running most constantly through Lower's essays on contemporary affairs is the complaint that materialism overpowers all higher ideals in Canadian — primarily English-Canadian — society. Before true Canadian nationhood can be achieved, such a base ideal must be expunged and proper goals to strive for be set before the people ("Our Shoddy Ideals" — Essay #13). "Canada and a Free Society" (Essay #14) argues in general terms that the best standards are those which make up the creed of liberalism.

8 | *I Came Back and I Am Content**

When I was a lad I remember a cousin of mine coming out from England, loitering a while with us, and then drifting off to Detroit. There his family still lives. His case was typical: in by the front door, out by the back.

For natives the door to the south opens even more readily than for immigrants. We all have relatives in the States. Apart from this moment, at which the movement is probably at an all-time low, thousands of the most energetic among us, the most skilled, the ablest, have gone southward, seldom to return.

They go for the rewards, most people would say for the dollar-and-cents rewards, because wages and profits are bigger there than here. That seems only half the story to me. They go for rewards, it is true, but not necessarily for monetary rewards. They go where they can find congenial work, where they find scope for their abilities, where their work is appreciated, where there is a vigorous current of life. They go because there is often little room and little demand for them in Canada. More often than not they go reluctantly.

Some come back and many others would come back if they could. Few ever get the chance.

I am one of those who came back. I lived four years in the United States. In so far as my day-to-day work went I was entirely at home there. I met with much kindness, witnessed much largeness of spirit, and made many good American friends. Doors had begun to open and I suppose I could have gone up the scale in American life as many another Canadian has done.

In my case a career in the United States would have offered a good life. I would not have become rich, but I would have had enough; I would have had my books, my friends, good libraries, and the possibility, if I had measured up, of wide recognition. No door would have been closed to me because of my Canadian birth. And yet I came back. I often wonder why.

I came back to a position which was inconspicuous and ill-paid, its working conditions at times intolerable. And I came back with no illusions. I was quite aware that I was coming back to a country on the edge of civilization. I did not hide from myself that Canada was a backwoods country at that time, not in the sense that unsubdued nature was everywhere close, but that almost everywhere, even in our great cities, a kind of backwoods mentality still held strong.

*Macleans, 1 July 1951, pp. 2, 47-48.

I came back to a country with virtually no original culture and with little taste, to a land where no piece of originality could get attention because there were no native standards to judge it by, where everything fresh and vital had to wait the approving nod of our "elders" in Great Britain and the United States before we dared have an opinion of it ourselves. There, incidentally, lies the real meaning of Charles G. D. Roberts's despairing line, "How long the trust in greatness not thine own?"

I knew that in the Canada of those days (we have moved a little bit since) the intellectual — and I suppose I am a member of that unfortunate species — had rather less prestige than in Ashanti. I knew that my fellow citizens, most of them, entertained a deep contempt for the more subtle shadings of civilization. I had been trained as an historian, and I was coming back to teach in a college. As an historian I knew I would continually have to be explaining my function to people who thought "history" is something in an elementary textbook. As a teacher in a college I was doomed to the label "professor," and I knew that "the professor," to people with half the ability and knowledge of the world that most professors possess, is often a figure of fun and if not, something sinister and either way, a man who must always be apologizing for existing.

I knew, that for most of the people among whom I would be thrown, yes, for the very students in my classes, books would be strange objects to be avoided when possible, abstract ideas, causes of deep suspicion.

I knew, in short, that I was coming back to a callow society whose shortcomings would always hit me in the eye, where consequently I would usually be unpopular and where many doors would be closed to me — coming back to a society which, in my blacker moments, I would almost hate.

And yet I came back. I was one of the few who ever get a chance to come back. Perhaps that last sentence puts it all in a nutshell, for there are not many Canadian exiles who do not feel the lash in it.

I remember a conversation with a friend of mine, another Canadian, in my American days. I remember saying to him. "I don't believe that I could take the final step and become an American citizen. For me, a Protestant, it would be like 'going over to Rome.'" My friend agreed.

That's as near, perhaps, as I can get to explaining why I came back.

I came back to the familiar, to my home. I came back to the adventure of building a nation. That's an exciting job. In an old society so many things have already been done: everything is formed, all the big decisions taken, the crowded centuries lie behind. Here, where there is little past to get in the way, we are building our world as we go along, things are mobile and flexible.

It was a tough job to make Canada the nation it is today. As an American friend of mine once said to me, "You people must be deeply attached to your own country or you wouldn't be willing to pay so much to keep it up."

It seemed to me that there were certain specific avenues along which I might go in my part of the job. I thought of the depth of misunderstanding, prejudice, and even hatred that existed between French and English. If one could do a little to alleviate that, that would be a life-work in itself. I thought of the gay abandon with which we conducted our immigration policies — seldom guided by other than material considerations, invariably viewing the immigrant as a mere "hand," rarely as a human soul, never stopping to ask ourselves what kind of society we, and the immigrant, were building. I thought of the complexities in the relationships between Canada and her mother country, relationships that had in them so much of filial devotion, so much of sincere emotion, and yet which, if not carefully shaped, could keep Canadians so long in the role of minor children that they might never grow up. Most of all I thought of the perils to our traditional free way of life that the First World War had revealed and which the Second was to make imminent. If a nation was to be built, it must be a free nation with a living faith in freedom and justice, a nation aware of itself, setting its course by its own nature and not merely seeking to become a pale copy of the republic alongside it.

Its own nature was obvious: a country of two cultures, a country of an incredibly difficult physical setting, one which could give a good life to its citizens but could never attain the size and wealth of the United States, a hard yet moderate country, without American flamboyance but with quiet and dependable qualities of its own, with humility. It seemed to me that those who wished could have a great part in making such a country and that it might be a good country.

I hope all this doesn't sound pretentious, nor as reflecting personal vanity. I really think it was the kind of reasoning that brought me back. It would bring many more back if modest competences were available. The proof: the way former Canadians rushed back during the war, either to the armed services or to technical places in the civil government.

It was because I wanted to take part in the job of building a new nation that I was glad that chance, when it brought me back to Canada, took me to the Prairies. Here was the newest part of Canada; a highly malleable society waiting for those who could show the way or put its ambition into words for it, and a part of Canada that was and is Canadian in a sense that the East is not. The eastern provinces have their separate colonial memories, carrying them back to the days before Confederation. The West has next to none of these. The eastern provinces were the parents of the Canadian federation; the western are its children.

No Canadian can know Canada unless he knows the West. I left New England with its comfortable towns and beautiful villages, its sea and its mountains, its dignified and established culture, for the harshness and rawness of the Canadian prairie. There is no use my pretending that I liked the prairie environment, but the wonder was that, living on that billiard table which is Manitoba, I felt more at home than in beautiful New England, hospitable though it had been to me. On the Prairies I was one of the family.

New England was not the only place to impart this dreamlike quality to everyday life, for it had been just the same in old England, where I had spent several years. I am of English parentage. But I am not a part of England. For me to live in England or the United States is to live in a more or less unreal world, to be only more or less alive. I know I am not alone in this feeling.

When I returned from the war, the ship was filled with Canadians who had not seen their native land in several years. As we came up to Quebec the familiar smell of sawn lumber drifted off to us. It brought back expressions of emotion that I had never expected from any of my reserved countrymen, expressions so intense that in a few cases they verged on the theatrical, though they were none the less genuine for that.

And so, after two long intervals abroad, in two different countries and at two different periods of my life, I came to rest for keeps here in Canada. I accepted its disabilities.

Canada, whatever we Canadians think, is not a country of the first importance. Therefore Canadians are not of the first importance. Americans are. It has been hard for Canadians abroad to get themselves recognized and separately identified. To foreigners they have been either English or Americans, depending on their manners. To the English, in spite of two wars, Canadians are still, as a rule, Americans.

I can hear someone saying: "Why, we grow five hundred million bushels of wheat. Look at our oil, our iron, our copper, our electric power, look at our skyscrapers, our big cities. This is the land of opportunity. What's this fellow complaining about?" Apart from the fact that a few of our big cities are worth looking at, none of these things in themselves make a society that is worth twenty-five cents. They are just means to an end.

Do Canadians have anything besides iron, copper, skyscrapers, etc., to be proud of? Is there anything in the word "Canadian" that stands for something deep and indestructible? Most people, whatever their origin, can grasp what it means for a man to be able to say "I am a Jew." That means something indomitable, an immortal spirit that has never been conquered, an inner ferment that has more than once revolutionized mankind.

If this country be just iron, copper, oil, and so on — merely a collection of material assets — if it has no original creative spirit of its own and cannot rise to one, it can have little future of importance, however many "opportunities" it may afford. And can anyone deny that, occasional cases excepted, Canada is still not far from a cultural and spiritual desert? Can it be denied that its people in the mass are highly Philistine, despising the intellect, able to understand only action, opaque to thought and to imaginative creative emotion?

These are the traits that Canadians usually, in pharisaical demeanour, reserve for Americans. No attitude could be more foolish. Those who know the United States at first hand and not merely through the artificial media of press, radio, and movie know that it is in that country, far more impressively than in Canada, that the greatness of the human spirit has been demonstrated. It is there that are to be found the music, the libraries, the civic and national pride, the fierce pursuit of liberty, the large-mindedness, the wide-ranging, imaginative spirit only occasionally encountered here.

Canadian, disprove this if you can.

And yet I came home, and others have, too. Why? I can speak only for myself. It's great fun, nation-building.

Home, that is the word. We Canadians have a strong sense of home. Not a strong sense of nationality — we are too narrow gauged for that. Our sense of home is our love of our neighbourhood.

There may be more people who feel like me than would usually be assumed: we Canadians don't wear our hearts on our sleeves, and most of us would rather die than let others know that we actually can feel, actually have enthusiasms and can be stirred. Yet occasionally, by accident, the cat slips out of the bag. I remember the simple storekeeper of Hawkestone, that cosy little village on the shores of Lake Simcoe, who exclaimed to me, after chatting about less favoured regions: "I don't know how I'd get along without that lake out there." He recoiled when the words came out and shut up tight, feeling that he hàd made a fool of himself to a stranger. But for once his inner self had glinted through. It may have been the inner self of many a staid citizen.

There was the equally simple farmer down on the shores of the Baïe des Chaleurs. He had once been out west, and he couldn't endure the flat prairies. He came home to New Brunswick, home to twenty acres of hillside, to hard work and a limited future. But the tall hills of Gaspé stared at him from across the bay. "When I came back," he confided to me, "all I could do was to sit and look at them there hills."

So I suppose it was "that lake out there" that really brought me home. And it must have been the lakes and woods of Ontario which brought me back to my native province. It was not the province as such, because I contend that, except in a legal sense, there is no such thing. There is no Ontario: there are just lakes, woods, hills, dales, farmland; and towns and villages with the good luck to be set in beautiful surroundings, and few of them aware of it.

For one who wanted the fun of nation-building, the Canadian West provided a more congenial environment than Ontario. The Prairies are wide and bracing; Ontario is stuffy and parochial. In Winnipeg a man can look eastward and see Montreal and the Atlantic steamers carrying prairie wheat to Europe. And he can look the other way, across the mountains, and see Vancouver and the Pacific. But in Toronto he can see only Toronto — or perhaps, by reflection, New York. In the Canadian West one gets a sense of the whole country, its whole magnificent expanse. But the East retreats into itself. As an inhabitant of what was, until recently, our farthest east, Nova Scotia, once said to me: "I'm not really interested in anything west of the Isthmus of Chignecto." Sometimes it seems as if the coats of arms of our eastern provinces should carry in their fields, as the heralds would put it, a "parish pump rampant."

But now for me it is Ontario and it's Lake Ontario.

> This eunuch sea
> This pastured, fenced nonentity ... .

So shouts our poet Earle Birney, who from British Columbia once migrated to Ontario and has now again put the miles between the eunuch sea and his mountain vastness.

And so here I am now, at last, washed up on the old Ontario strand, sitting in an old farmhouse, looking right out over the horizon of the eunuch sea. Sixty miles south, across those unbriny waves, lies New York State and the land that has swallowed so many of my countrymen. Just sixty miles to the big salaries, the big cities, the mild winters! Just sixty miles to the land of big achievements, the land where the world's destinies (ours included) are being decided — and being decided by people less capable, it would often seem, than ourselves! It wouldn't have been hard to get into that game; many another Canadian has done it.

Running the world (perhaps, I had better say, trying to run it) from Washington must be the biggest, most exciting game on earth. Any young Canadian who has the ability and the training can go down there and take a hand in it, nothing more certain — the funny thing is that all of them do not. Some of them, if not enough, stay here to get on with our own humble tasks.

Few people would argue that the great world nations are making times more pleasant for mankind. Great powers never have. They have never had records that impelled the little peoples to "up and join" them. No, the little peoples, the Swedes, the Swiss, the Dutch, the Danes, and others, have always had a very good conceit themselves. It has often been amusing to watch the giants in their folly. Dangerous, of course. But danger makes fun, too.

Well, here on Lake Ontario, I have a special reserved seat from which to watch Giant Number One. But I don't think I want to be part of him, even if he is big and strong. For here on the shore of Ontario — the north shore — I have found content.

9 | *The Social Sciences in the Post-War World**

Writing about things that have not yet occurred is always a hazardous task, but unless the scriptural injunction to take no thought for the morrow is taken rather literally, it is one that now and again has to be attempted. The social scientist, both as teacher and writer, like everyone else will be affected by the issue of the present war — it therefore behooves him to try and discover how. While no one can make a blueprint of the future, there probably will be fairly general agreement about some of the aspects it is likely to wear. Some measure of agreement may also be found among social scientists with regard to the nature of their calling and the way in which it is affected by the society in which they practise it.

It is commonly said that we stand at the end of an era, or indeed at the end of two eras — at the end of nineteenth-century individualism, sometimes called liberalism, and at the end of the longer period of individualism ushered into the world by the Renaissance and Reformation. It seems pretty clear that we stand at the end of nineteenth-century economic anarchy. Whether we stand at the end of Protestantism and free inquiry is another matter, not yet so evident. It is a common mistake to equate freedom with liberalism. Liberalism as a fairly definite philosophy was elaborated during the nineteenth century. It was European rather than Anglo-Saxon in origin and nature (as witness its anticlerical and antireligious tendencies on the continent) and was derived from our own older tradition — a more vital tradition for us — of legal "liberties," of the reign of law. Magna Carta, in other words, is older than the Declaration of the Rights of Man. This medieval tradition has never faltered in England itself and has been carried by Englishmen to the self-governing parts of the English world, where it wages continuous battle with the native influences of the environment.

In England itself the tumultuous forces of the nineteenth century enhanced the tradition of freedom, which fitted rather well into the new society of that period. England got many of the advantages of the frontier,

**Canadian Historical Review* 22 (March 1941): 1-13.

it must be remembered, without actually having a frontier experience herself, and likewise she avoided some of its less pleasant aspects, such as the crudities and amateurishness of its democracy. Her ruling class never lost control, and she therefore continued to receive the benefits of aristocracy. At the same time the rising business class found the traditional conceptions of law and order very well suited to its own interests and never manifested the slightest desire to break them down. "The English constitution is mainly a commentary on the law of real property," Maitland's well-known dictum goes. Thus, frontier anarchy never rolled across the seas to England; she kept her society tight and orderly.

The United States, on the other hand, came close to seeing the old medieval traditions swamped by the frontier. No country has ever committed itself more thoroughly to the maxim "every man for himself and the devil take the hindmost" than has the United States, a nation wherein has arisen the most completely atomized society in history. So far has this gone that the old social concepts of character, duty, loyalty, have tended to wear rather thin in American life. As C. A. Beard has remarked, from about the middle of the nineteenth century the old ethic was being crowded out by the new American morality, the morality of success.[1]

In Canada, where, because of the dispersion of population and of colonial imitativeness, general trends are much more difficult to trace than in the two older countries, there would seem to have been the characteristic compromise between English and American traits. The rigid English regard for the law certainly never possessed Canadians; neither did they go as far towards social anarchy as did the Americans. If the old traditions have not completely given way in Canada, it is probably mainly because the frontier has been less extensive, success not so appalling, and the influence of the steadier society of England more constant than across the line. Being somewhat off the main highway of ideas and of social forces, Canada usually has had the opportunity of seeing how they work out elsewhere before itself beginning to feel their full effects.

It is apparent that in the leading countries of the world, if not in the backwaters, the impulses released so vigorously in the nineteenth century began to run out in the twentieth. These impulses are often dubbed "capitalism," far too narrow a word, and people who use that appellation go on to say that the capitalist system or era is coming to a close. The truth would appear to be that something wider and deeper than mere economic change is occurring. The First Great War had much to do with increasing the speed of the change, even if it did not originate it, and this present war will similarly hasten the historic process. That some profound change

---

[1]See Charles A. Beard and Mary R. Beard, *The Rise of American Civilization* (New York: Macmillan, 1930), chapter 20, "The Triumph of Business Enterprise."

is occurring, the malaise of the last two decades, their indecision, apathy, irresponsibility, their economic cataclysms and political earthquakes, are sufficient testimony. What Hitler did in Germany, essentially, apart from his cruelties, was to end the confusion of purpose, the irresolution, the fumbling, that necessarily attend the senility of a social philosophy. Few of us like the unceremonious way in which he gave it the coup de grace, and we would hope ourselves to conduct a more dignified funeral, one less difficult for the attendants to bear, but we must admit that his expeditious hustling out of the old order gave him for the moment at least a great advantage over the rest of us, still perplexed as to how to do it.

Having ended the old order, he was able to present his countrymen with a new. It seemed a rather ugly baby at the time and has not increased in favour with God or man since, but no one can deny its strength and self-assurance. Meanwhile, we Westerners are still speculating. A new order is struggling to be born among us, but in genetics as in other things we cling to *laissez faire* ideas, so none of us knows much about what the infant may be like. That is the great problem on our hands at the moment, trying to divine the nature of the future, and as social scientists, perhaps even essaying to act as its midwives.

As a matter of prophecy it at least seems safe to suggest that whatever the result of the war, in the future the individual is going to have to subordinate himself to society more than he has done in the past. If our Western world is to be kept afloat it will surely be because of organizing skill, and organizing skill spells the death of our pleasant old social and political anarchy — for all of us except the organizers, anyway. Out of this a twofold problem emerges: in what kind of hands is the new society to be and how can it be built without losing the enduring values that our civilization has created? There is little hope of getting a really satisfactory answer to these questions yet, though certain guesses may be hazarded. In the first place it would seem futile to look for any universal order: each country will get the kind of régime that the political forces in it necessitate. Canada will certainly not have socialism, fascism, communism, or democracy just because Great Britain and the United States come to have something people may decide to call by one of these names. In fact, if history is any guide, the social process in Canada will lag behind by a generation or so and yet, of course, will not be entirely unaffected by events elsewhere. Our experience will inevitably be different, therefore, from that of either Great Britain or the United States. Our future will probably be organized by a different type of person from those who are doing the same task elsewhere and therefore in a different way. We shall not have the advantage of the mature political wisdom of the English civil service and governing classes, for example, or the semi-revolutionary, informed zeal of the American New Deal. So far the war has shifted power in Canada into the hands of men who represent social régimes preceding those now coming into existence in the other two countries, men who perhaps worship idols whose shrines tend to be deserted in their own temples, and it would seem likely that these men will manage to retain much of this power. The Canadian future, like the future of every other country, will therefore be organized in its own particular way.

The great problem, of course, is how to do the necessary job of organizing without losing the enduring values that Western civilization has created. It should not be beyond human ingenuity to put its house in order without sacrificing the spirit of freedom and the well-being that comes from this spirit and from it alone. We can make up our minds to a large measure of control in every area of life, but control and servitude are not necessarily to be equated. Controls accepted with a good heart and out of a sense of duty do not diminish the spirit of freedom. The member of a team is not a slave. But here again, every country will return a separate solution, depending upon its experience. We in Canada, for example, have had a good deal of freedom in the past, but it has been a haphazard kind of freedom. It has been mainly the freedom of the frontier, the freedom that comes from space, the freedom of retreat. Like our American cousins, if we did not like conditions where we were, we could "get out," "go west." We have rarely felt it our duty to stand and fight for our privileges. If unpleasant neighbours moved in next to us, we sold the old family mansion and moved into another. That process has resulted in the disappearance of the English-speaking Canadian from whole tracts of our countryside.

The freedom we have wanted and have understood has been the freedom to do as we like, to be left alone, not the freedom that emerges out of a close-knit society where everybody has his duties — and his rights. English society may be compared with a ship's company: the space is narrow and the ship has to be sailed; every member of the crew from captain to cabin boy has his allotted task, his severe duties, but also his unquestioned rights. He has a fierce sense of these rights. In fact, what makes the Englishman unpopular — and respected — the world over is his keen sense of his rights and his readiness to stand up for them. Not so the American and still less the Canadian: their freedom is much more like that of the Indian in the bush. It is a wilderness freedom, and of the great English tradition of ordered, legal freedom, we Canadians, despite the gallant efforts of our lawyers to transplant the whole English legal edifice to our soil, inherit only a fraction. It is not in our blood, for most of us are Irish or Scottish by descent, rather than English, and as such, have quite a different tradition. The proof of the unsubstantial character in Canada of this English heritage lies in our almost complete indifference to the abrogation of our formal legal edifice of freedom by our wartime legislation. The contrast with England is marked.

The social scientist must recognize this difference between the English and the Canadian scene before he begins making blueprints of the future, for the type of material he has to work with is very different from that of his English or his American colleagues. It is going to be exceedingly difficult to work out a closely organized Canadian society that shall at the same time have the spirit of freedom, far more so than in England.

We have already seen a vast increase in the edifice of control, both economic and political. The innumerable boards and commissions thrown up by the war go some distance towards establishing its mechanisms. They nearly all rest at the moment on the War Measures Act, a law which bestows complete and absolute power upon the dominion government. If at the close of the war the Dominion were suddenly to put off the powers it has assumed under this act, something like anarchy would result. It may therefore be safely assumed that since the operation of the act does not lapse until the government proclaims a state of peace, we shall, whether peace is arrived at abroad or not, continue to be in a legal state of war until the government thinks it safe to make the transition to a legal state of peace. We shall probably be governed under the War Measures Act long after the war is ended, long enough, at any rate, to effect a change from wartime control to peacetime control.

Control, if dubbed "democratic," seems to be acceptable to most people, not only economic control but also political. It is very difficult to decide on the real nature of a régime, and "democracy," "fascism," "communism," etc., may in essence merely be names. The only test is the spirit of the régime. If it stands for freedom and enlightenment, it does not matter much by what name it is called, but if it stands for repression, obscurantism, and privilege, it is all the more certain, especially in English-speaking countries, to insist on calling itself by a high-sounding traditional name. Thus, even if we here in Canada were to lose our democratic régime in spirit, we would be certain to continue having it in name. However that may be, at present we have a very complete degree of political control: control of opinion, of personal freedom, assembly, organization, movement, and residence, and no great reverence for due process of law. In these matters comparisons between Canada and either Great Britain or the United States are not in our favour. By our actions we display a grave lack of confidence in our historical English heritage. The future, therefore, will certainly not see a mere return to the past. A new kind of state is coming into existence in Canada, based on control, that is evident, and the unsolved problem is whether that state will permit a free community.

It is obvious that the nature of the state is a matter of supreme concern to the social scientist, not only as furnishing him with the phenomena that he seeks to describe but also, and perhaps more significantly, determining the conditions under which he describes them. Most social scientists like to think of themselves as detached observers, no more affected by the events and circumstances they are watching than is the astronomer by his stars. This is of course arrant nonsense: we are all part of the society in which we live, attached to it in a dozen ways and affected by it not only through our minds but also our hearts. And we cannot go away somewhere else and describe a society utterly alien to us, for there are very few who have either the opportunity, the ability, or the necessary detached penetration so to do. Even people who go off to observe the *Sexual Life of the Trobriand Islanders* tend to end up rather solidly on the side of the Trobrianders. The social scientist cannot, except by some tour de force of doubtful value, be an alien to the society he has chosen to study. There is an occasional Gibbon among historians (though we are without the comments of Roman historians on Gibbon's description of the empire, it must be remembered), but there are many more Macaulays. Practically all great history, as a matter of fact, has been written by persons who were of and from the society about which they were writing. It is just possible − I leave this to the experts − that Karl Marx would have made a better analysis of English society if he had been an Englishman.

We cannot escape our surroundings: they change, and we with them. The social sciences, in other words, and certainly social scientists, can never be completely detached, unprejudiced observers. Further, most social science must be limited and impermanent: it is the result of a limited observation by an imperfect observer of a limited scene, and therefore most writing, historical, economic, sociological, etc., is in the nature of an interim report, to be revised as occasion offers.

In Canada there is little attempt to be universal. We write about the Canadian scene. The strangers amongst us sometimes have tried to keep themselves, artificially, in the environment from which they have come, but eventually they too have taken to seeing the world through local eyes. The late Professor Waugh of McGill, for instance, did one or two volumes in European history after his arrival, but then he produced a life of Wolfe. For some time yet effective writing upon the social sciences in Canada, as in every other country, must be upon the Canadian social sciences, for a Canadian audience, and by persons "soaked" in the Canadian scene. This is amply proved by the fact that that is exactly the kind of writing we get.

The kind of writing is determined by and determines the kind of audience. "Who reads a Canadian book," it was asked some years ago, "except by mistake?" The question was a nasty one, for there was a good deal in the innuendo it contained. Who reads books on the various aspects of Canadian social science? Very few people indeed, and certainly among them, not many abroad. The amount of absence of interest in Canada on the part of the rest of the world is staggering. We Canadians are worthy, thrifty people, perfectly safe and constituting no problem to the countries in control of our destinies: we are therefore uninteresting and what we write about ourselves is also, for the most part, uninteresting — except to ourselves. The persons who read works on Canadian social science are therefore Canadian social scientists.

There is no reason to deplore this. The circle of readers is certainly small, but it is intelligent and it is not reading for mere pleasure, that is obvious. It is reading because it is trying to understand the Canadian scene. It is hard to believe that in these days of stress it is satisfied with mere understanding. The number of Canadians who wish knowledge for knowledge's sake must be severely limited: we are all too puritanical for that. Knowledge to us is power, and if we are trying to acquire knowledge of the Canadian scene it is because, at least in the backs of our heads, we have the notion that we can do something about it. In other words, here is a country, a society, in formation, and Canadian social scientists, like other human beings, find zest not only in understanding the processes of formation but in determining them. We are present at an exciting experiment, the beginning of a society, and we would be less than human if we did not wish to do something about determining its shape.

This same conclusion may be arrived at by another route. The Canadian historian is especially faced with this conundrum: What is Canada? What is it he is to describe? Is he to confine himself to the English in the Maritime provinces, to the French upon the St. Lawrence, to the Loyalists in Upper Canada, or can he bring a multitude of diverse phenomena under some general head? Can there be any such thing as *Canadian history?* Some of us have described economic activities that went on in the past in or about a certain geographical area now called the Dominion of Canada. These activities as often as not have been carried on by persons who have had only a fortuitous connection with the area. They have ransacked a region of natural wealth and have disappeared, leaving not a wrack behind. Their activities in a sense are the stuff of Canadian history in much the same way as were the activities of palm-oil traders on the Niger — who came one day and went the next — part of the history of the aborigines of that country. An area and its exploitation may be described, and that is a useful, if humble, task, but it is questionable if such description is history in the deepest sense. I certainly do not minimize the splendid accomplishments of my colleagues, who, individually and collectively, have achieved great things, especially in this last generation, but we must recognize that however able or sincere our efforts, we are not in a position to write great — and perhaps not even, real — history, and that because we stand at the beginning of an evolution rather than some distance along its course. What we write is not the sort of thing that the Canadian people (if there is one) feels in its bones. The Armada and Shakespeare and William

Pitt, Saint Louis, Joan of Arc, the Marseillaise are history, the stuff of life itself, the food great peoples live on. Our exercises in the description of times past, on the other hand, are in essence efforts to supply a history to a country that as yet has not got one, a kind of ready-made history, awaiting the arrival of a people to purchase it.

The objection that will be made to this statement is that writing of the type referred to is an act of scholarship and that scholarship is its own justification. Scholarship for whom, it may be asked? The audience for the kind of books most of us write is a very small one. They will be read by few persons indeed not interested in the Canadian scene. The audience must of necessity be that small group that can see in this geographical area so described its own home for the future (for very few of us can claim it for any length of time in the past). Canadian history in its deep and true sense is still to be written, must await writing indeed until there have been generations live and die here who have loved and suffered and triumphed together. Meanwhile the economic historian (still more the economist) is like the man who cuts the grass or cleans the windows: he performs meritorious but somewhat external services, and he certainly does not get into the life of the family. One wonders sometimes, indeed, if there is any family in this Canadian house, or whether it is not just an hotel. If it is, one economic historian, at any rate, is about ready to stop cleaning windows. If he (and I imagine, others) keep on, it is because writing what we call Canadian history is an act of faith. Thus, we come by another way to the essential truth that Canadian writing must be for Canadians (or Australian for Australians, for that matter, or all except the widest and greatest, even in the relatively narrow sphere of the social sciences, for the people out of whom it grows), and for that relatively small group among Canadians who are interested not only in what has taken place and is taking place but also in what is about to take place.

This small group is both passive and active. It provides the circle of readers for which its members write. It observes and records. It does more. It creates the scene and it creates the audience. It therefore seems to me that the social scientist in Canada must be more than a mere observer and recorder. He must be more than a mere scientist. He is a member of a group of workmen engaged in a common project. He must be to some extent an artist. Social science in Canada, in other words, is not so much like physical science as it is like medical science, both an art and a science. The social scientist will have something to do with creating and affecting society as well as with describing it.

If he refuses duty, he will probably be put aside as a classroom relic, for there will be little place for the mere academic monk in the strenuous future that is on all of us. We social scientists will be extremely lucky if we manage to keep our footholds at all. In the past a relatively stable world has permitted a certain detachment in many spheres of life. We have been able to indulge in the luxuries of free discussion and academic argument because there has been a certain amount of elbow room in society. Spacious periods in history permit learning and culture to flourish for their own sake: civilization wears them, as it were, like jewels in its hair. But in such periods, these marks of civilization easily degenerate and become the selfish retreats of persons attracted by them. Then sets in the last stage of liberalism, where social utility breaks down into mere individual selfishness, as in Renaissance Italy, or possibly this last decade or two here in the West. From these lax periods society purges itself by another wave of puritanism that restores the vigour of the academic disciplines in restoring their social utility.

It may be that we are confronting such a period now. It is unlikely that there will be much room for ceremonious debate in the storm up ahead. The call will be for action and there will be a high differential against mere reflection. A still heavier duty will therefore be imposed on the social scientist, who at one and the same time will have to supply most of the philosophy that arises out of reflection and constitute himself a man of deeds. If he abandons his post, there will be plenty of people ready to take over and "run the show," and he will end up as a person of small account. He may be content to sit and watch society go by, but it will get so far past him that his observations will not have much value.

The social scientist in the world about to be will have to have his position thought out very carefully. He will have to have his own ideas about the kind of world he would like to see come into existence, and he will have to be very clear as to the kind of job he is doing, both in his writing and in his teaching. The first thing a new order does in seeking to establish itself is to try to get hold of the schools and universities: *per contra,* an old order tries to maintain itself by tightening its control of them. Our teaching will undoubtedly be affected by the new world, just as we shall: the new world will change us, because we will be part of it, and it will change our teaching. It will not necessarily do this by coercion, though that possibility is not to be rejected, and it will certainly arise if we get too far out of step with the world around us. We shall therefore have to learn how to make reasonable compromise, which means that we shall have to know very definitely what we are doing in our classrooms.

Few subjects seem to be less debated among academics than the objects they have in view. Some have the comfortable view that there is certain traditional knowledge to be handed on. Others take refuge in "scholarship," though they do not appear to be very certain of the meaning of that term. Some equate it with this traditional knowledge, others with "culture," others with "widening the bounds of knowledge," or "productive scholarship," as the Americans term it. Nearly everyone either gets uncomfortable or indignant if the awkward question "Why?" is put. Yet in an atmosphere of increasing pressure that word is going to be put. So it is necessary for us to try and decide what we are doing in our classrooms.

There was a time when the schools of the land, of this gauche, democratic country, were trying to make "gentlemen"— the Rev. John Strachan's at Cornwall, for example. That effort has had its retribution: the few "gentlemen" that remain are rather divorced from our realities. Somewhat later on, when the first waves of democracy were washing in, students were being trained "to think." (They still are, without any startling degree of success.) Then, as we began to get a little leisure in the prosperity of the period before the last war, students were being steeped in "culture," which meant that they were acquiring affable men-of-the-world manners, the ability to talk pleasantly on a variety of interesting topics, to pose as epicures of literature and art. The question was not asked, "Whose culture are they being steeped in?" It was certainly not our own for we did not possess any of consequence. That pre-war generation was being immersed in the generalized culture of Western Europe, which to it was remote and somewhat artificial. Its training was generous and "liberal" in the best sense, as I can testify, but it was not exactly the training for young Canadians who had to meet the problems of their own time and place.

Since the last war our universities have moved immeasurable distances. The old ideas remain here and there, but the shallow exoticism of pre-war days has largely passed. In the social sciences at least, and probably in some of the other disciplines too, the student is being brought squarely up to the problems, past and present, of his own world. That world may be somewhat narrow. Canada is a secondary and second-rate country without much depth of experience: everyone admits that — too freely, sometimes. But that narrow world is our own. We have got to understand it well first, before we can get to grips with the realities of larger worlds, and we have still quite a long distance to go before we do understand it. For example, all the efforts of our scholarship, based as they are mainly on the Canadian scene, have as yet hardly begun to dissipate the mists of colonialism. Almost as I write these words, a senior student tells me that he would rather be governed by "Britain" than by "Canadian politicians." Asked to analyse the concept "Britain," he decides that it could not possibly include "Hore-Belisha," that in fact at the moment it consists of the concept "Churchill." In other words, he is completely hazy about the nature of the world he lives in and of our own institutions. There are thousands like him.

This is no argument for parochialism: the point simply is that there can be no true learning, no truth of any sort in the deepest sense, if the foundations are false. And the foundations are false when they are unreal, when they give us an untrue picture of the world we live in, that is, when the material we study is related in some artificial or fortuitous way to our own experience, which in the case of our students, happens to be their life here in Canada.

It would therefore seem to me that the classroom objective of the social scientist must simply be that of making clear to the student the kind of world he lives in, so that he may feel at home in it and may make his adjustments with it — and, it is to be hoped, may help in the process of adjusting it. Since there is so much difference of opinion about the nature of the world, this may be begging the question, though as a matter of fact among social scientists in Canada there is not a great deal of fundamental difference of opinion: there are many shades of opinion, but few irreconcilable differences. We all have an idea of the kind of world we would like to have; and most of us have some ideas about the kind of world we are likely to get.

Unless we regard ourselves as a class of people of absolutely no significance, who can have no effect upon society and owe no duty to it (and surely few of us would go that far), we must have some interest in bringing about the future we desire. In other words, by a third route we come back to the conviction that the social scientist in these pregnant days and in this malleable society of ours, cannot, if he is to exist, be a mere spectator, a mere dissector of society: he must also be a formative agent in society. He cannot, if he would, be a mere passenger on board ship. He must stand his watch on the bridge and help with the navigation — help lay out the course, which means that he must know where he wants to go. That task is laid on him: it is laid both on his pen and on his voice.

He will have to perform it as his conscience directs but he will refuse it at his peril.

10 | *The Massey Report**

Some communities grow; others are made. Canada is one that has been made, a country of a plan. Our original plan was Confederation: its blueprint, the British North America Act. Here was a carefully drawn document containing a scheme of government, an allocation of powers, a system of constitutional limitations coming close to a bill of rights, and an elaborate economic scaffolding for the construction of the future nation. In England,

*Canadian Banker 59 (Winter 1952): 22-32.

such matters had worked themselves out over the centuries and had never been put into a single precise public statement: in Canada, they were planned in advance.

There could have been no Canada without planning, planning of the most careful and ambitious nature. The British North America Act was but a beginning. True, it did contain provision for the means by which the Maritimes could be bound together with central Canada (the Inter-colonial Railway), but later on a much more complete programme had to be worked out. Within twenty years after Confederation it had been fought through Parliament, by the Conservative administrations of Sir John Macdonald. The programme devised a method for securing British Columbia and preventing the prairies from passing under American sovereignty, and the means chosen was planned as a kind of spinal column for the new country — the Canadian Pacific Railway. The financial structure of the new economy had to be rendered secure, and this was accomplished by that distinguished piece of planning, the Canadian Bank Act of 1871. This act, by erecting a national system of banking, prevented invasion and conquest by the banks of the United States. The most deliberate (and least systematic) piece of planning in the whole programme was the National Policy, which took the form of that most socialistic of all public devices, a protective tariff.

As we began, so we have gone on. At every critical juncture in our national life, when we have been faced with a choice between individualism and socialization, we have chosen socialization. The Liberals were defeated twice, in 1891 and in 1911, on their programme of rugged individualism, termed "reciprocity," "unrestricted reciprocity," or "commercial union." The individualists were defeated who would have allowed the Canadian Northern Railway system in 1917 to go bankrupt, let the consquences be what they might; and the Borden government embarked on that arduous road of nationalization along which we are still plodding. In Ontario, Sir Adam Beck won a victory over the non-planners, which was as decisive as a victory well could be, when he secured the establishment of the Ontario Hydro-Electric Commission. In like manner, each new and radical implement of public utility as it has come along has been the subject of a major struggle, and in each case victory has gone to the planners. Trans-Canada passenger aviation was taken out of the sphere of private interests and put into the public hands. The Bennett government established the Bank of Canada and began the transition from private to public broadcasting which has ended up with the Canadian Broadcasting Corporation. Canada has been planned.

These triumphs of socialization have not denied outlet to individual energies. Within the general planned pattern, individualism has made its own large contribution to Canadian life. But the point is that it has been within a general pattern. The Canadian people have, in fact, virtually without knowing it, worked out a way of life unique in the modern world: in their own practical, unvocal way, they have found a way of combining collectivism and individualism, the united effort of the community and the personal efforts of citizens. The illustrations are on every hand: C.P.R. alongside C.N.R., private air transport alongside T.C.A., private broadcasting alongside the C.B.C., and so on. The Canadian compromise may be destined to provide a solution for the major problem of our times, this stress between the general will as expressed in the state, and the multiplicity of individual wills, the *laissez faire* society.

It is lucky for us that our planning has been of a high order of practical efficiency. It has been planning with no fancy attitudes about it, good, solid, hammer-and-saw work such as befits a plain, puritan people. The result is that most of our national structure has proved to have good wearing qualities.

Why is it that a practical, unimaginative people should have embarked on this remarkable course, a course from which they show no sign of departing? The answer is plain: the one determining motive that runs through all Canadian history, in both French and English Canada, is simply never to become part of the United States. The friendliest and closest relations, yes, but absorption, never! The deduction from this fundamental psychology is equally simple: we must build a national home of our own, cost what it will.

No one would deny the cost. No task is easier than compiling lists of prices of articles on either side of the border showing the enormous differential in favour of the American. It is almost as easy to show the same kind of differential in rates of pay (especially salaries) and in cost of government. It becomes rather harder to show it in non-material areas, such as prestige, status, type of outlook, and cultural level, but it is not too hard to show it there, too. We Canadians pay and pay heavily every minute of the day for the privilege of remaining ourselves. At first sight it may seem hard to reconcile an apparently romantic attitude like this with our practical natures. We have, however, a good scriptural analogy for the problem involved: Satan, we are told, took Jesus up to a high mountain, and showed him cities of men: all these He could have, if He would but fall down and worship him. The moral fits us: material possessions are worth nothing if for them you surrender your soul.

Few of us soar into such high regions when thinking about national affairs, but to think straight about them we must have the idea in the back of our minds; and the writer is pretty sure that that is just where the average citizen of this country perpetually has it. Consequently, when it comes to one of the big decisions involving a choice between planning and individual enterprise, he is invariably in favour of planning, nationalism, socialism, public ownership, whatever you choose to call it. He is in favour of it because he knows individual enterprise, left to itself, leads, in Canada, to the abyss. If you let things slide in a country like this, there is no doubt about the direction they will slide in — straight into Uncle Sam's ample arms. That is just the spot we are determined to keep them out of.

Now what has all this to do with the Report of the Massey Commission? Simply this — that the commission is just one more exercise in this old Canadian preoccupation of planning our national home and that it comes precisely at that moment in history where one would logically expect it.

In a new country struggling forward against nature, the economic situation will first receive the major share of attention, as it did in Canada. But we had barely projected ourselves effectively across the continent before we were forced to face the problems that flooded in upon us from the outside world. With the opening of the First Great War in 1914, the political phases of life began to dominate the economic: they have gone on doing so increasingly. We had to work out the associations with one another of the sections into which nature has divided this country. We had to find a *modus vivendi* between the two races.

With great internal tension, as the conscription debates witness, we sought the *modus vivendi*. The fact that we came through the storm of two world wars witnesses to our having found it. Much remains to be done, naturally, for no human situation is ever static, but a less undemonstrative people than ourselves would probably by now be congratulating itself in no uncertain terms on the political miracle which it had accomplished. We take our unity in our stride, and we understand only dimly as yet the consequences that must follow from it. One of these consequences is the crossing of the next mountain range in national life: the expression in national life of the spirit which sustains it and which consciously or unconsciously permeates it.

At this point the Massey Report comes in, for the commission which made it was appointed in response, not to the personal desire of any one man, but to the feeling, to be sensed in a multitude of directions, that the time had come when the spirit of the Canadian community must find its voice.

By "finding its voice" I do not mean merely the writing of romantic novels on the Canadian scene or lyric poetry about it: I mean every kind of expression that a healthy organism requires: not only literary, artistic, and political, but economic, journalistic, and social expression, expression in amusements and sport. I think the Massey Commission means something of this sort, too. Every community that has risen to national height has found outlet for this vital expression of its way of life: this, in the widest sense, is what is meant by a national culture. American movie actresses and baseball mighties are part of the American culture. They are a necessary part, for the masses must have their representative figures. That is one of our serious lacks in Canada, though perhaps now being partially compensated for by the growth of the cult of the hockey hero.

The retort that we can well do without, shall we say, the Rita Hayworths is not adequate, for if our people do not possess such figures of their own, they simply crane their necks over the American fence to look at them. A mature culture gets every type of expression, from bottom to top. It is to be hoped that we may have a good share of the top; but there can be no top without bottom. A too-intellectual and too-aesthetic culture would be anaemic and rootless; it would not get far. This is probably what a writer in the *Peterborough Examiner* was warning about recently when he wrote:

> *Culture* "is a word which suggests to most Canadians pleasures and pursuits which are beyond their reach and of which they are at once afraid and contemptuous — (yet) *culture* means simply civilization — the state of life in which we find ourselves. Canadian culture will never soar beyond the Canadian people...."

The Massey Commission was not, of course, concerned with baseball players and movie stars. It had to think in more permanent terms, though in so doing it laid itself open to the danger I have indicated — alienation of the ordinary individual by being over his head. There is no quicker way to damnation in Canada than to be caught in "high-falutin'" attitudes, deservedly or not to earn the epithet "high-brow."

The Massey Report is therefore hardly for the man in the street (no reports of royal commissions are). It is aimed at a limited sector of the public and concerned with a limited, though large, sector of Canadian life. Its major interest, quite frankly, is in the more limited aspects of our cultural life, those that the butcher and the baker in all probability would label "high-brow." Does the presumed verdict of butcher and baker therefore damn the report? I do not think so. The meaning of the epithet "high-brow" depends on the point of view. Plenty of people, both trained and untrained, quickly become impatient with that which is beyond their range, the immediate utility of which they cannot see. As a "prof," I am a professional "high-brow" and in many circles damned in advance: what I think and say must, because I am a "prof," be dry-as-dust and mumbo-jumbo. It is possibly a healthy defensive attitude: we all tend to make a joke of matters beyond our range, refusing to take them too seriously, even atomic bombs. However, as a "prof" and a high-brow, I am unrepentant: I know with what armour-plating a tough education equips a man.

It is "high-browism" of this sort which, I think, marks the Massey

Report: its authors know the imperatives of life, and they know that the imperatives transcend the surface. Sure knowledge is written all over the document. No group not sure of themselves would have ventured to begin with a quotation from St. Augustine in the original Latin! Whether we understand it or not (and a translation is thoughtfully provided), this opening stamps its character on the report — and perhaps on the Canadian people, too, for it is hard to imagine public documents opening with Latin quotations being received with acclaim in many parts of the world. Its authors dare write a document like this because they know that first things must come first. Hence this extraordinary panorama of the cultural side of Canadian life which they spread before our eyes.

Many readers will have glanced through the report. For those who have not, it may be briefly outlined: It is divided into two parts. The first attempts to digest and recapitulate the evidence given before the commission. This part adds up, the commissioners believe, to a "sketch of the Canadian scene in its principal aspects" (p.268). They feel the better qualified to present their sketch of the Canadian scene because they are convinced that "in the hundreds of briefs which we received and in the thousands of pages of evidence which we gathered, we believe we heard the voice of Canada." The second part consists of recommendations, given in detail and in general, interspersed with expository sections of text. There are some seventy-five pages of useful appendices. Mention should also be made here of the companion volume, *Royal Commission Studies.* The report and the studies sell for $3.50 and $3.00 respectively, a price which unfortunately will greatly limit their circulation among a non-book buying people such as ourselves.

To deal briefly with the studies first, before undertaking an examination of the report itself: this volume consists of twenty-eight essays on a wide variety of topics, some written in French and some in English. A few titles will indicate the range: "The English Language in Canada," "La Presse de langue française au Canada," "Psychology," "National History," "The Teaching of Applied Science," "Architecture." Each essay is by an authority in the field; each is full of meat, and some are brilliant. Two may be singled out for the keenness of their analyses: "Canadian Letters" and "Philosophy."

The studies in their capable and mature approach indicate the spirit and standard of the report: they form in themselves a worthy addition to Canadian culture.

The report, however, can stand on its own feet, though no doubt its authors would gladly acknowledge their debt to the writers of the Studies. To continue its analysis: Part One is divided into five sections and each of these again into chapters. Section One, which is introductory, makes a logical beginning with a chapter on "The Forces of Geography." Section Two deals with Mass Media, Section Three with Voluntary Bodies and

Federal Agencies, Section Four with Scholarship, Science and the Arts and Section Five with cultural relations abroad.

Part Two follows the above divisions, in each case making its recommendations topic by topic.

Some sixty pages are given to mass media. Mass media are the agencies of communication designed to reach large bodies of people quickly — radio (which is put first), films, and the press. Most people are familiar with our Canadian problems in each of these areas. Any radio set will bring in a myriad of voices from the United States, or it will bring in some little local station playing cracked records as well as the Canadian Broadcasting Corporation. Any — all — film theatres bring in Hollywood and little else but Hollywood. The daily press brings in the American version of foreign news. Canadian periodical literature in competition with the American flood is so weak that it counts for little. The question, put metaphorically, is: "How long can a man's head be held under water before he drowns?"

The curious thing about this country is that its head has been under the surface of the American tide ever since the war of 1812 and that it still shows no signs of drowning. But to change the metaphor, may it not be becoming something like a fine old pine tree, sturdy and stalwart until the axe bites into it and reveals a hollow interior? There never were termites which so persistently nibbled away at the wood as these American agencies of mass persuasion do at our national existence. *Laissez faire,* of course, would allow things to take their course: it would allow the recent royal visit to be reported, in so far as it would have been reported, by the American radio. It would allow, as it does allow, Canadians to get their English news, and the reports of the Commonwealth conferences in which their own statesmen play leading roles, through American news agencies, clothed in American phraseology.

It did not take the commission long to rule out *laissez faire* in radio: it paid due deference to private stations (a pretty hard thing to do for those who have to suffer under them), but it came down unreservedly for the continuance of the national system of broadcasting. It is hard to see how it could do anything else. To give up the C.B.C. today would be cutting what is perhaps our main lifeline of national existence. When one remembers the struggles our founding fathers waged to keep the C.P.R. a Canadian railroad and to rear the whole structure that we call Canada, there could only be one nasty word for those who would sell the radio pass, the word reserved to all those who betray their country. The recommendations of the commission are therefore unreservedly in favour of the C.B.C., but they also provide for a continuance of this unique pattern of ours, with a line of private enterprise running alongside that of the nation. Private stations have their justification in their local service, the commission finds: it has no nod of approval for them simply on the ground that "they make money." The attitude brings us to the chasm, the huge chasm, on either side of which lie different measuring rods for values.

Thus on every chapter of the report the deepest philosophical issues impinge. We have it all over again in other terms in the section on Scholarship, Science and the Arts. Here are chapters on the Universities, on The Scholar and The Scientist, and on The Artist and the Writer. The latter chapter is sub-divided into twelve sections, each on a particular art.

Each of these sub-heads repeats the general theme: how can we maintain a Canadian community in any vital sense of the term against the unparalleled strength — in every aspect of life — of our great neighbour? Our universities year by year lose their best men to American universities, where salaries are sometimes twice as high: to replace them they bring in inexperienced young men from across the water at low wages, who take a lifetime to adapt themselves to Canadian life. Many of our ablest graduates go across the border. Canada suffers this great drain of blood year after year, and a weaker community is the result. The story is the same in the applied sciences and in the arts. A promising Canadian invariably ends up in New York. Presumably it is not much different in the world of business. How stop the issue of blood, how build a home for ourselves? How, for the creative spirits who do stay at home, moderate Canadian conservatism, fear of innovation, timidity, refusal to approve of any of our own until they have got the seal of approval from London or New York?

After the review come the recommendations. My own impression on reading over the report was that the commissioners would have to be something not far short of supermen if they were to find recommendations of a calibre equal to their accomplishments in analysis and exposition. I do not think they are supermen, and I do think that the recommendations are hardly up to the level of the remainder of the report, but nevertheless they seem to me of a high standard and the almost necessary deductions from the investigation conducted.

The first recommendation, and one by now probably familiar to most readers, has reference to radio. Put in a word, it is to continue the situation as it is, the C.B.C. to remain both a programming and a governing body, non-partisan and responsible to Parliament (not the government) alone. The reason given for this is that a neutral public regulating body could not fail to destroy the nature and purpose of the present system. It would tend to set up two systems, on equal footing, competing for radio channels and in the poor quality (i.e., popularity) of their programmes. Moreover, no evidence was presented that the C.B.C. Board of Governors is harsh or unjust. The C.B.C., the commission reminds us, is not merely one radio system among others: it is the nation itself in its broadcasting aspect, this role having been deliberately chosen.

There were many other important radio recommendations made for which space allows only a mention, especially those on advertising and finance. The financial recommendation for continuance of the license fee Parliament has recently implemented.

Programmes are to be conceived primarily in the national interest. (The commission does not use the approach "popular" vs. "classical" or "heavy" programmes.) Talks are considered to have been weak in comparison with music and drama, and it is recommended that this department be strengthened. If the writer may interject his own view here, may he express his agreement? C.B.C. drama is excellent, but some of it is pretentious ("high-falutin'" again) rather than of artistic excellence, and its appeal may be limited. A good "talk" on the other hand, put well, in comprehensible terms, will interest people at many levels.

A recommendation is made that the French network be extended to cover French-speaking districts in the West and the Maritimes. Justice demands that our French-speaking fellow-citizens have their language rights wherever they are in Canada.

Other recommendations include provision against too much centralization, extension of accompanying printed services, regional advisory councils and so on. Those who know the B.B.C. *Listener* know how great an auxiliary to broadcasts a good printed periodical can be.

The commission recommends control and operation of television services by the C.B.C. This recommendation is already being proceeded with: it is the only thing to do if our very hearths and homes are not to be captured as Hollywood captured our theatres.

The National Film Board, it is recommended, is to be continued along its present lines and extended. The commission evidently recognizes that the battle for that large section of the Canadian mind absorbed by "the movies" is lost: of all countries Canada is the most completely subjugated to Hollywood.

None of the present branches of the public service whose functions bear directly on the question of a national culture is overlooked by the commission; National Gallery, Museum, federal libraries, Archives, historic sites and monuments, all come in for examination and liberal suggestions. It is not too soon; for "this Canada of ours" in such matters is among the most backward countries in the world. Yet relief is in sight, for the change in attitude, insight, and taste which has taken place with the present administration is nothing short of revolutionary.

A large section of the report is devoted to scholarship, science, and the arts, about half of it dealing specifically with the universities and their problems. The commission is quick to recognize the key position of the university in a modern civilization. From it must come the leaders and the specialists in every walk of life, and without it this country could not continue long to weather the storms of the times. Government, in particular, is chained to the universities, dependent on them for the annual crop of young recruits of high calibre which its services require.

On the recommendations touching the universities action has already been taken and a substantial sum voted towards their support. This relief has come none too soon, for university salaries, never high compared with the business world and the income of certain professions such as medicine, are today, in view of the cost of living, far below the level of a dozen years ago. If government and business, through salary differentials, are to continue to be able to attract almost anyone away from the academic world, then our whole educational apparatus in this country stands in dire peril.

The last recommendation of the commission of which space permits notice is that advising the establishment of a Council for the Arts, Letters, Humanities, and Social Sciences "to stimulate and to help voluntary organizations within these fields, to foster Canada's cultural relations abroad, to perform the functions of a national commission for UNESCO, and to devise and administer a system of scholarships ...."

The groundwork for this recommendation is laid in pages 182-239, in many other less specific passages, and in the discussion immediately prefixed to the recommendation. One interesting influence on the decision was the examination of what other countries are doing, more particularly Great Britain. The generosity of national support to the Arts Council of Great Britain is strong testimony to the weight which the mature political mind of the Old Country attaches to things of the spirit, those intangibles upon which, in a much more subtle way than upon material things, a nation's existence depends. The Arts Council's functions would be those of encouraging, advising, and, in carefully investigated cases, extending money aid. A great society such as our Royal Society, struggling along year by year at only a minimum of efficiency, might then not have to go hat in hand to Americans for charity to help it keep alive. Nothing indeed is more degrading than the way in which Canadians trying to build a civilization here, and failing to secure help from our own people of means, are forced to accept assistance from across the line. It is to be hoped that the Arts Council, when and if established, will put an end to this state of affairs. It may be objected that it will mean a further dose of paternalism: the answer is that if we are to have a separate society we must expect just that, for our own wealthy people, with some honourable exceptions, have failed us.

The report of the commission is a classic document. The Canadian state now turns to the highest function of a state, building the spiritual structure (the word is not used in the religious sense) of a civilization, the material foundations of which it has already sturdily laid. If the builders can continue to be men and women of the calibre and vision of those who prepared this report, the work will go forward to brilliant achievement in future ages.

11 | *Is Distrust of Ability Formula for Success?**

It is a frequent assumption among people who have had some success that intellectual ability does not get its possessor far, that, in fact, a good item of equipment for success in life is a reasonable degree of stodginess. Not stupidity, just dullness; solid grey reliability without any trimmings seems to be the desirable quality. A good, heavy-axe man inspires confidence; the razor-sharp fellow evidently is a rogue.

Those who write accounts of a great man during his lifetime, when it is still necessary to bring the giant down somewhere within range of the average, invariably discover that "he stood forty-third in his class, or second from the bottom." They have discovered this about both Roosevelt and Woodrow Wilson, I believe. As time goes by, it is not so necessary to advertise these virtues, and the individual's place in his class tends to move up. William Ewart Gladstone, impeccable on every count, was a "double first" in his day, which is now remote enough to allow this bit of scandal to creep out. Our own Edward Blake was a first class in Classics at the University of Toronto, but possibly this is the explanation of his notorious unpopularity. Sir Winston Churchill is still well down in his school class; people like him better that way.

There is no doubt about one disability of ability: its unpopularity. A young man whose natural endowments go farther and deeper than his fellows either has to keep them to himself or make a bit of fun of it and at least pretend that he never does any work; other young people still accept the fellow "that's smart," providing he pulls it off with a kind of effortless expertise.

Young women, of course, cannot forgive other young women who go to the top; they are betrayers of their sex. But few young women are so simple; they are all at least clever enough to know that however clever they really are, they must not seem to be as clever as their young men.

Young fellows who are "in a class by themselves" are apt to cause people to shake their heads. Especially if they are individualistic and non-conformist, as persons of that type nearly always are, they may become

*Saturday Night, 23 April 1955, pp. 7-8.

the subjects of dire forebodings on the part of their elders. "He's not like other boys." Dreadful fate!

Occasionally a youth comes along whose credentials are so obvious that non-acceptance is impossible. An Ernest MacMillan conducting a large choir in his early teens is evidently something so far beyond the ordinary person's reach that no attitude but respect is possible. This is not the case in the commoner phenomenon of the young fellow who merely leads his class, reads an infinity of books that his schoolmates have never heard of, knows far too much for their comfort, and is not interested in sport.

What really happens when the young lads grow up? Is it the respectably dull who usually get on? Of course it is hard to find out in the case of any prominent man just what his youthful record was. No respectable millionaire will plead guilty to having got beyond Grade Five: he always began as an errand boy. (I began as an errand boy myself, but that did not seem to bring me any closer to becoming a millionaire.) What about our native aristocracy of presidents, managers, and senior executives generally? They are the substantial men of the community. Were there any scholarship winners among them? If so, would they ever admit it?

A notable contrast in the matter is presented by those who run our universities in comparison with those who merely teach in them. As a professor, you constantly keep your eye open for able youth. When you find someone who indisputably "has the goods," you back him for all you're worth, hoping that one day he will come back and succeed you. You forget all about the individual to whom you gave 50 (a bare pass) because you didn't want to leave him at 49. Then by and by this person, being a good fellow or having got in with the right people or for a dozen other reasons, such as being determined and stubborn, of excellent judgment and much wordly wisdom, turns up as a super-substantial citizen and is necessarily appointed to the board of governors. As such, he is now in a sense "the boss" of his former professor. Here is a clear case of the disabilities of ability, for the man of outstanding intellect is not as a rule much interested in making himself a mere man of substance.

It is the same in politics. Nowadays many of our best graduates go into the civil service; some day they are sure to become deputy ministers. As such, their duty will be to advise — and cajole — their ministers. And who may their ministers be? Well, very likely the fellows they knew back in their college days who managed to get through with very thin C's and then went on to become undistinguished lawyers. But as such they got to know all the boys back home, went up through the regular succession of municipal offices, and eventually landed in Parliament. Then if they possessed gravity and dignity and came from the properly strategic riding, someday they caught the PM's eye and found themselves "The Honourable."

The "A" men always seem fated to be ruled by the "B's" (when it isn't the "C's"); more push, less inhibition; not so much sicklying o'er with the pale cast of thought.

Examples could be piled up. I am sure they represent a distinction commonly made in life, that between sheer intellectual ability and the collection of qualities marking the man nearer to the average. The towering intellect, more often than not, does not seem to go with those qualities — it frequently insists on going off on its own incalculable course, to the confusion of ordinary people. That is why we find it hard to tolerate the genius in politics. The Lloyd Georges and the Disraelis have never been popular. Good, stupid Mr. Baldwin was.

We Canadians too, I think, like our prime ministers with a good large infusion of stupidity or, at least, of mediocrity. Borden and King were ideal. Macdonald carried off his innate ability under a cloak of "hurrah-boy" good fellowship. Laurier, however, was the rare combination of dignity and the common touch with high ability, to which, when it occurs, most men bow down.

The disabilities of ability are real. It is not fun to live under half a cloud all your life, or at least to have people run away from you because they are afraid of you. It is not overly pleasant, though probably it does not matter much, to be denied the higher posts simply because you don't line up easily with the other fellows. Why see at all if you see too far? And at that point we come to the prophet, the poet, the saint, whose hard fate it is to be each in his own way so gifted as half to destroy his gifts.

But where would society get to without its prophets, its poets and its saints?

12 | *Speaking to Each Other**

Pour ce discours présidentiel, en tenant compte du sujet général de notre séance présente, j'ai choisi comme titre « Speaking to Each Other » : « En Parlant les uns aux autres ». Je l'ai fait parce que notre sujet général est » Specialized Speech » : « La Langue Spécialisée » et parce que s'il n'y a que deux langues officielles dans ce pays, il y a dans notre Société environ une vingtaine ou plus de langues spécialisées. Il y a la langue des physiciens de plusieurs variétés, la langue des botanistes, celle des

*Delivered as the presidential address to the Royal Society of Canada and published in the *Proceedings and Transactions,* 3rd series, 56 (1962): 69-80.

humanistes, des sociologues, etc. Est-ce que les membres de cette Société peuvent parler les uns avec les autres? J'en doute. Est-ce que c'est une bonne chose? Je sais que ce n'est pas une bonne chose. Si nous sommes des hommes instruits, si nous formons une élite, si nous sommes tous dévoués à la connaissance, nous devrions pouvoir nous parler les uns aux autres.

Cette affaire de compréhension va au dehors de la communication verbale. Elle va au dehors de l'homme lui-même. Je peux parler avec mon chien: je suis sûr qu'il me comprend! Sur le plan humain, un homme et sa femme peuvent rester chez eux toute la soirée sans rien dire, mais ils se comprennent. Le langage est important, mais il n'est pas tout. J'espère que nous Canadiens, héritiers de deux fières traditions, pourront un jour rester seuls toute la soirée, pour ainsi dire, sans parler, mais en nous comprenant les uns les autres. Nous ne devrions pas parler seulement avec notre langue, mais, il faut l'espérer, aussi avec nos coeurs, avec nos coeurs tout canadiens.

On a dit que chaque langue humaine est « une classification d'expérience. ». Tous les hommes, même les plus primitifs, font une large variété des mêmes distinctions fondamentales grammaticales comme le *singulier* et le *pluriel.* Parmi les langues sauvages de notre pays, appellées souvent par erreur « primitives, » il y a des raffinements d'expérience que nous-mêmes ne possédons pas. Quand un Indien de la tribu Cree ou Ojibway veut dire « vous et moi, » le pronom de la première personne du pluriel, il se sert d'une forme — « kelananow » — et quand il veut dire « il et moi » ou « ils et nous, » il se sert d'une autre forme — « nelanan. » Je crois que cette distinction très utilitaire on trouve aussi parmi les langues Dravidiennes de l'Inde du Sud. Ces peuples ont ainsi organisé leurs expériences: ils ont inventé une langue spécialisée.

Touchant les deux langues de ce pays, nous savons qu'elles ont beaucoup en commun: beaucoup de mots, beaucoup de phrases. Presque tout le vocabulaire des sciences par exemple leur est commun. Dans les deux langues on peut enfoncer des idiomes qui résument les jugements que l'un fait sur l'autre. Les Anglais disent « take French leave, » mais les Français tournent les tables en disant « filer à l'Anglaise. » Il y a des autres exemples semblables.

Prenez les termes anglais de la loi; notre « common law » est principalement la loi normande qui a été imposée aux Anglais par leurs conquérants normands pendant les onzièmes et douzièmes siècles. Comme résultat, les termes légaux en anglais sont presque tous français: nous parlons du *jury,* de « marriage », d'un inquest, d'une mortgage, d'un escheat, un conseil, en fait d'une couronne et d'une parlement, etc. Dans la période du dix-neuvième siècle beaucoup des mots anglais au Canada ont passé dans la langue française du Canada. Les deux langues sont mêlées; elles ont été mêlées plusieurs fois dans les neuf siècles depuis la conquête normande. Leur formes présentes reflètent cette expérience: la langue, c'est la classification de l'expérience.

Il n'est pas seulement les deux langues qui ont été mêlées il y tant de siècles: c'est aussi les institutions publiques; en un autre lieu j'ai écrit sur le sujet de « the French Origins of English Freedom » : « Les Origines françaises de la liberté anglaise. »[1] Je ne veux pas ici répéter ce que j'y ai dit, mais en bref c'était que les institutions qui ont garanti au monde moderne ses plus précieuses possessions publiques s'élèvaient du combat du moyen âge entre les nobles normands en Angleterre et le roi normand-français.

Il me semble que l'origine française de la liberté anglaise est un point majeur pour un pays comme le nôtre, ou les deux races, dont les longues histoires ont tant en commun, se trouvent depuis deux cents ans en des parentés permanentes. Soit en Europe, soit en Amérique, les Anglais et les Français se sont battus les uns contre les autres pendant des siècles. Les Français ont conquis l'Angleterre. Les Anglais ont conquis la France. Les Anglais ont adopté, à moitié, la langue française. Aujourd'hui, les Français du Canada ont emprunté des centaines de mots anglais. Et il faut se souvenir que depuis deux cents ans, c'est au Canada que les deux peuples se battent l'un contre l'autre, seulement par des mots. Si deux races dans le monde entier devraient se comprendre l'une l'autre, il me semble que c'est les deux races du Canada, avec leur longue association intime. Vous n'avez qu'a considérer cette Société, avec ses quatre-vingts années d'association toujours paisible, ses successions d'office et ses amitiés réelles et souvent profondes. Nous avons deux langues, mais nous sommes engagés dans la tâche commune de « classifier notre expérience » et en cette tâche, nous trouverons en temps, pas la même langue, ni une langue mêlée et hybride, mais une langue commune, moyen de penser que nos deux langues refléteront et qui grandira de notre ouvrage commun, de nos tâches communes, et ôse-je le dire, du sens que nous avons d'avoir un commun pays, notre pays, le Canada.

Nous sommes ici des hommes d'une vaste sophistication, et nos tentatives de communications s'étendent beaucoup plus loin que le simple moyen de parler. Sur le grand champ de communication profonde que nous appelons *la connaissance,* il est maintenant nécessaire que je vous dirige le vue.

I have spoken about "Language as a classification of Experience." That topic fits in with our topic of the year, "Specialized Speech." In this address, I should like to extend its limits and push it further, into some consideration of the vast topic of *knowledge.*

---

[1]*Culture* 9 (March 1948): 18-28.

But first, let me recall to you that this is the eightieth year of our Society: we are already becoming venerable. And if our affairs are conducted wisely, as I am sure they will be, we shall become not only venerable, but more and more effective. Associations and other corporate bodies do not incur the human disabilities of age: they may go on as long as the encircling protection of the body politic to which they belong continues, and they should be able to draw continuously on their experience.

I suppose our exemplar has always been the Royal Society of Great Britain, which this year reckons itself in the 302nd year of its age. We differ from the Royal Society in that our range is wider and in that we do not have world-wide prestige. But we have much more prestige than when we began, and in another eighty years, we shall have more.

I make this reference to the Royal Society in part for a personal reason, which I hope you will indulge. On October 17, 1667, there was elected to the Royal Society a person of my name, one Dr. Richard Lower. I suppose I am vaguely of his family. The Thompson *History of the Royal Society*[2] states that he was the man who first explained the reason for the difference in the colour between venous and arterial blood. He also performed an experiment in blood transfusion, the first such to be performed, I believe, when he turned the blood of a sheep into a man (nothing is said about what happened to the man!). As one source puts it: "They introduced with no apparent ill effect nine or ten ounces of blood from the artery of a sheep into a man variously described as 'a harmless lunatic' and 'an eccentric scholar'" — perhaps the two terms mean the same thing![3]

According to our by-laws the president has one chief duty and that is to deliver an address at the annual meeting: he is conscripted to deliver an address, so that must mean that his hearers are conscripted to listen to it. Such being the case, it would seem common sense that the address should be in terms that everyone present can understand. Does this mean he ought to struggle to put something about his own discipline into words of one syllable or that he should select a theme that somehow or other includes all disciplines? If the president cannot address all fellows because there is no common language, which means there is no common ground, then we have no Society, but only a collection of various professionals. If we cannot talk to each other, then we do not form a community.

The point forces consideration of the problem: How does the specialist communicate with other specialists having other specialties? If he cannot communicate, he remains locked up in a world of his own. I do not intend

[2]Thomas Thomson, *History of the Royal Society* (London: Printed for R. Baldwin, 1812), p. 106.
[3]Dorothy Stimson, *Scientists and Amateurs: A History of the Royal Society* (London: Sigma Books, 1949), p. 86.

to say much directly about "jargon," for it is being discussed in other papers, but it is surely evident that specialized language has its place in all intellectual work: the language of the mathematician is probably the most striking example. I myself would make a distinction between jargon for the sake of jargon (which is probably the defence of the unsure man, who tries to hide behind it) and convenient verbal shorthand. I would make a further distinction between technical writing which employs language with skill and perhaps artistry, and merely careless, sloppy expression. Clear writing, technical or otherwise, is surely a reflection of, and a stimulus to, clear thinking.

Some time ago I was asked by a young economist why the Royal Society continued to exist: he contended that the professional societies had deprived it of any excuse for survival. The attitude is natural and if the Royal Society is to flourish, logical reasons for our existence must be found.

I think the key to our dilemma will be found in the following words of the president of Harvard University[4]:

> A strong university is a very complicated institution with an amazing number of departments serving a variety of interests. It is easy to deplore its lack of distinct, easily recognizable unity. It is more difficult to see grandeur and beauty, richness, excitement and meaning lying within such multifarious activity. But they are there. And there is also more unity than at first meets the eye. There is, at least, as a rule, a wide-spread, unrelenting hunger for excellence which compels all or almost all who work there and gives them a sense of participating in a common enterprise, different as may be their fields of interests and their definitions of excellence.

Our problem is how are we in this Society to make real and vivid that which the president proclaims as marking a great university, unity. How are we to find any unity in modern knowledge, with its astronomical scope and its infinite divisions?

Unity can be found, it seems to me, in a conception of knowledge, in our attitude as educated men towards knowledge, and in attempts to grasp its place and significance in human affairs. Such attempts will also give us logical reasons for our Society's existence.

The term "science," itself, I suppose, represents a groping after unity for it is applied to a large number of fields, not because they are intimately related to each other, but because they have certain aspects of procedure and methodology in common. Unless we merely mean "organized

---

[4]*Report of the President of Harvard College and Reports of the Departments, 1958-59*, Official Register of Harvard University 57, no. 24 (September 1960), p. 18.

knowledge," there is, however, strictly speaking, no such subject as "science": the term is too vast to have unity. But there are innumerable interconnections and associations, and these do not stop at the so-called "laboratory" or "experimental" sciences. Chemistry extends into geology, but geology and geography, because of their preoccupation with the concept of time, have associations with those other "time" disciplines, archaeology and history. Similarly the progression from biology to physiology to psychology to sociology, economics, and political science represents a series of fairly gradual transitions. Here is one approach to unity, then, the canvassing of relations and interconnections.

But canvassing of relations and interconnections does not get us overly far, for that can soon lead merely to new disciplines. It is some other kind of unity that it seems to me we should seek.

Perhaps I could convey what I have in mind by a figure. Old Jeremy Bentham, among his other bits of prowess, worked out a plan for a perfect prison. The building was to consist of wings radiating out from a centre like the spokes of a wheel: at the centre one or two observers could keep watch down the wings and thus see all that was going on. This he called his "Panoptikon." Now knowledge, it seems to me, is a species of "Panoptikon" in reverse. Men of knowledge are on the spokes of the wheel looking in towards the centre, trying to see what lies there. They are all, in other words, gazing at the same point. But what is that point?

We give the point many names, but most of us recognize its existence: we call it "reality," "nature," "the essence or nature of being," "the scheme of things." We call it "truth," or simply "God." And I suppose it is in the attempt that each makes in his own way to get a glimpse of what lies at the centre of things that we find unity. The unity of knowledge and of those who seek it, in other words, comes not from the subject matter of the quest but from its goal.

The listener will say: "But this means that you require all men of knowledge to be philosophers." I suppose that is just what I do imply, but by the term philosopher, I do not mean merely the person devoted to the discipline formally so-called. Rather, those who keep the ultimate goal in mind and use the quest as their direction-finder. Certain it is that if we each go our different directions and get lost in the interest and detail of our own special fields, we shall have a hard job justifying the existence of a Society such as ours.

Few would deny that the major mark of our present age is that which is our concern here: knowledge. Knowledge — whether you call it "science," "learning," "education," or merely technology — and its necessary condition, free inquiry, marks and dominates the modern world. We all are aware, too, of how recent a situation this is, even though it has come about gradually and most of its roots may be traced far back. The mass and amount of knowledge is a matter of three or at most four centuries, and most of it is much more recent than that. At present, knowledge appears to be expanding in geometrical progression. So giant are its strides that the suggestion often is heard that knowledge can furnish us with a complete way of life, adequate to all circumstances, with an answer to all questions, that is, that it can give us the same solution for our lives as religion formerly did.

One side of man's nature drives him to know: this may be mere ape-like curiosity or it may have a greater name. Whatever it is, man is hopelessly curious and, I suppose, this trait has outranked reason or practical purposes in building up our accumulations of knowledge.

Another side of our nature drives us to fear that very accomplishment that makes us men, the power of knowledge. There has never been an age or clime in which men have not feared knowledge even as they have sought it. It is only in our own day, in this age of knowledge, that the fear has been substantially reduced, and some of it still remains. The dilemma receives classic form in the Bible story: the apple (the fruit of knowledge), the tempting serpent (man's curiosity), Eve, Adam, and the expulsion from Paradise. "Earning our bread by the sweat of our brow" and the other consequences of the expulsion follow in due sequence.

The myth is Hebrew. The Hebrews were not conspicuous accumulators of knowledge. Their gift was spirituality. It was through the spirit that they hoped to regain the lost Paradise. Of the making of many books, there was for them no end, and it was all a vanity unto the spirit.

The Greeks took a different view. Their Promethean myth contained a note of triumph: Prometheus had stolen fire from heaven and successfully defied the gods. He, too, however, received his punishment: knowledge is to be had at a great price. About Greek culture at its height, so signally concerned with knowledge, we find a modern note, something that calls to us across the centuries; and this a little examination identifies in the fact that for a brief moment in history, then, as now, the mind was free, or almost so. Man has seldom consented to cast off the chains he has imposed on his own mind, and some would say that that is because he discerns how dangerous the liberation is. But these two periods, that of Athens at its best and our own, are surely unique in that they provide for as much freedom for the mind as man is ever likely to get.

To both cases there are sharp limitations. Socrates was put to death: his mind was too free. Not only that: there was, it would seem, an area of mind closed and barred. The Greek, pushed far enough, came to a door called "impiety," and his mind was such that he could not go through that door.

In his discussion of Greek mathematical thought, Oswald Spengler argues that the Greek mind differed from that of the moderns in that it thought in terms of specific, cognizable form, such as the temple, the statue, or the whole number. He builds up his whole case for a distinct classical "culture" (in his technical sense of that term), with its beginning, its efflorescence, and its end, around this concept. He says that "in considering the relations between, say, diagonal and side in a rectangle, the Greek would suddenly be brought up against a sort of number, an irrational number, which was fundamentally alien to the classical soul, and was consequently feared as a secret of its own existence too dangerous to be unveiled."[5]

He adds: "There is a singular and significant late-Greek legend, according to which the man who first published the hidden mystery of the irrational perished by shipwreck, 'for the unspeakable and the formless must be left hidden forever.'"[6]

We do not need to go all the way with Spengler's semi-mystical approach to understand that there were limitations to what the Greeks thought they ought to inquire about. With our own Christian era, the limitations become more apparent and more formidable. No story is more familiar: Christianity gave a complete way of life, a complete account of the world and of the course of history from creation to destruction to infinity. It gave final answers to everything. It became difficult to see why other knowledge or inquiry was necessary. Independent inquiry became of all conduct the most dangerous, the most reprehensible, and the most sternly prohibited.

But prohibitions cannot stop man using his head or following the desires of his heart. There are few barriers that cannot be outflanked. For centuries, few frontal assaults, none of them effective, were made on the barriers, but outflanking movements were many. Briefly summarizing, one might say that these took three forms: one respectable and recognized, a kind of boring from within; another troublesome but sufficiently within the law to be conditionally allowable; and the third, suspected, hindered, and its suppression attempted. There were many shadings, and the classification is rough.

The respected and allowable form of inquiry was that which was taken in the schools, that which gradually grew into the great body of scholastic philosophy. Within the schools there was much liberty of thought within well-worn channels. The results remain to us in the vast, acute, and fundamental philosophical inquiries of the great medieval thinkers, such as St. Thomas Aquinas. What they did in exploring, defining, and classifying almost the entire field of human experience as it then stood needs no eulogy from me. For our purposes, their significance lies in their making

---

[5]Oswald Spengler, *The Decline of the West* (New York: Alfred Knopf, 1939), I: 65.
[6]There is a comparable reference in Horace where the poet adjures his friend "not to be tempted by the Babylonian numbers" ("Tu ne ... Babylonias temptaris numeros. . . . ."), *Odes*, 1, xi.

a considerable breach in the walls that barred the way to free inquiry and in carrying man some distance in the direction of an intellectually satisfying view of the universe.

The conditionally allowable phenomenon was the mystical experience. Since he claims to have a private vision of reality, the mystic always presents a difficulty to constituted orthodoxy.

What he believes has reached him by some channel other than sensory impression. He reports on his vision, but he cannot describe it. He cannot communicate to us what this is, this "total reality," this "one" with which he has been in touch. But he himself is sure of the validity of his experience.

Philosophers argue over the constitution of nature. In that profound and beautiful book of MacNeile Dixon, *The Human Situation,* there is a chapter, "The One and the Many," which puts the opposing views: Are phenomena discrete and separate in origin and nature or is everything part of some great whole? The mystic claims to *know,* because he has seen! He has looked on the "One." Ordinary mortals have to be content with something less. But there are few, I venture to say, who, as they have speculated on the busy life moving everywhere about them, have not had some feeling that "all this is part of some one thing, a manifestation of something that transcends all its details." It is this reality at the heart of things that the mystic thinks he has gazed upon, and it is also this, surely, which the men of knowledge seek, when they investigate nature and try to roll back her bounds.

The third type of attempt to push out beyond that which was allowed by orthodoxy consisted of all those practices lumped together in condemnation by medieval man as "the black arts," everything from the crudest charlatanry through the various forms of magic up to alchemy and astronomy, the search for the philosopher's stone, and all the rest. Whoever might engage in them, be he a Roger Bacon himself, was apt to be suspect: he was acquiring knowledge not provided by revelation, what might be called "bootleg knowledge," seeking some kind of short cut to that which in due course, when the Great Divide was crossed, would be made known to all.

It is remarkable that under such restraint, learning — non-literary learning included — progressed, but progress it did, and at the very peak of medievalism. I read, for example — and this takes me beyond my depth, since it relates to mathematics — that Nicolas of Oresme (1323-1382), bishop of Lisieux, "was the first Westerner who used co-ordinates, so to say, 'elastically' and the first to employ fractional powers."[7] Roger Bacon is supposed to have had notions about steam-engines and aircraft. As Spengler says of such men: "These meditative discoverers in their cells, who with

---

[7]Spengler, *The Decline of the West,* 1: 73.

prayer and fasting wrung God's secret out of him, felt that they were serving God thereby.... But for all of them, too, there was the truly Faustian danger of the Devil's having a hand in the game.[8]

With the Renaissance, many restraints on learning disappeared, but old habits died hard and men were still to suffer, some of them with their lives, for the unorthodox learning which they expounded.

In the seventeenth century, however, the old stops on knowledge were largely replaced by mere ridicule. This century, that great classical age of science, saw many academies founded, among them, the Royal Society of England. The Royal Society had its share of ridicule to face, but hard words break no bones, not even if they are uttered by a Dean Swift. Swift's *Gulliver's Third Voyage* took him to Laputa, where he found, you will remember, that a man at the Grand Academy "sought to extract sunbeams from cucumbers to be placed in vials and released as needed."

The most sustained and telling piece of fun-making in England was by the dramatist Thomas Shadwell in his play *The Virtuoso* (1673). Sir Nicholas Gimcrack, the hero, has

> in his laboratory ... a frog in a bowl of water, tyed with a packthread by the loins, which packthread Sir Nicholas holds with his teeth, lying upon his belly on a table, and as the frog strikes, he strikes, and his swimming master stands by to tell him when he does well or ill. "I swim most exquisitely on land," says Sir Nicholas. But does he intend to practise in the water? "Never, Sir," he answers, "I hate the water .... I never come upon the water, Sir." "Then there will be no use in swimming?" says his questioner. "I content myself with the speculative part of swimming, I care not for the practice." Sir Nicholas rejoins, "I seldom bring anything to use: 'tis not my way. Knowledge is my ultimate end."[9]

A more serious attack on knowledge has not yet run its course. This was the rating given to it by the educational theorists. Practically all of them rated knowledge low. "I judge learning the meanest piece of education," said Bishop Burnet. John Locke supported him: "Virtue is the first and most necessary of those endowments that belong to a man or a gentleman. Reading, writing and learning I allow to be necessary, but yet not the chief business." Although learning was a great help towards producing both virtue and wisdom in "well-disposed minds," nevertheless "in others not so disposed, it helps them only to be more foolish or worse men."[10]

---

[8]Ibid., 2: 501.
[9]Quoted in Stimson, *Scientists and Amateurs,* p. 93.
[10]Quoted in George C. Brauer, *The Education of a Gentleman, 1660-1775* (New York: Bookman Associates, 1959), p. 18ff.

Those who were to be educated cordially agreed: knowledge was the mark of the pedant and the prig. A century onward, a famous voice was raised to reinforce their point of view:

> A set o' dull, conceited asses
> Confuse their brains in college classes
> They gang in stirks and come out asses
>   Plain truth to speak
> And syn they think to climb Parnassus
>   By dint o' Greek.

Still another century on, in the 1850's, Lord Palmerston, prime minister of Great Britain, could refer airily to Germany as "a land of damned professors."

It was to be well into the nineteenth century before the two elements in education, knowledge and "virtue," were got into proper balance, if indeed they ever have been! Few of us even today would like to take a downright stand for knowledge as primary, at least not until men have got well beyond that stage in their education where it could be taken for granted that they were already virtuous!

We are not yet done with the fear of knowledge. Consider the storms that were raised in the nineteenth century, storms that have echoed on into the twentieth, over the doctrine of evolution. Think of the last majestic attempt to erect a barrier against free inquiry once and for all, an attempt that failed, as all such attempts must fail. I refer to Pio Nono and his celebrated *Syllabus of Errors,* a condemnation *in toto* of everything that could be called "liberal" as of 1860, that is, of free inquiry as such. He was just another King Canute, for the waves of knowledge had advanced too far to go back at any man's bidding. But he by no means stood alone. The novelist Peacock, writing in 1860, put this same fear of knowledge from another angle in making one of his characters say "I almost think it is the ultimate destiny of science to annihilate the human race." That destiny seems to be becoming clearer.

Whatever the consequences may be, today knowledge has scored a complete victory. We are in the full tide of so-called Faustian man, exploring, triumphant man, man achieving for the sake of achieving. Faust, according to Goethe, is one who

> Vom Himmel — fordert die schönsten Sterne
> Und von der Erde jede höchste Lust.[11]

There is now no domain into which the mind of investigating, curious man may not and does not penetrate. There are for the inquirer no sacred

---

[11]"From heaven demanding the finest stars / and from earth every keenest desire."

things, no Holies of Holies. Nothing is barred from scientific investigation, or, for that matter, from popular discussion, as almost any of our student newspapers bears out. "Where are the reticences of yester-year?" an old man plaintively asks. Gone to join the snows of yester-year, I suppose.

But right on our heels comes fear again, fear this time not so much of that which it is not lawful to know, but of what we actually do know. We all live with Damocles' sword hanging over our heads, and we wonder whether that other classical myth does not also have its significance for us, the myth of Icarus, who flew too near the sun and had his wings melted off, perishing ingloriously. We are gripped with fear today, all the nations of the earth, fear of what knowledge may do to us.

Knowledge has gone so far and in so many directions that it is no wonder we speculate and wonder whether it cannot go the whole way, whether it cannot in time reveal the ultimate secrets of creation to us, and whether *ad interim* it cannot furnish us with an entire way of life, answering all needs, meeting all expectations, rising to every emergency, straightening out every quandary. When I was a boy, I was much impressed by those lines from Tennyson's *Ulysses:*

> To follow knowledge like a sinking star
> Beyond the utmost bounds of human thought.

I used to think that if one could only know completely, then he could *do* completely, that all could be set right through knowing. Knowledge would indeed be power. I could not then see the flaw in my thinking. It is plain enough now: knowledge will not overcome the perversity of man. The intellect is a sharp tool, but it *is* a tool, and it may cut our fingers. It has been finely said that "we know so much intellectually that we are in danger of becoming the prisoners of our knowledge. We suffer from a hubris of the mind. We have abolished the superstition of the heart only to install a superstition of the intellect in its place."[12]

Yet there is always the hope that if we only have the chance, we may discover enough about the human animal to straighten him out: our belief in the power of knowledge is persistent. To many a man it has given a vision of knowledge as the complete arbitrator of his destinies. Herbert Spencer, I believe, used mathematical methods in deciding whether or not he should get married, adding up the pluses and minuses on either side of the equation, and basing his decision on the result: he has found few imitators. A recent newspaper editorial — and how surprising to find such an editorial in a Canadian newspaper — comments on this point: "Descartes toyed with the idea that mathematics could solve social problems. Thomas

[12]Laurens Van der Post, *The Heart of the Hunter* (London: Hogarth Press, 1961), p. 138.
[13]*Ottawa Journal* quoted in *Kingston Whig-standard.*

Hobbes applied algebra to ethics. The 19th century, understandably, once believed that science held the key to an earthly paradise.... We should know better."[13] Knowledge, there can be little doubt about it, though expanding with almost the speed of light, is in the stage of diminishing returns — it is not "paying off" in its former way: it may be turning from a blessing to a curse.

If the stone of knowledge does not roll down the hill again under its own weight, knowledge will go on accumulating and expanding. What the situation will be in a century, two centuries, who can conceive? But, however bulky it may become, will knowledge give us the complete way of life? Knowledge comes, but wisdom lingers. Will knowledge ever become a religion, with answers for every question and solace for every hurt?

Some are bold enough to believe so. Here is an extract from a review of *The Humanist Frame*:[14]

> The new unity of mankind requires a new ethic grounded in facts and potentialities of science rather than in the *ex cathedra* pronouncements of a Jewish Jehovah or a deified Karl Marx. Conservative estimates indicate that the present world population of 2,800 millions may rise to over 6,000 millions in less than forty years. The social cataclysm which such figures imply will not be evaded by the issue of Papal encyclicals on the sinfulness of birth control or by blandly proclaiming the undoubted truth that the productive resources of the world are not yet fully realized. Sooner or later, we must face the issue: WHAT ARE PEOPLE FOR? We need an ethic which will offer some rational measure of the value of more people versus more food, of individual variety versus mass standardization, of enjoyment for the young and healthy versus protective care for the weak and the sick and the dying. Christian philanthropy is tolerable only when it is inefficient. Applied with rigour under modern conditions, it would lead simply to the survival of the unfittest.... Somehow we must learn to make ethical decisions without becoming entangled in reverence and awe, for only then can we fully admit that as knowledge increases, the foundations of morality are continually changed.... This kind of operational ethic requires that we be just as much on our guard against the enticing certainties of an apocalyptic future as against the worn-out authority of a traditional past.

In other words, knowledge is to dominate every nook and cranny of life. It sounds uncomfortably like Orwell's *1984*.

Yet we all know that in most of its areas life goes on much as always,

[14]J. Huxley, ed., *The Humanist Frame* (London: Allen and Unwin, 1961), as reviewed in the *New Statesman and Nation,* 29 September 1961, 438.

with the same guides, for what they are worth, of common sense and good intentions. We know, too, that the supreme creative achievements of mankind, a symphony of Beethoven, or his great opera *Fidelio* with its trumpet call for freedom, do not come primarily from intellectual knowledge. They spring out of the depths.

We can come to no conclusion. The intellect asks "how?" "when?" "where?" and it finds many an answer. It also asks the more difficult question "why?" To that it is not likely to get an answer.

Men may soon get to the moon. "Why?"

Knowledge and man! I struggle with the immensity of the theme. It is too big for me. It may be too big for any man. One thing that perhaps I can say, as an historian, is that we cannot take things as they are for granted. Times may change. Long ground-swells, I think, exist in history, which bend an age whatever its intentions. If we begin with formlessness and disorder, we may get society ordered on the basis of an evangelical dynamic, such as the pietism of the eleventh or the nineteenth centuries. Intellectualizing processes erode away the emotional drive and substitute cool objectivity, freedom to investigate. These are the knowledge-accumulating generations. Freedom means freedom for everybody, and it easily passes over into freedom for everybody to go in every direction. That way disintegration lies. And with disintegration may go all the great values, and accumulation of knowledge among them We can take nothing for granted.

We can take nothing for granted — except the portentous development that lies behind us, for, like Ulysses, before us

> ... gleams that untravelled world
> Whose margin fades forever and forever when I move.

13 | *Our Shoddy Ideals**

Prosperity really appears to have emerged from "just around the corner" and to be toying with the idea of staying with us a while. We shall be glad to see more of it, not only for our own individual reasons but because it may help to solve so many pressing public problems. Depressions, like diseases, always produce a vast number of proposed remedies. Some of these are helpful, most of them are nothing but nostrums. But just as

*Maclean's's, 1 November, 1937, pp. 24, 39-40.

physicians are still mainly occupying themselves with trying to cure rather than to prevent diseases, so also most of our social experts — our financiers, economists, and legislators — devote the best part of their time trying to heal our wounds rather than to uncovering the roots of the trouble.

Unfortunately, it is going to take more than the usual commercial and financial medicines to get society over the illness of which the last depression has been so painful a manifestation. It is not going to be a matter of merely finding work for everybody and then going back to our comfortable old ways. We are faced with something more intricate than that. This country is somewhat in the position of a youth who has inherited a fortune, has never developed a sense of responsibility, and who, just as he reaches manhood, suddenly discovers that his money is nearly all gone and he will have to reconstruct his whole scheme of life.

In other words, we grew up in what was for the most part a peaceful world, where we could each go about our business of looking after our own particular selves. We had, as a colony of Great Britain, a powerful and rather indulgent parent to protect us; and, in our own right, the riches of half a continent to squander. Today the world is no longer peaceful, our parent very justly thinks that his adult offspring ought to be able to look after himself, and much of our natural wealth has been dissipated. We, therefore, like the irresponsible individual, either have to reform or suffer the consequences.

A pioneer people have many assets and a pioneer society has many virtues, but there is also a debit side in the ledger. Inevitably in a new country the individual takes on undue importance. The world as he knows it is open to him, it is his to possess; and, being human, he proceeds to possess it. He becomes impatient with everything that stands in the way of his desires. In other words, the old social restraints which the settlers brought across the sea with them tend to go by the board. Society is loosely organized, population is sparse, and communities unstable; a man is here today and gone tomorrow. Hence the people of a new country cannot appreciate the wisdom and essential justice of so many of the ways of life which their ancestors built up during the centuries.

A new world means elbow room for everyone to develop in the direction of his essential nature; and, human nature being what it is, some very unlovely qualities make their appearance. The one preoccupation of a pioneer people is to better their condition. Inevitably everything tends to be sacrificed to material ends. To acquire possessions, to "make money" as our illuminating North American phrase has it, becomes the chief end of man. Everything gives way to that — morals, culture, and religion. In fact, each of these becomes coloured by the dominating motive. It is not immoral to be dishonest, providing you can "get away with it"; indeed it is admirable and "smart." It is, on the other hand — in the full blast of pioneer exploitation, at any rate — effeminate and silly to waste your time on reading or to take an interest in art. It is worse still to be a writer, authorship being a faintly immoral occupation. But it is definitely in line with God's purpose, the pioneer parson teaches, for a man to acquire wealth. That is a sign that "God is prospering him."

Life in a pioneer community is hard, and few people attain the goal so constantly kept in mind. Those who do succeed by industry, thrift, a certain level of integrity, and more commonly by helping themselves to the riches which nature has provided. At least it is in this latter way that the really great fortunes have been made. When the strong man seizes a great area of virgin land, or a timber limit, or a water power, he of course does it through the medium of government, and it is these occasions which have provided our major political scandals. But nobody really is shocked, for every pioneer knows in his heart that he would have done the same thing if he had had the opportunity. The wealth is there, belonging to no one in particular, and there is not a sufficiently integrated society to prevent the strong man from taking it. The small man merely envies him a bit and proceeds to do what he can in the same direction, keeping before his mind's eye the wealthy man and his buccaneering ways as his ideal. It will probably be better for everyone when we have got this job of thievery over and done with. When there is nothing left to steal, we may have a chance of developing into a reasonably honest people.

These things are common to nearly all pioneer societies. In others than our own they have been balanced to some degree by additional factors. Thus in colonial New England, religion was such a dominating force that for a time it provided the goal and ideal of the community, until it became somewhat overpowered by the all-consuming American materialism of the nineteenth century. But Puritan New England gave this continent a large share of its spiritual and educational heritage; it had a way of life that had much room for non-material factors, and upon which in many respects the American nation has been built.

In Australia, a country which was built on the singularly unpromising foundation of convicts and gold miners, spiritual salvation of a sort has been found in the determination to build a "white Australia," no matter what the cost. Whether or not we sympathize with the racial pride which steadfastly refuses to create an Oriental problem or indeed a foreign problem of any sort, despite the temptations of quick development, cheap labour, and greater population, we must admire the hard, enduring attitude which characterizes the Australian in respect to his racial heritage.

That attitude is not one which we Canadians could assume. In the great days of immigration, we scarcely gave a thought to any aspect of our future save the material one of increasing our wealth. Whether immigrants were suitable or unsuitable, assimilable or not, did not bother us; the main thing was that we hoped that, by adding to our population, they would increase the wealth of those of us who were already here and that they would form a source of exploitable cheap labour. That selfish and nearsighted attitude is working its retribution now, for the unassimilated and unattached immigrant, through no fault of his own, constitutes a major factor in our present economic, social and political problems.

But our carelessness and lack of foresight in respect to the settlement of our country are only one example among many that might be cited in support of the contention that the very warp and woof of English-Canadian mentality is spun out of a crass materialism which in its heyday could scarcely see any objective, racial, religious, or political, that could outrank the all-consuming desire for mere wealth. The American materialist has often redeemed his conduct by a certain dash of imagination, a certain capacity for acting in a large and constructive way — witness such things as the foundations, libraries, and universities founded by American rich men.

None of these things have redeemed the materialism of the average Canadian. Few of our rich men endow libraries or found universities. The Canadian has acted, and does act, on a smaller stage than his American counterpart, imitating only the latter's sorriest tricks. He has summed up life into the task of acquiring possessions, getting a good job, being as much like other comfortable and respectable people as possible. Little love of country has redeemed him, for his ties to his country have been the thinnest. He has, for example, thought it almost the normal thing for his young people to go across the line and become Americans and for his old people to go over there to retire, taking along with them their experience and the money they have made in Canada. He has not been brought up in a creed of Canadianism as an American has in the creed of Americanism. The old English sanctions, such as the tradition of freedom and tolerance or the responsibility of the rich man toward the state, his duty to serve it, which keep society healthy in the mother country and which curb the excesses of even the grossest "businessman," have had little force here. They have been shoved to one side in the mind of the average Canadian, and if he understands them at all he pays only lip service to them.

A proof of this statement lies in the astonishing equanimity with which the Canadian people, year after year, decade after decade, receive the succession of revelations of corruption which have always bedevilled our politics. Each set tries to prove itself white by blackening the other set. But we all know very well that both are black. Most of us enjoy seeing the mud thrown and do not blame either of them, for we would boodle too if we had the chance.

And now this individualism and materialism are rotting, leaving nothing behind. These unstable foundations of the state have given way. In his more pessimistic moments one is inclined to think that this Canadian people, hardly adolescent as peoples go, is worn out already, spiritually exhausted, without ideals, without valid traditions, without vitality for creation, without even any very evident interest in its own fate.

That may be too extreme — the writer hopes it is — but a glance round our institutional life is not reassuring. The two historic parties blunder along, the bankrupt heirs of a dead past; there is nothing in either of them to stir the imagination, and day by day they lose their attraction for thoughtful people and for the generation growing up. They are dominated by elderly gentlemen egotistically puttering about in an age which bears little resemblance to that of their youth and which they with difficulty understand. As the late Principal Grant suggested some years ago, the old game of ins-and-outs is almost over, and no longer engages the interest of the spectators. The third party is well-meaning but "half-baked," its policies inspired by a rather nebulous humanitarianism which has already attracted to it an undue number of cranks.

Provincialism grows apace. Little knots of officials in the provincial capitals launch lawsuits which they feel confident will be decided by a distant authority against the Dominion. Few citizens protest, and the combination of self-seeking provincial authorities at home and a distant court jealous of Canadian nationalism, steadily whittles away the powers of the central government. One of these days either the edifice of Confederation will break up into its original fragments; or, to preserve it, those of us who care for our country will have to go through what the United States endured from 1861 to 1865.

Our society, the society of that English-speaking Canada which eighty years or so ago seemed to have been permanently established on the strong basis of a vigorous yeoman stock, carries on with the momentum it then acquired. Upper Canada and the other English-speaking provinces were built upon an assertive Protestantism, a provincial place in the British Empire with the heritage of British tradition thereby implied, popular education as an instrument in advancing the interests of the individual, and the strong self-dependence of the pioneer. These ideals sufficed for our fathers; they gave them a sense of stability and enabled them to live without harassing doubts.

But they have never been revamped, hardly even examined. And yet today the fire has gone out of Protestantism, the church cannot give us those certainties it gave to a previous generation, and unless in some way it can pull itself together, its future is of the darkest.

English-speaking Catholicism seems in little better case; for, while the dogmatic framework remains untouched, the individual Catholic has been affected by the forces of the day to an extent but little less than his Protestant contemporary. In Quebec, where a strong peasant society still preserves itself almost aloof from outside influences, that is not the case, for a separate language, nationality, a corporate sense, and historical traditions of validity and vitality have given to the French Canadian elements of stability which the English Canadian lacks. The French Canadian does not worship the English god, "High Standard of Living," but at an older and on the whole a more satisfactory shrine, wherein the objects of devotion are not money-making but the land, the race, and immemorial ways.

Our school system was originally a fine accomplishment for a pioneer people, and it is on record that even in their poorest days the people of Upper Canada were always ready to find money for education. That does not mean that they, like the Jew, were driven by fierce intellectual hunger; it simply indicates that they understood the hardness of their lot as pioneers and were determined that life for their children should be easier. Education was a key to ease. But education is no longer a simple highroad to the professions. In its lower levels, it is fast becoming a mechanical device for turning out robots to operate typewriters or perform other routine duties in the precincts of the temples of that which but yesterday was our national religion — business. Probably never in their history have our schools been more efficient in the discharge of their humdrum day-to-day duties, never have children written more clearly, spelled more correctly, or added up figures so speedily. But never, either, has the school been so barren in respect to that task which of all other tasks it exists for — the elaboration of a philosophy of society and the equipment of the pupil with that philosophy; in other words, the turning out not of sharp tools but of citizens, and of citizens who know why they are citizens.

In older countries, the fundamentals of national life are unceasingly re-examined, and every outstanding teacher brings to aid his efforts his conception of the nature of the state. But in Canada there seems to be a divorce between the school and political philosophy, and the teacher who has a clear-cut conception of the kind of state he would like to build with the material passing through his hands must be a *rara avis* indeed. In the West we try to make Canadians out of "New Canadians." But who has ever told us what is meant by the term "Canadian?" Every Frenchman understands the content of the concept of "La France," every English-born person knows the force of the appeal to be "British" — the word conjures up almost a complete theory of conduct. What does it mean to be "Canadian?"

Again, our people, true to the materialistic training which bids them place the acquisition of things and the comforts of life above the natural human instincts, seem to be doing their best to secure, through the limitation of families, their own extinction. In the West, two or three generations will probably have seen this process go so far, through the difference in birthrate between the "new" and the "old" Canadians, that the descendants of the latter will have become a small minority, possibly a pleasantly rich minority, but in essentials like the original New Englanders today — shoved aside in their own country.

In the old days, church, school, and home gave children a working philosophy; oriented them toward themselves, each other, and the state. It was elementary but it sufficed; and these agencies knew what they were doing, they were sure of themselves. Today the three are weak. There is nothing to give the child save a threadbare creed and the dull routine of the school curriculum. There is no longer a clear goal to point to. "Work hard and you'll get rich and in due course go to Heaven" won't take us very far today. Even a simple child would laugh at that. Consequently the generation growing up drifts about, not bound together by the older ties, a set of atoms, sheep without a shepherd, save in so far as the movie, the comic strip, and the athletic hero constitute shepherds and supply what does duty for a code of conduct.

We have any number of "priests" — that is, guardians of things as they are — in this country, but few prophets. We ask the "priest" — or parson — for bread and he gives us a stale sermon. We ask the politician, and his bread gives us indigestion. We have also any number of quacks and cranks vending political and religious patent medicines. But we have no great unifying national purpose. Where there is no vision, the people perish.

In the war years, we had just that — a creed, something that man could passionately believe in, fight for, and die for. But that was a creed for an emergency; and when the emergency passed, so did our fine idealism, gradually filtered away by the steady drip of disillusionment. Today there are those among us who have a creed they can passionately believe in — a political and economic heresy that it is hardly safe to mention in ordinary circles, communism — and if necessary die for. Their appeal is to the underdog. What have the older Canadians, the top dogs, to offset it? What have we to believe in, and if necessary die for? The Conservative and Liberal parties? Business? Pleasant, fatuous, little bridge parties?

These things are our lives. They are our shoddy ideals.

We used to believe in the Union Jack. In its complete vagueness, its ability to cover half a dozen kinds of contradictory behaviour, complete self-sacrifice combined with utter selfishness, it served our Anglo-Saxon mentality rather well. But even that naive old colonialism, which was ever ready to do and die in causes which did not concern it and which it did not understand, is passing. Mere blatant imperialism is not what it was, not even in Ontario.

Whether we like it or not, we are being separated from our mother's apron strings. We have got to face the dreadful ordeal of nationhood. What have we got to face it with? No nation known to the writer exists without some more or less coherent body of doctrine. What is ours?

14 | *Canada and a Free Society: Liberalism, its Nature and Prospects**

Our twentieth-century world reminds the historian of that of the sixteenth — the same destruction of old institutions, the same recasting of ideas, the same endless controversies, and similar wars of religion. I am addressing historians: it is just possible, therefore, that you will bear with me when I refer to history. I admit, your tolerance, if accorded, will be exceptional, for nothing seems to bore the Canadian people, with their pretensions to being "practical" and "realistic," more than a suggestion that to find wisdom we might turn to one of the chief components of wisdom — experience. I am not convinced, however, that a people who have so far destroyed the earth they live by as to bring down on themselves the disastrous floods which, this spring, have been only worse than usual have any large claim to wisdom. Appeals to history, therefore, are apt to meet with, at most, strained politeness. Among those who teach the subject, however, that statement may not hold.

My own tendency, when looking at a big social problem, is to take a rapid glance over the evolution of our civilization during the last thousand years or so and try to plot on this chart of the ship's course the point at which she now is. To do this requires, for my present subject, consideration of two wide epochs: the Middle Ages as a whole, culminating in the disturbances of the sixteenth century; and the period since then, with its current disturbances.

The end of the "Dark Ages" saw Europe emerging out of barbarism into the comparative light of medievalism. Few people realize how magnificent was the structure reared in those centuries after 1,000 A.D.: a supreme architecture, a revitalized church with a new philosophy, two great new legal systems, new military methods, several of the modern nation-states, and constant frontier expansion to the east. In some respects medieval Europe was as active and creative as modern America. The usual picture painted, of men reflecting so sombrely on the life to come that they had not time left over to live, is the most utter nonsense.

Intensity of life and the spirit of accomplishment — what we here in America call "drive" — produced their inevitable results, a high seriousness. This was reflected first of all in the intellectual revolution of the late twelfth and the thirteenth centuries and then in various other move-

---

*Delivered to the annual meeting of the Ontario Educational Association in 1948 and published in the *Annual Report* (1948): 68-75.

ments of expansion. The medieval scholar tackled his problems just as assiduously as does the modern scientist. And he provided for the science of the day a satisfactory philosophical and rational basis in the work of St. Thomas Aquinas. From the period of Abelard, or say 1150 until the impulse began to run out, or say 1400, Europeans were building a great new dynamic civilization. Naturally they were in earnest. The Middle Ages began with the moral austerities of St. Bernard and they produced Dominicans and Franciscans, devoted to the austerity of poverty, to say nothing of the intellectual austerities of the Thomist philosophy. It seems to me that periods of intense accomplishment, which invariably are accompanied by this austere attitude towards life, may well be called puritan periods.

Puritanism, however, always runs out. Sooner or later, accomplishment fulfils itself. One has time to sit down and rest. The country house succeeds the castle. Hymn singing develops into music. A more spacious life of this sort began to come in as the Middle Ages wore on, at first along Europe's front street, Italy, later spreading north. We usually dub this phase of European history the Renaissance. I am not a specialist in the period, but the name seems to me to be wrong. The Italian Renaissance does not mean so much the beginning of an age as the end of one. The starkness and earnestness of medievalism gave way to something more genial: the Middle Ages grew up and ripened. In fact they rapidly got over-ripe. Italian civilization from the eleventh to the sixteenth centuries ran through all the stages of growth right through to degeneracy. The severity of a Dante gave way to the literary and antiquarian curiosity of a Petrarch, and a century after Petrarch along came the Renaissance popes, with their drunken parties and their bastards. The solid North German, Luther, journeying down to the metropolis from the north-east European backwoods, was frankly shocked at what he found at Rome. Any city where Benvenuto Cellinis could live and the *Decameron* be read, where pardons and poisoners could be bought, could hardly be called austere, or, if you like, intolerant. Renaissance Rome seems to have been about as free, in the anarchic sense of the word, as it was well possible for a city to be. Other Italian cities were more or less like it, and the attempt of Savonarola, in Florence, to turn back the hands of the clock and re-impose twelfth century puritanism was a failure.

My interpretation of this sequence, for what it is worth, is simply this: the drive that built the Middle Ages was running down, and naturally ran down soonest where its job was most completely done, in the Italian metropolitan centres. Puritanism had come down through characteristic stages, first to tolerant intellectualism, and next to hedonism, or paganism. No wonder the man from the German backwoods was disgusted. As a Wittenberg frontiersman, with the Slav barbarian not far away, he had been accustomed to the same tense and active atmosphere that had characterized Italy generations before, when her cities had been fighting to cast out the German hordes of Barbarossa. So he went home, and, without any idea of where it would all lead to, nailed his theses on the church door.

Now here *was* the beginning of something. The Renaissance, it seems to me, was the end of an age — puritanism going up in smoke — but the Reformation was the beginning of one. It was the real rebirth — the rebirth of energy, of zeal, of faith, or crudity, in short a new puritanism, with little concern for Renaissance freedom, a puritanism begun on the frontier, in revolt against big-city goings on.

I have put this down, not so much for its own sake as because it seems to me to throw some light on the processes of history and to help us with our problem here and now. For it may be we are again living in one of those uneasy ages when a new world is just about to be born. The Reformation, calling out so many new values and energies, began a fresh cycle in human affairs. It interjected controversy and dispute which tore Europe apart, but it gave to Europe — to Catholic Europe as well as Protestant — immense accessions of vitality. It was the first and the greatest of the modern revolutions, and like most revolutions, it produced a new puritanism, a new sense of accomplishment. This was not confined to one side. Reformation may have generated Counter-Reformation, but both represented new supplies of energy, often manifested in similar guise. It is striking, for example, how similar the puritanism of the French Counter-Reformation turns out to be, on analysis, to its better known rival across the Channel. The spirit of both the Old World societies was transferred to the New, where apart from intrinsic differences between Catholic and Protestant, the frowns of a Bishop Laval on balls and stage plays do not seem very different from those of the fathers of a Boston Sunday.

Medieval civilization, in Italy at least, with its sense of accomplishment, its intellectualism, its terminal paganism, at last had its day, and its end was marked by the gorgeous sunset of the Renaissance: beauty often seems to come out of social degeneration. Is our modern civilization, which we usually regard as beginning about the time of the Renaissance, and which has lasted about the same length of time as that which preceded it, to follow the same course? There are plenty of people ready to predict this. It has become almost fashionable to say that modern civilization begins with this new release of energy marking the sixteenth century, enormously accentuated by the discoveries, and is marked chiefly by individualism, as compared with the communalism of the medieval world. It represents, it is said, the helter-skelter rush to grab the good things of the outer world — its gold, its furs, its forests, its lands.

This individualism is then equated with "liberalism" — with a small "l," of course. This, if I understand her correctly, is what the English Catholic intellectual, Miss Barbara Ward, would say. She is in the school of Belloc and Chesterton, which cannot agree with our conventional concept of freedom and sees in the raw individualism of the nineteenth century — "rugged individualism" — and the insensitiveness of certain sections (the highly vocal "free enterprisers" of the moment) of "business" today little but evil and the destruction of human values. Miss Ward would see the end of this long cycle in the great wars of our time and would look in replacement for something like the brotherhood of man under the aegis of the church universal. From the other side, we have Harold Laski, writing his *Rise of European Liberalism,* chiefly, it would seem, in order to have the satisfaction of predicting its decline. He sees in its stead some kind of secular collectivism.[1] Let's face this fact. Is the civilization of which we form a part, beyond which few Canadian imaginations can travel, is this free civilization of ours doomed, and will it, too, go up in revolutionary flames?

There have been many secondary eddies in the four centuries' flood. In France, Counter-Reformation zeal and austerity — Catholic puritanism, as I have called it — ran out with the Enlightenment of the eighteenth century, whose central figure was Voltaire, the man, you may remember, whose slogan comes as close to the essence of what, it seems to me, genuinely may be called liberalism as anything can: "I may not agree with what you have to say, but I shall fight for your right to say it." The Enlightenment lasted a generation or two and then France, unable to find its way through the autocracy of the ancient régime to a broader conception of government, exploded in revolution.

Again, in the nineteenth and twentieth centuries, France ran through a similar cycle: the zeal and discipline of Napoleonic effort sank down to middle-class complacency and comfort under Louis Philippe: the middle classes possessed France for the rest of the century, but responsibility to society was not as prominent a characteristic of theirs, it would seem, as the individualism of business or family; and so we have the torn, pathetic France of the present generation never freer intellectually and morally, but close to anarchy, and so with its freedom hanging in the balance.

In England, Puritanism was chased out with the Restoration, and there was, for a brief period, just such a carnival as had occurred in Italy at the height of the Renaissance: its coincidence with a brilliant literary period cannot be ignored. Restoration license was moderated by the Revolution of 1688: the boys were called in from recess. With James II and Louis XIV both disposed of, the way was open for the long, genial summer afternoon of the eighteenth century. But it, in its turn, gave way under the blows of the Industrial Revolution and the great wars with France.

[1] Barbara Ward, *Democracy, East and West* (London: Bureau of Current Affairs, 1947); Harold Laski, *Rise of European Liberalism* (London: Allen and Unwin, 1936).

The pressures of the age were marked by the rise of Wesleyanism, humanitarianism, and the evangelical revival in the Church of England. These
made the nineteenth century; and the nineteenth century, that supreme
age of accomplishment, was puritan. It is the fashion just now, especially
in England, to turn and rend the Victorians: modern Englishmen might
remember that whereas their grandfathers saw the rise of a great structure,
they only see its fall. Puritanism, Stuart or Victorian, is not a spirit which
fits a period of disintegration.

Is that what is implied for our own day, disintegration? Has the strong
spirit of accomplishment, in church, in state, in practical endeavour, which,
no one can deny, characterized the nineteenth century, run out? If some
aspects of our society here in North America are examined, they do not
make for complacency. The essential puritanism of the pioneers of this
continent, whether expressed in morals or simply in morale, tamed nature,
built railways, cities, and a vast new society. A century ago every man
was the architect of his own fortune, and every American boy could go
from log-cabin to White House. The continent, or at least that more fortunate part of it which is the United States, was bathed in golden sunshine.
By the end of the nineteenth century, people were becoming content
to drop down a stage from "striking pay dirt" and "getting into the big
money," and were looking for good jobs. Since then, the job psychology
has marked the continent. It has become particularly conspicuous in Canada,
where opportunities have always been fewer. In neither country today is
puritanism what it was. We in Canada, and, I suppose, great regions in
the United States too, have lost much of the stern old drive of accomplishment and reach out instead for security. That is youth's cry — security.
It is the cry of the petty bourgeoisie, the lower middle class. The big
bourgeoisie who were subduing the continent — the Stors, Vanderbilts, Van
Hornes, Mountstephens, Holts, Huntingdons, Hearsts, and Fords — never
asked for security. They asked for the earth. They passed, and today the
little man inherits, the petty bourgeoisie. He has always asked for security.
He has never wanted more than to sit quietly and comfortably under his
own vine and fig tree, with his family round him. All he wants is a nice
car and a nice little house, with a nice electric refrigerator and a nice
radio — it doesn't really matter much what kind of programme comes
over it — and a backyard, a bowling club where he can gossip with his
neighbours. He has never wanted responsibility. Our average voter, he is
essentially irresponsible.

The little man with his innocent little wants and his slender stock
of ideas or culture, with little understanding of anything at all except what
goes on under his nose, is the typical Canadian today. As the ordinary
"man in the street," he has displaced the pioneer, the immigrant, the farmer.
It is because he is the little man, with the little man's addictions, that

he is so often shouldered aside by the immigrant, who finds it easy to establish himself in Canadian life. The immigrant, by the very fact of immigration, has, for a time, to live precariously and dangerously, the little man just slides into a comfortable rut.

Unfortunately he has rarely been allowed to realize his little dream. And so today, when he asks for security, he is confronted with another war. "It is because modern man, having made himself God, has invented the concept of a realm on earth where everyone will be perpetually happy, perpetually cared for, and free of want and fear from the cradle to the grave, that we are all so insecure."[2] It would improve the quotation a little, I think, if it were altered to read "It is because the little man, having climbed up on the shoulders of those among him who in stature are Gods, has dreamed of a realm on earth, where everyone will be perpetually happy, perpetually cared for, and free of want and fear from the cradle to the grave, that we are all so insecure."

The people who climb to power are never concerned with quiet lives. That is the secret: the people who climb to power are not concerned with quiet lives. They may be driven by some great ideal, or by sheer personal ambition, or by a deep sense of responsibility, or by any or all of these, but they will certainly dominate the little man. The Lloyd Georges, the Roosevelts, the Churchills, the Hitlers, the Stalins, the John Lewises have at least this in common, that they keep on the job every day and all day, and far from wishing to go back and see the apple blossoms in Warwickshire once again, as did pathetic Mr. Baldwin, they get their lives out of the excitement of the game. They may or may not be great and good men, these giants: the one thing they all must do is to serve their own career. So the little man looks on and cheers and asks them to provide him with security, which they may or may not do.

Security, even for the masses, however, is no universal ideal. I have suggested that civilization may move from the phase of drive and accomplishment to a phase of genial speciousness and tolerance, not unmarked by complacence. I have also suggested that the next phase is hedonism — the selfishness and materialism of paganism — and that this stage sometimes has sunset glows of cultural brilliance. Is this last stage to be found here in America? Is our universal motto still "anything for a quiet life," or are we moving into this last stage, paganism? A glance back over the last thirty years may give some data on that.

In the interval between the two wars, both Canadians and Americans seemed to be preoccupied with kicking their institutions to pieces. To the average man politicians became figures of fun. Professors always had been that. Ministers became "old sticks," the bottom fell out of religion, out

[2]Dorothy Thompson, "The President's Speech," *Globe and Mail*, 23 March 1948.

of large areas of Protestantism, at any rate, and that is the only creed for which I can venture to speak. Education became more and more diluted. The result is that while today we have more people in the upper ranges of education than ever before, we are probably turning out fewer educated people. From the point of view of appreciation of reality, sound learning, and urbanity of culture, our educational system in its old liberal areas, in my darker moods, seems to me not far from one big bluff.

I should not have expanded on education — though that's a stab that toucheth Caesar closer — especially as the democratization of education does not indicate a return to paganism, although its demoralization, with the consequent drop in intellectual standards, does. But I would have the right to let myself go on another diagnostic factor, the position of woman and the relationship of the sexes. The generation of women of the period before the first world war won freedom for women, or "women's rights"; I can see little evidence that their daughters set much value on that freedom. "Votes for women" has not altered the political position — if it has, it has not necessarily altered it for the better, women being even more apathetic politically than men. The young women of this generation seem to be going in two directions: one, the old-fashioned route to becoming wives and mothers — and good ones — the other, an equally conventional, though not as commendable, route to "liberty" in the especial feminine sense of the term. That route is marked by the rising divorce rate, increase of illegitimacy, and other such phenomena; these sexual phenomena invariably come out into the open in the pagan stage of civilization. When this trend has run its course — and there has been plenty of experience of it in the past — society may pull itself up sharply again, as it did at the close of the eighteenth century, and start off on a new cycle of puritanism. This seems to be what is happening in Russia, where the freedom of woman, with no discernible limits for the few years after the initial revolution, seems to be rapidly shrinking again.

I would never suggest that we Canadians have been getting rid of our bourgeois inhibitions as quickly as our American friends. The great metropolitan civilization of the continent with its constant exhibitions in "smart-aleckism" is not our creation. Our divorce rate is still relatively modest — though we are learning fast and we are far less puritan than we used to be. It is not, it must be admitted, an edifying sight to see this rude backwoodsman, Jack Canuck, casting overboard his taboos. He does not go in for sipping vintage wines; he gets his hard liquor down with the old familiar jerk of the arm and then begins to swear. Our climate is against an elegant paganism. In mid-January we cannot go in for the fluttery pirouetting of southern California where no pretty girl, one gathers, ever wears anything but the scantiest of bathing suits.

Since this continent is highly equalitarian, American puritanism naturally exhibits itself in popular, or mass, phenomena, most clearly seen in the media which educate our young. Please do not be under the misapprehension, ladies and gentlemen, that you, or their parents, educate our young. Our young are either confined to the ivory tower of school and home until they break out of it or are educated from the beginning in that culture which possesses their souls, the culture of which the movie, the comic strip, the sport page and the slave music which grinds mournfully and demoralizingly out of radio and juke box, are the ear marks. These are the major cultural accomplishments of the continent, because this continent is frantically equalitarian, and will accept little that savours of favouritism, selection, gradation, aristocracy, in culture. Our North American cultural accomplishments − and despite equalitarianism they are great − have to be smuggled in, as it were, and are largely repudiated by the masses, whose popular culture dominates.

It may, then, be that we are somewhere near the end of a cycle and that the years ahead are going to see all our traditional institutions and social morals tested as they never have been before. There is no doubt of the presence in our midst of revolutionary forces both conscious and unconscious. Unfortunately, our characteristic social pattern, petty-bourgeoisism, has little more power to stand up under their shock than it has had in Hollywood or in Czechoslovakia. In Hollywood and like places, petty bourgeois morals have gone by the board; in Czechoslovakia, petty bourgeois parties. Just being a good fellow will not save you from coming under the domination of men with a determination to seize power. How then are we going to escape the fate of other peoples − the loss of the free institutions of which we are the beneficiaries but not the creators? How shall we make the dangerous crossing from the end of our cycle, with its paganism, to the beginning of another, with its new sense of drive and purpose, and carry our free institutions with us? We shall not escape unless we can find a fighting creed, something in which we believe, not tepidly, but passionately. The Nazi assault was only the first round, I am afraid; this time, freedom is going to be threatened in her very dwelling place, and largely because her children are complacent, or stupid, or gullible. Talking about the black future, a friend of mine said to me the other day: "The idea of another war just makes me tired." I said to him that was why there was the possibility of another war, because people like him were tired − because they want to run away from the battle.

Where is the trumpet call that will rally such people, what is the creed of freedom to which men can be attached as passionately as men are attached to that of unfreedom? It cannot be found in the irresponsibilities of mere individualism, which is anarchy. I suggest to you that it will be found somewhere within that much abused term liberalism, which is what most of us mean, I suppose, when we use the word *democracy*. I hope it is unnecessary to remind you that I am not using the word in a party sense. Let me examine it, for within it somewhere is contained all that we need to know in respect to the title of this address "Canada and a Free Society."

First of all, a few things which I cannot believe liberalism, in any really vital sense, to be: I cannot believe it to be mere tolerance. It is often said that the dilemma of our liberal societies consists in the fact that, as liberals believing in freedom, we can take no measures against those who employ the agencies of liberalism — civil liberties — to destroy liberty. That is what happened in the association of one particular form of economic society with *the* good society. Communism, for example, despite all its philosophical apparatus, seems to be simply a blueprint, bed-of-Procrustes recipe for society. If individuals are too long for the state's Procrustean bed, cut them down to fit; if too short, stretch them out. Communism, as demonstrated in Slavic Europe, would seem therefore, to provide the most effective method yet devised for dealing with labour. Capitalists who complain about labour should become communists at once, take over the state, and treat their labour force as labour is treated where men who really mean business are in power.

Capitalism, on the other hand, I cannot fit into the conventional economic definitions which associate it with individualism, and both it and individualism with liberalism. It seems to me to be simply the old human instinct for power and pelf, which can be associated with any type of organization of society whatsoever. You can have *laissez faire,* or small capitalism, big business capitalism, ecclesiastical capitalism, feudal capitalism, staple trade capitalism, banking or finance capitalism, state capitalism, such as we have here in Ontario with our Hydro, and communistic capitalism. In every age and clime man's acquisitive and power instincts have been much the same low cunning. They have asserted themselves whatever the form of society, and they always will.

But, surely, here is the point: in every age and clime, since men have been men, there have been codes of conduct — even the savage Iroquois had his high code of honour — and everywhere, as soon as man has been able to command his thoughts sufficiently to be able to think in abstract terms, there has come out the idea of justice. It is the just society which is the quest, and justice must include freedom. A favourite quotation of mine puts it: "What doth the Lord require of thee, O man, but to do justice, to love mercy and to walk humbly with thy God?" That, it seems to me, is the essence of the matter.

It is the pride of the English-speaking world to claim that for some centuries past it has been more concerned with justice than have most other sectors of mankind. That may be sheer racial conceit, but whether we have thought these matters out or not, and perhaps just because we have been fortunately situated, we do seem to have got farther along the road to a decent society than most other sectors of mankind. God knows we have fallen far short of perfection, but in every English-speaking society there have always been people who have forwarded the quest. It is our pride, too, that our move forward toward justice has been rooted in freedom. Here, surely, is content for the word *liberalism:* the objective of a just society rooted in freedom. That it is our objective might be proved quite simply: I don't suppose there is a man in this country who would dare to express his preference for any other objective.

Why have we moved along this road, and how best can we keep in the path we have trod? I account for our institutions and the spirit which inspires them under three heads.

1. Legal. Centuries ago, the Roman Catholic Frenchmen who were building England worked out the basis of the common law. Our legal institutions have come down from that distant period; and when Norman Frenchmen became English, our law became English too. Incidentally, race apparently had little to do with it. Much more important than race was the nice balance between the medieval king and his barons, which, by preventing the domination of either, brought forth compromise and a constitution, a constitution embodied in numerous great documents, of which Magna Carta is only one.

2. Political. After medieval bishops, barons, and kings (in order) had built up the common law, the processes of politics brought into existence the great institution of Parliament. Parliament, at first merely a weak emanation of the royal will, became hallowed by time; representative government, one of the profoundest of political devices, became the fibre of English life. Three centuries after its origin, and three centuries ago, Parliament found itself strong enough to stand on its own feet. In the revolutions of the seventeenth century it wrenched the power from the Stuart kings. The result was another outstanding compromise which we call "parliamentary sovereignty" or "limited monarchy." The English-speaking peoples have spent centuries perfecting this device. Whether in the form of parliament at Westminster or Ottawa, or of the congress at Washington, parliamentary government, I am convinced, remains one of the strongest, most subtle, most elastic guarantees of a just society that the mind of man has devised or can devise.

3. Religion. Last year this association heard an excellent paper by Professor Saunders, which based democracy on the Christian religion. Here is the greatest of debates.

Science in its inexorable march seems to fasten upon mankind a rigorous determinism. Are we but creatures of relentless fate, mere pieces of motor mechanism, bundles of chemical reactions? If so, why do we not obey to the uttermost what seems to be the law of all the rest of life, be begotten and beget, eat and be eaten? Why did ever a prophet arise to enjoin us to do justice and love mercy? Why were not Hitler and his friends acting quite legitimately when they killed off human beings as we kill chickens? Why is the Russian secret police and its midnight arrests, its slave labour camps, why is all this reprehensible? We can find no pity in the animal world .... Why introduce it into the human, which is animal too? How in the face of nature can any case be made out for the tender squeamishness of the Christian ethic? We cut live dogs to pieces in order that humanity may benefit. Why should not Germans cut live slaves to pieces in order that a super-race may benefit? Is this Christianity, this Western liberalism of ours, just softness? After all, in the totality of things, one event is very much like another, the death of a fly or of a hundred thousand Japanese at Hiroshima, or the death of a star. How justify these human emotions − pity, sympathy, generosity −− which are so transient in the transient experience of a transient species?

I wish I could get what man never has got, the final answer to such questions. If there be no such answer, then is the strongest wolf justified by his strength? Here is the *real* dilemma of liberalism. Can it find some free will for man in the midst of all this cosmic determinism? How are you going to convince the pagan or your dog, if he could speak, that man is the child of God and so of special intrinsic worth? Are all men brothers? They are if they are the children of God. Then is not all life an emanation from God and is not the Hindu right, who refuses to injure any living thing?

If I cannot get any final answer to this question of questions I can at least drop down a step and still find good fighting ground. If I cannot prove beyond the peradventure of a doubt that man is a child of God and that, as such, every individual man has a special and unique value in the sight of God, I can at least find an empiric test and say that society works best if we believe so. We can leave out the rest of life for a moment and just admit that the destructive impulses of men can best be curbed by agreement to curb them − in the interest of all. "In a state of nature the life of man is nasty, brutish, and short." Men, therefore, come together and found a civil society, subject to law. It was atheistic old Thomas Hobbes who took that view; perhaps then we may find our best justification for liberalism, if not our most exalted, in sheer necessity. But who can minimize the reinforcement which the Christian ethic has supplied, the intensity of application, the fervour, the devotion, the dignity, and the splendour with which it has surrounded our species?

Of one thing I am sure: if everyone were seized of the impelling implications of the Christian ethic, if it were possible for men to live up in small degree to the mark it sets us, we would not be here canvassing the problem of Canada and a free society. For we would know the truth, and the truth would make us free. Unfortunately, being humans, with the infinite limitations of humans, we can only pursue the truth, not attain it. But in pursuit, may we not at least ensure for those who come after us, a heritage at least as worthy as that which we were given? Will these traditions of ours which have carried us through so many centuries and have outlived the storms of revolution and the threats of social degeneration alike, not carry us through once more into another great cycle wherein, whatever its nature, freedom and justice will still be our watchwords? If we are true to them, I think they will.

IV.

Nationalism

Since entering the academic community Arthur Lower has written upon a variety of current questions in his effort to help build a Canadian nation based upon liberal principles. First, studying how a culture develops and recognizing that there are two ways of life in the country made him question whether it was possible for such divergent people to share a common nationality. Second, during the thirties there was a great debate concerning Canada's identity and Canada's relationship with other nations. As he berated his countrymen for opting for shoddy ideals, so he rebuked them for not believing in themselves ("Canadians: 'Good Second Bests'" — Essay #15). The essay "Bonnie Chairlie's Gone Awa'" (Essay #16), written in response to R. B. Bennett's departure for Britain, is a classic angry blast at the Canadian colonial mentality. Instead of dependency, he felt Canadians should foster a mature, self-reliant nationalism. Only through this "National Policy ... Revised Version" (Essay #17) could Canadians develop a unique culture and provide the nation with a *raison d'être*.

As publicist, Lower was also concerned to deal with questions at various levels. Debate at the theoretical level among the élite would be sterile if it were not brought to a practical level of the average person. In "What This Country Needs Is Ten New Provinces" (Essay #18), he speculated on the future of Canada and argued that to achieve greater national spiritual unity the provinces should be divided into twenty smaller units. As provincial power was de-emphasized, national power would be stressed and national awareness fostered. In "If We Joined the U.S.A." (Essay #19), he set forth the practical considerations of a Canadian union with the United States. While material gains might accrue, he rejected union because it would cost Canadians their souls. Saving their souls involved understanding their situation. "The Forest: Heart of a Nation" (Essay #20) gives Canadians a brief lesson on one factor shaping the Canadian character.

15 | *Canadians*
     | *'Good Second Bests'**

Some months ago, I came in for a good deal of scolding because of a chance remark of mine to the effect that Canadians were "very good second bests." Having had time to think it over, I've decided to stick to my opinion.

No doubt I will come in for more scolding.

The major trouble with Canadians — English Canadians, not French — is that they don't believe in themselves, are not interested in themselves, hardly know that they themselves exist.

Just yesterday, a young lady came from school and informed her parents, "Half the kids in our room didn't know who the prime minister of Canada was. They all know about Eisenhower." When she went to get her hair cut, the barber asked this same young lady if she wanted it "like Mamie." "Mamie" Eisenhower, he meant.

Don't such things put the situation in a nutshell? To a large group of Canadians, it would be all one whether they continue as a people or just cease to exist. They don't know who their prime minister is — and they don't know why they have one, either.

If people are not sure whether they are alive or not — and that is another way of putting it — it's hard to see how they can amount to a great deal.

English-speaking Canadians would appear to be the people for whom the undertaker's advertisement was written: "Why go around half-dead when we can bury you at cut-rate prices?"

I am aware that my fellow-citizens eat, sleep, wear clothes, and exhibit all the other familiar traits of living beings, and when you meet them as individuals, they are kindly and well-meaning. But do kindliness and good intentions make people anything more than second bests? I don't think they do.

Of course, I am not thinking of people as individual John Smiths and William Joneses, but of their character all taken together. I am not thinking of Mr. Brown or Mr. Johnson but of Mr. Canadian, and he's the man it seems to me who can be described as second best.

Mr. Canadian is an honest, decent fellow. He works just as hard as anyone else. He is a faithful husband and father and a loyal supporter of the local hockey team. His range does not take him much beyond that

**New Liberty*, November 1953, pp. 15, 63-66, 68.

local team, though. He doesn't think in large terms. He is hitched up pretty tight to the spot whereon he sits.

I don't want to rob the ordinary man of his honourable share in the big things that have been done in this country. But it was not the ordinary man who worked out our system of government, achieved Confederation, dreamed the C.P.R. into existence. The men who did these things were not second bests — but they were few! And today "half the kids in our room" would not know the name of a single one of them!

Despite our failure to understand that we really do exist, we have, for a people who are only half alive, many hard-wearing qualities. We are patient and long-suffering — aside from a little grumbling about taxes, don't we leave it all to the politicians? We don't wear our hearts on our sleeves, like some that could be mentioned. No, we know how to conceal our feelings, our deepest feelings. In fact no people hates a display of feeling as much as does our own. Canadian faces, it often seems to me, are masks. I often wish I could see beneath them and understand something of what is going on behind them.

I sometimes wonder if anything of importance is going on behind those masks of faces, whether real emotion, as distinct from the sloppy exhibitions of emotion which we all dislike, is warming these hearts, whether thoughts beyond the most immediate are stirring these brains, whether there are visions, intimations of beauty, all the qualities that make men not merely pleasant but significant. I don't know. But unless some yeast is fermenting, my charge will hold good.

I suppose there never was a period in man's experience of greater interest than the present. Big things are happening everywhere. Great dangers threaten. The Canadian sky, however, remains unclouded. One seldom hears on Canadian lips such words as "Korea," "atomic bomb," and so on.

When the "Red Dean" attempted to speak in London, Ontario, some students of the local university answered him, not with arguments, but with cowbells.

"How would the students of a certain other university have answered him?" one of them was asked.

"Oh, they would have been too apathetic to have answered him at all," came the reply.

Well, a first-rate people would not be apathetic: it would be concerned with these great world issues. Fancy such men not being answered in Great Britain! Go to a British political meeting and hear how even the best of speakers get heckled — heckled not with cowbells but with searching questions. Go to a Canadian political meeting — but what's the use of saying that? No one ever goes to a Canadian political meeting — the audiences are all watching American movies.

Take another field, industry. The "National Policy" was established seventy-five years ago to encourage Canadian industry. It did encourage it, and Canadian industry gradually grew up to a respectable height. But if you will make an analysis of Canadian industry today, that industry still sheltering under the protective tariff of the national policy, what will you find? Much of it, most of it in the key areas, not Canadian at all, but American. Canadian industry has become largely a branch plant industry, and no one takes orders more willingly from his American boss than does the Canadian businessman. When a great Canadian retail organization recently shared its field with a still greater American, no one publicly expressed a word of regret: the process of being swallowed and digested is evidently a pleasant one.

Can you think of any thing that distinguishes a Canadian enterprise from an American, anyway? Except the poorer quality of the product, I mean. Our industry has been without originality and without inventiveness, mostly merely a pale reflection of American creativeness.

Well, the man who takes orders and gets his ideas ready-made — is he first class?

Take our press. Many of us are loyal "Britishers." Yet when our prime minister goes to London to a "family" gathering, the more important reports of the meeting come through an American news agency. The principal accounts of the Coronation were given to Canadians by Americans. Our press slavishly incorporates American terms as if they were our own, speaking of "regimental combat teams" when our word is "brigade," and so on.

And yet, our press is one of the brighter spots on the Canadian horizon.

Take our attitude toward books. What Canadian ever buys a book anyway? Why buy books when there is gasoline to be bought? Most Canadians, for all our expensive schooling, handle a book as if it might bite them.

Most of us judge books by the numbers of pictures in them and the brightness of their covers. "The only kind of novel that will really go in Canada," said a publisher to me once, "is one with plenty of sex in it." No longer getting the benefit of sermons and Bible reading, as did our grandfathers, more and more of us are living in an intellectual vacuum. In so far as the written word goes, most modern Canadians are about as advanced as Sitting Bull's Sioux Indians.

Sioux Indians in big cars! Canadian "civilization"!

When it comes to the world of action, as contrasted with that of thought or ideas or reflection, it's a different matter. I don't know anyone I'd rather have with me in a tight spot than a fellow Canadian. Get your canoe broken in a rapids far from civilization, and he's your man. Cheerful and resourceful when it's nature and nature's dangers he's facing. And he has carried these qualities over into warfare. No better soldier ever existed.

But put these same resourceful men into contact with human problems — well, it's like the backwoodsman coming into town. He may get dressed up in city clothes, but he acts like a backwoodsman all the same.

The two peoples with whom our lot is cast, the English and American, present marked contrasts to ourselves. There is a strong dash of originality in both. They are inventive peoples. When you go into a store here in Canada and buy some useful gadget, of one thing you can be sure — it was not invented in Canada; it was thought up by some ingenious Yankee.

Is there a piece of original industrial design in the whole country, I wonder?

You go into a gadget store — and collectively, they occupy a big section of our main streets — and you go into an American store. In some sections of the country, you go into a chain grocery store — and again you go into an American store. You go into a good hotel — and the chances are good you go into an American hotel.

Leadership of American business in industries calling for large supplies of risk capital — in oil, for example — is understandable. But what of a country than can hardly run its own corner stores?

Cross the line into the United States at most points along the long border (I have crossed it in twenty-two different places that I can remember), and you will not have gone far before you find yourself in a land of well-kept farms and of towns with wide, tree-shaded streets, big dwelling lots, plenty of space about well-painted houses. A big contrast to our own crowded towns and untidy countryside, our relatively narrow streets and relatively crowded houses. Vision lies all over many great American cities and many smaller American towns. Over their Canadian counterparts lies lack of vision.

Why the difference? The explanation does not lie entirely in difference of wealth.

Go to the New England coast and you will see in the old towns there — like Marblehead — the narrow, crowded streets of colonial days. Motor inland from the coast and when you get back beyond the line of settlement at the time of the American Revolution — say in western Massachusetts — the streets get wide, the towns open and well-spaced. Why? Because when the Americans took their national destinies in their own hands, their minds enlarged with their tasks and with their future. They carried big, generous ideas along with them to the Pacific coast, and these are reflected in the appearance of their communities.

Now I know that there is nothing the average Canadian wants to hear less than praise of his neighbours, the Americans. All he wants to do is to imitate them!

Why did we not imitate our neighbours then in the layout of our towns? Think of that narrow, gloomy cavern that serves as the main street of Toronto, second city of Canada! Think of the unimaginative way in which the streets of North Vancouver charge full tilt up the mountainside from the water's edge. Then compare that with the imagination shown in the layout of the neighbouring "British Properties," where you can climb to the top of a mountain almost without knowing that you are going uphill. If it is unpopular to find good in what our American neighbours do, may I be allowed a word of praise for this imaginative piece of British planning? But why could we not have done it ourselves?

A few generous layouts we do have in Canada — London, Saskatoon, and by some strange chance, the main street of the little town of Smith's Falls, Ontario. These are all recognizable as of American dimensions, and they give character to each of these places. But too often, our towns and cities reflect the narrow colonial minds which laid them out. What they needed, and what they did not get, and now may never get, was the generous creative fire of a national vision. Good second-best cities!

My fellow-citizens remind me of the first stage of one of those experiments we used to do in high school physics. A pile of iron filings would be spread out on a paper. There the filings would lie, all higgledy-piggledy, in confused disarray. Then a magnet would be passed under the paper. At once, the filings arranged themselves in orderly rows and columns, following the magnetic lines of force. I'm afraid that what we lack is the magnet passed under us: in other words, we have not experienced the pull into order of a great creative national purpose.

That is why we are second bests.

The English handed down to us the secrets of self-government. We pride ourselves on being able to govern ourselves, on Canada being a free country and so on, but I wonder how well we would run our country if it had not been for the centuries of experience that the English handed over to us. Have we added much to the talents of which we, in the Biblical figure, have been made the stewards?

I don't want to run my own people down, but it is plain to me that as long as we are just "copy-cats," fearful of working things out for ourselves, taking over from other people the things they have invented for themselves — whether such things be their songs or their slang — wearing, so to speak, other peoples' hand-me-downs, we can never be a first-rate people ourselves.

One of my students said to me the other day that we seem to be developing more pride in ourselves "now that the Americans are taking more notice of us — all these articles that have been in American magazines on Canada, and so on." Someone else chipped in, "Now that Americans tell us we are not dead, we are beginning to believe that we must be alive!"

But why do we wait for Americans to discover that we must be alive?

Our big job in Canada is to build a new country; a new community, if you like that word better. It is a gigantic task. It calls for all the effort, all the imagination, that any group of men can bring to it. On this great half-continent of ours, we have to build our home. We have to build it not for a day, but for centuries. Most men take pride in building their homes. We Canadians are an especially home-loving people. Yet our national home does not seem to rank very high in our thoughts — we keep thinking, instead, of the parental house across the seas or of the magnificent mansion of our neighbours. But we have no option about the job. We have to build our home, and our children's home.

Until Canadians can catch that vision and put all they have into it, it will be fair, it seems to me, to go on describing them as "very good second bests."

16 | *Bonnie Chairlie's Gone Awa'**

It was almost theatrically appropriate that the last good-byes should be said to him here on board ship in Halifax harbour, among the citizens of the town in which his formative days had been spent. He was thinking, as his words showed (though his history was somewhat inaccurate), of that day 190 years ago when from another ship's cabin in this harbour, another Statesman of Empire, as everybody here puts it, launched the infant capital upon its course. Here, among the stalwart Bluenoses, with their ruddy faces, their quiet manners and their wing collars, was to take place the apotheosis of this modern "Statesman of Empire." The chariot of fire was to swoop down and snatch Elijah up into heaven from their very midst.

Six young ladies enter, bearing flowers. All well and truly, if somewhat publicly, kissed. Mr. Bennett's kisses provoke no domestic discords. The ship's orchestra crashes out boldly in a sort of omelet of "favourite tunes from the operas" — anything, one wonders apprehensively, to do with the speech to come? The chairman makes appropriate, if not overly original, remarks. The great man rises.

Mr. Bennett had something for everybody. For youth he reiterated his own bare, puritan creed — work hard and stick to it! For Nova Scotians, a warning against provincialism — a courageous utterance in a province whose interest in itself is so intense. For Canadians, a badly needed call to love of country. And for imperialists, a blast on the trumpet that shall yet make fall the walls of Jericho. No idle felicitations here. No, indeed.

**Canadian Forum* 19 (May 1939): 44-46.

The prophet was never more prophetic-like, never more sternly called sinners to repentance. He would have been a great power in prayer.

His audience smiled appreciatively at his complimentary references to Nova Scotia, tried to look appropriately serious when he spoke of their duty to the whole of Canada, even Ontario, though some expressions seemed to indicate that that was going a bit too far, and wriggled uncomfortably when he told them that they, the assembled democrats before him, were the people responsible for the extravagances of democracies (there was a stab that touched Caesar closer). When he poured out his feelings on what is always referred to here as "the heart of Empire," some of them, the platoons of colonels present, anyway, beamed with religious exaltation. "Hear, hear," a voice exclaimed, or was it "amen"?

Then we all filed out and shook hands. The band played "Bonnie Chairlie's gone awa.'" Shortly afterward the Chariot of Fire sounded her whistle and put to sea, bound for "the heart of Empire," or heaven (in Halifax it seems all one).

For years past, Mr. Bennett has dazzled us with his fiery lightnings, his sudden onslaughts, his as sudden retreats. Now, having put off responsibility, he has been revealing himself, his mind, and his heart to his countrymen as he has moved across Canada. He has put his philosophy before us. Duty, honesty, courage, hard work, traditional loyalties, these are the man. Little compromise here, little suavity — the hard-hitting creed and manner of the rising west engrafted on the parochial east. Not the kind of thing one finds "in the heart of Empire." But strong withal, and confident.

"It was almost the same speech I heard him make here forty-five years ago, when we were students together," said an old gentleman as we came out. "Consistent, anyway." But not quite the same speech. In the intervening years, he has discovered Canada. The discovery has obtruded itself into the speech and the creed. Mr. Bennett talks the traditional language of United Empire Toryism, but he has had to find room also for a new concept, Canada. It does not fit in too well, but it will not be dislodged. One may suspect that it may expand.

, Why, then, is he leaving us, this elder stateman? Because Tory Loyalism is still only colonialism and cannot really reconcile itself to finding its centre here. Canada is only a stopping place, and when Canadians "make good," why (after a colonial way of thinking) should they not go back to the land of heart's desire? There, in the country houses that they buy, they will at last have reached the goal to which all good imperialists look forward. Having leaped over the centuries at true pioneer speed, from poverty to prime minister, they may then leap across the Atlantic and continue the process by playing at being aristocrats.

So Mr. Bennett having done his turn of duty — and all will admit that it was a good turn, done with right, good will — is off from among us, to where life is more congenial. He advises us all to be good Canadians. Is there not a saying about deeds and words? Have perchance our French co-citizens some reason for saying that we English-speaking Canadians are not primarily Canadians at all, merely Englishmen overseas?

At any rate the Montclare is by now in Heaven.

17 | *National Policy ... Revised Version**

A recent writer has termed this country the "unwanted step-child" of England. It is both less and more than a stepchild. From one point of view it is the illegitimate offspring of a French mother by an English father: from another it is the child of a couple now divorced, England and the United States. Whoever its progenitors, none of them has ever wanted the baby. Though the father, John Bull, took it until it came to manhood, he carried out his duties with reluctance. Since even in extreme cases it is hard to extinguish filial respect, there have always been many of our citizens who deem the paternal establishment more worthy of their affections than their own family hearth. Although we are now growing up, many of our people still hold this point of view. Generally speaking, they are those who shrink from the implications of our historical development and who are motivated by much the same psychology as marks the maiden trembling on the brink of womanhood, afraid of the results of her own growth, anxious to delay the inevitable moment of maturity.

But nations, like individuals, must obey the laws of life and accept responsibility for their own fate. If they linger too long at their mother's apron strings, they find their vitality and initiative sapped. They may become not maidens in their mother's house, but sour old maids. Eventually, if they are to have vigorous health, they must win through to control of their own life.

If the community has control of its own political life, it constitutes a state: if it has control of its own economic life, it is thereby a stronger state. We in Canada have not complete control of our own economic life and in the nature of things possibly cannot hope to have. Much of our natural wealth is controlled by outsiders, chiefly Americans, and there is not much doubt but that in ordinary times of peace American interests

**Manitoba Arts Review* 3 (Spring 1943): 5-14.

established in Canada exert a considerable influence in determining policy. A large American paper company, some years ago, succeeded, it is said, in frustrating agreement on the sane limitation of paper output, but most economists regard this interior control by outsiders as a passing phase of development. It may cease as we secure accessions of capital.

There is one aspect of our national economic life which, it seems fairly safe to say, we shall never be able to control: we shall always be dependent on foreign markets, and consequently our economic ups and downs will reflect those of the outside world. For a country which produces so large a quantity of primary products as we do and which by its very physical nature can never have a dense population, this is inevitable. But there are comparatively few countries of which it is not true to some degree, and it is only the huge world states of the United States and Russia that would seem to have a chance in the future to keep a large degree of control over their own economic life.

It is when we turn to our general mode of life, what might be called our "culture," or our "civilization," that we enter the sphere in which our national achievement is weakest. Yet this is the very sphere in which we must look for our nationalism to justify itself. Certainly, mere material accomplishment cannot justify the effort and expense involved in creating this new nation.

As one observes the Canadian scene, it is sometimes hard for him to discern anything in it of a distinctive quality, and it is an old assertion that you cannot tell Canadians from Americans. The best answer to that is a period of residence in the United States. If anyone wishes a guide to the differences between the two peoples, let him sit for a while in the House of Representatives in Washington. The tumult and shouting will soon convince him that he is not in Canada. Or again, the wide open democracy of the United States requires even a president to bow to the press in a way that would make our Canadian public men shudder. The truth is our Canadian character is somewhat different from that of the American, and it seems to be growing more different. It is colder, less spontaneous, less imaginative, takes more kindly to steady routine. It throws up in considerably less profusion than does the American the vapid hedonists who constitute one of the most well-marked products of modern urban life. That may simply be because of fewer opportunities; it may also be because of the terrific load of inhibitions carried around inside himself by the average Canadian. Compared with the American, the Canadian is dour and silent. If he has any emotions, he buries them so deeply that it is hardly too much to say that no one has yet succeeded in discovering them. Having been brought up in a harder school than his neighbour, he perhaps takes more thought for the morrow. He is industrious, thrifty, and reliable but without much initiative — because without much imagination — and hence a better follower than a leader. He is not as sentimental as the American. His pulse is slow: he is slow to love and slow to hate. He is incapable of hero-worship, whereas the American is much given to it. He is infinitely more cautious and conservative than the American, timid, not bold of spirit, and hence lacking in power of decision and magnetism of personality. He is a good steady cart-horse, not a race-horse. These differences, not very flattering to ourselves, are great enough to suggest that if we have not yet got control of our own cultural life, we at least have formed something of a national type, which is a considerable step towards a national civilization.

Though appearances are all against us, it has often been noted that almost our entire popular culture — the day-to-day life of the people — is American. Rotarians, realtors, morticians, educational fads, fraternities, college yells, our courses in dress-making and sandwich-making leading to degrees all come from across the line. Of course there never has been a time when we have not been, in this sense, "Americanized." The Loyalists, after all, were Americans, and they never abandoned the ways of life they brought with them from the States. Into these ways of life later arrivals fitted and the border was always wide open.

At present the circumstances of the time are opening the door to an older set of influences, those from England. The war introduces among us once more the panoply of English aristocratic life, its military traditions and usages. It is as difficult for us to make headway against these as against popular American influences. Thus it is only in a narrow and nominal sense that we have a Canadian navy, army, and air force. In these areas our native way of life is submerged in the British. In ordinary civil society, especially in peacetime, English influence is confined to a few well-defined fields. Our system of law and government, the etiquette of the "best circles," the clothes of men who pay much attention to clothes, the amusements of the few, a select list of reading — indulged in by another "few" — and the classics of English literature come from Great Britain.

In some of the minor subjects we make curious compromises. Our table manners, for example. Older people do not keep their fork in their right hand as do the Americans, but our younger people do. None of us eat dessert (which we do not call "a sweet") off a flat plate, with fork and spoon, as do the English. We do not stand in the open air bareheaded in the presence of ladies, as do our American cousins. In fact we have distinctly less courtliness towards the ladies than have they. On the other hand, this country is not the man's paradise that England is. If American husbands are "lap-dogs" as Herr Einstein avers, English wives are still often — well, definitely not heads of the house. There is in these domestic matters, as in so many others in Canada, a tendency to be half-way between the other two countries.

It seems unreasonable to expect a distinctive way of life to emerge until all our jarring human elements are in some measure fused, until a reasonably homogeneous society has been attained. And in Canada there are more than the normal supply of discordant human elements. There are the two chief races, one of them concentrated in the Province of Quebec and cutting off the English of the Maritime provinces from those further west. There are in the western provinces great blocks of peoples of different origins, whose amalgamation will not have been completely accomplished for several generations and which when it is accomplished will have produced a new type of Canadian, neither Anglo-Saxon nor European. Within the main groups, even within the English-speaking group, there are numerous half-assimilated sub-groups.

The wonder is that with a bare majority of people of English-speaking origin and with a considerable minority of native-born of English-speaking origin, we have achieved our present degree of unity. Whether we can go on to the next stage and from political unity achieve cultural unity is a difficult question to answer. Probably we cannot. Probably the time has gone by for any large nation to achieve it. Among the old nations, France seemed to have it to a considerable degree, though she has lost it now. Great Britain never has had it, still less the "United Kingdom." In his *Autobiographies*, W. B. Yeats describes his desire for a "Unity of Being," a "Unity of Culture," and his conviction that "Nations, races, and individual men are unified by an image, or bundle of related images, symbolical of [a] state of mind" and that "a nation, as distinguished from a crowd of chance comers [was] bound together by this interchange." He concludes, nevertheless, that "the dream of my early manhood, that a modern nation can return to a Unity of Culture, is false; though it may be we can achieve it for some small circle of men and women, . . ."[1]

With French, English and fifty-seven other varieties of people in our midst, perhaps we may as well give up the dream of cultural unity. But it may not be too late to achieve two principal unities, a unity of French culture and a unity of English, or "non-French." That depends on how wisely the problem of the various immigrant groups is handled and on whether our infant society is submerged or not by a new immigration after the war.

Some will say that despite our divergences of culture, many cultural fruits have been gathered even on the Prairies, where diversity is greatest. That may be granted, though they nearly all have been of the same type — novels that deal with man's struggle against a stubborn nature, against the soil. While some of them are of genuine merit, the type of literature they represent is possible in any new country where graphic problems

---

[1]W. B. Yeats, *Autobiographies* (London: Macmillan, 1926), pp. 241, 326, 363.

present themselves. But it is essentially a pioneer literature, much of it written by pioneers from abroad, and makes its appeal to an audience which reads it in somewhat the same way as a Victorian England read stories of missionary adventure in the South Seas. Frederick Philip Grove as a literary phenomenon is comparable to Mrs. Moodie and her *Roughing it in the Bush* (though from a literary standpoint the comparison is in Grove's favour). The test of a native literature will come after pioneer days are gone.

A certain unity of society, a certain unity of culture, English-speaking Canada has of course already achieved. It will rapidly achieve more. Both in everyday matters and in what is often unfortunately called "the higher life," something that might be described as an English-Canadian way of life is recognizable. Indeed in some respects, the racial gulf has been bridged and a Canadian way of life has been achieved, one which is neither French, English (in the sense of English-speaking), British, or American. We have a national game, hockey, that is as much our own as baseball is American. One may find himself quite at home in a French-Canadian household, and with his French-Canadian friends he need not feel himself a stranger: our mentality is in many ways more alike than is English-Canadian and British (which are really very far apart) or in certain respects even English-Canadian and American. Thus a friend of the writer can say: "les élites des deux races se connaissent, se comprennent, se respectent et même s'aiment d'une amitié raisonnée mais véritable." French-Canadian particularism may give way some day, if we do not meet it with too rigorous an English-Canadian nationalism and too narrow a Protestantism.

Why emphasize this abstraction "cultural unity"? Because until a homogeneous society has been achieved, neither the individual nor the group can live a satisfactory and reasonably harmonious life. As a social animal, man's most powerful motives for action are those that spring from his relations with his fellows. He wishes their approbation and good will. The complete individualist, the pure egoist, the man entirely indifferent to what other people think of him or how they treat him, probably does not exist. Now if instead of a close-knit group, there are just various people dumped down in the same geographical area, a good many of these incentives disappear and life becomes an unhappy matter of every man for himself. "The bonds of society" are very real and keep many a man in line who otherwise would be a nasty customer. They are not only negative, however, and it seems unreasonable to expect that any work of much value can be done in too individualistic a setting. That is obvious enough in concrete things. An engineer does not build a great bridge merely for his own satisfaction: his bridge-building is definitely a social task, only made possible by a considerable measure of agreement on the part of society about ends. It is only when one comes to the immaterial, the abstract or cultural, that it does not seem quite so clear. But no author writes entirely for himself, every musician hopes to hear his music played, and every preacher likes to have a congregation.

In Canada, despite some promise of a better condition, we suffer from something very close to social anarchy. While the pressure of the war keeps minor affairs in the background and imposes a temporary unanimity over a wide area of conduct and speech, it is not difficult to see that beneath it there are few matters upon which the country as a whole finds itself in agreement and there are only relatively few public matters that do not provoke dissension. The mail received by the Canadian Broadcasting Corporation would probably bear interesting testimony to the prevalence of anarchy even in relatively minor matters: probably not a speech, not a concert, not a comedian is broadcast but there is someone to take violent exception, and as often as not because he represents a group of some sort or other that objects in principle to the kind of thing that has been broadcast. There are, naturally, parallel disagreements everywhere, but in older countries greater agreement about the fundamentals of civilized life has usually been arrived at than has been here.

Still, notwithstanding the above, remarkable progress towards unity of civilization has been made, especially within the last generation. Not so very many years ago a great church used to set itself steadfastly against the theatre in an effort, more or less conscious, to keep its people within a community of their own. That attitude has gone — though one might say, cynically, so has the theatre. Before the last war English-speaking Canada was habitually torn between "wets" and "drys": we have come closer to good sense on that question. A short quarter of a century ago, nationwide organizations were few: there were the churches, the railroads, a few large companies, the banks, the political parties. Periodicals, such as there were, circulated narrowly, newspapers were invariably for their local districts. Today, one picks up a copy of the *Dalhousie Review,* published in Halifax, and notices in it a long poem by a resident of Nanaimo.

Our universities have done a good deal, not only in actual instruction, but through the common interests of the instructors. For example, practically all the instructors in history in the universities and colleges of this country are personally acquainted with each other. Their association meets every year: there they exchange their views: their periodical keeps them in touch with each other's work. They form a little national community of penetrating influence, whose interests are anything but sectional. There are many other such bodies. More generally, and of more significance, young men and women everywhere — and some older ones too — as the writer can testify from personal observation in many parts of the country, are coming to regard themselves as *Canadians,* without qualifications. As a result, wherever one goes, he feels he is among his own people. The Canadian, that is, is already a recognizable species of human. Canada, unlike the United States, where men are lost in the crowd, has some of the advantages of a small population. Her nucleus of educated men, of leaders, is comparatively compact.

But in what other country are there more obstacles to a genuinely indigenous way of life? We are open to foreign influences from every side. In a world so crowded and so astonishingly creative as ours, it becomes harder and harder for new plants to reach up to the sunlight. If one attempts to write here in Canada, he may be sure that some Englishman or American has already said much the same thing and published it to a wider circulation than anything printed in Canada can have. If he writes with special reference to the Canadian scene, he limits himself to a narrow audience. So in most other lines of productive endeavour, men find themselves crowded away from their own firesides by strangers.

It seems impossible to suggest a way out, except the persistent cultivation of our own garden. But here again, there must be overcome within the country itself, the dead and discouraging weight of colonialism. If our people take for granted that the really good things, whether books, boots, or battleships, must come from abroad, we are never going to have much that is worth-while inside the country.

Most people would admit that it is desirable to end this distrust of ourselves, this unwillingness to face the implications of our own development, this seeing life through other people's eyes, but would be puzzled if asked to name the means. The analysis here made may suggest them. Our salvation lies in the direction of self-reliance.

Self-reliance in politics means independence. It does not mean the termination of cordial relations with the other countries of the Commonwealth. It does not mean refusal to co-operate with them. But it does mean the making of our own decisions. It means that we must arrive at some rational conception of our national interest, one on which there is reasonable measure of agreement. We can never be either self-reliant or independent as long as we are torn between so many conflicting opinions and sentiments as we are at present. Self-reliance in detail means the invention of a device for amending our own constitution, the abolition of appeals to the Privy Council, a flag of our own, national fighting services of our own. Self-reliance means making our own foreign policy and being prepared to look after ourselves in times of trouble like the present. Surely this struggle and our demonstrated military capacity should end forever the miserable old sentiment so often heard about our need for other people's protection. The plain fact of the matter is that we do not so much receive protection as give it.

Self-reliance means ending our dependence on the United States for all the manifestations of the ordinary life of the people, for our popular folk-culture. It means our own popular heroes and heroines. We need our own Charlie MacCarthys! We need not only our popular hockey players, but our own dance music, our movie stars and our radio comedians — all points for the popular imagination to focus on.

Self-reliance means ending our dependence on the United States for the absorption of the surplus of our young intellectuals. Let us find — or make, if necessary — places at home for our highly trained and highly gifted young men. Let that trek to the professions and the universities of the south, to its stage and to its pulpits, so marked in Canadian history, now temporarily ended by the war, never be resumed.

Self-reliance in culture would involve revamping our education: it would have to become more consciously national — or "communal," if you don't like "national." Many good people will be shocked at this suggestion but it does not mean that we must preach hatred to others just because we set out to know ourselves. It is not that the flag would have to be waved more vigorously, for that is a shallow kind of nationalism, but rather that the present educational philosophy — if there is one — would have to be revised out of recognition. At present it is individualistic and materialistic, or if not, it is of the opposite extreme, resting on an idealism so vague and broad as to be sentimental and meaningless. At present most children are sent to school to improve their chances of "getting on," and those who go beyond the elementary school, do so, as a rule, in order that they may get the better jobs. A few in the upper reaches decide to devote themselves to "service," whatever that may be. "Service" should mean very directly the service of the state and of the community, that is, of the nation. It should mean not merely humanitarianism, which in itself is not enough, but good town councillors, good members of committees trying to do necessary and tiresome civic tasks. This ideal of education, perhaps being forced on us by the exigencies of the war, would make it a privilege and a responsibility, not merely an agency for individual advancement.

Self-reliance in culture would mean a revaluation of the whole English literary heritage. Our debt to that heritage is great, but we must not allow ourselves to be overwhelmed by that debt. The English literary and historical heritage we shall always use and appreciate, but let us learn to look at it objectively. A great deal of life can be seen through the eyes of a Wordsworth, a Bernard Shaw, or for that matter those of a John Galsworthy. But the life we see through John Galsworthy's eyes, interesting as it is, is not our life. He wrote primarily as an Englishman for Englishmen, not for Canadians. Thus we cannot see the whole of life through the eyes of the English giants: we cannot, indeed, see Canadian life at all, any more than we can see Canada in great European painting. There is a field in which we have got our eyes open, painting, but not, except in a minor way, in literature. Self-reliance, then, in the field of the written word, implies a frank recognition that English literature is no longer our own literature but one following a different course and inspired by different traditions, one to be looked at with somewhat alien eyes.

What advantages are to be derived from such a programme, one that may seem drastic? In the first place, whether we like it or not, we are following such a programme, for it is impossible to stem the currents that were set going when this Dominion was established, and hence, as it gradually realizes itself, it necessarily departs from or remolds the traditions under which it was born.

Possibly just now we are at a crucial stage in the process. Heretofore we have been strongly conscious of certain English traditions — and they have served well — but the generation coming up knows little of them and cannot make use of them. It must get a set of traditions of its own; that is, it must work out a way of life for itself. Take the important field of civil liberty. Up to the present we Canadians have not felt that there was any distinction between "British" liberty and the kind that we enjoyed. "The rights of Englishmen" followed us here, and they have in considerable measure been maintained. But who can find among our people today much vital knowledge of or interest in the "rights of Englishmen" or indeed in the abstraction "freedom"? How many protest when freedom of the press is curtailed and the traditional law in respect to trial before imprisonment is superseded? A few individuals may object, but there is no mass movement of protest, no universal roar of indignation. This battle has to be fought out all over again on Canadian soil and a new concept of liberty worked out, one based on local circumstances. Our old traditions help in that battle but they cannot function as substitutes for the new, and those who have been fighting on that front know how little result is achieved by urging them as specific precedents.

In the second place, justification for a programme of independence and self-reliance is to be found in the intangible advantages to personality. It is as necessary to health for a people to integrate their personality as it is for an individual. Sometimes the individual sensitive to such things feels drowned in the immensity and depth of the general cultural heritage of the world: at those times, he sighs for a little island where he can cultivate and understand his own garden. Understanding it, he can then begin to look at other people's and will appreciate them all the more because he does understand his own. But he will not be in the position of a man without a garden admitted into that of his rich neighbour, to admire and then depart.

Political independence we have, but a certain degree of cultural in-breeding would hasten the completion of the task begun in 1867, the creation of a new nation. It would hasten the making of a people with institutions and traditions of their own, a people who would not be merely imitative but by being true to themselves might be productive of good to others. Political independence combined with some degree of cultural independence would give us perhaps that psychological independence that at present we Canadians so signally lack. The combination might result in a people who, if it had lost a certain part of the whole world, would have gained its own soul and that, on unimpeachable authority, is a commendable end.

18 | *What This Country Needs Is Ten New Provinces**

Every time one picks up a paper, he sees something to remind him of the perpetual feud between Ottawa and the provincial capitals. Some provincial premier is always shaking his fist at the prime minister. Premier Duplessis of Quebec has lately won a sweeping electoral victory with frantic shouts of defiance at the big, bad wolf of Ottawa. Premier Macdonald came right out in the Liberal convention and told Mr. King that he had better not try to gobble up Nova Scotia. And Premier Drew's heroism in shielding Ontario from the villains at the national capital is well known.

Outsiders, witnessing one of these displays of provincial defiance, might think that the country was falling apart. They would be wrong. What they see is simply a phase of normal family life. There never was a family where the children did not occasionally attribute the blackest and cruelest of motives to the parents. So with provincial governments.

The wonder is not that there is bickering and plenty of it, but that great sprawling continental states such as ours (or the United States, or Australia) hang together at all. The only possible device that could keep together free peoples, scattered over immense areas, is federalism. Even Russia has found it expedient to go in for what it terms federalism. Apparently, however rigid the dictatorship there, it cannot run things in detail all the way through from Moscow to Vladivostok.

In all such countries the story is much the same: jealousy and distrust of the central government, ostentatious ignorance on the part of the older or wealthier toward the newer or poorer. Even in Britain, a composite state, Scotsmen in the pages of *Punch* invariably are humorous figures uttering queer expressions like "Och" or "Aye." In the United States, good New Englanders affect to know nothing of what lies west of the Hudson River.

**Maclean's*, 15 October 1948, pp. 7, 77-79.

For all our localism, we Canadians have never dissolved in civil war as did the United States. Yet most of us recognize that our federation works far from perfectly. Perhaps the most popular panacea among us is the one that goes something like this:

"The trouble with this country is that it has too much government. We have 9 provincial parliaments with several hundred members — there'll be 10 when Newfoundland comes in plus a federal Parliament with 255. There are also separate systems of courts for each province. We would get cheaper government if some of the provinces were combined, so that we could cut down on the salary list of members and cabinet ministers."

Sometimes the proposal is to revive the old project for uniting the three Maritime provinces, sometimes it is suggested that the three prairie provinces be combined. The idea of fewer provinces, I contend, is not only impracticable but dangerous. It would be better for this country if we had not fewer and larger provinces, but more and smaller.

The original conception on which Canada was founded was that there should be a central government for common affairs and local governments for ordinary matters. Money and the post office naturally fell to Ottawa; private property and relationships between landlord and tenant as naturally fell to the provinces. But other ideas came in to distort the picture.

Into the British North America Act there had crept the provision that every province should have the control of its natural resources. Here was an avenue by which provincial governments were to be carried far beyond their indicated functions. Today, thanks mainly to the generosity of successive administrations at Ottawa and the pugnacity of various provincial premiers, all the provinces, with the exception of the Maritimes, are territorial giants. All consist of small settled regions to the south, with great, unrelated tracts of wilderness to the north. Provincial governments administer these distant territories much as the government of an empire administers distant colonies.

In thus apportioning the soil of Canada, the federal government could say, "Well, the Americans do the same thing: they have divided all their territory into states, until now the national government has virtually no territory to administer directly." The American example, I submit, was misleading. Most of the United States is, to a greater or lesser degree, arable. When a new state was set up, it was eventually settled more or less continuously. But in Canada, there was never any expectation that the stretches of the north would be settled, nor will they ever be, except in favourable patches here and there. They will always be administrative areas pure and simple. This is an essential difference between Canada and the United States, and from it arises the essential difference between an American state and a Canadian province. The American state with one conspicuous exception, Texas, is a relatively small and homogeneous local area, whereas six Canadian provinces out of the nine are great imperial domains.

The orthodox defence for this extension of provincial boundaries is that it is in line with the idea of provincial rights. But does it have anything to do with provincial rights? When, in the early years of this century, people rushed out onto the western plains, local government had to be provided for them. It was wise, prudent, and just in 1905 to erect the two new provinces of Alberta and Saskatchewan. These provinces, in providing law, order, and local services for their inhabitants, exemplified the intrinsic meaning of "provincial rights." But what had the extension of their boundaries to 60 degrees north, far into the wastes of the Pre-Cambrian Shield, to do with "provincial rights"?

What we have done in Canada, by our system of large provinces, is to have reduced the original idea of Confederation to a kind of League of Nations. At Washington, where forty-eight states are dealt with, even the greatest of the states counts for little in itself. New York, with a population about as large as all Canada's, has only some 12 per cent of the total population. Compare Ontario's with its 33 per cent. In the U.S. the federal government has never feared a state. What it has feared has been the section, by which Americans mean vast regions like the South. But in 1940, when a hostile resolution was directed against him from the legislature of a great province — Ontario — Mr. King thought it prudent to dissolve and secure the people's re-confirmation of his mandate.

In Canada, the original aim, as expressed in the British North America Act, was for a strong central government and for local governments with limited local powers. But the Canadian people were not ready for any great degree of cohesion, and the Privy Council obligingly co-operated in weakening the federal government; the provinces retained their wilderness lands — in the United States these had been surrendered to the national government by the North-West Ordinance of 1785 — and so we took the path of decentralization. Today this has gone so far that we cannot get important things done unless we assemble a conference of Dominion and provinces, which meets with the stage-setting of an international conclave (and like such bodies, frequently breaks up in disagreement). That is, in addition to nine provincial governments and one federal, ten in all, we are gradually evolving an eleventh — a super-government based on this combined get-together and a super-government, not of elected representatives, but of premiers and officials.

And yet the proposals for fewer provinces "to save expense" keep coming up. Suppose we could save the cost of three or four legislatures and of some scores of legislators, what would that amount to? No more than a few millions a year at most, for cutting down the number of M.P.P.'s would not reduce other expenditure, such as that on schools and roads.

And can anyone contend that a great province would be more economical than a small? The exact reverse appears to be true. Government in a small province like Nova Scotia is parsimony itself compared with the prodigality of Ontario or British Columbia. What is more, in a relatively small community a man can feel close to his government and can in some measure keep tab on it. It is to be suspected that the most expensive and the least efficient governments in Canada are those of the larger provinces.

So much for expense; next for the way of achieving fewer provinces. If the proposal is to amalgamate the three Maritime provinces, just ask any Maritimer one question. "Where will the capital be?" If any agreement can be secured on this, then the next step in union may be proceeded with. As to the proposal to amalgamate the three prairie provinces, which still comes up occasionally, consider the vast area to be administered. It is 1,000 miles from Winnipeg to the Rockies, the largest stretch of continuously settled country in all Canada. If it is unwise to centralize affairs too rigidly at Ottawa — which few would deny — it is equally unwise to centralize them too rigidly at the capital of a vast province.

Not long ago, the school board of Orillia, so the press report ran, virtually threw in its hand. It was impossible, the statement went, for a local community, through its school board, any longer to have much control of its schools; it was bound hand and foot by the provincial department of education. Instances of the same kind of bureaucracy could be multiplied. The provincial governments themselves are guilty of too much centralization. Through centralization they are slowly destroying municipal institutions, the very springs of democracy.

If Canada were reduced to a few great provinces, what we would have would be the incorporation in legal form of "the sections," those great divisions of our country which each in themselves have a certain species of unity: the Appalachian Atlantic, the French St. Lawrence, the Lakes, the Prairies, the Pacific Coast. If this were done, the end would not be far to seek: each section would begin to take on "national" characteristics and would build up understandings ("alliances") with other sections against its neighbours. The end would be disintegration.

If instead of nine provinces we had nineteen or twenty, each would be reduced in importance. Each would speak with less weight at Ottawa. The situation would approximate to that in the United States. There would be no more of the undignified brawling between the premier of Ontario and the prime minister, because the premier would be cut down in stature and would no longer be a rival.

I can hear the shrieks of indignation with which such a proposal will be greeted. I once happened to propound some such scheme to a French-speaking senator. "How about dividing Quebec into North Quebec and South Quebec," I said, "with the St. Lawrence as the dividing line?" He was plainly shocked. "That would be murder!" the senator replied.

Now in the case of Quebec, division might possibly be a kind of murder, for many French-speaking Canadians regard "Quebec" as being synonymous with the French race. The notion is not valid, since there are three-quarters of a million people of French descent outside the province and 630,000 of non-French within it. Still, it cannot be denied that Quebec presents a special case, for it is the organized expression of our country's second culture, and our two cultures provide us with our major domestic complexity.

Now, since I am a friend of the French-speaking people of Canada, rather than of the Province of Quebec, I have no hesitation in adding to the gravity of my crime by suggesting that we might consider the division of Quebec not into two provinces, but three or four. The island of Montreal and the neighbouring islands at the confluence of the Ottawa River, plus the "bite" that Quebec makes into Ontario at that spot and the City of Montreal's immediate northern hinterland, might in themselves make a suitable province. This province could be called Montreal. The great northern farm and mining lands east from the Ontario boundary would make another, which we could provisionally dub Abitibi. Quebec north of the St. Lawrence River could become what extreme French nationalists sometimes seem to desire — a little province called Laurentia. Quebec south of the river would appropriately be called Richelieu.

How about the other provinces?

It all depends on one's conception of a province. If a province is a community with a life and will of its own, its people bound together by strong ties of blood and history, then division might possibly be likened to murder. But then a province becomes virtually a nation. If a province is primarily a convenient administrative area, division may be merely a judicious re-arrangement in the interests of the country as a whole.

In practice, of course, provinces are a little of both. Quebec and Nova Scotia lean heavily in the direction of the integrated community, and that is why both are invariably more or less restive in Confederation. Alberta, under its Social Credit government, has been given a push in the same direction. Prince Edward Island is a community. New Brunswick's loyalties seem to go out to the Maritimes as a section, in distinction to New Brunswick as a province. In the West, the Rocky Mountains tend to make British Columbia a world apart, but on the Prairies, the overriding conception is again sectional rather than provincial — "the West," as contrasted with "the East." Ontario is a case in itself and demands separate consideration.

"Well, if not murder, division would at least so weaken the provinces that they would be an easy prey to Ottawa and would lose all their provincial rights," I can hear provincialists saying. "For example, they might lose the right to supervise insurance companies" A job like looking after insurance companies, which usually operate in many provinces (and there are many such jobs) could be done better at Ottawa. Rights such as supervising insurance often represent little more than the importance, position, and desire for power of a group of officials. When it comes to fear for "provincial rights" one has only to ask which government has been the protector of the weaker provinces. Neither Ontario nor Quebec has been willing to forego many privileges in their favour.

In Canada as it is today, only the three Maritime provinces are small enough in area and population to make Confederation work comfortably. While there is much wilderness land in two of them, they all form more or less compact and homogeneous communities, Nova Scotia and "The Island" especially so.

There is also a good deal to be said for the three prairie provinces, especially Manitoba. Manitobans, as contrasted with Nova Scotians, have no intense provincial loyalty; they are generalized Canadians. In Winnipeg one looks both ways, east and west; he sees Montreal in one direction and Vancouver in the other. Yet all three prairie provinces are probably inconveniently large, and their wilderness lands, while well administered, provide no financial support for them. It might have been wiser, when the old Northwest Territories were being divided up into provinces, to have set up four rather than three. The new province perhaps could be called Athabaska, extending from Edmonton northwest into the Peace River country.

One of the most awkward areas in Canada is British Columbia. Here are over 350,000 square miles of mountain, forest, valley, sea-coast, with great islands on one side and, jabbed into Alberta on the other, a stretch of the plains. Is there any logic about all this? Is "British Columbia" anything but a space upon the map? Half its population lives within a few miles of Granville Street, Vancouver. The other half lives in the dozens of distant interior valleys, over on "the Island," up and down the coast. Whatever unity the province possesses, and here as elsewhere a provincial type has arisen, has been conferred by the sea and by the railways built by the Canadian people. A strong theoretical case could be made out for carving B.C. into three provinces. We could start with the Columbia River watershed on the east — the triangle in the south-east corner of the present province — and call this Okanagan. On the west, "the Island" would make a neat province by itself. A more compact, although still large, British Columbia would remain, sacrificing a northern slice to the new province of Athabaska.

Finally among our provinces, there is the crowning anomaly of Ontario, a province stretching 1,000 miles north and south, 1,400 east and west, and with 33 per cent of the country's total population. If that 33 per cent were more or less evenly distributed, Ontario would just be another large, rangy unit. But Ontario follows within itself the same "pocket" arrangement of people (and therefore of political importance) as the country as a whole.

Southern Ontario (the peninsula between Lakes Huron and Ontario) crams nearly 3,000,000 people into 23,000 square miles — a population density of 125 to the square mile. "New" Ontario (the area north of Lake Nipissing) has barely 1.3 inhabitants for each of its 310,000 square miles. Between these extremes, there are roughly fifty persons to the square mile in the Ottawa and St. Lawrence valleys and seven to the square mile in the other districts of "old" Ontario.

Within the peninsula of "old" Ontario, there is an inner ring, centring on the western end of Lake Ontario. Here seven contiguous counties have a population of a million and a half, or nearly 40 per cent of that of the entire province. Here lies the great metropolitan tract of Toronto-Hamilton.

Ontario, it may be said, is not unique in these respects. Huge area and "pockets" of population are equally characteristic of Quebec. But Ontario affords a marked contrast to Quebec. Quebec, as cradle of the French race in America, stands for an idea — the maintenance and expansion of the French race. Quebec, right through to Hudson Strait, is the "patrimony" of its children.

Not so Ontario. The average resident of Ontario has no consciousness whatsoever of being an "Ontarian." The Ottawa Valley hardly knows that south-western Ontario exists. Living in western Ontario — not Western Ontario, around London, which is not west at all, but west from Lake Superior — one thinks of "the East" just as the Manitobans do, and all his connections are with the Prairies.

The other day, a young woman from New Liskeard exclaimed: "The people down here seem entirely different from us; we don't seem to have much in common with these people down in the south. We're more like westerners." The young lady certainly had no "Ontario" feeling about her.

All across the north, from Lake Timiskaming to the Lake of the Woods, "Toronto" and "the government" seem shadowy. Many local inhabitants would say that the chief function of the government was to hand out the natural resources of the region to its favourites, as distant imperial powers so often have done.

In the older areas of Ontario, as I know them, affection never centres on the province but on the "old home town," or in rare cases, on the county. It's hardly too much to say that, except as a legal and constitutional entity, Ontario does not exist. The province is an administrative machine without a soul, and whoever captures this great, throbbing machine is able to wield enormous power. Inevitably, every premier feels he has to make out a good case for himself; so whatever his party, he shakes his powerful fist at Ottawa.

The place of Ontario within Canada bears certain resemblances to the place of the old kingdom of Prussia within the German Empire. Prussia contained something like half of the population of the whole empire and some such percentage of its area. Yet Prussia was a composite — a collection of bits and pieces composed of many little territories around the original nucleus of Brandenburg. It had been the driving power of this hard, northern people, headed by their "junker" aristocrats which had made the empire.

It was Ontario's driving power which forced the creation of the Dominion, compelling the sister province, Quebec, to come along. Quebec is Canada's Bavaria. Bavaria was the only one of the old German kingdoms that was strong enough to stand alone. Ontario represents the hard, dynamic, Protestant, Prussian north; Quebec, the easy-going, temperamental, Bavarian, Catholic south. Ontario, like Prussia, contains an inordinate proportion of the people and resources of the whole country. And in Ontario, politics has lately tended to become something of a mere struggle for power, with the strategically placed running the show, sometimes from behind the scenes. As long as the old Prussia existed, the German Empire's inner unity was precarious.

It may be lucky for Canada that Ontario does not have an intensive corporate character. If it were as conscious of itself as Nova Scotia, it would probably destroy the Dominion. As it is, the average Ontarian just assumes that he is a Canadian — people from other provinces may or may not be — and lets it go at that.

All this amounts to saying that modern Ontario is too big, too complex. Its government has to handle all sorts of matters that are not provincial in character. It runs a railway, immigration schemes, has semi-diplomatic relations with neighbouring states. Should it be broken up?

Ontario would make four or five nice-sized provinces, none of them so powerful as to excite the jealousy of the rest of the country. I would suggest the following tentative divisions, which correspond roughly with the natural divisions as I have given them above:

The Province of St. Lawrence: to consist in the triangle lying between the Ottawa and St. Lawrence rivers, with a western boundary approximately following the height of land between the Ottawa River and Lake Huron. It would run from about Mattawa on the Ottawa River through Madawaska, which lies just south of Algonquin Park, and then southward along highway 62 to Madoc and Belleville.

Hurontario: the heart of the present Province of Ontario. This province would adjoin St. Lawrence and would rest on the Georgian Bay, Lake Ontario, the Niagara River and Lake Erie, as far as the Grand River. The dividing line between it and the south-western peninsula would be the Grand River and thence northward on a line through Arthur, to Owen Sound. How natural this unit is can be shown easily — just look in the Toronto papers and see the maps they publish of their distribution by truck and carrier. Where the Toronto paper goes as the predominant newspaper reading of the community, there lies the edge of the Toronto metropolitan area.

Huron-Erie: the south-western peninsula, from the line indicated to Lakes Erie and Huron. My name is not a good one, but I am not wedded to it. London is the natural centre of this region. Anyone taking the short train trip from Toronto to London, if he is sensitive to such things, can feel that he has crossed some kind of boundary. The south-western peninsula has a genuine life of its own, which has been put into a most interesting book — Fred Landon's, *Western Ontario and the American Frontier.*[1]

Timiskaming: The region north of North Bay to Cochrane, thence westward to Hearst and south to Sault Ste. Marie. Here is a vast and rapidly growing area, with a life of its own, distinct in flavour and atmosphere, whose people are quite conscious of their own identity. Timiskaming would meet St. Lawrence and Hurontario at the confluence of the Ottawa and Mattawa rivers. Here, from the high lookout at the edge of highway 17, overlooking the historic route of Champlain and the fur traders, Canadians of the future could stand and see four provinces, Hurontario, St. Lawrence, Timiskaming, and North Quebec.

Superior: This is the most difficult to designate as it almost comes down to saying "all the rest." But communities such as Geraldton and Beardmore, both near Lake Nipigon, are tied in with the two cities at the head of the lakes, Port Arthur and Fort William, and these in turn with the Dryden-Kenora area. This province would not have a large population, but neither would it be controlled by a government in a distant metropolitan city. The vast stretches of its hinterland should probably go back where they belong — to the administration of Ottawa.

This scheme of partition is merely roughed out here: innumerable modifications would be necessary in detail.

The real point is: would the inhabitants of Ontario worry very much if the present province were so divided? Would there be any cries of murder? Except for the persons at Queen's Park, both in the ministry and the civil service, and those others whose interests are best served by a quiet and unknown hinterland, the average resident, especially if he lived more than a hundred miles from Toronto, might not be greatly concerned.

Readjustment would give us nineteen or twenty provinces, (after Newfoundland comes in) instead of ten. No one of them would have more than 15 per cent of the total population: no one would be identified in the same close way with a cultural minority. That minority, instead of seeking to barricade itself behind the ramparts of a provincial government, would fight out its cause in the general arena of the nation — more success-

[1]Fred Landon, *Western Ontario and the American Frontier* (Toronto: Ryerson, 1941).

fully, I think, for we are coming to realize that the term *Canadian* is for us wider than either the term *English* or the term *French*.

Things as they are make it unlikely that this multiplication of provinces will take place, but the essence of my suggestion is, nevertheless, valid. New Canada will never become a nation in the most intense and fruitful sense of that word until the provinces revert to what national subdivisions naturally should be — local authorities guarding local rights. Then we shall have some chance of realizing the idea dear to an increasing number within our land — the spiritual unity of our whole country.

19 | *If We Joined the U.S.A.* *

Every few years old Satan comes around to us Canadians, displaying the glittering rewards he has for a little easy submission: these invariably wear such labels as "Commercial Union," "Unrestricted Reciprocity," or, simply, "Reciprocity." He has been back again recently and this time his package is marked "Customs Union."

We used to assume that Satan was merely baiting a trap for us; if we fell into it, the unpitying hunter, Uncle Sam, would come along and take our hide. Canada would be annexed and would disappear. As a result, we got used to throwing Satan out, along with his glittering packages. We did this in two famous general elections, 1891 and 1911, and on various minor occasions. But it is usually forgotten that for 12 years, from 1854 to 1866, there actually was *reciprocity.* While the customs houses were not closed up, a wide measure of free trade existed between the two countries and Canada prospered as never before and seldom since. Maybe the bait which Satan sets deserves examination. Maybe he is not Satan at all, but Santa Claus.

Whatever the temptation, we have always retained our freedom in tariff matters. Now, however, the dollar crisis, added to external disturbances, is once more turning the thoughts of some Canadians toward a customs union, and many Americans, including some influential politicians and publishers, also favour the idea.

Today we may acquit Uncle Sam of being a hunter. Still, closer associations with the best of neighbours, when changes in legal relationship are involved, are not to be entered upon lightly and must be examined carefully.

* *Maclean's,* 15 June 1948, pp 7-8, 71-74.

A customs union is a peculiarly intimate form of relationship, and we must know what it would really mean and how it would actually affect our economy and society.

"Trade naturally flows north and south"; this phrase is repeated millions of times a year in this country. Like many other clichés, it is accepted without much examination. Does trade naturally flow north and south? It does not: I implore my fellow Canadians to cease repeating shibboleths and begin looking at facts. The facts are simple and physical: the St. Lawrence River and the Great Lakes. These are the arteries of trade. Our grain would go out by the Great Lakes if there were not a single railroad north of the Lakes.

Trade "naturally" flows over the border, too. Trade flows in every direction. Most "naturally" of all — in any area capable of producing surpluses — it flows from the interior of the continent to its edges, down the natural and man-made highways to the great ports. For us, a customs union would alter this "flow" in detail, but would not terminate it.

"If there were no tariffs, our industries would all be drawn south of the line." Gallons of ink have been spent in arguing this point, so it is impossible to do much more here than notice it. It was American holders of timber limits in Canada who fought for the 1935 reciprocity agreement; Canadian lumbermen were indifferent. It was a fight between two sets of Americans, one having timber limits on one side of the line, one on the other. The reciprocity agreement enabled the American owners to slaughter the Canadian forests in happy abandon, reaping quick profits from their sales in the American market. American tariffs against Canadian raw materials have constituted measures of conservation, holding up the exhaustion of our supplies.

Of course, the great consuming centres of the United States will get much of our wealth anyway. Cornell University is said to have been built out of the pine forests of Simcoe County. There are American colleges today which are similar happy recipients (through donors) of funds derived from Canadian raw materials — a wealth that passes right by equally deserving but much poorer Canadian institutions. The position would not be altered by a customs union, except in that it is just conceivable that the spirit of public generosity so marked among wealthy Americans might prove catching! This, however, it is not safe to count upon.

The reciprocity proposals of 1911 were defeated because Canadian manufacturers feared for their own survival. It is on manufactures, rather than raw materials, that the debate really centres. Under a customs union, how much of our industry would disappear? That is the crux of the question. And it cannot be answered. Undoubtedly the readjustment would be great. Many American branch plants might close (a proud people might see these as symbols of alien domination, anyway, though we do not). But the present trend toward decentralization of industry, based on electric power and cheap transportation, might compensate for any that were closed. Canada has passed the infant stage in industrialization. Many native Canadian firms might expand into the United States without losing their Canadian identity, as they usually do at present when they follow this course. The western farmer and many other farmers would get supplies much more cheaply than now. With the several hundred dollars saved on a car, for example, the farmer, and other car owners, would buy more services: there would be advances in medical care, in education, in merchandising facilities, and so on.

One other matter of importance: under a customs union, the United States would find it difficult to discriminate against us when the pressure goes on oil, coal, freight cars, and other such articles for which we partly depend on American sources of supply.

The pros and cons are endless but, everything considered, Canada, I imagine, would gain materially from a continental economy.

But we have never made our decisions on such a basis. We have always looked to the more indirect results, the political, constitutional, legal results: remarkably enough, even to the cultural results.

The first political consequence, so it is always said, would be that our tariffs would be made in Washington. I don't see how this could be escaped: directly or indirectly, they would be. Perhaps representations made by Ottawa might be listened to; more probably, they would be overborne by powerful American "pressure groups." It is just possible that the bargain struck would include some kind of tariff board, under which we could retain some type of veto right. Or it might prove possible for us to go on making our own tariff arrangements with countries outside the Canada-U.S. union, providing goods imported from abroad were segregated and not allowed to cross the present American boundary. The exact devices would be for the experts to work out. Persistence might save us some tariff autonomy.

Exchange and finance would almost necessarily follow goods and go on to a continental basis. Would this involve a currency union? At present, an American presented with a Canadian coin drops it as it it were a hornet. A currency union would at least avoid this — because there would no longer be Canadian coins. Would we miss them? I have yet to meet the Canadian who has any great objection to taking American money.

Our banks would certainly have to readjust themselves to a different atmosphere: this would be highly painful. It might involve ending internal exchange charges — there are none in the United States. On the whole, Canadian banks should not be much afraid, for Canadians seem made for this sad business of finance in its secondary rungs (not its more daring) and, moreover, our banking structure at the moment, it would seem to an avowed amateur, possesses no great degree of independence. However, it did get us through the storms of 1933 without the horrors which came to Americans. So, here again, we come to a balance.

The real difficulty, of course, in the whole situation, even allowing due weight to the profits which reside in the tariff and the employment it is supposed to give, is the fear that commercial union would lead to political union. Disguise it as we may, it is the old bogey of annexation with which we are dealing.

The twelve years' experience from 1854 to 1866 would suggest that the more prosperous Canada is the better able she is to resist tendencies toward union. Would the experience be repeated under a modern customs union?

One of the first demands that would follow a customs union would be a demand for common citizenship. A common citizenship would at least eliminate the border-crossing nuisance. But it would not eliminate questions of residence and domicile: just as people from one province today have to "qualify" in another for residential rights, such as voting, so they would still have to qualify on moving from Ontario to Ohio, or from North Dakota to Manitoba. It would take more than a common citizenship to abolish that favourite perplexity of the lawyers, domicile. A common citizenship would not be a decisive factor, one way or the other.

It is when we come to symbols of citizenship that we get into dangerous territory. Would our fighting forces put on American uniforms? A whole division did so during the closing stages of the last war without anyone objecting very much. Union or no union, what would happen if the pressure were to go on again? Common heroes? Would we have to stop naming our schools "King George" or "Winston Churchill" and begin calling them "Abraham Lincoln?" There is no reason to think we would, though we would be more respected (especially in England) if we dug up a few heroes of our own and quit borrowing those of Great Britain. Would we have to rewrite our popular historical legends and, for example, depict the war of 1812 as an American triumph? Why would we have to do anything like that? Both peoples would still be at liberty to misrepresent their history as much as they wished, just as English Canadians and French Canadians today misrepresent it. This kind of history — the kind too often taught in the schools — is not strikingly dissimilar from Jack-the-Giant-Killer stories anyway.

It is symbols like flags and national anthems that make the real trouble. Would it be fair to put it this way: that since we Canadians have none of our own, adopting the American flag and national anthem would simply involve switching over from one set of exterior symbols to another? Many would not accept this view, but it is to be feared that simply because they have never been able to acquire symbols of their own, symbols growing out of their own native soil, they might, under suitable pressure, be the first to accept still another non-native set. We must never forget that the only really big annexation movement set on foot in this country, that of 1849, was sponsored by the wealthy English-speaking group in Montreal, who a year or two previously had been vociferous in their cries of "loyalty."

Just at present there would be fierce resistance to a suggestion of a change of flag, though it cannot be sustained that Canadians dislike the American flag: it flies too freely here for that to be so. If talk of union ever comes to anything, it will be precisely because there is an unfilled vacuum between the Union Jack and the Stars and Stripes: if that space were filled with something to which all Canadians without exception could give their undivided allegiance, discussions like this would be unnecessary.

If we were to go on from a common citizenship to a common flag, we would be precious close to complete political union. The debate at this point requires relentless application of its own logic: where would we get to under political union?

Would we have a common government? Would Ottawa cease to function? Would they lock up the Parliament Buildings? Anyone who has been in Edinburgh can see what an abandoned capital looks like — a city bravely trying to keep up appearances after the reality has fled. Abandoning Ottawa would be pretty hard to take.

Could we avoid abandoning Ottawa by having some kind of government within a government? An American friend of mine, in a moment of unusual candor, once said to me: "We fought a civil war to prevent certain states arrogating special privileges to themselves." His implication was plain: "Come in, if you like, but not as a nation."

If we decided to accept such terms, tearing up the concept of Canada, and becoming states of the union, then what? Eighteen senators at Washington? Eighteen senators would speak with a far more powerful voice, one would think, than one ambassador — if they spoke with the same voice. But who could imagine eighteen senators speaking with the same voice? No, our senators at Washington would simply speak for their individual neighbourhoods, not for a dead idea, Canada.

But would we get eighteen? Would Prince Edward Island get two? That is hard to believe. Our proportionate share is more like nine. As to members of the House of Representatives, our share (1940 figures of population) would be 38, out of a total house of 473. The three Maritime provinces together would be entitled to three representatives, Quebec ten, Ontario twelve, Manitoba two and so on. Of course, before numbers were fixed, a prolonged party battle would be fought at Washington. Each party would attempt to forecast the political complexion of a particular Canadian region and to act accordingly. The Democrats might fight for an over-representation of the West, hoping that from it they would get recruits to offset the agrarian Republicans of their own West. The Republicans would certainly try to shove up the figures of representatives from the Toronto area.

It is evident that we could not take it for granted that all our provinces would become states. If it were proposed to telescope the Maritimes into one or two states, what reaction could be expected from Maritimers?

Integral political union would involve acceptance of the American constitution in its entirety, president, fixed terms, and all. Provincial rights would be rearranged, becoming broader in some respects, narrower in others. Ontario bellows loudly in Ottawa's ear; her voice would be little more than a whisper at Washington. The special and official place of the French language in Canada would disappear, though in Quebec there would be nothing to prevent its position remaining as strong as it is now. There would be no constitutional guarantees for separate schools, unless these could be made a special condition within the basic arrangement.

An important part of the American constitution is its Bill of Rights. We do not have a bill of rights in Canada guaranteeing civil liberties. While we have not too much to complain of, it may be that liberty is safer under the written American constitution of 1789 and the great tradition built up since 1776 than under our own powerful type of government. The point is debatable and the debate is endless.

Here are some other considerations, of a political or related nature, which deserve to be well pondered; it is impossible to do more than enumerate them:

1. Our representatives at Ottawa are remote enough from the average man as it is: they would be much more remote at Washington.

2. The average congressman (not senator) at Washington has little prestige: membership in the House of Representatives would actually be a "comedown" from membership in the House of Commons.

3. The American system of government would be found strange and alien by the average Canadian.

4. Canadians might fail to identify themselves satisfactorily with the American party system. How many of us could work with illiberal Southern Democrats, for example? That might expose us to the dangers of wandering around in a kind of party no man's land, our weight not great enough to tell very much in any direction.

5. From our point of view, we would find the American party system inflexible. That has some real disadvantages, especially in these troubled times. For example, it has not proved possible to set up in the United States a reformist third party. The result has been that the Communists have crowded into this gap and have put up another false front around Henry Wallace, which may go far. The Canadian system allowed of the emergence of a reformist, or social, democratic party, the CCF, in response

to the plainly discerned tendencies of the age, and this party takes the shock: it acts as a lightning conductor, as witness the Communists' elephantine efforts to make use of it.

6. No feeling is more common among Canadians who attend American conventions than the oppressiveness of mere size: in these huge gatherings one feels lost in the crowd. Politically, union might well mean that we Canadians would be "lost in the crowd," recognizing few whom we knew, filled with a feeling of helplessness because of the mere size of the show. Canada is at least a manageable political unit, large as it is, and it is still possible for Canadians in similar lines of endeavour to know all their fellows, from coast to coast. In the United States, when they put in sugar rationing, it took an army of 27,000 people to run it. We avoid some of the evils of being a giant.

7. Washington is normally a bedlam. A strong expression? Well, just go to Washington. Go to the House of Representatives. The average Canadian will wonder how any country can exist, let alone be well governed, with such an atmosphere prevalent. There is another side to the story, of course, and things do get done and often well done. But anarchy is always rife. Take this uneasy period we at present face, with all the bolts and tumblers in the American combination lock out of alignment and working efficiency to be restored only by the general election of next November, no matter what happens in the interval. The normal atmosphere of Washington approximates that of bedlam.

8. Could our provinces retain their judicial system? We appoint judges, the Americans elect. We usually consider our system the better. However, the quip an American made should be noted: "In the United States," he said, "we at least appoint the successful candidate as judge: in Canada, I gather, it is the defeated candidate whom you appoint."

9. While certain incidents suggest that American "third degree" methods are not unheard-of among our police, there is little reason to believe that they are customary. With union, would the American police system "slop over" into Canada, together with their system of law enforcement generally? Such things would be pretty hard to keep out. Would bribing minor officials, corrupting the courts, and so on become common here? This is a well-worn topic and it seems to me to present too much of a temptation for us to fall into our old attitude of complacent superiority to make it wise to put much emphasis upon it, unless it be fully discussed and investigated, which it cannot be here.

10. Could we avoid the American legal system, with its technicalities and its endless delays? Our provinces would keep their own laws, and the spirit of their administration would continue. But what of the criminal law, now common to all Canada; under union, would each province write its own, adding to the confusion already existing in a country where theo-

retically there may be forty-nine different kinds of murder?

Political union would not be all disadvantage. There would be some tangible advantages: these also must be enumerated:

1. Members of Congress are not bound by party considerations to stick to their party line through thick and thin: there is probably a good deal more plain speech and genuine expression of opinion at Washington than there is at Ottawa.

2. We would be citizens of a great power. How much would Austrians or Czechs give for the possibility of such a membership? As citizens of a great power, with the world's destiny depending on us, we would acquire a greater sense of responsibility in international affairs than we now possess. If Americans in foreign affairs are adolescents, Canadians are no more than boys of nine. Membership in the Commonwealth does not give us responsibility or the privilege of decision, for there, too, decision rests on a great power and we avoid interfering — just as we do, also, at present, with the United States.

3. We would become members of a country which is more of a "grass-roots" democracy than our own. In the United States, power grows out of the people's will to a degree hardly credible to the average Canadian. Anyone who knows the American scene well can supply evidence of this.

4. Our fighting forces would, by and large, be in a more familiar medium than heretofore, better adapted to our highly democratic society than they are at present, with the traditions of aristocracy that infuse them.

5. We might as well have the game as the name. We shall certainly incur all the results of American policy — especially of its mistakes. As J. V. McAree remarked in the *Globe and Mail* not long ago: in the case of another world war "the United States will be in it from the beginning and, of course, Canada will be too." If we are so completely tied up as all that — and there is not the slightest indication that Canadians desire anything else — then, perhaps, we ought to think about getting the benefits of American budgets, American weapons, and of unity of command.

6. Union would open big careers to Canadians. This is not an unworthy motive: it had a good deal to do with bringing about Confederation. Now, again, as before, possibly some of our big men may feel "crowded" on the mere Canadian stage. I am sure many a Canadian businessman would like to be a director of United States Steel. Many a military man would like to command something higher than a corps.

The most important — and the most elusive — factors in a country's life are not tangible, but intangible. Because they touch the roots of life, they are hardest to discuss and, whatever language is used, it will appeal to the fewest people. But the spiritual realities which stand behind them, however inadequately I voice them, will settle our national fate.

The intangible advantages of union with the United States do not directly affect the average man very much. But they are of profound importance for the sensitive and the creative spirit, on whom the inadequacies of Canadian life weigh heavily. For such, merger in a real nation, with a genuine national spirit and tradition behind it, would flush out many of the shoddinesses of Canadian life — its imitativeness, its divided loyalties, its deep-rooted colonialism (and perhaps its parochialism), its hangdog submissiveness to the greater world beyond its borders. Submissiveness? Yes, and an illustration: In a recent issue of *Maclean's*, a letter writer chided Beverley Baxter for a little mild criticism of Winston Churchill: that was "presumptuous."

Merger might get rid of our polite hypocrisies — the conceit that, somehow or other, we are more "refined," less "materialistic" than our neighbours. It might relieve our sorry subjection to another country's culture, though only through the hard process of drowning whatever native culture we have in that other country's. At any rate, the American movies, such as they are, would be our movies and their popular heroines, ours. When we supplied an actress to Hollywood, she would not, as now, be lost to us. Nine-tenths of our people live, move, and have their being in American popular culture anyway. Personally, I loathe American popular culture, with its mournful croakings and croonings, but I don't count, for I am only a "prof" lost in the crowd (dare I exercise a "prof's" prerogative at this point and shout out words that few will understand: *odi profanum vulgus?*). So maybe it would be better for the average Canadian to quit watching the baseball game through the knothole in the fence and walk up and pay for his ticket.

Of culture in the non-popular sense, the culture of educated people, we have in Canada no oversupply, either native or imported. Our native culture — and it is only by its cultural creativeness that, in the long run, a country can justify its existence — is a tender plant. We have done magnificently in political and legal institutions. We have done creditably in medicine and science. We have done rather well in painting. We are beginning to make a literature of our own and even some music. We show some promise in the scholarly world. But in none of these fields, except the first, have we gone far as yet, and a distinctively Canadian culture and way of life, as there is a distinctively American, has not yet decisively manifested itself. A large part of the explanation for this lies in the mentality of our people. "Can any good thing come out of Nazareth?" Canadians seem to ask themselves. We oscillate between a touchy vanity and the servility that accompanies deep self-distrust; we have little deep pride. We sometimes seem afraid to allow anything really native to grow up: for generations, for example, the universities, admittedly among our most conservative institutions, have imported teaching talent from Great Britain and Europe, all too often turning aside their own promising young men and forcing them into exile in the United States. The result has been unreality and colonialism in one of the most vital areas, higher education.

We export our best, carelessly and casually, whether they be professors, writers, or athletes, and then wonder why they so quickly forget us, out-Americaning the Americans in their scorn of the backward fringe of settlement "up north." Such attitudes do not make for a healthy community, one rejoicing in its strength, confident in its destiny.

It may be that to become American would be to have the gates of imagination and creativeness open up to us. It may be that the power, the vitality of American life would thaw this frozen northern ground and that in the end, whatever we have worth-while about us would not be submerged, but would come out stronger, more valid than before. On the other hand, the frozen north might continue full of frozen northerners, still living on the thin gruel of unrealistic notions of superiority.

And yet, that north! The illimitable wilderness, its shining lakes! Those waves I've fought with on the Gulf of Georgia, or on Nipigon or Simcoe, those far blue hills down the St. Lawrence! Those simple, kindly people! Whatever their shortcomings, they are mine.

Intellectually, I am afraid the balance may not be difficult to strike, as the points I have enumerated go to suggest. But is cold logic the whole story? When you are faced with decision, there wells up within you that which renders rational argument difficult, and you think of another unfortunate country, spiritually torn, too, though perhaps not so tragically as ours, a country whose course, so similar to our own, has been touched off by the English historian Trevelyan, in words with which this article must close:

"For two centuries and a half after Bannockburn, Scotland remained a desperately poor, savage, bloodstained land .... Her democratic instincts had prevented her from being annexed to England, who would have given her wealth and civilization .... What then had Scotland gained by resisting ...? Nothing at all — except her soul, and whatsoever things might come in the end from preserving that."

20 | *The Forest: Heart of a Nation**

In Canada, the forest is always with us. It is our great national physical fact. It has played a vast part in our lives. Once it was cursed; today it

Canada Month, November 1963, pp. 21-23.

should be praised. On that occasion of national praising which is coming up, our Centennial, due homage should be paid to the forest, for out of it Canada has been hewn.

Drive for a few miles from almost any Canadian city and you are in the bush. The only major exceptions are the places in south-western Ontario and those in the central prairies. From Victoria and Vancouver, you can almost throw a stone into the mountain forests: in fact, I have been told that one of the hazards of life in the safe, staid city of Victoria consists of cougars straying into the outskirts and carrying off the children! Not far from Vancouver, grizzlies are to be found. Edmonton is some distance away from the Rockies, but not Calgary. The forest of the Canadian Shield is only an hour's drive from Winnipeg. At the Lakehead the bush is right at one's door. Even Toronto is only a hundred miles south of the Muskoka country, still nearly all forest. Ottawa is practically in the bush, and bears still nose around the late Mackenzie King's artificial ruins at Kingsmere, ten miles off. Halifax and Saint John are on the edge of good moose-hunting, Quebec and Montreal not much farther off. There can be some truth in the story that two Englishmen once turned up in a fashionable Toronto hotel all equipped for bear-hunting. Why not? They would not have had far to go.

The forest that begins a bit to the north of our cities goes on for hundreds of miles. Eventually it peters out, conquered by the Arctic cold; and beyond lies the infinite tundra, extending as far as land goes. Considered as a whole, the Canadian forest covers something like three or four thousand miles from east to west and anything up to fifteen hundred from south to north. In places it is thick and in places it is thin: here the trees make good lumber, there they are almost worthless. But the forest is always there, just over the back fence.

We have been doing our best for the past three centuries, first French, then French and English combined, to push the forest back: burn it, cut it, root it out, get rid of it in whatever way we could. So far we have not succeeded except in limited areas. We have cleared a little of eastern Canada; next to nothing, really, compared to its total area: but we have hardly touched British Columbia. The Prairies nature had cleared for us.

In the business of clearing, we have put on one of the most abominable spectacles of waste, greed, and sheer destructiveness that the Western world has known. We plundered the lordly pine of eastern Canada, and even now we are slaughtering the giant Douglas firs of the Pacific coast. We have let fire run through thousands of square miles, destroying not only the trees but the very earth itself. And still the forest stands. It stands unconquerable, for as we destroy in one area, it comes up in another. It is unlikely that our destructive propensities will ever reduce all our rocky country to a desert, mainly because there is so much of it; but also and hopefully because today we are slowly learning a little sense.

Our pioneers saw in every tree an enemy. Get the wretched things out of the way in order to let sunlight into the precious soil beneath! Others among them saw the northern and the mountain forests as "inexhaustible." Inexhaustible they are, in the sense just suggested above; but not inexhaustible of good, merchantable timber. So as exhaustion of that approached, conservation measures began. These have not gone far yet, but they will go further, and they may well result in the Canadian of the future having a country whose forests are almost as large as those which the settlers encountered (and probably more productive). Canada will remain a forest country.

Before there were settlers, when the discoverers first looked on the New World, they were everywhere confronted with a coast line of shaggy, unbroken forest. How could they have known that they would have to go over a thousand miles inland before they emerged from it. After the sea-coast, every river brought the same story — forest, forest, forest! Think of the men who first coasted the Great Lakes — the Champlains, the Radissons! As far as they went — and farther — there stretched out before them the illimitable forest. Only La Verendrye, a century and a quarter after the founding of Quebec, got out beyond the forest into the prairies.

Formidable enemy though it was, the forest was life to New France, for within it lived the beaver. The fur trade on which the colony depended was the beaver trade, and the beaver trade was merely a reflection of the forest. In a later time the forest began its second great age with lumbering.

Lumbering on a considerable scale began about the year 1800, and every year saw it grow in importance until, within a generation, it had become Canada's most important industry. The lumber trade furnished employment for thousands of lumberjacks, river drivers, and sailors. Those who were successful in it often became very rich men (Booths or Eddys or Bronsons or Gilmours), and their accumulations of capital presumably passed into the general economy of the country. Out of lumbering, that is, out of the forest, arose cities and towns with churches and schools. Quebec, Ottawa, Saint John, and other places have literally been hewn out of the forest. Vancouver is still being so hewn: it is still a forest city, a lumber town much of whose wealth consists in the trees it commands.

In Ottawa, for our Centennial, they are creating what they call a "mile of living history." Are they aware that the Sussex Street of Ottawa, 1867, was a mere echo of the forest? Along with polite restorations of shop-fronts, are they putting back what was there in 1867 — the mud, the hordes of fighting, drunken lumberjacks, the prostitutes? (After the late government's restoration of Dawson City's theatre-brothels, it is possible that they may be.) The point is that the forest gave us our entire background, not just the nice parts of it.

Canada's forest heritage has not ceased with the lumbering. By the time the best of the pine was cut in eastern Canada, a way had been found to make paper out of spruce and balsam, and today the forest gives us still another great industry, the support of innumerable little towns and some big ones — the pulp and paper industry. The oldtime lumberman plundered the forest: the modern pulp and paper company, which has much capital invested in expensive plants and processes, surely can be counted on to regard it as a permanent resource: if it does not, it must be shortsighted indeed. Pulp and paper making today is among Canada's leading industries.

But the forest has still other gifts for us. Through the forest flow rivers, and rivers must in their course descend to the sea. As they come down off the highlands, dashing over rapids and falls, they present us with waterpower. Not three-quarters of a century ago we could not use it. Today we light our houses and turn our factory wheels with hydro-electricity. Cut off the forests and turn the rocks on which they stand into deserts, and you will reduce the flow of our streams to a trickle. Hydro-electricity is as much a forest product as is lumber itself. And it is a singularly beneficent one, for to conserve stream-flow, it is necessary to conserve the forest: here is a case of all things working together for good. Many industries are destructive of nature (think how our waters are being polluted); hydro-electricity must conserve and encourage her.

Without these practical uses the forest would still have a large part to play in our lives, for it gives us the finest and most beautiful of recreational and sport settings; and to those whose hearts are attuned to it, it affords that communion with the mysterious something of solitude that gives life its deepest significance. It is no accident that the forest has been the subject of innumerable legends, tales, poems, histories. Wordsworth exclaimed: "There is a spirit in the woods!" That may be!

"This is the forest primeval, the murmuring pines and the hemlocks." "There is a pleasure in the pathless woods" where some can hear "the horns of elfland faintly blowing." The mythology and poetry of the forest is richer in the Old World than in the New; but in the Old World the forest is a past glory rather than a present: it has been so tamed, so reduced to servitude by man that its age of poetry has passed, or almost passed.

That is not the case in Canada: the forest is at our doors, unconquerable. Its poetic celebrations have already been worthy. Read Isabella Valancy Crawford's "Malcolm's Katie," if you want a nice sample. Here are a few lines:

> . . . the scouts of winter ran
> From the ice-belted north, and whistling shafts

Struck maple and struck sumach — and a blaze
Ran swift from leaf to leaf, from bough to bough;
Till round the forest flash'd a belt of flame
And inward licked its tongues of red and gold
To the deep, tranced inmost heart of all ....

A fair share of our nineteenth-century verse was, in fact, inspired by the forest. Most of our modern poets, it is true, seem interested only in women's thighs, but the forest will have its turn again: it will find its voice again. And within it, as from the beginning, are all nature's creatures: the moose, the deer, the bear, the wolf, and many more. And one could add, the Indian, for many of our Indians are still forest dwellers; they still follow the way of life that their fathers followed, still practise most of the ancient forest skills.

This forest that lies at our doors is not just any forest: it is our own unique forest, ours in its hugeness and its variety. Nowhere else on earth can be found, for example, an equivalent to our Canadian Shield, those hundreds of thousands of square miles of forest, rock, river, and lake to the north. How many lakes are there in Canada? Can anyone have any idea? Hundreds of thousands probably; everything from the little mountain tarn to the Great Lakes themselves. And not only the Great Lakes, but the other great lakes: Great Slave, Great Bear, Athabaska, Winnipeg. And those middling lakes that in other countries would be reckoned great: Nipigon, pearl of lakes, Nipissing, Lake of the Woods, Mickikamau, Simcoe, and dozens of others: all forest lakes, all jewels, as it were, in the crown of the Canadian forest.

These forest lakes of ours are far more than opportunities for economic exploitation: to increasing thousands of people, they are life itself. They have set up a way of life that is our own, a Canadian way of life, almost a unique way of life. For numbers of them now support, encourage, and invigorate huge summer colonies whose members swim, paddle, fish, or simply gaze! When I was a boy, our use of the lakes, not having at its disposal modern methods of transport, was much more restricted than it is today. But already a summer was not complete without a week or two of "camping," with meals cooked over open fires and beds made of shakedown materials on the native earth. From that, people rapidly expanded into the summer cottage, so that today our northern forests and our ocean shores contain tens of thousands of these more-or-less-elaborate dwellings. Recreational housing is common throughout the world: in Europe and in many parts of the United States it has evolved into the fashionable resort and as such has no particular significance. But in Canada, with some exceptions, it has retained most of its simplicity and carries its numberless occupants back to a simpler way of life. Who is to estimate the weight of all this in making a nation? There must be relatively few Canadians who are completely and entirely urban. There must be few who have not had at least a snatch of acquaintance with the outdoors. And there are huge numbers, city dwellers though they may be, to whom canoe and camp, axe and gun, are familiar and loved objects.

Such associations must pass into conduct: they help to give us a certain youthfulness and freshness. They avert from us the jaded urbanism of the great crowded ghettoes of the world.

I could grow rhapsodic on the subject of our Canadian forest lakes. I think of summers I have spent on them; of that pine-clad point on Neboquazi Lake, far north of Sudbury; of West Shining Tree, with its innumerable arms stretching in all directions; of Okwakenda and Nashokwakeda, off the Metagami River; of Barrington and Allenwater away to the north-west of Port Arthur. I think of all the lakes of our Rideau chain here near Kingston. A friend of mine has a little place in a beautiful bay on Devil's Lake. Great granite bluff on one side, splendid timber — beech and maple mostly — on the other. We often paddle across it together, and the last time I was up there with him, I was proud to demonstrate my ability still to "throw" a canoe.

But I am only one of thousands.

In less than four years we shall be celebrating our Centennial — if we have not torn ourselves apart before that! Are we going to celebrate a hundred years of repulsive city building — giant, ugly sprawling cities, complete with slums and a new crop of vulgar rich every year? Are we going to celebrate a century of ransacking our treasure house for lumber and minerals? (For ransacking, read "destroying.") Are we going to celebrate the triumphs of avid mining men in destroying our national parks? Are we going to celebrate the growth of industries so successful that they turn our rivers and lakes into sewers? Are we even going to celebrate our annual hundreds of millions of bushels of wheat? In other words, are we going to celebrate out tawdry shortcomings and our merely material accomplishments? If so, we shall not be celebrating very much, and it will be fitting for the Centennial to tail off into a gigantic beard-growing contest.

It is to be hoped, however, that the good sense and innate propriety of the Canadian people will lead them to celebrate deeper aspects of their existence than these. It is to be hoped that they will show some ability to recognize their own existence as a people, some ability to transcend the miserable sectional and racial bickerings that rend us. Then may it be suggested that if this can be done, due and loved recognition be given to the place the forest has occupied in our story?

May we have, as they had when the Prince of Wales went to Ottawa in 1861, "lumbermen's arches"? May it even be possible to take some of our celebrities down a real good rapids? The prince went through the lumber slides on the Ottawa River, and it is recorded that the royal feet were not even wetted. Then just below Capital Hill, he met the assembled lumbermen on a huge raft in mid-river, and they read an address to him, which concluded "God bless Queen Victoria: May Your Royal Highness long remain the Prince of Wales"! He did! Just over forty years, in fact. An English reporter of the event commented on the flashing paddles from the fleets of canoes gathered about the raft and on the wild, strange song that went up in greeting to the prince.

A friend of mine, an ardent forest lover and canoeist, suggested to me more or less in fun that we should begin a widely advertised trip from North Bay in the Centennial year and time it to arrive under Capital Hill July 1, 1967. Canoe and canoeists would then come triumphantly up the slope by the canal locks and approach the multitudes on the Hill to hear the politicians' speeches. Arrived there, we would respectfully offer them a ceremonial paddle. My friend has retraced most of the old voyageur routes and has paddled Lake Superior in his canoe. He is a true coureur de bois. I am an Ojibway chief myself, *Kinegago Kakanoodon* — "He who writes the story of his people" — and of this I am prouder than of my degree of Doctor of Literature. So the two of us should have some claim to the role (but readers may be sure the politicians will not be yielding any limelight).

Whatever is done, or not done, in 1967, let us have some recognition of the forest and "the hearts that beneath it lept like the roe when it hears in the woodland the horn of the hunter." It is from the forest and its neighbouring farmlands that much of the sturdiness, the self-reliance (and the self-contained natures) of the Canadians have come. Let us celebrate the forest, write stories about it, make poems in its praise. Let us cross the paddle and the axe in national symbolism. For the forest, our parent, will be here long after we have gone, and it will provide in the future, as in the past, much of our national fabric and more than its share of our national well-being.

V.

Biculturalism

The "two ways of life" thesis means not only that the existence of French and English Canada should be recognized, but also that that historical fact should not disappear in the future. It has been generally recognized that Arthur Lower has done more than any other historian, English or French, to bridge the gaps of ignorance and intolerance between the two races in Canada and thus helped make the continued existence of this duality within a unity a continuing paradox. In "Two Ways of Life" (Essay #5), he attempted to analyse the structure of these two life styles for an academic audience. The same year he tried through "Two Nations or Two Nationalities" (Essay #21), in *Culture,* a journal reaching a bilingual audience, to answer the obvious question: given the two ways of life, did Canada have a future? His conclusion was optimistic: knowledge and tolerance were the keys to continued national existence. Friction was inevitable, but it could be lived with, were the desire for a Canadian nation in thriving condition. On the practical level, "Would Canada Be Better Off without Quebec?" (Essay #22) assessed the costs of separatism for both Canada and Quebec.

A Note on Quebec Today

How far the institutions of the two peoples have flowed together in the last two centuries remains an intriguing problem. I would think that down to a quite late period, say the 1880's, certainly to Confederation, the acceptance of English parliamentary government was almost complete in Quebec. L.-J. Papineau's attempt to secure an elected Legislative Council (which preceded the Rebellion of 1837) had little survival value — if we except the similar move in the 1850's which did establish such a Council, and with very little effect, the Commons remaining the centre of the parliamentary system. Dissent rose after Confederation on specific issues (such as the French school issue in New Brunswick, the Red River affair, the North West Rebellions of 1885). As French Canadian national feeling strengthened, some antagonism showed itself towards English parliamentary institutions. It would have been remarkable if it had not. But even in our own day, the amount of hostility is quite small: there have been certain voices raised for a different kind of Supreme Court and for a more effective Senate, but these have not been strong. French Canada has more or less contented itself with symbolic gestures, such as, among others, its provincial flag and its National Assembly, together with its strong feeling about language. This despite *separatism*.

The major change I see since the so-called "quiet revolution" is the vast weakening that has occurred in the power and status of the Roman Catholic Church. Whether nationalism without the support of a deep religious faith will prove strong enough to resist the North American vortex, who is to say? If it does, the inner cohesiveness requisite will make for a disciplined, rather than a free, society. In that case, the underlying French tradition might easily assert itself in the establishment of some kind of authoritarian society. If it does not resist, then the dissolving forces of "the media" in all their awfulness, may work the same horrors in French Canada as in English Canada. There is a third possibility: French Canada may some day accept its fate as a member of the Canadian Confederation and join with English Canada in a movement of survival and self-discovery. There is a considerable hope for this, providing the extremists can be kept at arms length, and the mutual elements of distrust ruthlessly exposed and then, with luck, obliterated. At any rate, most people who know both groups recognize at once their large area of common identity. If proof were needed, the fate of the *separatistes* since the 1960's could be cited: their support was minimal. It is one thing to brandish a stick and another to use it. Where they tried to use their stick with the violence culminating in kidnapping and murder, they quickly lost support.

It is unsafe to indulge in predictions, even short range predictions, but at the moment of writing, I retain my hopes for a joint, if at times stormy, future.

A.R.M.L.
October, 1974

21 | *Two Nations or Two Nationalities**

A house divided against itself cannot stand. If the legal entity called Canada is to go on existing and to be transmuted into a spiritual entity called Canada, the two main races must come to some sort of understanding with each other. It may be that the concept *Canada* has not enough value in it for either to make this worth-while. If so, it will disappear, and the

Culture 4 (December 1943): 470-81.

two groups will submerge their identity in the general continental sea. That is a course that has often been plotted but never followed. Is it not then a fairly safe prediction that it will not be followed? There is enough in Canada's past to assure her of a future. The original question therefore returns: how can a reasonable future be assured?

In writing for a bilingual audience, I may be permitted to begin by defining my terms, particularly as the leading word in this article is one that bears different meanings in French and English. The French meaning, as I understand it, of the word *nation* comes closer to the Latin original whose root is the verb *nascor,* "to be born." *Une nation* is a group of people who are born of common ancestors. The word will hardly bear this meaning in English. The correct translation of *la nation métis,* for example, would be "The Métis people," a "people" being a blood group in too advanced a state of culture to be referred to as a "tribe." The English use of the word *nation* stresses the idea of political sovereignty but does not place overmuch emphasis on the idea of blood, that is, descent or "race." In no sense could the United States be thought of as a blood group, but there is no question of the existence of the American nation. Any group of persons who come together in a social compact, forming themselves into a civil society for more or less definite ends, and with control over their own destiny, whatever their origins, would be, in the English sense, a nation. Thus England and Scotland, voluntarily united in 1707, form the "British nation."

To the word *nationality* in English attach, first, a purely legal meaning — you are of Canadian nationality if you are a Canadian citizen — and secondly the social meaning of a group whose members recognize their sameness, that is, are possessed of the necessary element of self-consciousness, but who do not constitute a state. I do not consider that it would be correct today to speak of the Scottish nation, but rather of the Scottish nationality. Similarly in Canada: in English usage, it would be legitimate to refer to persons of French-Canadian nationality but not to the French-Canadian nation.

Another word, often on French lips, is *race.* It is a tragic word. Not only does it excite passions leading to wars, but despite the monumental labours of a whole generation of pedantic German asses, it can be given no satisfactory scientific content. We speak of the human race, meaning the species *homo sapiens;* of the negro race, meaning a variety of mankind with more or less black skins (and the same blood groups as ourselves); of the Alpine race, meaning people whose homelands extend from central France to central Asia and who have broad (Brachycephalic) heads, medium complexion, and medium stature, but who may include anyone from a Swiss to a Tartar; of the German race, meaning dark people from Austria, light people from Prussia, people speaking German, Dutch, Russian, and

Hungarian, broadheads and longheads, Goerings and Goebbels, obviously rather a silly term, despite libraries of *Rassenwissenchaft*. Racialists the world over talk in terms of purity of *breed*, but there are few communities indeed where men are not hopeless mongrels. Among these exceptions, two stand out, Japan and French Canada. Neither one has had much fresh blood since the original society was begun some 2,500 years ago in one case and 300 in the other. These two may therefore with a little more justice than most talk of *race:* whether they have benefited from their isolation is another matter; to the biologist, in-breeding has its merits and its defects, and he will make you out a long list of both.

Nature, no doubt, is always trying to establish fresh breeds, or new species, and perhaps a "race," if left to itself for the next fifty thousand years, might become a new species. For ordinary human purposes, it seems to be so much a product of time and place that it is better to think in social rather than biological terms. "A people" may therefore be defined as a group of men who have achieved sufficient homogeneity to enable them to live a common life, not a mysterious blood group, *(ein Volk!)*. If a people — or several peoples — can find enough in common to enable them to live *by consent* (the phrase is crucial) under a common form of government in reasonable harmony, then they may be thought of as a nation. The important point is not some mysterious doctrine of blood, which may be left to Hitler, but social harmony.

Now it is not debatable that in Canada, people do live under a common government and by consent. They have been living that way for quite a long time. If they did not find their way of life more or less to their satisfaction, the struggle to change it would be much more violent than anything we have witnessed in Canada so far. In the last 180 years there have been many high-tempered debates, much acrimony, some riots, and one small squib of a rebellion. As the course of human affairs goes, that is a rather good record. Compare France itself. Compare Italy since Napoleon's campaign of 1798, with the ferment around its secret societies of the 1820's, the wars against Austria of the 1830's, the 1840's, the 1850's, against France or the Papacy, its innumerable local revolutions, capped by the long turmoil since 1922. Where divisive forces are great enough, armed outbreak is sure to be the result. If there has been little armed outbreak in Canada that argues that the divisive forces, while they may be annoying, are not of first importance. To paraphrase the famous *mot* of M. Thiers, "Canada is that form of polity which divides French and English the least."

Like St. Paul unto Caesar, I make my appeal unto history. While I cannot commit myself completely to the doctrine of predestination, few historians can fail to feel a strong tendency to believe that what has been will be, that the broad lines of a society's life, as evidenced by the past, are likely to continue into the future. Exceptions, it is true, there are, such as revolutionary upheavals that seem to cut across the path of evolution. Yet we are told that even in Russia, the old manner of life of the Russian people is still plainly discernible: Russians are still Russians. So with us here in Canada: whatever our personal predilections may be, the chances are that we shall go stumbling along on the path we have been following.

The people of Canada have been compressed in this mould of a common history for nearly two centuries. What has resulted? Are they like, shall we say, sawdust, which falls out again as soon as the mould is taken off? Or are they like metal, which has hardened into the shape of the mould? I would suggest that they are more like metal than sawdust. If we could imagine the hand of history removed from us, I do not think we would just fall apart into separate grains. Nor might we be as hard and as formed as metal. We would be somewhere between, but nearer metal than sawdust. In other words, it seems to me that the mould of history has shaped what may be called a Canadian people, a people of two wings to be sure, French and English, but nevertheless a people. Through acting together and against each other, through pressures from within and without, we have taken on a shape. We have developed institutions that are our own. No French Canadian will claim that his public institutions are French, nor will he admit that they are British except in point of derivation. French-speaking Canadians have taken originally English (a much more legitimate term than "British") institutions, worked them and shaped them until they now serve them as their own. So with English-speaking Canadians. It is often overlooked that for most of the English-speaking pioneers (who came from the fringes of the British Isles), English institutions were not exactly their own. The Highland Scots, for example, who have played a large part in Canadian history, were of another culture, and to them English institutions were almost as foreign as they were to the French. Of course, the English tradition of common law and free government was more familiar to the non-metropolitan people of English speech than to those of French, but the point is that, in each case, the old institutions had to be worked over and made our own. Our parliamentary system, our federal system, our courts of law, have long since become Canadian, neither English, French, nor British.

A very wise old lawyer once said to me, in discussing the rise of the American nation: "What made the American nation? It was the Constitution that made the American nation." I cannot go quite that far. It seems to me that there must be deeper things in addition to a legal framework if a new society is to emerge. But he was correct up to a point. A common form of government does put a common print on everybody living under it. In Canada both French and English have since 1774 been under the same criminal law. Both take for granted fair trials in open court, the right of cross-examination of witnesses, and so on. Both have the same conception of crime — neither one shares the rather nonchalant attitude of neighbours towards homicide. Such things do not of themselves make a people, but they give a common basis for action, common norms of conduct, and these take us a long way. It seems to me our institutions of government, if they have not created something vital, have provided an atmosphere in which anything vital can grow relatively easily.

Discussion, the life-blood of freedom, has perhaps had a greater significance than formal institutions. There is a passage in Sir Richard Cartwright's *Reminiscences* in which he talks about the old peripatetic Parliament of the Union. His opinion was that the English members profited greatly from their residence in Quebec: the French people were hospitable and friendly, and the M.P.'s soon understood that not every noisy orator was to be taken at his face value. The result was that they acquired qualities of sympathy and tolerance that went far to ease the strains between the two races.[1] Parliament in consequence became — as it has remained — one of the chief media for mutual understanding. Very few men going to Parliament today can fail to become better and bigger Canadians. (It is unfortunate that so many M.P.'s have to delay beginning their education until they get elected.)

Apart from Parliament, discussion in the daily press, even when bitter, has gradually served to bring about common attitudes in a good many areas of life. It is rather difficult to engage in a controversy with any man without hearing a little of what he says, even if you disagree with it. We have been discussing the same things in Canada now for a good deal more than a century. I do not claim that we have settled many of our differences, merely that a century of discussion has begun to elucidate them. That may seem like rather slow progress, but I am not sure that it is: societies take an interminable time in forming, and one of the factors in making the process slow is the inability of one given group of people to grasp what the grievances of another are. Sometimes, as with the English and Irish, that is never done, but my opinion would be that the attitude of French-speaking Canadians is gradually being grasped among the English-speaking. The process has not gone very far yet, but there are more people today than before who can grasp imaginatively the psychology of a minority group that fears for its survival.

On the other hand, I have seen practically no evidence that French-speaking Canadians have any understanding of the problems of their

[1]Sir Richard Cartwright, *Reminiscences* (Toronto: W. Briggs, 1912).

English-speaking brethren, or any desire to understand them.[2] That, it seems
to me, is regrettable, for the two groups should be making common cause
against those in their midst who cannot respond to the challenge of this
great country but try to hide themselves away in snobbish colonialism or
narrow parochialism. French Canadians do not understand how difficult
it is for an English-speaking person to be a Canadian, *tout court:* how
he is pulled apart by the appeal of the race, so strong both from south
and east. After all, it is asking a lot to expect people to abandon membership
in a great world group of some two hundred millions, in order to retreat
into a peculiar little self-contained society of eleven. It would be fantastic
to expect the English ever to cut such cultural and historical ties completely,
and there therefore must be distinct limits to separatism. Culturally, the
same is more or less true for the French, though few French-speaking
Canadians whom I know seem to worry very much about their inclusion
in the greater world of French culture: they find a life that seems adequate
in their own group, or, many of them, in another world society, the Roman
Catholic church.

French-speaking Canadians often accuse English Canadians of not
being Canadians at all, but Englishmen overseas. The accusation in many
cases is just, but does not a similar charge lie against those French-speaking
persons who cannot rise to the challenge of the whole of Canada and
persist in curtailing their loyalties to the Province of Quebec or the French
race in Canada? "Canadian" as the term has been used historically by
French-speaking Canadians is as much to be condemned as "British."
Neither one answers to the reality that is Canada.

I doubt very much if English Canadians will ever be content to confine
themselves entirely to their own group, for there are too many spiritual
and material riches to be sought outside it, and in their awareness of the
outer world they are in a way the least parochial of peoples. However,
they can become a satisfactory sub-group, for their own country — and
to some extent their own Canadian culture — can provide for them means
of self-expression adequate to the majority of life's situations. The important
thing in the formation of a new society is not to cut off communication
with the outer world — to violate history — but to refuse to be overwhelmed
by the accomplishments of older societies, to believe that the new society
has its contribution to make to mankind and then to go ahead and make
it. To put the matter on a personal basis, I, like most other English-speaking
persons, have learned to write English prose at the feet of the great English

[2]One happy exception has recently appeared in the article by Father D'Eschambault in this
journal (A. D'Eschambault, "National Unity and its Implications," *Culture* 4 (1943): 196.),
though if Father D'Eschambault will allow me to say so, I do not think he has succeeded
in getting very far into the spirit of English-Canadianism especially as reflected in education.

classical authors; however, because they wrote so well, I shall not allow myself to be frightened out of writing. I shall go ahead and say what I have to say. So with forming a society. It need not cut itself off from its past, but it must "say what it has to say."

At the same time, it would be highly desirable if members of the two groups in Canada could say what they had to say rather more to each other than they at present do. They speak to each other in Parliament, and they are beginning to speak to each other through the pages of this periodical. But if they could speak more, they would abuse less. I suggest we are losing several heaven-sent opportunities in Canada: we know little or nothing about each other's books; why not? Why not a little more translation? Then there is the radio. We have established French and English networks that destroy it as a medium of nationalism. Of course, indiscriminate nationwide broadcasting in both languages is not very practicable, but surely many special programmes could be arranged for the men of good will on both sides. The language question is not an insuperable obstacle. Till the end of time, I suppose, French will speak French, and English, English, and I do not see why that cannot be taken for granted. But for mutual broadcasting there is no difficulty in finding bilingual persons by the thousands on the French side, and it would be possible to scrape up a few even on the English.

I do not make such proposals out of mere sentimentality, such as has marked so much "bon-entente-ism" in the past. I know just how empty that sort of thing can be — and how much better (because more courteously) the French can carry it off than the English. I suggest discussion — and I would not worry too much if there were a good deal of hard hitting in it — simply because out of discussion there must eventually, if there is any basis of agreement at all, come some measure of understanding. And if understanding, compromise. A better word, with more Christian charity in it, is tolerance. I think that eventually we may manage to make our respective points of view more or less understood. Then, like George Brown and John A. Macdonald, after their celebrated meeting of 1864, we may discover what excellent fellows we are.

The obvious rejoinder to all this is that it is all a matter of expediency, that there is nothing of deep spiritual significance drawing the two races together in Canada and therefore no enduring basis for the Canadian nation. I will grant that they do not have in common the deep human experiences of language and faith — though in the matter of faith it must be remembered that there are many Roman Catholics who are not French, and it must be hoped that Christianity is still a larger term than either Catholicism or Protestantism. (We would very soon find out something about our common Christianity if we had to undergo, shall we say, a Japanese conquest.) I will even grant that in their ultimate philosophy English Protestantism and French Catholicism are irreconcilable. I will not, however, grant that just because I differ from my neighbour in my theology, it is inevitable that I must some day cut his throat. Religion is an absolute, and humanity has plenty of expedients for avoiding the logical results of its absolutes; its daily life is rarely passed in the domain of the absolute. Nor will I grant that a common history and a common environment are not deep spiritual forces. I think they are. I feel that the magnificent outlook from the Citadel at Quebec is mine, too, along with my French-speaking friends: it is part of me as well as part of them. If they will come up to inland Manitoulin with me some day, or the Nipigon, I will show them a part of their Canada that will take their breath away too. If man cannot get profound spiritual experiences from the world of nature around him, he may not be able to get them anywhere else. The common country, in its beauty, its expanse, its challenge, most assuredly provides a common spiritual experience.

Environment and history work the same subtle magic. You cannot cancel out Lafontaine and Baldwin: they exist. You cannot cancel out a hundred years of more of less satisfactory co-operation. English and French may not be an ideally mated married couple; I do not think they are: they are not soul-mates, but they have managed to rub along, with their "spats" at times and even their fights, but still they have managed to live together. Even much unhappier marriages (Czechs and Germans, for example) build up associations that it is rather hard to tear down.

Environment represents the mould of geography, and with us it is compelling. All the hot talk of the separatists will not separate the St. Lawrence River from Lake Ontario. The St. Lawrence and the Lakes are a great highway leading into the heart of Canada: along that highway flows the golden harvest of the West, wheat on its way to Europe. It makes little difference whether we agree or whether we do not: the St. Lawrence and the Lakes are going to be there, and they will force some kind of unity of the people living along them, whether those people like it or not. In time to come that part of Canada lying above Three Rivers, with its unique advantages in water transportation and electric power, will be a highly integrated and closely settled region. The forces of geographical and economic determinism will not ask permission of French and English for that. The two peoples will be thrown across each other's path in every conceivable way. They can keep up a continual dog fight if they like and make life thoroughly miserable for each other. Or if they can muster enough common sense, they can manage to live in peace. There is no guarantee that the common sense will be forthcoming — except that a good measure of it, when it has come to the pinch, usually has been in the past. If it continues to be displayed, the two peoples can go on, and let us hope, improve their understanding of and friendship for each other.

That will bring no millenium. I do not see why we should expect a millenium in Canada. Any society that I know anything about always has plenty of points of friction and its individual members always have plenty of grievances. No doubt French and English will go to the crack of doom airing their grievences against each other: in the year 2443, no doubt the French will be complaining that they cannot get their due share of public positions because the English take them all, and the English will be complaining that the French are so unreasonable as to wish to speak a foreign language when they could have the privilege of speaking English. We shall get used to this by and by — the first two hundred years or so are always the worst — and we shall come to understand that, having to live together anyway, we may as well make the best of it.

Does this give the basis for a Canadian nation? It at least shows that Canada, already a going concern for three-quarters of a century, can continue to be one. Providing we win not only this present war but the next, our existence as a political community is assured. But what kind of existence? Economically a very good one. We are better off than nearly any other of the world's peoples just now, and if we wish, we can still further improve our lot: the war and its associated activities, with the good times they have brought, and the enormous increase in our productive powers, have proved that. Politically our future should be no more eventful than that of other strong communities. There will be growing pains, naturally, and there will be sharp adjustments to be made, especially between the two races: "incidents" will continue to occur; drastic differences over policy, especially foreign policy, will continue to manifest themselves. But the drastic differences of 1917 and of 1941 did not break up the country, which preserved substantial unity of action despite them. These storms blow up and as a rule blow over: it is completely wrong to believe that they indicate an impossible situation. Obviously they do not or we could not go on. Every one of them has been adjusted in some way or other. Not logically, of course. I should hope my French readers are too logical to expect logical solutions to political questions. Canadian life can only go on by compromise, and as a rule by illogical, make-shift compromise that violates all logical conceptions and, while it satisfies no one, drives no one to desperation. If this is a bad situation, what is a better one?

Simply because the situation is not ideal, I hope no one will begin talking nonsense about "Laurentia," separation, annexation, and so on. No human situation is ever ideal, and in the kind of world we face small units will be very much worse off than big. We are at one of the sharp transition points of history: these have always been accompanied by war and revolution. Pandora's box having been opened, is it reasonable to believe that the gigantic winds let loose during the last twenty-five years can be quietly put back? Is it not far more reasonable to assume that they will continue to blow violently about the earth for a long time yet? With good luck, we on this North American continent may be spared from actual first-hand contact with their results in the form of war on our own soil, as we are being spared today, but we shall certainly incur their secondary incidence. How foolish it would be, then, to allow ourselves to be provoked by pique into a defenceless parochialism.

Nothing will contribute more effectively to the emergence of a genuine nationhood than some measure of agreement on the broad lines of foreign policy. It is time for all those that love their country and put its best interests first to turn on the offenders against her and sternly subdue them. They are to be found on both wings; those people who cannot be genuinely loyal to Canada because they put another loyalty first — the colonials and imperialists who would make us a subordinate people — and those who cannot catch the vision because they put a section or a race first — the parochialists. Neither set of persons can be regarded as true Canadians. In this covetous world it is therefore the duty of all those who wish for the welfare of this group of eleven million people with half a continent at its disposal to think in the terms that these conditions impose, to think in realistic and not in sentimental terms. Let us once realize ourselves as Canadians, owing unlimited allegiance to the political and historical structure we have created, and then all else will fall into line: there will be found a place for the affections of men for their birthplace and their province and a place for co-operation with other nations to the common good. "The best interests of Canada" need be neither parochial nor selfish. "To thine own self be true," says Shakespeare, "thou canst not then be false to any man."

Persons whose faith fails them, who doubt the wisdom of continuing "the experiment" because of racial squabbles, should remember that history does not afford important examples of dissolution by consent. Norway and Sweden, it is true, parted company, but they had never been more than separate countries under a common crown. Belgium had to fight her way out of the kingdom of Holland, Poland out of Russia, Ireland out of the United Kingdom, Greece out of Turkey, and so on. The Southern States tried to fight their way out of the American Union and failed. The present Russian constitution theoretically allows a Soviet Republic to secede, but we all know how much meaning that has. Once a political union is made, it is exceedingly difficult to unmake, and innocent people who imagine that a province of Canada could secede without a major disturbance ought to study their history a little more closely. The dissolution of a political body is just as painful an experience as the dissolution of a physical body, and it is most unlikely that the experiment would ever be made unless conditions became very much worse than anything we are likely to encounter. Certainly the kind of racial bickering we have had in Canada up to the present could never justify such a last resort.

We are not a great power; most likely we never shall be a great power. But we are a power of very respectable weight indeed, as the present war has proved, and if we can only get more confidence in ourselves, we can play a large part in world affairs, quite large enough to satisfy reasonable ambitions. But we must get rid of our colonial sense of inferiority and that applies to French just as much as to English: French-Canadian colonialism takes a different form from English, but it is just as marked. While there is no space to analyse it here at length, the frequent inability to distinguish between English Canadians and the English is one illustration; the frequency of suggestions that it is British interests which determine our actions, another. Both French and English colonialism must disappear, and we must solve our own problems in our own terms. Then we shall take our own place in the world, and a very good place it will be.

I therefore see no reason for believing that we cannot have a Canadian nation because we have two races which are so divergent. We can have one if we want to have one: and it will probably turn out that it will be much easier and much more sensible to allow things to take their course, which will involve the strengthening of the political society known as Canada, than to do a right about turn and try to destroy that society. That, however, does not involve unity of culture. There seems little likelihood of that. French and English will continue to follow their own ways of life, but moulded by a common environment and a common history. Their literatures, if not their other arts, will develop separately. But it is not unreasonable to believe that springing from substantially the same sources, they will tend to resemble each other. In fact they already do: Ringet's *Trente Arpents* is quite similar in conception and expression to Martha Ostenso's *Wild Geese*. They will be variants of the same fundamental.

That is not to say that French-speaking and English-speaking Canadians will all love one another like brothers. They will not: they are far too different in temperament for that, and there are far too many historical ghosts not yet laid. However, men of good will on both sides will continue to make it their business to lay these ghosts, and the area of understanding and good feeling can still be greatly enlarged: at present it embraces parliamentarians, and a small body of the liberally educated. In the future this range can be extended — to the professions, to journalists, to school teachers and so on. Understanding will not come of itself, and there will be many shocks and rebuffs on both sides. But those Canadians who take the ethics of Christianity seriously can do nothing else than work for understanding and for tolerance, for have we not all been taught that "thou shalt love thy neighbour as thyself"?

22 | *Would Canada Be Better Off without Quebec?**

I write what follows not because I advocate Canadian separation. This I would not for moment do; in fact, I would regard separation as the greatest possible calamity. Nor do I write out of any enmity toward my French fellow-citizens. I have many good French-speaking friends, and I have no reason for regarding them in any other light than my English-speaking friends. We are all Canadians together, and my fondest hope for years past has been that the two peoples could gain sufficient understanding of each other and sufficient mutual tolerance to enable Canadians to think of themselves, not as two, but as one with two parts. I have advocated the fullest extension of linguistic privileges throughout Canada, including school rights, and every other measure that would relieve my French-speaking fellow-citizens of any occasion for feeling "second best."

If now I try to sum up the bill that might be presented to the Province of Quebec as the price for its leaving Confederation, I do so only because the constant talk of separation by extremists — and the almost equally constant remarks with implications of separatism on the part of people who do not put themselves down as separatists — makes me feel that we had better take a hard, realistic look at what the separation of Quebec from the rest of Canada might involve. It is always best frankly and courageously to face the worst possibilities, rather than merely to hope that the storm will blow over.

But let me repeat, I do so in no spirit of enmity toward my fellow-citizens of French speech. And also, I do not confuse the Province of Quebec with the French-speaking people of Canada. The two things are quite distinct. Quebec is a province, a geographical and historical entity. It is virtually that old New France which passed from French rule with the capitulation at Montreal in 1760. The French-speaking people of Canada, on the other hand, are to be found in every province, and no feat of political magic could possibly separate them from their English-speaking fellow-citizens. What follows, then, is an objective attempt to consider what situation might arise if Quebec, the province, insisted on leaving Canada.

Instead of recoiling in horror at the possibility of an independent

**Maclean's*, 14 December 1964, pp. 27, 51-52.

Quebec, I believe English Canadians should be seriously considering whether their interests would be better served with Quebec out of Confederation. French Canadians, after all, are not the only nationalists north of the international boundary; English Canada has national aspirations, too, and it is possible that it would be in a better position to fulfil them if Quebec, politically speaking, were out of the picture.

I am not advocating separatism and I am not indulging in a hymn of hate against "the French," but I *am* suggesting that the so-called "dialogue" between Canada's two peoples might be a great deal more fruitful if we considered separation at least as a possibility and tried in hard-headed fashion to see what it involved. Although it is desirable to try to save most marriages, it is only realistic to consider the possibility that the marriage contracted in 1867 might, in the course of events, end in divorce. There are only so many concessions that the central government can make to Quebec nationalism; and it is possible that the point could be reached where no further peace offerings could be made.

English Canada, for instance, might agree to allow the ten provinces to appoint senators to the national parliament on a "rep-by-pop" basis. But would it be willing to go farther? Already there are demands from Quebec for more than that. The Montreal branch of the Saint Jean Baptiste Society and Daniel Johnson, leader of Quebec's Union Nationale opposition, are among those who have suggested transforming the Senate into a "chamber of two nations," with half the senators from Quebec and the other half from English Canada. Few English Canadians would accept this proposal. It would probably involve the subordination of the House of Commons to the Senate, and it would mean that Canada's two "nations" would be held together by only the most tenuous of links.

If Canada is to stay united, then in the interests of simple justice a change should be made in the field of education. Provincial school laws should be revised to provide for the right to educate French-speaking schoolchildren in their own language. But such a relaxation will not occur if "separate schools" are once more merely identified with Roman Catholic schools; for the sectarian issue − as opposed to the linguistic − would reawaken most of the old bitterness.

If the idea of separation were to be frankly accepted, hard bargains would have to be driven. Since the demand would come from Quebec, it would be up to Quebec to present its proposals and for the rest of the country to decide whether or not to accept them. If Quebec wished to get out of the bargain it made in 1867, it would only be fair for it to be ready to pay for the privilege.

What would the payment be? No one can say with exactitude, but unless the rest of Canada ignored its own interests, the price would be high.

To begin with, Canada cannot afford to be broken in two by a foreign power on the banks of the St. Lawrence. It is virtually certain that as one of its first steps, an independent state of Quebec would establish its own system of tariffs and surround itself with a ring of custom houses, complete with all the familiar bureaucratic annoyances. But far more serious than that, speaking in hard terms, Canada cannot afford to have its overseas trade and relationships subject to interference at the Port of Montreal by a foreign, and perhaps unfriendly, government. A bill of divorce, therefore, would by necessity require Quebec to renounce any rights to establish border customs offices and to control the Port of Montreal and the St. Lawrence Seaway.

There would also have to be insistance that Quebec pay a pro rata share of the national debt. On March 31, 1964, the net debt totaled somewhat more than fifteeen billion dollars. Quebec's share (census of 1961) would thus be four and a quarter billion dollars. Nor is that the extent of the financial burden it would have to assume. It would also be fair for it to pay its share of the C.N.R. debt which in September of this year was near a billion and three-quarter millions of dollars.

Canada would also have to exact from Quebec firm military and strategic concessions in return for separation. A ready and unhampered right of military, air, and naval access to the Gulf of St. Lawrence and the Port of Quebec would be required. And to assure continuity in trade and in political and social relations, there would have to be a guaranteed right-of-way between Ontario and the Maritime provinces.

Quebec as an independent state would have little claim to the territory of Ungava, for this was given to it by Canada as a whole when there was no thought of it (Quebec) being anything else than a "province" like other provinces. Ungava never formed part of the original "New France."

Some will ask: what about the "English" of Quebec? Could the rest of Canada, in negotiating a separation agreement, abandon them to the mercies of a new nationalist government? The short answer, in my view, is yes.

While Canada would probably be disposed to make the best bargain it could for them, it would be pointless to worry too much over the non-French groups of Quebec, the majority of whom live on the island of Montreal. No "English" newspaper or institution — apart from such small groups as centred on Dr. Frank Scott at McGill's faculty of law — said a public word against the Duplessis régime. In South Africa, the English-language press has at least spoken out courageously against the oppressive racial policies of the Verwoerd government; but no such English voice was ever raised in Quebec against Duplessis. With individual exceptions, the non-French groups of Montreal, split into a dozen sub-groups with little relationship to each other, are morally and spiritually bankrupt. Collectively, they are hardly worth fighting for.

In similar fashion Quebec would have to abandon the French minorities in the rest of Canada. These minorities would no longer be able to claim collective rights.

For the rest of Canada, freedom from Quebec might well be freedom from a millstone. Were the brakes off, there are a dozen different directions in which rapid moves forward could be made — morally, economically, and legally. Foreign policy would take on a simplicity and unanimity that at present it cannot have. Why should "Canada" keep in step with "Quebec," a collectivity whose attitudes are so remote from, and in some respects so out of tune with, the modern world?

The answer most frequently heard is that, without Quebec, the rest of Canada would instantly be absorbed by the United States. Leaving aside the interesting question of whether the U.S. would *want* to absorb it, one may disagree.

Today, as always, there are two factors preventing English-speaking Canada from becoming a genuine community with enough agreement within itself, enough common will, to act effectively in vital matters. One is the U.S. The other is the Province of Quebec.

Far from facing absorption, a Canada without Quebec might soon find its feet against the U.S. In deep essentials, it would speak with one voice, as it cannot do now. And added fears of absorption would make absorption even less likely. English Canadians today have gone far enough on the road to nationalism to preserve them from becoming Americans. Quebec does not help in this respect. Today it hinders.

There is another point to be faced very sternly and coldly. The present tide of emotion in Quebec could eventually break the dikes, and Canada, our common country, might be faced with another Fort Sumter. To me, this would be the ultimate catastrophe, the destruction of my country. Let us, before it becomes too late, reckon up the accounts.

VI.

Civil Liberties

Arthur Lower's "two ways of life" thesis sits in easy juxtaposition with his more practical concerns for the liberties of the individual. The imposition of restrictions upon personal freedom during World War II, as well as several incidents of the cold war such as the Gouzenko and Norman cases, caused him to direct his work towards the defence of liberty. In a brief to the committee of the Senate on human rights (Essay #23), he reviewed the history of the institutions of freedom in Canada. "Is the RCMP a Threat to Our Liberty?" (Essay #24) was typical of his efforts to make the average Canadian aware of the threats to his personal freedom. In "Some Reflections on a Bill of Rights" (Essay #25), he argued in favour of such legislation as essential for the defence of personal liberty.

23 | Brief to the Committee of the Senate on Human Rights*

Our Canadian society and its government, as everyone is aware, rest on two historic traditions, the French and the English. These two traditions have been subjected to the forces of our North American environment for many generations, with the result that both have altered considerably from their original form. Each has also influenced the other, so that we have in Canada today a certain admixture of French and English institutions, baked together, as it were, in the oven of the North American environment. The result is that our Canadian system of society and government cannot be described in simple words such as "French" or "English." It is Canadian.

But of course the original historical traditions are still easily discernible, and they must be understood if their results in producing our new Canadian tradition are to be understood. I would, therefore, like to set out what

*Canada, Parliament, Senate, *Proceedings of the Special Committee on Human Rights and Fundamental Freedoms* (Ottawa: Kings Printer, 1950), pp. 311-25. Reproduced by permission.

seems to me, speaking as an historian, to be the gist of the French and English traditions respectively, and then to draw certain deductions from this material with respect to civil liberties.

The former kingdom of France, as it existed before the French Revolution, was forged out of the disorder of feudalism by the French kings. Many centuries ago, disorder in the land of France was so great that the ordinary, average man was willing to pay almost any price for peace and quiet. The price he paid for the repression of the feudal baron by the king was the absolutism of the king. France developed the institutions of an absolute monarchy. This admitted of no compromise between private right and public right, and public right, that is to say, the authority of the Crown, everywhere prevailed. If by the seventeenth century, the century in which Canada was founded, any tradition of liberty remained, it lay in those provinces of France which had never lost their provincial assemblies or estates (known as *les pays d'états*) and in certain of the towns and cities which had charter rights or rights as *communes*.

It was the absolute conception of the French state which was transferred to Canada. In 1663 when the Province of Canada was formed by Louis XIV, no assembly was given to it: it became what was known in France as a *pays d'élection*. This had important consequences in the nature of Canadian life, which will be referred to below. Nor were any of the rights and privileges of the historic *communes* of France transferred to Canada; Quebec, Montreal, Three Rivers, the three towns of the old régime, being under the direct administration of the intendant and his deputies.

France, however, although an absolute monarchy, never became a totalitarian state, for the king always had a great rival in the state which he could never entirely subdue to his will, namely, the church. It has been well said that where church and state exist together on co-ordinate terms, liberty cannot entirely perish.

Nor was France lacking in another modifier of absolutism, namely, the system of law. It is important to understand the general nature of the old French legal system because it was this system which was inherited by French Canada and has come down in some respects unchanged to the present day in the Province of Quebec. France of the old régime derived her law from three principal sources. There was first of all immemorial custom. Each province had its custom, and in the course of time these came to be codified and written down. One of the most sophisticated of these customary codes was that of the capital, Paris. It was the Custom of Paris (*coutûme de Paris*) which in 1663 was officially declared to be the law of Canada.

The second source of French law was Roman law (*lex scripta*). The Roman law is one of the world's great systems of jurisprudence, and it has usually been considered also to have been one of the strongest instruments of absolute government. One of its leading maxims is that "the will of the prince has the force of law." This gives an opportunity for absolute conceptions to grow up, and it is significant that those countries which have developed absolute governments have been Roman law countries. One of the most important aspects of Roman law has been the nature of its processes of trial. Generally speaking, Roman law regards a trial as a scientific investigation in which no method of getting at the truth is neglected. A trial under Roman law is an *investigation,* an *inquiry,* an *inquest,* an *inquisition.* Men learned in the law conduct the trial. It being the sole objective to arrive at the truth, the liberal safeguards afforded private parties under English common law did not develop. Thus under Roman law trials could be conducted in secret, though they were not necessarily so conducted; anyone could be questioned, his evidence recorded, and later an accusation preferred against him, and, after the accusation had been preferred, he could again be forced to testify. There was no requirement by which witnesses were examined in the presence of the accused, and, of course, there was nothing like the jury system. And, behind the power of judge and court, there lay the device by which men could be forced to speak, the black shadow of *torture (la question)*.

These Roman law methods have gone all over Europe with the exception of England and, I think, the Scandinavian countries. The countries of western Europe, such as Holland and France, have today greatly modified them, but even in these countries the old Roman law traditions give their tone to the general legal atmosphere. It can readily be seen that under Roman law the tendency would be to give to the person subjected to its processes a minimum of protection against the authorities. This came out very well in a remark of one of the attorneys general of France, made after the celebrated criminal ordinance of the 1680's. "Were I accused," said he, "of stealing the Steeples of Notre Dame Cathedral, I would not attempt to defend myself against the charge; I would begin my defence by running away." Accusation, that is to say, meant condemnation.

The third source of French law consisted in the edicts and ordinances of the king or those of his deputies throughout France. For purposes of administration, the Crown employed the officials known as intendants who had legal powers of a very wide nature relating to justice, police, and finance. On all of these they could issue their own ordinances, subject to the eventual approval of the Crown. The result was that in addition to the many highly formal and elaborate pieces of legislation originating from the Crown itself, which tended to form what in English would be called a code of statute law, there were every year innumerable subordinate pieces of legislation issued by the intendants on every conceivable subject. This was the system that was introduced into Canada in 1663, a system consisting of the legislation of the king of France and of local legislation mostly put out by the intendant. To those brought up in English ideas, the whole system was fluid, depending on the will of the officials in charge. There was nothing like the formal solemnity of English processes of legislation. Echoes of this type of government, where the official was both judge, jury, and legislator, were to be heard in the imperial pronouncement made at a recent trial in Montreal, when the governing official is reported as having in substance declared that because a man acted in a manner displeasing to the authorities in one area of conduct, he was therefore deprived of his privileges in another and completely separate area.

Such was the law of France as introduced into Canada in 1663; it was the basis of the government of Canada as a province of France until the cession of 1763. During this time there were superimposed upon the structure of French law innumerable pieces of Canadian legislation and innumerable local court decisions which were built into Canadian law. Since there was no printing press in Canada until after the cession of 1763, the laws of Canada were mostly carried in the memories of the legal profession, and owing to this the English were unable to make head or tail of the Canadian legal structure when they took over.

Despite the formal absolutism of Canada as a province of France, nobody would suggest that the Canadians were an unfree people. For one thing the Crown of France kept justice cheap, and everybody had the privilege of waging lawsuits against his neighbour if he wished. The impression is that most people availed themselves of this privilege, for Canadians are described by everyone at litigious and insistent on their rights against their seigneurs and against their priests. They also had their own ways of balking the will of the authorities, the government or the intendant. Thus it is on record that despite the instructions of the king to the intendant that the city of Montreal should be surrounded by walls and that the citizens should pay the cost of the construction, year after year the people of Montreal managed somehow or other to get out of the tax which was proposed. They believed not only in no taxation without representation, but even more strongly in no taxation.

There was, of course, another recourse against French absolutism and that was, to put it tersely, the bush: every Canadian who felt the pressure of authority too severely could get out and to the *pays d'en haut*, go Indian, become a coureur de bois, etc. Between their own natural stubbornness and sense of freedom and the infinite space which the new continent afforded, the Canadians proved difficult to coerce, and every official used to remark on the difference between them and the people of France in this respect.

The North American environment, it is evident, was having its effect, and a natural democracy was growing up in Canada, even under the formal institutions of absolutism. Of course, sooner or later the absolute authority would have caught up with the inhabitants, bush or no bush, and then they would have found that they had no formal theoretical defence against it. This is the vast difference between Canadians in the French régime and Americans in the colonial period: the Americans had formal institutions of government and freedom which they had brought with them from England and which they were later to use as the foundation of their own national institutions. The Canadians had nothing but the institutions of French absolutism and such evasions as the wilderness might procure for them. Their fate would have been either to have passed under absolute government or to have rebelled and made a revolution as their fellows in France did a generation after the English Conquest. That, however, leads us into the realm of speculation. The hard fact is that French Canada entered the English period without formal institutions of freedom: its citizens had no legal rights against the state.

The question is whether, in the two centuries since the conquest, French Canada has managed to incorporate the institutions which were grafted upon it by the rough process of conquest. Have they become, as they are in English Canada, the bone and fibre of the community?

This is very much to be doubted. One of the honourable members of this committee in examining a gentleman who presented one of the briefs seemed to find it incredible that a police officer should not have the power to prevent the distribution of pamphlets within his jurisdiction, if he considered them to be improper to be distributed publicly.[1] Almost any English Canadian would find it incredible that a police officer should have this power, because to the English Canadian the police officer acts within a very limited range of authority and could not possibly be entrusted with wide discretion, since what he does must be done under the law. I hope I am not pressing this point too far when I suggest that a willingness to give discretionary power to the police officer indicates a survival of the mentality of the old régime, when the authorities, either as intendants or *sub-delegués*, or captains of militia, could exercise almost any kind of discretion without necessarily having specific authority for it.

Of course, there are obviously many areas of Canadian life in which French Canada has adopted English institutions in the most intimate and thorough-going way, particularly such areas as Parliament and representative government generally. It is hard to say what the exact influence of the last two centuries has been in the life of French Canada, and some opinion upon this might perhaps better be deferred until the English institutions themselves have been examined.

It cannot be too emphatically pointed out that the French and English

---

[1]Canada, Parliament, Senate, *Proceedings of the Special Committee on Human Rights and Fundamental Freedoms* (Ottawa: King's Printer, 1950), pp. 154-55.

traditions began at almost the same point: they began in the feudal monarchy of the France of the eleventh century. William the Conqueror was a Frenchman, the vassal of the king of France. All his conceptions were French. So far as I know, no king of England for three hundred years after the Norman Conquest in 1066 was able to speak English. Yet this was the formative period during which all the characteristic English institutions grew up. English institutions — that is to say the common law, the writ system, royal justice, the courts, the jury system, the system of trial, criminal law, the land law, the law of property and of succession to property, the council, the House of Lords, the House of Commons, and innumerable minor institutions — all these were forged by medieval, French-speaking Roman Catholics. English institutions, in their origins, are mostly French.

But since the Middle Ages, the two countries have had very different histories and have diverged widely, so that English institutions have come to have their own genius which is as different as can be from anything that the France of the pre-revolutionary period knew, and that is the only France we are concerned with, for it is the true motherland of French Canada, not the modern republican and democratic France, whose institutions have been copied in turn in large part from those of England.

England was much smaller than France, and because of this from the first there was a much higher degree of public order. This public order represented an equipoise between king and feudal baron. The evidences of this equipoise or balance are to be seen in the many formal legal settlements of their differences. When king and baronage fought each other in England, the result was not complete triumph by either party, but compromise. It is these compromises which are embodied in the historic documents that constitute for England, her fundamental law. These documents are numerous. I name, among others, the Charter of Liberties of Henry I, 1100; Magna Carta, 1215; The Provision of Oxford, 1258; The Confirmation of the Charters, 1297. The very essence of Magna Carta is that it is an agreement between the king and his barons that the customs which have always obtained will continue to obtain. But Magna Carta is only the most prominent of these documents, for they all point in the same direction. Magna Carta came to be symbolic, and on each occasion when a king's hand got too heavy, the invariable recourse was to ask for another confirmation of the Great Charter. Its details were soon forgotten, though reissued at frequent intervals through the whole medieval period, but it came to stand for the idea that there was a point beyond which the king could not go, that the king had to behave himself in accordance with custom, and that in the last resort there was a principle in the state more powerful than he was. In testimony to this principle, two medieval kings, Edward II and Richard II were deposed. The Bills of Accusation against Richard II contained as the main charge the accusation that he had said that "the laws of England were in his own breast." By the year of his deposition, 1399, Englishmen had decided that the laws of England had to be in the statute book.

By the year just mentioned, 1399, England had secured a fundamental law, the fundamental law stated in the Charter and particularly the idea contained in its famous thirty-ninth section:

> No freeman shall be captured or imprisoned or disseised or outlawed or exiled or in any way destroyed, nor will we go against him or send against him, except by the lawful judgment of his peers or by the law of the land.
>
> Nullus liber homo capiatur aut imprisonetur aut dissaisietur aut utlagetur aut exulatur aut aliquomodo destrauatur, nec contra eum ibimus nec mittemus vel per legale iudicium pariorium suorum vel per legum terrae.

The very essence of this section consists in the rule of law. While the word "freemen" was originally used in the feudal sense and no doubt did not include the bulk of the people of England, yet as time went on the class of freemen got larger and larger until eventually it came to include every British subject. The fundamental law of England, therefore, simply consists in the concept that at all times the rule of law shall prevail and that there cannot be anywhere in the state arbitrary authority. After the Middle Ages closed, England experienced nearly a century of revolution, and it was during this period, which consisted of the great revolutions against the Stuarts, that the spirit which we still possess was infused into the historic institutions which had already been established.

When Englishmen left England and came to America to found their colonies, they had very clear ideas as to what these historic institutions were. They brought out with them and were ready to assert what they called "the laws of England." They insisted on the "rights of Englishmen," and this many years before King Charles's head was cut off. Both Massachusetts and Virginia were founded before the outbreak of the English Civil War, that is to say, before the parliamentary monarchy had been established. But the inhabitants of both these colonies soon asserted their rights as Englishmen, and these rights consisted in representative institutions and the English common law. Representative institutions and common law developed in America according to their own genius and today have become rather different in the United States from what they are in the parent land.

No doubt they would have developed in much the same way in England if it had not been for the attempt of the Stuart kings, Charles I and James II, to revamp the institutions and common law to their own advantage and bring England nearer to the model then prevailing on the continent of Europe, which model was absolute monarchical government. The result of the attempts of the Stuart kings to impose this type of régime on England was that Charles I lost his head and James II lost his crown. A new king and queen, William III and Mary, daughter of James II, were brought in and accepted the monarchy in their joint names. They also accepted the famous statement which went with it, the Declaration of Rights. This statement, which was passed into law as the Bill of Rights of 1688, was looked upon as the fundamental law of the revolution, that is, the fundamental law of parliamentary monarchy, and although it is true that it is an act of Parliament and can theoretically be changed by another act of Parliament, yet it was part of the settlement, and the Crown of England today rests on that settlement. It would be an arguable point that if the Bill of Rights were changed in any serious way then the whole pact made in 1688 between the people of England and their new sovereigns would be repudiated and that the present reigning house would then cease to have valid title to the Crown. The Hanoverian Succession, the Bill of Rights, and that other great document of the period, the Act of Succession, all go together, and it is difficult to see how one could be changed in any serious particular without invalidating the others.

The parliamentary monarchy is a familiar story, and no one would now waste much time in championing the rights of Parliament against the king. The battle of liberty has shifted into other areas. One of the main areas is the battle of Parliament, or rather those it represents — the people — against those in control of the Crown, that is to say the executive or the cabinet. The cabinet is the modern Crown and it is rapidly assuming a far more powerful place than the Stuarts ever had, and also a more intrinsically irresponsible one. If the Stuart revolution ever had to be re-enacted, the parliamentary side will be the same old side, but the place of the Crown will be taken by the prime minister and his colleagues. It is difficult to foresee the necessity of cutting off the head of any prime minister of Canada, but the fact that it might some day be necessary to proceed to stringent measures against the chief executive is possibly a salutary check on the propensity of all those in public office to increase both their power and their importance.

The modern struggle for liberty centres in the stuggle between the executive and the people or their representatives. In this struggle the people have various historic weapons in their hands. I have pointed out one, and perhaps the chief one — the fundamental idea that law and not personal will is the principle of the state. There are many others; among them representative government is probably the most important.

It is impossible in a short document to debate the pros and cons of representative government. We all know both its shortcomings and excellences. Its shortcomings arise from the weakness of human nature and from the severe discipline of the modern political party. Despite such difficulties most people recognize that representative government manages to impose a check upon the executive tendency towards despotism which no other instrument can. All I could add here would be an exhortation to members of Parliament to remember the great traditions that lie behind Parliament and to cultivate the independence of character and of decision which their predecessors have shown over the last seven centuries at various critical stages of the history of the English-speaking world.

In the day-to-day working of our institutions, nothing has been more practically important than the English system of law. It furnishes the strongest possible contrast with the French system of law, particularly in the nature of its trials. Historically, the English trial is a free-for-all between plaintiff and defendant waged in the presence of neighbours. Here the words of Magna Carta still strictly apply, "nor will we go against him *... except by lawful judgment of his peers or by the law of the land."* The law of the land means immemorial custom, which assumes that a man must have his chance to confront those who make accusation against him, to examine them in public, and at a given moment to appeal to a group of his neighbours to decide whether he is guilty or innocent — the jury. Trial in open court, the right to confront hostile witnesses, the right to plead guilty or not guilty, and then to keep silent (not to have to testify against oneself), the right to put oneself on the country (that is to say, appeal to the jury), all these are immemorial English rights. The essence of trial is publicity. All these rights were established many centuries ago, long before parliamentary monarchy made its appearance, and they have been carried out from England to the ends of the earth. They are so deeply rooted in people of English descent that it is difficult for them to envisage any other kind of public trial.

That is why the spy investigations of a few years ago made such a profound impression on English Canada. In their secrecy, their denial of legal counsel to the accused, their fact of virtually making the accused testify against themselves, they cut across the most deep-rooted conceptions. They were Roman law proceedings. One of the most popular acts of the Long Parliament before the Civil War of 1642 was the destruction of what were called the Prerogative Courts, prominent among which was the Star Chamber. The animus against the Star Chamber was precisely because the proceedings were Roman law proceedings. In the Star Chamber men could be required to testify against themselves, and if they would not speak, the use of torture was not unknown, and all this could be done in secret. Three centuries ago Englishmen unceremoniously expelled Roman law proceedings, with their nasty suggestion of torture always hanging in their background, and have never allowed them to come back. The antagonism shown in Canada to the method of conducting the spy investigation (and certainly not because Canadians looked with favour on the spies) is possibly a guarantee that Roman law proceedings will not be allowed to get a serious hold in those provinces of Canada in which the common law historically prevails.

In Quebec, with its Roman law traditions, the outlook is much more uncertain. I am quite sure no English province would pass a Padlock Law. Those French-speaking Canadians who know my record, and many of them do, know I am actuated by nothing but sincere friendship for French Canada, and in passing an opinion upon the Padlock Law I certainly do not condemn the French-speaking people of Canada. I regard the Padlock Law as their affliction and know that many of my personal friends feel a deep sense of personal humiliation because it is on the statute books of their province. One of the members of this honourable committee expressed the view that those who protest against the Padlock Law are insulting the Province of Quebec.[2] On the contrary, it is those who have passed and supported such arbitrary measures as the Padlock Law, which are in complete antithesis of the spirit of free institutions, who are insulting the Province of Quebec and who are, incidentally, by such measures taking the surest course to ensure mounting success for that political creed against which those measures have been enacted.

It is a sure instinct for the safe course to trust to the historic processes of trial. Justice at times may miscarry, and naturally judges are human beings, but the guarantee of publicity, the assurance that somehow or other you can get your case heard, and the innumerable devices of freedom with which the citizen has been surrounded, are the unique monument of the English-speaking race, its greatest contribution to the world's civilization. I wish to pay this unreserved tribute to the legal tradition we have inherited from England and to enjoin upon all members of the legal profession their duty to preserve it in unsullied form.

During the last century and a half or so, this country has been more or less self-governing and has taken the traditions which it received from France and England and made them its own. In some cases there has been some amalgamation, but in most it has been a matter of adaptation. One thinks at once of the way in which the British system of parliamentary government was adapted to Canadian usage, principally through the two great devices of responsible government and federalism. Both these great achievements were the work of both races. With responsible government we associate the names of Louis Hippolyte Lafontaine and Robert Baldwin, to say nothing of others scarcely less prominent. With federalism we as-

[2]Ibid., pp. 29-30, and see also pp. 109, 241 for further remarks on the subject by Senator Gouin and pp. 240-43 for similar remarks by Senator David.

sociate the names of many, among others John A. Macdonald and George Etienne Cartier. Those are the specific Canadian accomplishments in public institutions, but the legal systems, which had existed previously were simply continued. Thus the English provinces of Canada are common law provinces, and the Province of Quebec has the laws of Canada as they were guaranteed to it by the Quebec Act of 1774 and as they have been added to since.

It should be carefully noted that federalism, as expressed in the British North America Act, took many things for granted. Among others it took for granted the whole background of common law institutions which the English-speaking Canadians had brought overseas with them, just as the New Englanders brought out with them in 1630 the laws of England, the rights of Englishmen. So the English-speaking Canadians in 1867 felt secure in their possession of the historical rights and privileges under English law. Those included not only the obvious and specific institutions such as representative government, trial by jury, and habeas corpus, but also all those freedoms which the common law had taken for granted and for which Englishmen had had to fight their king in the seventeenth century. In 1867, when the British North America Act was passed, it would not have appeared necessary to many people to state that British subjects were possessed of freedom of speech or of freedom of assembly. Such rights were taken for granted and if documentary evidence of their existence were needed the Bill of Rights of 1688 could be pointed to.

In the period since Confederation, we have got a considerable distance further away from our English origins. Unfortunately, there are not many of us Canadians who can substitute for inherited tradition a sound knowledge of history. In the period since Confederation our population has been reinforced by hundreds of thousands of people from countries ouside the English tradition. The result is that today the average man is probably not as aware of his historic rights and privileges as was his great-grandfather. To the average Canadian today, the execution of Charles I, the abdication of James II, the Petition of Rights, the Bill of Rights, the Act of Succession, and other great fundamental documents such as these are hardly known: they may get cursory mention in school-days, but they are hardly part of our bone and fibre, so to speak. Responsible government and Confederation we framed ourselves, and while no doubt the ordinary man could not give a very reasoned explanation of these institutions, yet the average citizen may be said to *feel* how Confederation works: while he cannot distinguish between the powers that belong to the Dominion and those that belong to the provinces, he has a measure of appreciation of how the two governments work in relationship to each other.

But he knows only in the vaguest way that he has other rights which have come down to him through other channels. He more or less takes it for granted that he has the right to say what he likes but can hardly cite chapter and verse for this right. This is probably the outstanding difference between the people of Canada and the people of England, for in England battle after battle has been fought, either to preserve those fundamental rights or to win them, and each battle has renewed the memory of all previous battles. For example, when, a generation ago, the struggle for women's suffrage was taking place in England, much resistance was offered to "votes for women," and many scenes of struggle and a certain degree of violence ensued. Women quickly reminded themselves of the struggle their ancestors had waged against Charles I or the struggle for the reform of Parliament in 1832. This relatively minor struggle for political freedom produced a review of the whole course of the historic English struggle for freedom. Nothing of the sort occured in Canada. Most people simply assumed that if women wanted suffrage, they ought to have it, and in all provinces except Quebec it came without any fight worth talking about. This has been the invariable course of the struggle for political privilege in Canada: our freedom has come easily and the result has been that we have neither understood very clearly whence it has come, nor valued it too highly once we have got it.

The United States resembles England in this respect: it has had to fight for its freedom, and, like England, its victories in the cause of liberty have been marked by great resounding documents and declarations which can never be lost sight of. No American can ever forget the ringing words of the Declaration of Independence — "We hold these truths to be self-evident...." — no American ever forgets the solemn declarations in the first ten amendments to the American Constitution, the so-called Bill of Rights. The Americans have had the great good fortune to produce men at various times in their history capable of enunciating in eloquent words this fundamental principle of a free society. I refer to such figures as Thomas Jefferson, Abraham Lincoln, and Franklin Roosevelt. The British too, of course, have been conspicuous in this respect, and no one can discuss a subject like this without having come to mind the extraordinary eloquence of Mr. Churchill in this last war. It is of the utmost importance to the health of a free society that from time to time the principles upon which it is founded be restated. Such men as I have named have made these restatements for Great Britain and the United States. What of Canada?

In English Canada hardly a figure comes to mind whose words have risen above the pedestrian level in such matters, certainly not since Confederation. English Canada is a land conspicuously lacking in prophets. Before Confederation this was not quite so true, for in those days, the abuses in government produced men like Joseph Howe, Robert Baldwin, and William Lyon Mackenzie.

In French Canada, I am happy to say, the great tradition of freedom has found eloquent utterance. A small people who can produce a Louis-Joseph Papineau, a Louis Lafontaine, and a Sir Wilfred Laurier have nothing to be ashamed of. I like particularly to dwell on an incident in Laurier's career which concerned the Salvation Army. When the Army first began to hold its processions in the city of Quebec about fifty years ago, it was met with obstruction and abuse of much the same type as the minor Protestant sects are encountering in the Province of Quebec today. Laurier faced the situation squarely; he wrote to the mayor of Quebec "the Army must be allowed to march; if necessary I myself will march at the head of the procession." No consideration of votes, no other mere party considerations, deterred Laurier from acting in the interest of freedom and tolerance and in line with what he considered his Christian duty.

That, alas, was fifty years ago.

Each of the three men I have mentioned — Papineau, Lafontaine and Laurier — were steeped in the English tradition of freedom. In their persons, French Canada took over and made its own the English tradition of freedom. It would be difficult to see how French Canada could today repudiate that tradition, together with its institutional expression, without repudiating these three great Canadian sons and to repudiate them would be to repudiate itself. Papineaus, Lafontaines, and Lauriers would have made short work of Padlock Laws. The measure of the greatness of their successors may well lay in their ability to follow in their footsteps. It is to be noted with gratitude that the present prime minister has himself recently made a public gesture that ranks with the courageous attitude of Sir Wilfrid. In his recent pronouncement against racial intolerance Mr. St. Laurent is proving himself a worthy successor of his great predecessors.

If our Canadian tradition can be summarized, then we would have to say that it represents a half-formed amalgamation of English and French traditions, plus a certain admixture of our own native development. We would have to add that today it is in the position of rapidly forgetting its European origins in the process of building its own nationhood but that it is lacking great and eloquent exposition of the doctrine of liberty. What Canada needs at the moment is something which will summarize her vital traditions, that is to say, the tradition of freedom, and place it, as it were, within the reach of the ordinary plain man.

I can think of no more effective method of bringing our traditions within the ordinary man's grasp than to forge some kind of public restatement. If we were to encounter a severe crisis of liberty, such as England encountered in 1940, then we might hear some Churchillian voice sounding out of Ottawa. That would be one way of restating our traditions. Another way would be to put them in a public document. The British have done this many times, and the Americans have done it on at least two occasions.

It has been on such things as this rather than upon a "high standard of living" that free nations have been built.

My concrete suggestion is that the committee, in its report, attempt to frame such a document. I suggest to the committee that it get the statement of principles first and worry about its constitutional form second. Many of the briefs submitted have elaborated the principles which ought to go into such a statement, and the exceedingly carefully worked-over Declaration of Human Rights constitutes an example. Surely out of all the material on hand the essential statements which underlie a free society can easily be found.

If space permitted it would be a congenial task for me to go further and to indicate to the committee that, as Canon Seeley stated in his eloquent submission,[3] another historic source for principles of freedom and liberalism and of a still more revered nature is to be found: it would not be difficult to show that these principles of a free society are based in the first instance on the Christian view of man, the Christian concept of the individual dignity of man, and the essential worth of every human soul. In other words, both our English and French tradition of a just society is founded upon this still wider tradition of a Christian society. It is obviously very difficult to legislate into force the precepts of the Christian religion. Yet these precepts are not any the less influential because they cannot be enforced. We cannot require by law a man to love his neighbour as himself, but the very existence of that great commandment through the centuries has had a powerful effect, to put it mildly, in making men hate their neighbours rather less than they normally would. It is much the same with the precepts of freedom.

If we state that one of our ideals is to preserve a free society and that a reasonable measure of freedom of speech is necessary to that end, then we can have a mark to shoot at. Our declaration gets into the schools and becomes part of the up-bringing of the rising generation. No one is simple enough to believe a mere declaration will make a free society, but it is far better to have the declaration, because it so powerfully reinforces the efforts of those attempting to keep society free. It might be more difficult than it is to deal with thieves if we did not have the original commandment "Thou shalt not steal."

All this can be summed up in repeating that what we need in Canada at the moment is a powerful and cogent restatement of the principles upon which our society is founded. We need this restatement because our people have been too long without conscious contact with these principles, because we have taken them too much for granted, because there are far too few people in the Canadian state, both French and English, who really are

[3] Ibid., pp. 129-35.

alive to their importance. The stream cannot go on forever flowing through arid territory without tributaries coming in; sooner or later it will dry up. It is in considerable danger just now of drying up — not because many people are consciously trying to assail it, but because its spiritual roots are not receiving adequate nourishment. It is submitted that a statement of the type that I have suggested would have its place in securing the needed nourishment.

The constitutional question of a bill of rights is too large a matter to be argued here, and most considerations which affect it have been brought forward in one or other of the briefs submitted. Possibly I may be allowed to summarize some of the general points heretofore made.

1. Canada is a country of fundamental law, not a country of parliamentary sovereignty, such as Great Britain. The British North America Act is our fundamental legal document. The Privy Council opinion is that somewhere within the powers of dominion Parliament and provincial legislatures lies all legislative power. Yet the limitations on each of these bodies are so patent that it seems to me only a cliché to speak of Canadian parliamentary sovereignty. It is true that in time of war the dominion Parliament, or rather the dominion government (a very different thing), becomes practically sovereign. But at other times the dominion Parliament is far from being a sovereign body for its sovereign powers are limited by the wide range of powers named in section 92 of the British North America Act and other sections of the act.

Similarly, no provincial legislature is sovereign because of the existence of the dominion Parliament. It is a very different thing to say that the two sets of bodies put together are sovereign than to say that either one in itself is sovereign, We have only a limited version of parliamentary sovereignty in Canada, and almost every clause of the British North America Act testifies to the limitations placed upon our legislative bodies. Our lawyers have been so steeped in the British tradition that they have not been able, for the most part, to see the essential divergence which has occurred between it and our own. The essence of that divergence is that Canada is a country based on fundamental law, a fundamental law which preserves large areas of their power from the dominion Parliament or from the provincial legislatures or, indeed, in practice from both, for it is rather absurd to talk about parliamentary sovereignty when everybody knows that, even if the desire existed to do so, it would be virtually impossible to alter the provisions in our Constitution which conferred legal rights upon Quebec's Roman Catholics and Protestants in education and legal rights upon the use of the French language. Canada, I repeat, and in this I disagree with practically every expert whom I have encountered, is not a country of parliamentary sovereignty, but a country of fundamental law.

2. Canada's fundamental law, as contained in the British North America

Act, assures community rights but does not assure individual rights. It, therefore, needs over-hauling and remodelling in order to incorporate within it the historic rights preserved by the English constitution through the agency of great constitutional documents and by the American Constitution through the Constitution itself.

3. The meaning of the property and civil rights clause of section 92 of the British North America Act has been elucidated in briefs already presented to the committee. Its history can be briefly given. When in 1774 the Quebec Act restored to Canada the "Laws of Canada," it specifically provided for matters concerning property and civil rights, which were to be decided according to the "Laws of Canada." In doing this it simply lifted a phrase from the old French law and, as Professor Scott has shown, made provision for dealing with family matters, family property, and that sort of thing under the law to which the people of Canada had long been accustomed. It did not even include under this law mercantile rights or business law. The phrase "property and civil rights" passed into the law of the old Province of Lower Canada and was transferred to the list of provincial powers when the Confederation proposals were written down. It has virtually nothing to do with civil liberties, which are an entirely different matter. Over some eighty years of historical ignorance, our courts have succeeded in building into the words "property and civil rights" completely unwarranted conceptions. The consequence is that people have got the impression that the provinces are in control of all the ordinary historic liberties. If so they have had control conferred upon them by the misunderstandings of the courts. To the layman it would appear plain that since men usually lose their civil liberties by some contravention of the criminal law, civil liberties, for the most part, must be the concern of the Parliament of Canada.

There is the wider consideration that Canada, as a federation proceeding from the people of Canada, can only be made to work if its citizens have the freest possible opportunity for discussion, assembly, printing, and so on. Mr. Justice Canon in his Alberta press case brought this principle out, and it is now an important milestone in Canadian legal history.[4] It is possible that the judicial decision alone is enough. I would imagine that the more formal statement of the necessity for civil liberties as wide as the Dominion is preferable.

The only reference to the question of sovereignty which I have seen in the committee's proceeding is a reference by the chairman to the words in the British North America Act: "the Government of Canada shall be

---

[4]In the Supreme Court of Canada [1938], S.C.R. 100. See Peter H. Russell, ed., *Leading Constitutional Decisions, Cases on the British North America Act,* Carleton Library No. 23 (Toronto: McClelland and Stewart, [1965]), pp. 171-75.

vested in the Queen." He considers these "the strongest words in the Act," and with this statement I agree. But does this mean that we have in Canada the historic English monarchy without special application to our own circumstances? If it is the monarchy which is regulated by the Acts of Succession, 1701 and 1936, then I suspect we have the historic monarchy, for these two acts, one of which provided for the Hanoverian succession and the other for the succession of George VI, effectively dispose of any suggestion that the monarchy is aught but the symbol of the people's will. There is no mysticism about the monarchy. The monarch is the symbolic head of the state, maintained in office, as the case of Edward VIII proved, only as long as he acts in accordance with the wishes of the people.

It is fair to say, then, that we have in Canada not only parliamentary monarchy, but a monarchy growing out of the will of the people of Canada and, therefore, a monarch upon whom any conditions that the people of Canada desire may be imposed. If the people of Canada, therefore, desire to limit the freedom of the executive by a general statement of their rights, there is nothing in the nature of the monarchy, in the nature of the principle of sovereignty, to prevent their doing so.

5. "The all-powerful modern executive": I have suggested above that we have arrived at a point where the executive has become exceedingly powerful and in some respects irresponsible. Many people might wish to challenge this point of view, but there is no space here to debate it at length. However, my view is that, under modern parliamentary conditions, the executive, that is to say the cabinet, represents such an extreme concentration of power that it is able for most of the time to impose its will not only upon the individual member, but on Parliament as a whole. Moreover, the executive is so removed from the average voter that the idea of responsible government becomes considerably watered down. It has been said, and, I think, well said, that what we have under our system of government in Canada is the election every five years of something resembling dictatorship.

Fortunately for us in Canada, the dictators whom we elect do not have many qualities that normally come with dictators; therein lies our liberty. Nevertheless, as Shakespeare said, "appetite grows by what it feeds on," and of no appetite is this more true than the appetite for power. Liberty is rarely threatened from the circumference, invariably from the centre. It is not the few rabid sectaries, Christian Brethren, Jehovah's Witnesses, etc., who are threatening the liberties of Quebec: it is the government which enacts Padlock Laws which threatens those liberties. Incidentally, when I was in Germany in the summer of 1949, I found pamphlets widely distributed which pictured Quebec as a place where no liberty of religious opinion was tolerated, an unfree country compared to free Germany. That is not a very pleasant reputation for a Canadian province to have abroad ("Stadt Quebeck, stelle deine Zeugen! Keine Gottesdienst freiheit in der Stadt Quebeck!" — "City of Quebec, station thy witnesses. No freedom of religious service in the city of Quebec!").[5]

These may be strong words but I wish to emphasize them. The threat to liberty comes from people in power, not from people out of power. What the good citizen has to do always is to watch out for his governors whether these be called civil servants, bureaucrats, policemen, or cabinet ministers. I am not waging war upon individual cabinet ministers, among whom there are just as ardent devotees of freedom as I am. I am simply suggesting that office is always a dangerous thing to those holding it and that we shall always do well to maintain and increase the curbs upon persons in power. The whole trend of the times seems to be in favour of increasing the powers of the state. Whatever public declarations we make, or documents we have, we shall do well if we keep the flood from tearing down the dikes. But we must not abandon the effort to build up our dikes of liberty, and one of the best methods of proceeding, surely, is to put formal limitations upon our governors.

The man in office invariably wants more power; he always wants a sharp sword to cut through the difficulties of the moment, and it is only human nature that he should do so. It is often difficult to advance good reasons against some measure which will result in an increase in efficiency. But those who are accustomed to such measures in social and historical terms know very well that efficiency can easily be the death of liberty. Liberty was safe in Canada in the old days under our good old easy-going civil service and when our politicians did not take themselves too seriously. Today with brilliant minds thronging into the civil service and with the sense of pressure and crisis in the atmosphere and the increasing seriousness with which ministers have to take themselves, liberty becomes a much battered hulk.

I sum up this point by again asserting that *the danger to liberty is to be found not among those out of office, but among those in office.* If we can succeed in restraining the hand of the official, we shall have gone some distance in assuring ourselves of a free society.

I have put down all this material in the hope that it may be of some assistance to the committee, and I am quite aware that it does not constitute the last word on the subject. It is however, I think, a fair review of the historic background and draws some fair deductions from that background. It is not urged in any partisan spirit or party sense. It is urged simply because, as an historian, I think I can see trends in the past and consequently may be in some position to predict the trends of the future. Liberty is

---

[5] *Erwachet!* 27, no. 6, 22 March 1949.

at all times easily lost and hardly won. It is eternal vigilance that we need.

I exhort the committee to address itself to the task of framing a general statement of liberties and to the further task of deciding the wisest way in which such a statement can be made an integral part of Canadian national life. Since we are already a fundamental law state, I can see no objection in going further in that direction and writing into our fundamental law the well-worn list of rights which the two senior democracies, Great Britain and the United States, have many times enunciated.

24 | *Is the RCMP a Threat to Our Liberty?**

Canadians have the habit of assuming that they are on the side of the angels and that Americans rush in where angels fear to tread. Consequently, when something dramatic occurs like Herbert Norman's suicide, we usually take for granted that Canada is right and the United States wrong.

I wonder if many of us stop to ask what results we expect from righteous indignation. Do we expect to put things right, to change American conduct, the course of American action, American policy? Or are we just letting off steam? If we would only pause a moment to reflect, we would have to admit that however much indigation we generate, few Americans will be aware of it, and especially that the conduct of American congressional committees will not be affected by it. It takes little first hand knowledge of the United States to make anyone understand that.

So if we expect to influence American processes of government (except at the highest levels, where our government can make direct representations), we might just as well save our breath.

What we ought to do, and what most of the time we don't do, is to see that our government and its servants behave themselves. We are supposed to be a self-governing people. I wonder if we really are — that is, beyond electioneering and the outbursts on sensational issues. The Norman affair revealed to us an important branch of our government handing on rumour and hearsay to the American secret police. Being American secret police, the latter find it difficult to keep secrets. And so our officially collected hearsay pops up in a congressional committee, with the tragic result we all know.

Whose fault is that?

The circumstances are still fresh in memory. According to the press

Maclean's, 6 July 1957, pp. 8, 57-58.

(and that is just about the only source of information for the ordinary citizen):

> In October 1950, the RCMP informed the appropriate U.S. security agencies that it had a report from one of its secret agents mentioning Mr. Norman as a member of the Canadian Communist party in 1940. But three months later, the RCMP, after extensive enquiries, reported to the U.S. security agencies that its secret agent's information was a case of "mistaken identity or unfounded rumour by an unidentified sub-source" and it was therefore deleting the earlier reference to Mr. Norman being a communist party member ten years earlier.
> —Canadian Press, April 17, 1957

Few more damning statements about an agency of government can ever have been published. Here is a responsible branch collecting any and all types of hearsay and rumour from "unidentified sub-sources" — in other words, tittle-tattle passed on by irresponsible gossiping — and handing it over to the American secret police, whence it later turns up in congressional committees which, whatever their purpose, publicize it throughout the world. And then over there in alien Egypt, a young Canadian diplomat, this strain added to others, takes his own life!

Again, one may ask, where is the onus of Mr. Norman's death, in so far as the public has been allowed to know the facts, to be placed?

Why blame the Americans?

The budget of the RCMP has increased many times over during recent years; so has its strength:

	Budget	Uniformed Strength	Specials
1925-26	$ 2,251,000	876	87
1935-36	6,165,000	2,364	136
1945-46	12,059,000	2,456	173
1955-56	36,557,000	4,569	362

What is all this money and all these men being used for? The RCMP has a fine tradition, inherited from old North West Mounted Police days. But traditions do not just go on: they have to be maintained. And now that the RCMP has become a universal police force, it cannot expect to retain the dashing military reputation it had when it was a frontier constabulary. It is still in part a frontier constabulary, but it is also a municipal police force, a provincial police force (eight provinces out of ten), an anti-drug-traffic organization, and a secret police. Its service as a municipal and provincial police force brings a dangerous degree of centralization in our police forces. A government that had a long-range vision of popular liberty would not allow it: that, however, is another story. It is as a secret police that the RCMP's role contrasts most sharply with its old functions. Musical rides and brilliant uniforms do not go well with the habits of the investigator and the spy. When the police collect rumour from "unidentified sub-sources" and treat it seriously (fancy the stacks of it that must be filed away in Ottawa), it is hard to see how they can be distinguished from secret police in other countries, most of them of evil repute.

Yet apparently rumour-collecting is one of the RCMP's functions. Worse still, it hands this trash over to representatives of a foreign power, for them to use at their discretion. Surely such activity is more dangerous to our liberty than the threats it is supposed to guard us against.

Those who have watched Canadian affairs over the years will probably date the beginnings of the decline of the RCMP from the Depression years.

I remember calling at a government building in Ottawa during the Imperial Economic Conference of 1932. The old ex-dominion policeman on the door was all dressed up in a new uniform, with a heavy revolver at his side. I said to him: "You look very dangerous with that weapon; have you tried it on anybody yet?" "No," he replied, drawing it from its holster, "as a matter of fact, they didn't issue us any ammunition for it." We both laughed.

One can still laugh with the policeman in most of our Ottawa buildings, for the pleasant old atmosphere of confidence is by no means gone. And, moreover, when one has official business with the RCMP, he is invariably politely and correctly received. But an incident from the later 1930's perhaps indicates the trend. A friend of mine told me at the time that he had been meeting with a few other men — privately — in a municipal building to discuss foreign affairs. One day the janitor said to him that a Mountie had been round inviting him to listen at the keyhole, as it were, on the allegation that "those fellows are Communists." So apparently things were changing.

And then came the emphasis on "security" during the war, with the people ready to give unlimited elbow-room to the military and the police because of the threats from Hitler. With the atmosphere like that, there came at the end of the war the famous "spy trials," which predisposed a large section of the public to decisive action against suspects. After those held for inquisition had been kept incommunicado for some time, a man said to me, "They must be guilty or they wouldn't have arrested them." How much did it mean to him that one of the finest of our traditions is that a man is innocent until he is proved guilty?

Has all this tempted us Canadians to begin taking leaves out of Nazi and Communist books?

I once had an interview with the Russian OGPU, at that time the name for their secret police: two, in fact; one at a station halfway between Moscow and Leningrad about two in the morning, the other on the Finnish border. I certainly would not wish to fall into the clutches of those lads!

We do not expect our federal police to turn into an OGPU. But we would be poor citizens if we were not aware of the direction in which a police force which is maintained mainly for political purposes leads. It leads, and perhaps speedily, toward the dreaded secret police of these older, unfree countries, and it must be pretty hard to keep out of it all the practices associated with such forces — the secret interviews, the *agents provocateurs,* the spies, the midnight arrests, the inquisitions. And these must sooner or later drag in their wake the whole list of horrors — the cruelties to extort confessions (that is, torture), the brainwashing, all that against which we are ready to fight. Wouldn't it be ironic if we found ourselves fighting for it? "Can it happen here?" Of course it can, and the greater our ignorance of what goes on behind closed official doors, the more quickly it is likely to happen.

Here again, it is possible that the tradition of the RCMP may be our salvation and its own, for in its origins it was more a military than a police force. We assume that our soldiers are citizens, imbued with the same attitude as the rest of us, and I think we are right. Let us hope that we can make the same assumption about our political police.

But then there is this business of collecting hearsay. Is that soldierly conduct? Collecting careless and casual hearsay? From "unidentified sub-sources"? Then, inability to trace the rumour, casualness in reporting it to the American political police. Meanwhile an able servant of Canadian diplomacy takes his own life.

One wonders how far this tie-in with the FBI has gone. Have our police been playing the same subordinate role to it as our Teamsters' unions have played to Dave Beck? One gets used to labour unions being controlled from across the line, but it comes with something of a shock to think the same sort of thing may be happening to branches of our government.

But, says the reader, the RCMP is under the minister of justice, a responsible cabinet minister. The answer to that one is simple: many modern branches of government, thanks to the complexity of their affairs, are virtually laws unto themselves and ministerial interference can neither be frequent nor effective. It would take a strong minister indeed to assert himself against the organized police. Let him, for example, try to cut down the money they demand from him! As often as not, now that bureaucracy has grown so portentously, the servant of the state, whether civil servant or policeman, is not in reality so much responsible to the minister as the minister is to him. So the RCMP, a powerful and wealthy branch of government, for practical purposes can be assumed to be an autonomous body; as long as some general ministerial assent lies somewhere in the background, it is probably not far from a law unto itself.

The sooner this state of things is ended the better. Only a vigilant public opinion, reflected in genuine parliamentary control, will end it. The sooner we citizens insist that our servants cease to disseminate hearsay under the guise of official duty, the better it will be for this country of ours.

25 | *Some Reflections on a Bill of Rights**

Objection: We already have a bill of rights: it became the Declaration of Rights and forms part of the Revolution settlement of 1688. It is an integral part of "The Protestant Succession" and cannot be upset without upsetting that.

Answer: Unfortunately, the Declaration has been caught up in the doctrine of parliamentary supremacy, and over two centuries of usage prevent its being restored as fundamental law.

Query: Is the doctrine of fundamental law quite dead? Fundamental rights are implicit in all our assumptions. In Canada, the B.N.A. Act and amendments, plus the Statute of Westminster, are fundamental law. Could not the Declaration of Rights be joined to them?

Answer: If so, it must be made explicit, and restored to its place. But it may be admitted, quite freely, that in Canada there are limitations to the doctrine of parliamentary supremacy: these lie in the point made above and in the very nature of federalism. It would, therefore, be no wide departure for us to enlarge our fundamental law (our "constitution") by explicitly mentioning in it that English structure of law which nearest approaches fundamental law, namely, the Revolution settlement; this consists essentially in two things: (*a*) the change of dynasty, and (*b*) bound up with (*a*), and as integral a part of it as enactment at the time could make it, is the Declaration of Rights.

The Declaration of Rights was repeated almost verbatim in the first ten amendments of the American Constitution.

Neither of these, the Declaration of Rights nor the Bill of Rights in the first ten amendments is sufficient in itself for the language is somewhat archaic, the prohibitions are not definite enough, and their range is too negative. What is necessary is a revamping, with modern terminology, enlargement, and exactitude, and especially a positive statement of rights or list of rights.

The question to be initially faced is whether a bill of rights should be a simple statute or whether it should be a constitutional amendment. The latter is preferable, but at our Canadian rate of proceeding, it will take many years to effect. A statute, on the other hand, is repealable. Yet such a statute would constitute a declaration of principle, it would give a text from which to preach, it would form one additional hurdle for Parliament to take when it next consented to abrogation of civil liberties,

**Fortnightly Law Journal* 16 (15 February, 1 March 1947): 216-218, 234-237.

and it would make that abrogation a much more solemn thing than it has hitherto been.

What should be contended for? As to practical procedure, the utmost that one could envisage in this winter of 1947 would be to secure a debate, to be followed by a parliamentary committee of investigation: at this, briefs and suggestions could be presented.

What should be contended for at such a committee?

1. Repeal of the War Measures Act.

A long argument can be made against the wisdom of this act. The principal criticism is that it constitutes an abrogation of the powers of Parliament. It is as complete a power of attorney as Hitler ever got out of the Reichstag: in fact, the procedure involving it is very similar to Nazi procedure. Only our good luck has saved us during two wars from very bitter experiences. As the sense of freedom in our people is gradually weakened (and how greatly it has weakened in the last generation), it will be possible for authorities to go farther and farther. Another crisis would certainly see the power of Parliament further cut into: it would see a more complete abrogation of civil rights, and one more harshly enforced. It would enhance the power of the police: and the third degree, heretofore only having its toe in the Canadian door (as in the electric light incident at Ottawa during the espionage detentions), would probably come right in. The War Measures Act is the head and shoulders of the offending.

2. Strengthening of safeguards against arbitrary arrest and detention.

Once abandon the theory of freedom from arbitrary imprisonment (secured by habeas corpus), and you abandon everything. Men can be picked up as they habitually are in Russia and Germany, and spirited away, God knows where. Dead men tell no tales. Who is to say whether a man arrested and not produced in court is dead or alive? The struggle to throw safeguards around Section 21 of the War Measures Defence of Canada Regulations was long and only partially successful. It may be conceded guardedly that the state needs extra powers during a war (though the United States did not resort to such arbitrary measures as did Canada), but they must be surrounded with all proper safeguards. It is difficult to see why habeas corpus should be suspended by such regulations as Section 21. Let those detained be brought into court in the ordinary way. If the state cannot proceed with trial owing to the danger from enemies (such as comes from revelation of information), let the minister make a statement and let the court test that statement. It should not be beyond legal ingenuity to devise proper machinery for preserving justice. The essential thing is to guard against secret imprisonment: this is much more invidious than imprisonment without trial.

3. Revision of the Official Secrets Act.

As this act stands, virtually no one accused under it can have a chance against the state. As in the case of Wing Commander Poland, it is possible to cite the act against a person who merely has the name of the agent of a foreign power on his telephone pad. The good sense of the trial court prevailed in this case, despite the previous exhortations of the commission urging guilt, but that may not always occur. The Official Secrets Act, in terms of pure law, taken at its face value, and without allowing for the common sense interpretations of the courts, might just as well read: "all persons against whom a charge is laid are *ipso facto* guilty."

No time should be lost in taking out of the Act the un-British principle that presumption of guilt exists until innocence is proved.

It is no argument to bring forward the British statute as justification. British circumstances are not necessarily the same as ours. Moreover, British legislation and regulation of this type seems, as a rule, to be wiser and less arbitrary than ours. The British Defence of the Realm Acts, and the regulations under them, have been better drawn and have left more scope to historic principle than have the Canadian War Measures Act and Defence Regulations. The British acts have not been in the blanket terms of our War Measures Act but have been subject to parliamentary safeguards. In Great Britain, these are real: the British Parliament is less amenable to cabinet authority than is the Canadian; there is a wider range of independent judgment contained in it, and its members share the instinctive feeling for what is socially expedient which characterizes their very old and mature community and contrasts with our own, which is easily swept off its feet by unusual situations.

Moreover, the British themselves could normally plead greater necessity than can we. It is to be suspected that the severity of our measures of late years comes not from necessity (after all Great Britain was closer to the war than was Canada) but from the hysteria of an inexperienced and frustrated people. Certainly government will now have a hard time convincing people that the safety of the state was endangered by the actions of a few misguided spies. The conduct of government, from prime minister to royal commission, over the espionage case, bore every appearance of hysteria, when it did not bear the appearance, as unfortunately in certain quarters it did, of sheer persecution.

It is consequently difficult to argue for the *necessity* of the Official Secrets Act in its present form.

4. Revision of the Public Inquiries Act.

Under the present law, apparently, a royal commission can be made into a device for requiring a man to testify against himself, as did most of those detained in seclusion and examined in respect to espionage. The act can be made into an instrument to extort evidence. Heretofore, in so far as the layman can ascertain, the dirty work has been done by the police. With the recent royal commission in respect to espionage, it was assumed by two justices of the Supreme Court. Revision should render it impossible for heretofore respected judges so to besmirch themselves in future, by removing the right of examination in secret and without counsel.

War Measures Act, Official Secrets Act, the Inquiries Act (in the latest use to which it has been put), and similar legislation constitute for Canada the blueprints of dictatorship.

5. The passage of a statute reaffirming the rights enunciated in the Declaration of Rights and extending and making more explicit such rights. See above as to the relative merits of a statute and a constitutional amendment. It is here argued that a half-loaf is better than no bread. The entire subject is unfamiliar to the Canadian people and to most of their legislators: our task at first is exploratory and educative. A statute, it must be admitted, would be a great gain and could be used to argue for conversion into an amendment.

6. The exploration of the phrase "the safety of the state."

Salus populi suprema lex literally means *the welfare of the state is the supreme law. Leges silent inter armes* would more exactly express what the authorities have recently had in mind. Or more colloquially "Just you trust me."

Such phrases might be contrasted with the equally valid maxim *fiat justitia, ruat coelum; let justice be done, though the heavens fall.*

Safety of the state is a familiar continental maxim: it may well have strayed into Canadian life through our French continental door, with its basis in Roman law, its authoritative structure, and its lack of knowledge of the personal guarantees of freedom which are the glory of our British inheritance. It was upon a closely allied maxim from Roman law that the French state itself was built: *Quod principi placuit, legis vigorem habet: the will of the prince has the force of law.* In Canada for *prince,* read *minister of justice.*

"Safety of the state" equates to the ill-omened phrase "reasons of state." Napoleon had the Duc d'Enghien murdered "for reasons of state," in other words to suit his own convenience and remove a possible rival. Hitler and Goering had murders performed in the thousands to secure the "safety of the state." The disturbances of June, 1934, constitute a case in point. After no one yet knows how many people had been slaughtered, when an attempt to overthrow the régime failed (not, it is true by espionage, but by force), Hitler put the point very neatly: "I was for one moment, in my own person, the supreme court of appeal of the German people."

That, of course, is exactly the point to which "reasons of state," considerations based solely on "the safety of the state," to the neglect of justice, invariably lead: they lead logically to the firing squad. It is not suggested that any Canadian minister of today has either the desire or the courage to employ the firing squad: ministers of the day are patently humane and peaceable men. But with sufficient practice, ministers of the future might overcome such disabilities. Our rulers, in general, seem singularly blind to the lessons of history and quite unable to plot their position on the chart of social process. It would seem obvious that the arbitrary experiences of the past few years have shaken our historical position of freedom, and yet the head of the government which has been in power during this period not long ago could make a ringing declaration (over the air) in favour of liberty, just as if the whole structure were as unharmed as in the days of his youth. It is not unfair to characterize this as unawareness of the social process. Once our feet are set on the slopes of arbitrary conduct − slopes built up in Canada of such legislation as the War Measures Act, the Official Secrets Act, and, apparently, the Inquiries Act − it is difficult to avoid sliding, at varying rates of speed, until the bottom is reached. At the bottom lies the supersession of the rule of law, and its concomitant, the firing squad.

"Safety of the state" is a newcomer in English law. In fact, British institutions hardly know the concept "state." Our official word is "crown," and it is on the semi-personal concept of the Crown that our maxims of state have been built up. They invariably reflect, not the ruthlessness and arbitrary will of Roman law, but paternalistic justice: "The king can do no wrong" (that is, if he did, the subject could not proceed against him, would have no "remedy," and for every wrong there must be a remedy); "the King is the fountain of justice." It is maxims such as these that embody the spirit of our institutions, not the foreign interloper, "safety of the state."

It is nevertheless not suggested that government can afford to forget " the safety of the state": that is obviously one of its primary considerations. What has to be decided is whether considerations of safety demand the abrogation of the laws. This will no doubt always be a matter of opinion, the timid and conservative invariably being for strong measures, while the generous-minded, the unsuspicious, and the courageous will always be inclined to minimize peril. In this subject, we are on the line between law and ethics, for whether we invoke a given measure or not depends ultimately upon our sense of right and wrong, justice, fair-dealing, magnanimity, and courage.

However, surely no one will deny that resort to severe measures must never be taken except in extreme cases.

The case against our wartime structure of law and its reflections in peacetime (failure to repeal War Measures Act, continuance of Official Secrets Act, etc.) is that these extreme measures were resorted to without sufficient examination, with too little regard for their consequences, without sufficient sense of the kind of régime they were rendering possible, and probably without sufficient justification in the circumstances. There was not any immediate danger of Canada's being invaded by Germany. It is hard to believe that there was any grave danger of the safety of the state being imperilled by the activities of the spies. If the authorities say there was such danger, let them prove it: they have no right to ask citizens to take it on faith. Certainly the results of the spy trials do not prove it. The simple truth seems to be that there are always men in places of authority who prefer short cuts, who are timorous and therefore avail themselves of power, who are impatient of parliamentary methods, who wish "to get things done," or who, by reason of something within themselves, some instinct for power, some egotism, actually desire to bring in authoritarian methods. In September, 1939, many motives such as these conjoined to bring in the War Measures Act and the extremely severe Defence of Canada Regulations: but these were brought in deliberately, and no one could fail to see that they brought our legal edifice very close to absolutism. In the winter of 1946 it seems more likely that government, alarmed by a state of affairs without precedent in Canada but with innumerable precedents in older and less innocent communities, allowed itself to be stampeded. It is time now to examine our situation coolly, in the manner of adults rather than adolescents, and take measures against repetition of the attacks against our traditional liberties.

The above may be summarized in the observation that the safety of the state is best preserved by the least possible departure from the principles of the common law and the well-worn principles which underlie our entire conception of life. The safety of the state is naturally the concern of every loyal citizen (it is that which causes us to rally to the colours), but it can be just as much endangered by hasty legislation and panicky or oversevere regulations as by the external enemy.

It is therefore suggested that the phrase be used as little as possible in the future and that, where it is used, safeguards be thrown about it. It should not be sufficient to state that A.B. was acting in a manner prejudicial to the safety of the state (which may have meant that he was simply scribbling idly on a telephone pad), but that he was doing such and such, conversing with such a one, uttering certain words; in other words, persons accused should be accused of specific wrongdoing, not of an extremely general intent.

The contents of a statute containing a bill of rights:

1. A Canadian bill of rights should, first of all, affirm the linguistic and religious rights enacted into the B.N.A. Act. These are expressions of fundamental law just as truly as are the first ten amendments of the American Constitution.

It would be a fine, generous gesture if the Canadian people would consent to the extension of the language clauses by adding to the B.N.A. Act, section 133, the words: "The official languages of Canada shall be English and French."

2. Secondly, the bill of rights should affirm the historic rights of the subject against the Crown. These are conveniently summarized in the third amendment to the American Constitution, which adds to them a guarantee of religious freedom: — "Congress shall make no law respecting an establishment of religion, or prohibiting the free exercise thereof; or abridging the freedom of speech, or of the press; or the right of the people peaceably to assemble, and to petition the government for redress of grievances."

And in the fourth: "The right of the people to be secure in their persons, houses, papers and effects, against unreasonable searches and seizures, shall not be violated, and no Warrants shall issue but upon probable cause, supported by Oath or affirmation, and particularly describing the place to be searched and the person or things to be seized."

And in the fifth: "No person ... shall be compelled in any Criminal Case to be a witness against himself, nor be deprived of life, liberty or property without due process of law." And in the sixth: "In all criminal prosecutions, the accused shall enjoy the right to a speedy and public trial, by an impartial jury ... and to be informed of the nature and cause of the accusation; to be confronted with the witnesses against him ... and to have the Assistance of Counsel for his defence."

And in the eighth: "Excessive bail shall not be required, nor excessive fines imposed ...." And in the ninth: "The enumeration in this Constitution of certain rights, shall not be construed to deny or disparage others retained by the people."

It would require little adaptation to make the American Bill of Rights (which, it must be emphasized, is the English Declaration of Rights of 1688 reshaped and extended) fit the Canadian situation. If it be argued that abstract statements do not, in fact, secure liberty, the reply is that, during the war just ended, the American Constitution did equally, in fact, constitute a sheet-anchor and that there was in the United States little of the authoritarian legislation by which the rights of Canadians were taken away. It would have been quite impossible to have had the law of the land transmuted into some sixty arbitrary war regulations, as was done in Canada. It would have been impossible, in face of the Constitution, to get legislation authorizing secret imprisonment or abridging the freedom of speech. History does not record that the United States, by reason of its failure to cast its ancient liberties on the sacrificial pyre, suffered any undue consequences.

3. Thirdly, a bill of rights should state the principle of the equality of all citizens.

Over the years, Canada has developed a system of graded citizenship, some persons enjoying full rights in every respect, others enjoying the protection of the laws but being denied the specific attributes of the citizen in a democracy, namely the franchise. More especially now that we have made the classification "Canadian citizen" a legal concept, we cannot deny by our conduct that which we solemnly affirm by our words. The tacit assumption upon which the idea of citizenship rests is that all persons capable of performing duties have correlative rights. This is the very foundation stone of democracy. Not long ago, the older conception was referred to in Parliament, namely that government and Parliament are emanations of the king's will. This view, which is still the formal basis of our law, though now of antiquarian interest only, was at once vigorously repudiated by representatives of the leading opposition parties, both conservative and radical, who strongly emphasized that Canada is a democratic state, namely one in which government proceeds from the will of the governed.

In an age very different from our own, it was possible for government to rest upon the monarch because he was regarded as the chosen of God. Now that we unreservedly accept the doctrine of the sovereignty of the people, it is difficult to see how "the people" can be divided up, some to govern, others to be governed. Such a division shifts the sanction for government to the mere basis of power: that group which is strong enough disfranchises at its discretion other groups in weaker positions and presumably would have no cause for complaint if, the positions being reversed, it was itself disfranchised. The equality of all Canadian citizens should be affirmed. The right of banishment recently conferred on the federal government by the Privy Council in its decision on the deportation of Japanese Canadians should be surrendered by the Crown: a clause in the bill of rights should specifically state that a Canadian citizen may not be banished from Canada. This decision of the Judicial Committee would seem virtually to restore the early medieval punishment of outlawry, since if a citizen is banished and is then found on Canadian soil, he presumably possesses no rights under the law. Banishment should be abolished.

This affirmation has nothing to do with the conditions which may be required of those seeking to becoming citizens. Every state naturally has the right to scrutinize the qualifications of those seeking to become its citizens. But to discriminate between its native-born citizens, awarding degrees of excellence (or privilege) should be anathema.

4. Fourthly, a bill of rights should take note of specifically modern requirements. It should extend the liberty of assembly to the liberty to organize, thus giving to labour the rights it has won by its efforts up to date. It should extend liberty of speech and the press to liberty of broadcasting.

An important question to be decided is as to whether a Canadian bill of rights should include the broad statements of the Atlantic Charter, with its "freedoms." Could these statements be couched in the realistic phrasing of our former bills of rights, with their terse and specific assertions? It should be noted that the American bill takes the form of assuming certain fundamentals as existing and guaranteeing against their violation: "The right of the people to be secure in their persons, etc., shall not be violated."

It is much more difficult to cast rights in positive form. Suppose, for example, a bill of rights contains some such clause as "The right of the citizen to a subsistence at a reasonable level of well-being, secured through his right to be at all times employed, is hereby guaranteed" (this is the "right to work" idea, nowadays much mooted); will such a clause be of practical value? It will certainly not keep the state out of economic difficulties. It is much easier to guarantee negatives than positives. On the other hand, such enunciations of general principle have their value, for they affirm the creed upon which the state is founded. No one can deny the immense influence of "We hold these truths to be self-evident, that all men are born free and equal, and equally entitled to the pursuit of life, liberty and happiness...." However far the United States may have wandered from this profession of faith, it is from time to time brought sharply back to it, and no one can officially repudiate it: it was this profession which lay at the base of the abolition of slavery and which inspires much of the progressive thought and action of that country today. Similarly, there is reason to believe that the saying "Whatsoever ye would that others should do unto you, that do ye unto them" has not been without its effect. It is an injunction, and neither it nor any of the ethic which it represents can be enforced in a court. "A new commandment give I unto you, that ye love one another." Here is a commandment which cannot in any respect be enforced, but which millions of men try to obey, which, indeed, colours every aspect of our Western lives. The enunciations of humanitarian principle such as "the guarantee of the right to work" are similar to our traditional ethical injunctions, have about the same effect (though infinitely less potent), and serve the same general purpose.

Consideration at this point should be given to the Declaration of Human Rights which is likely to be framed by the United Nations. It will no doubt also be another mark to shoot at, rather than compelling law. Whether it should be embodied in a Canadian bill of rights is an open question. On the whole it would seem more consistent with our traditions, legal and political, if our declaration were to be kept to relatively small dimensions and the well-worn rights (which really are all-inclusive) reasserted, with appropriate amplifications.

The difficulty in framing a new bill of rights would be that once the subject was opened, a tremendous array of rights would be certain to be put forward, some wise, some foolish, some forward-looking, others merely defensive of vested interests. For this reason, the bill would have to be carefully drawn in relatively general language, for it could not be allowed to become a retrogressive measure.

A second difficulty sure to be raised would be that such a measure would invade provincial jurisdiction, with its control over civil rights. But it is quite obvious that a federation must have its own area of civil right (as the Supreme Court recognized in its decision on the Alberta press case some years ago): a federation is a nicely balanced mechanism, which can exist only so long as all its constituents are able to put forward their point of view. It was no mere coincidence which caused Hitler, as one of his first major acts, to destroy the German Federation (*Deutsches Bund*) and set up a unitary system. Under a unitary system, there can be dictatorship, but not under a federal system. In order to maintain a federation, the means to balance and elasticity must be preserved: these lie in the area of discussion. Grant free discussion, and eventually you grant everything else.

> Rights of citizenship are civil rights and they are not comprehensible within a province. They are Dominion Civil Rights and as such must be under the custody of the Dominion. There are certain underlying conceptions on which the structure of Confederation is built. Some of these are: the principle of judicial review: responsible government, the combined function of working the Courts, the provinces administering justice and constituting the Courts, the Judges being appointed by the Dominion.... Is democratic government ... an implied requirement of our constitution? What does democratic government in this sense connote?
>
> A fourth condition for a national unit presents another aspect of Dominion Civil Rights. This country was founded in the full flood of the British conception of liberty. In the nineteenth century not only had Great Britain enshrined freedom as the guiding principle of her own domestic life but also her government on more than one occasion had shown its sympathy for other peoples struggling to be free. It was the peculiar glory of British institutions at the time of Confederation that they incorporated within them the spirit of individual freedom: freedom, national and individual, was the accepted foundation of the state.... But while the spirit of English institutions was freedom, a legal development had gradually been taking place that put their complete custody in the hands of parliament.... Fundamental law had by the period of Confederation been swept into the net of parliamentary supremacy.... But the rights were regarded as completely established and as substantially inalienable in fact. Not so in the United States, where the constitution was made eighty years before Confederation, at a time when they did not deem that constitutional liberties had been completely established, as they had in Britain and the colonies.... The Americans therefore thought it advisable to set them out specifically.

But the Fathers of Confederation, in the different circumstances of 1867, did not consider such specific provison to be necessary, especially when disallowance and reservation were there to protect them. The necessities of our situation, with nine Provinces, imperatively require equality everywhere to some minimum degree — some common rights of Canadian citizenship. Such rights must be beyond provincial interference, whether or not they are embodied in a Bill of Rights. The British North America Act was a product of its times. Whatever there was of freedom in British institutions in 1867 passed into ours. We, in Canada, were the heirs of all the liberties won in previous centuries. It was inconceivable that the bodies set up for the government of Canada and its Provinces, any more than that of Great Britain itself, would betray this fundamental of all British and Canadian life. Had not Creasy just said that Magna Carta had provided freedom to the utmost "for everyone that breathes English air"? To the people of the time, there seemed no more need to recapitulate those rights and incorporate them in an act than there was to incorporate the ten commandments, English liberty was taken for granted. It was basic in our constitution.

It may therefore be asserted that in the British North America Act, by the very necessities of its existence, there must be found embodied as rights of Canadians as such, those fundamentals historically known as the liberties of the subject. These liberties are traditional. They are the warp and woof of our way of life, as that of all other English-speaking communities, and a part of the democratic system and philosophy. They are the foundation of our conception of citizenship and of the institutional structure of the Dominion and all its Provinces, that is to say, of representative and parliamentary government and the reign of law among a free people, as opposed to the conception and exercise of dictatorial will. To the Fathers it was unthinkable that they should ever be in danger from any British legislature, for that legislature was simply a manifestation of the free men who stood behind it. These rights, to them, were too plain to need expression, they were underlying, basic, implicit and unchallengeable. The Fathers therefore, felt no necessity of especially referring to or safeguarding in express language the traditional and fundamental liberties of the subject from provincial curtailment of annihilation.

The spirit of the times has now changed and experience has shown that the liberties of the subject are no longer completely safe in the legislative hands of the Provinces. What of the Dominion? If the legislature represents the "will of the people" recent experience has tended to show that "the will of the people" may not necessarily be in the direction of traditional liberty. But shall established liberty on that account be jettisoned? Liberties sometimes have to be maintained not by, but against, majorities.[1]

Time works strange changes: the above arguments were mostly directed to the preservation of freedom as against the encroachments of the provinces. Today, and for some years past, it has been from the authorities of the Dominion that the threat has come. "The law of England is the law of liberty." The dominion authorities have during the last eight years, at one time or another, obtained from a subservient, or at least, an uninformed and short-sighted Parliament, legislation that could not conceivably have been obtained from any English-speaking legislature of the period of Confederation. Legislation such as the War Measures Act has had no parallel in English history since the act by which an equally subservient Parliament gave Henry VIII power to legislate by proclamations.[2]

Legislation such as the Official Secrets Act, with its shameless repudiation of the English heritage, would have made Peel or Gladstone turn in their graves. The time evidently has come when our freely elected Parliaments can no longer be depended upon to stand firmly against infringement of the liberty of the subject. The new despotism is indeed again upon us. It does not come this time in the form of a king with extravagant claims of divine right, but in the form of a cabinet with equally extravagant assertions about the safety of the state. Behind the Tudor and Stuart kings, who came so close to erecting an absolute monarchy in England, stood the great administrators ever seeking to extend their powers. A Cecil might wish to extend his powers merely that he might do his job more efficiently, and thereby give better government. A Strafford might wish to extend his powers for efficiency, it is true, but for something more, because he believed in power and objected to the fumbling and confusions of popular government. Behind our present-day cabinet, which has far more power than Charles I ever thought of assuming, stand similar serried ranks of administrators, men who, without any particular animus against democracy, steadily entrench on it, merely in order that they may do their jobs more efficiently. And the modern state has behind it a power not possessed by the Stuarts: a state police of whose conduct the ordinary citizen is unaware, just as he is unaware of the ideas which govern those who are in control of it. Such men may be in every respect estimable. They may be liberty-loving citizens. Or they may be obsessed with desire for power. They may, as police, feel the necessity for results overruling the stumbling

---

[1]From Coyne, Lower and MacFarlane, Brief submitted to the Royal Commission on Dominion-Provincial Relations, Winnipeg, Manitoba, 8 December 1937, mimeographed.
[2]See Lord Hewart, *The New Despotism* (London: Ernest Benn, 1929) and the Royal Commission of Inquiry on the charges contained in his book.

methods of freedom. Whatever they may be, the citizen does not know their nature or their methods. All he can be sure of is that power "grows on what it feeds on."

However high the marks to be given to our modern cabinet — and for public spirit, integrity, and a sense of duty, they should be high marks — it is impossible to refrain from the suspicion that it may sometimes be the slave rather than the master of the administrative system standing behind it. Join to this the extreme degree of power wielded by our cabinet, and it seems obvious that some further protection must now be given to the citizen against the state.

Evidently the time has come for the insertion of a new principle into our democracy. And this new principle will be found to be the reassertion of an old. We can no longer depend solely on the omnicompetent Parliament. It has shown heretofore only slightly more sense of liberty than have the masses. We cannot easily rest on the doctrine of parliamentary supremacy. We must return to older doctrines. In our necessities, it is not so much Parliament that is serving us in its omnicompetence as bodies whose very conservatism causes them to rest on portions of that older tradition. Those bodies are the courts with their basis of common law, the great seventeenth-century weapon which proved so effectual in a struggle similar to that with which we are here faced, the struggle against overwhelming authority. We must get back to the principles of common law, and in returning to them we shall find ourselves resting also on another great body of doctrine, a body of doctrine upon which the strong neighbouring nation still rests. That body of doctrine is the natural rights philosophy of the eighteenth century, and it is enshrined in the Declaration of Independence, and the first ten amendments of the American Constitution.

In passing a bill of rights, the Canadian Parliament would go far to redeem itself from its past negligences. A bill of rights would once again enshrine freedom as the basis of our state. It would say to all and sundry that there are principles in life, principles which a mere counting of noses cannot alter, principles for which men have died. We have fought two wars for "freedom." Could there be anything more ironical than that, in seeking "freedom" at the ends of the earth, we should have trampled the life out of her here at home?

VII.

Immigration

Lower's long-standing interest in immigration arose from his concern with the question of what factors shaped a community. He made a series of studies of the various facets of the movements of people and the impact of that movement upon the formation of a culture. The major conclusion of his demographic and social studies is set forth in "The Case Against Immigration" (Essay #26). Immigrants make a permanent contribution to the population of a country only when there is an economic need for their labour. Government policies which subsidize immigration regardless of domestic conditions do more harm than good. Under these policies the unnecessary increase in labour supply only contributes to keeping standards of living at a low level. This latter factor causes the more energetic native labour to seek a field presenting the opportunity for higher living conditions, in Canada's case, the United States. This continuing influx and exodus provides neither a permanent increase in population nor continuity between generations. This pattern has prevented the development, especially in English Canada, of a population with deep roots in the country, and its concomitant, the lack of a sense of belonging, is a key factor in the failure to develop a Canadian identity.

26 | The Case Against Immigration*

The question of immigration has been discussed in Canada too little from the standpoint of the large general problem of which it forms a part, that of the peopling of the North American continent as a whole. It is therefore proposed to present a brief resumé of the history of population in Canada in the hope that certain principles will emerge which can be applied to our present problem.

In that it has been their lot to play a significant part in the greatest

*Queen's Quarterly 37 (Summer 1930): 557-74.

occurrence in history, the creation of a new world, Canadians are a privileged people. The surge and roll of the flood of humanity as it has burst over this continent has not only constituted a drama of heroic proportions but has also provided unparalleled opportunities for observing how man as an animal disperses himself about the world and how as a human being he creates societies. When Englishmen first came to America, they had a continent before them. They proceeded to occupy it, and by the time of the Revolution the original settlers had increased to some three million persons. With almost mathematical regularity they had doubled their numbers each twenty-five years. In this striking performance, immigration had played a very small part. Massachusetts, for example, which was the most populous province in 1760, received all told, during the 130 years from its founding, probably not more than 50,000 immigrants or considerably less than an average of 500 per year. The reasons for the increase in numbers of the colonists are obvious. They were a healthy stock, and there was land enough and to spare. It was very easy for a young man just starting life to obtain enough land to live on. If he were to use it, it was essential for him to marry and surround himself with a family. The story of the growth of population in that oft-misunderstood province, New France, is similar. Except in the period before 1715, one of almost constant warfare, during the eighteenth century the population doubled regularly in slightly less than twenty-six years. There was virtually no immigration. Under British rule the experience was similar, and the population of the Province of Lower Canada continued until 1851 to double every twenty-five or twenty-six years. In this period also there was little immigration, for newcomers were, as a rule, deterred from settlement in a French province and proceeded farther west. In English America and in French America, the population doubled about every twenty-five years. It would seem, therefore, that this rate of increase was normal for a healthy young community having plenty of room for expansion.

From 1851 onward the rate of increase of the population of Lower Canada, or the Province of Quebec, declined rapidly. At any time in the fifty years from 1851 to 1901 the rate was such as to double the population not in twenty-five years but in ninety years. There was no abrupt decrease in the birth rate or increase in the death rate. There was, however, a fairly considerable increase in immigration over the earlier period. Why then was the old rate not maintained?

In Upper Canada, during the thirty-seven years from 1814 to 1851, the population increased at such a rate as to double itself every twelve years. This was an experience which was quite comparable with that of the new states then being settled and which has not been equalled in Canada since, even in our western provinces. During this period there was extensive immigration. It is difficult to determine the exact amount because many of those recorded as immigrants passed on to the western states, but a rough estimate of the annual arrivals who remained in the country would be from fifteen to twenty thousand. There is no doubt that these numbers affected the rate at which the population of Upper Canada grew, though they did not by any means account for the entire growth. After 1851, or more markedly after 1861, Ontario shared the experience of Quebec, and a population which in the nineteen years prior to 1861 had tripled actually required fifty years to double itself.

It was about the middle of the century that people began to leave Canada and go to the United States. In 1850, there were in the United States 147,000 natives of British North America; in 1920, there were over one million Canadian-born residents in that country. Save for the first two decades of the twentieth century, the increase has been continuous and regular. During those fifty years of something unpleasantly like stagnation, approximately one out of every two children born in Canada sooner or later found his way to the United States. The surprising concomitant of this large emigration was a large immigration. During the decade of the eighties, for example, no less than 886,177 newcomers sought our shores. The same conditions which were drawing away our native-born were likewise drawing away the immigrant, and it is therefore not surprising to find that in this decade the immigrant population increased by only some 40,000. It is obvious, therefore, that no amount of immigration could compensate for the forces which were keeping our population almost stationary. The sole bright spot on the horizon was in the West. With the completion of the Canadian Pacific Railway, a national achievement scarcely less significant than Confederation itself, population began to pour out upon the western plains, and Manitoba grew at a rate recalling that of Upper Canada before 1850.

The new century saw a third period open in the history of Canada's population. Here one is on familiar ground, for everyone remembers something of the spectacular growth after 1900, especially in the three western prairie provinces. From 1900 to 1914 conditions in the West were very similar to those in the East before 1850; in both cases there were large areas of vacant land suitable for agriculture. It required little persuasion to induce people to come and possess them. In 1914 we entered a fourth period of population growth. From 1914 to 1919 we received very few immigrants; from 1919 to the present we have been receiving 100,000 or more a year. Our population has been increasing at about the same rate as it did prior to the opening of the West, or perhaps a little faster.

A glance back over the last century and a quarter reveals three well-marked periods in the history of Canadian expansion and the beginning of a fourth, a half-century of rapid settlement and growth, a half-century — to give it the best name possible — of consolidation, and a quarter-century of swift development. During the first of these periods, 1800-1850, all the provinces grew rapidly at approximately equal rates. Immigration, small in amount if judged by present standards, was important, though the provinces which did not receive many immigrants were not very much slower in their rates of growth than those which received the most. During the second period, 1850-1900, despite a considerably larger annual immigration than in the first, population increased very slowly and emigration went on continuously. During the third period, 1900-1921, the population of the majority of the provinces increased rapidly. Emigration fell off but did not cease, and immigration became very large. But, as in the earlier period, most of the immigrants went away again.

Like all other things, the growth of human population is determined by natural law. Doubtless in a state of nature the numbers of the human species would tend over a long period to become stationary: they would respond to conditions in precisely the same ways as those of other species of animal. When food was abundant they would increase; when conditions were hard they would decrease through starvation and disease. Though they are obscured by the complications of our civilization, these basic principles still operate. Even in the most sophisticated modern countries, population responds very directly to the means of subsistence. The England of the nineteenth century, for example, with the world's markets at her feet and the ability to command wealth from every quarter of the globe, increased her population very rapidly. Today, in the face of a bitterly competitive world, English trade is fairly stationary and the population of England is increasing very slowly. Mankind responds to the means of subsistence as surely as the crops to the sunshine and the rain.

With the long experience to which we in Canada may refer — almost alone among nations we have records of our population from the beginnings of our history — we should be able to determine very accurately the laws of our growth. They must necessarily be only special applications of the general law just enunciated. As such they are not mysterious but are perfectly patent to those who take the trouble to inquire into them. In ordinary discussions of immigration, however, they are invariably almost completely disregarded.

In his report for 1856, the commissioner of crown lands for the Province of Canada, in the course of a survey of the lands still remaining to the Crown, remarked that "Government has now no more lands to offer to settlers in that part of the province considered the most favourable for settlers and where by far the greater part of the sale and settlement of public lands has hitherto taken place." After giving a careful survey of the settled and unsettled regions of the province, he comes to the conclusion that the future progress of settlement must be slow and adds that "not only very many European emigrants but also a great and increasing number of the young men of the province and even the older settlers prefer (to the poor lands remaining in Canada) the easier livelihood that is to be earned by cultivating the [American] prairies of the west." Here lies the explanation of the dramatic change in Canadian conditions which occurred about 1850. Once the good and available lands were taken up, population had to stop growing. Our population was obeying the first law of growth and, not finding means of subsistence in Canada, was taking itself off to a region where it could find it.

From about 1860 to 1895, save for the infant West, comparatively few new sources of wealth were tapped in Canada. Agriculture, since there was no more good land, could not expand to any marked degree; that other Canadian staple, lumber, with the exhaustion of the white pine forests, could not increase very much in importance; mining was slight, and manufacturing was in its infancy. The perfectly natural result was a very slow increase in population, an increase which was not affected in the slightest, positively or negatively, by the efforts made to secure immigrants and by the large number of immigrants who actually did come. But when the West was opened the old story was repeated; large areas of fertile land were rendered available and population bounded forward.

It seems obvious then that one of the fundamental conditions of the growth of population in Canada has been the availability of large areas of good land, and, since we no longer have areas comparable with our original domain, we may rest assured that we shall never again have an expansion of settlement comparable with that of the periods before 1850 and after 1900. We may dismiss from our minds any notion that the spectacular days of twenty years ago will be repeated. For a good many years we probably will have expansion by settlement, but we must be content to see settlement go forward modestly.

In the modern world the land does not constitute the sole means of subsistence, and consequently we have many examples of countries in which population responds to industrial development rather than to new areas of fertile soil. In this respect Germany has been conspicuous, and with the great growth in her industry which occurred from 1871 onward, her population increased by leaps and bounds. In Canada we have also had our industrial development, and it is therefore pertinent to inquire into its bearing on the growth of our population. For two generations or more all Canadians have been brought up in the faith that we have vast natural resources. This is doubtless true, but we have seldom paused to ask ourselves why it is that these resources have been so slowly developed. The reason is not far to seek. We have scarcely a natural resource which has not been extremely hard to utilize. A century ago there was no more fertile land on the continent than in western Ontario, but how difficult it was in the days before railways, before even the St. Lawrence canals were cut, for the farmer of Upper Canada to take full advantage of the good crops he could grow. It is at present only by reason of a most highly developed and delicately organized system of transportation that the crops of western Canada can be marketed. The old Red River Colony, for example, lay stagnant for half a century, unable, until it found an outlet, to utilize the "vast natural resources" which lay about it. After many years of effort and large expenditures of capital, the mineral wealth of our north country is now becoming available, but to win it has involved hard fighting, fighting against the woods and rocks of the pre-Cambrian wilderness, fighting against the rigours of a northern climate. How easy of access and development compared with these northern minerals of ours are the coal and iron deposits of the United States! Difficult development means slow development, and slow development of natural wealth means slow growth of population.

Apart from the presence or absence of internal difficulties, the growth of every new country depends upon the outlets it can find for its products.

The most important feature of economic life in a newly settled community is its commercial connection with the rest of the world. On this more than upon any other circumstance depends its prosperity. The history of modern colonization does not show a single case where a newly-settled country has enjoyed any considerable economic prosperity or made notable social progress without a flourishing commerce with other communities. This dominance of foreign commerce in economic affairs may be considered the most characteristic feature of colonial economy.

If this dictum be applied to Canada it will be apparent at once that with respect to our economic organization we are still pretty much in the colonial stage. This is the explanation of that phenomenon with which our politicians like to flatter their audiences, namely, the high rank which Canada takes in the *per capita* amount of foreign trade. Older nations find in themselves a market which absorbs a large part of their total production, but with us the home market can absorb only a fraction of our production. We are raising on an average now some four hundred million bushels of wheat a year, but we can manage to use only about one-fifth of this ourselves. The remainder must be sold abroad. It is similar with most of our primary products; the limits of the home market for manufactured goods, likewise, are soon reached. In the case of the United States a home market very quickly grew up, but we, because of natural factors over which we have no control, cannot expand indefinitely within ourselves. We cannot look forward to the day when we shall consume all our own wheat, all our own paper, all our own nickel, and we therefore must depend for our growth upon the increase of the demand of other peoples for our products. This fact was intuitively grasped by the Canadian pioneer whose frequent prayer was said to be, "Give us a good harvest and a bloody war in Europe." We have always had hectic prosperity during periods of war, simply because war meant large, if temporary, increase in consumption abroad. We have also, unfortunately, usually had to "sober up" from the orgy of production after peace has been made.

The relationship between our growth and foreign demand is nicely illustrated by conditions in Canada since 1914. We had our war period of feverish prosperity. On the conclusion of the war, after a brief boom, came the reaction; European markets disappeared, and our own productive machine slowed down. The effect on population was evident at once. The index number of employment fell rapidly. American immigration figures indicated that large numbers of people were leaving this country. These figures are confirmed by the 1926 census of our three prairie provinces. For a few years after the war European conditions were most uncertain, and the prices of agricultural products were distinctly below the level of those goods the farmer was obliged to buy. The situation reacted definitely and inevitably on the growth of the three provinces. For the five years, 1916-1921, years of little or no immigration, their population increased by 15.19 per cent, a rapid rate. In the five years, 1921-1926, when immigration was considerable, they increased by 5.46 per cent, a rate poorer than that of the Dominion in the period of stagnation prior to 1896. Since 1926, now that conditions abroad are better, growth has begun again. But in the future as in the past the growth in population of the western provinces will depend upon the success they have in marketing their products, and no amount of immigration will affect that growth in the slightest degree.

Two deductions regarding the growth of population in Canada may therefore be set forth.

1. Our population grows rapidly when there are large areas of fertile land available for settlement.

2. Otherwise, it will grow in proportion to the demand of the rest of the world for our products.

These are the laws of Canadian growth.

It is now desirable, as an aid in formulating a definite policy, to make some inquiry into the rate at which the country is likely to grow in the future. From 1861 to 1881 the annual growth was 1.7 per cent; from 1881 to 1901, it was 1.15 per cent; from 1901 to 1911 it was 3.7 per cent; from 1911 to 1921 it was 2.1 per cent; an average for the sixty years of 1.91 per cent, an average rendered unduly high by the great influx after 1900 which cannot be repeated. We have no dominion figures for the period since 1921, but our three western provinces during the first half of this period increased by about 1 per cent per annum, slightly less than the worst previous experience of the Dominion as a whole. We shall probably do a little better than that during the present five years, 1926 to 1931, but even providing we do very well we shall probably not grow at the rate of 2 per cent per annum for the ten years 1921 to 1931. The annual rate of increase in the United States at present is between 1 and 1.5 per cent, and I do not think we can hope to grow at a much faster rate than they are doing, more particularly as our chief market, Great Britain, is fast approaching a stationary population. It would, therefore, seem that if Canada continues to grow at the rate of 1.5 per cent per annum, adding about 135,000 persons to its total every year, it will be doing very well.

Where are we to get the people who will provide an increase at this rate of growth? It happens that at present our natural increase, that is the surplus of births over deaths, is approximately 135,000, or 1.5 per cent per annum. Obviously, then, we do not need to go outside our own borders for the population that we shall need for our future growth. The conclusion, therefore, is justified that we have no need of immigration to increase our population, and if immigrants in large numbers continue to come to us there can be only one result. Our own people, those who are born in the country, will have to go away. The presence or absence of immigration will not affect in the slightest degree the rate at which the country will grow, for this is dependent upon natural causes which we cannot influence much more than we can influence the weather.

It would appear to be very probable that we should be able to provide from our own population for a rate of growth much greater than that above named. During the nineteenth century, nearly every important nation in Europe except France increased its population at a rapid rate, much more rapid indeed than the rate at which Canada was growing at the same time, but in no single case was there any dependence on immigration. On the contrary, during these years there were large emigrations from nearly all these countries. In some years Great Britain sent abroad several hundred thousands of persons, yet at the same time her own population increased by leaps and bounds. The same is true of Germany. Both these countries, standing square in the stream of modern industrial development and well-placed geographically, met all their multifarious demands for men from their own stores and had great abundance to spare. Their increase in population was directly due to the increase in their productive capacity and in their markets. So will it be with Canada. It is very easy to get the cart of population before the horse of production and this, unfortunately, is frequently done. People do not make jobs but jobs make people, and if the number of jobs in this country increases rapidly in the future, we do not need to worry about there being plenty of people on hand to fill them. We have been curiously blind to this rather obvious fact in the past, and Canadians seem to have been oppressed by a fear that if they did not import people constantly, and in large numbers, the country would not be adequately peopled.

Strange as it may seem, had we never had a single immigrant come within our borders since Confederation, sixty-three years ago, it is probable that our population today would not be materially different from what it is. Save under exceptional and limited circumstances, immigration does not increase population. This seeming paradox is capable of proof, and the proof lies in the fact that, except when we had large areas of vacant land to be filled up very quickly, our immigrant population simply displaced the native-born. This is a process that has been happening for years in Canada and is happening today. During the decade of the eighties the natural increase of our population was between 800,000 and 900,000. We received therefore from both sources roughly one and three-quarter millions of people. Of these we retained about one-half million. As we must have retained some of the immigrants who came to us as well as some of our natural increase, it is obvious that among those who left us were a great many of our native-born. Probably as many as 60 or 70 per cent of the people born in Canada in the decade of the eighties left the country. The immigration of the eighties, therefore, was not an accession to the population; it was simply the exchange of one set of persons for another.

In the opening decade of the twentieth century, there was an immigration of 1,800,000 and a natural increase of 850,000. Yet there was an increase in total population of only 1,800,000. During this decade, therefore, we had 850,000 people more than we could accommodate. Fortunately for ourselves, we managed to export them. Since there was a substantial increase in the immigrant-born population of the country during that decade, it follows that the exports must have consisted very largely of native-born.

During the five years 1921 to 1926, there came to the three prairie provinces about 180,000 immigrants. The natural increase of the three provinces was about 150,000. Their total increase should have been 330,000, but it was only 111,000. It would appear, therefore, that 220,000 must have gone away. It is significant that a number equal to the whole 180,000 immigrants together with 40,000 of the people born in these provinces in the years 1921 to 1926 simply disappeared into space. It is known that every immigrant who came here during those years did not so disappear. Those who remained with us must therefore have pushed out an equivalent number of the native-born. Once more, immigration had had no effect whatsoever in increasing population. It had simply dislocated it. The persons who were already here and who may be presumed to have spent time and money in learning to adapt themselves to this Western country were replaced by persons who had not done these things but who would have to do them in the future. The same type of social adjustment which had already taken place would have to be repeated.

The country, in short, may be likened to a ship which can carry only a fixed number of people, crew and passengers. If she takes on a number of passengers in excess of her complement, there is only one way of compensating for it; some of the crew must be left behind. We in Canada for sixty years past have been taking on so many passengers, that is immigrants, that we have had to keep leaving many of the crew behind. To provide room in the ship of state for immigrants we have had to embark a large proportion of our own children for the voyage of life in another vessel, the good ship *United States.*

The objection may be raised that if we had not had immigration in our bad years, our own people would have gone away, and we should have had an actual decrease in population. This, however, will not stand. It has already been shown that the country's population is determined by its productions and the success it has in marketing them abroad. While a certain number of people would have gone away, because we had more than we could use, this number would have only been sufficient to compensate for the adverse economic conditions of the period. Regardless of immigration during the period 1921-1926, the population of the three prairie provinces in 1926 would have been the same.

The case against immigration then is, briefly, that immigration is unnecessary. Save under exceptional circumstances which are not likely to recur again, we have had and will have in this country sufficient manpower to develop its resources. In five years out of six we have had more than sufficient manpower, as is proved by the fact that we continuously export manpower. We cannot use all the manpower we have. We sent emigrants to the United States sixty years ago; we have sent them every year since, and we are still sending them. The compensations we have received from American immigration can easily be shown to be small. Under these circumstances it would seem to be absurd to refer to Canada as an under-populated country. It is, in fact, most of the time over-populated. The existence of large open spaces is not synonymous with under-population. The Arctic lands, for example, are empty, but under present conditions they are not under-populated. Nature seems to maintain a very nice balance between the number of people in a region and the number of people which that region can support. Let population rush up beyond the land's resources as it did in Ireland in the first half of the last century, and there comes the inevitable reckoning, emigration or starvation. Let a land be empty, as were the Prairies a few years ago, and if men can get in, they come rolling in like a flood until it is filled. This country, since it has invariably more people than it can use, is therefore as a rule over-populated. We have been fortunate in having a great outlet for our surplus population so close at hand, otherwise we would soon experience the ills of overpopulation and the more fortunate, as in England today, would be engaged in supporting the less fortunate.

Those who think we must bring in immigrants to compensate for our loss of population do so because they do not realize that the initial cause of the loss is the inability of the country at any given time to support the people who go away. Under these circumstances it is plain that immigration does not act as a cure for the disease but in fact aggravates it. Immigration into the country is not a compensation for the emigration of our own people from it, which every Canadian deplores, but itself is a cause of that emigration.

In the days of good Queen Bess, Sir Thomas Gresham, founder of the Royal Exchange, formulated the important monetary law which has since borne his name. "Cheap money will drive out dear money," said Sir Thomas, by which he meant that in times when the currency system is not satisfactory, a depreciated currency will circulate and people will keep in their possession the sound money that comes their way. If he had directed his thought to immigration, Sir Thomas might have stated his law thus: "Cheap men will drive out dear."

Everyone is familiar with this "Gresham's Law of Immigration," in its application to Orientals. The white labourer cannot compete with the Oriental, and the only way to prevent the country being swamped by Asiatics is to limit their migration to our country. We are willing to admit the principle as applied to Asiatics because of a difference in colour. It is more difficult to grasp the application of the law to persons whose skin is the same colour as our own. But whether they be of different race or not, "cheap" men will always drive our "dear" men. The man with the higher standard of living cannot compete with the man with the lower. In this sense, virtually all immigrants are "cheap" men, for on arriving in this country they are not in a position to bargain for the sale of their labour. They must get a livelihood on what terms they can. In this respect, people from the Mother Country differ from other immigrants only in degree. Their standard of living is higher than that of foreigners, but it is not as high as that of the native-born. If it were they would not emigrate. Thus they compete with the Canadian and innocently displace him in many walks of life. The result is that the people born in this country, because of competition with the immigrant, whether that immigrant be English-speaking or not, tend to go over the border in greater numbers than if there were no immigration.

The immigrant's handicap is the employer's advantage, for the employer gets a man who at all costs must hold his job. He may, probably, get a more highly skilled workman. Old-country craftsmen are better trained than Canadians; Canadians, on the other hand receive a warm welcome in the United States for similar reasons. In the motherland, where jobs are few and a man dare not risk the loss of the one he has, a man must be efficient. In Canada, fear of being out of work is not so great, and a willing person can always make a living in some manner. There is therefore a greater spirit of independence. In the United States, conditions have advanced a stage farther, and as a rule, one can not only get work but can find employment more or less to his liking. This tends to create a still greater independence on the part of the employed person, hence the warm welcome there to Canadians who are described as "reliable," which means, that coming from a land where opportunities are not as great as those in the United States, they are more afraid of losing their jobs than are the native-born Americans.

One may assume that Canadians wish to see Canada a nation and possessed of all the best attributes of nationhood. If it be true that the chief result of immigration is to drive out the native-born, much evil must come of this constant renewal of blood generation after generation. About one million people, native-born and immigrants have left this country within the last six or seven years. That means that our population coming in by the front door of the St. Lawrence and going out by the back door of the international boundary is essentially shifting and unstable. A surprisingly large number of persons thus never get a chance to adapt themselves to the country. This state of permanent social dislocation does not promote the making by Canada of a contribution to the world's civilization worthy of her possibilities. A man has just nicely fitted himself into Canadian ways; he has begun to think in Canadian terms and to understand Canadian problems when off he goes or, if he should remain his children, his more accurately adjusted self, leave our shores.

Wholesale immigration, productive as it is of wholesale emigration, turns our country into a training ground for American citizens. We instruct our newcomers in the ways of the continent; teach them, often at considerable pains, to fit themselves into our social structure; we educate their children at great expense to the state and then send them across the border. When they become American citizens, they are welcomed as highly manufactured products, finished at the expense of another country. Meanwhile we in Canada have brought in another batch of raw material which out of the goodness of our hearts we proceed to prepare for our American friends.

The enormous magnet to the south will always draw away some of our children, but the only way in which we can resist its attractions will be by creating a drawing power of our own. It is possible that if our standard of living were not being continuously depressed by the arrival of the immigrant, opportunities would be relatively equal on both sides of the line. A continental, rather than a national, standard of living would then obtain, and we would be more likely to retain all the population which our natural resources justify our having.

It seems plain that since we do not need immigration we should discontinue all the various attempts now being made to secure it. There should not be one cent of public money spent on securing immigrants of any type. Steamship transportation should be made not easier but more difficult. No one should be allowed to come here who does not come on his own initiative, and even the immigration of this class of person should be selective.

For generations the Canadian people have been pursuing the will o' the wisp of immigration; for generations they have been telling themselves that theirs is an under-populated country, a country which year after year with monotonous regularity sends thousands of its citizens abroad! That it would be better to have a larger population is a point on which we are all agreed, but we cannot lift ourselves by our bootstraps. As the world demands our products our population will grow, and nature will add the cubit to our national stature which we by taking thought cannot acquire.

VIII.

Education

Arthur Lower, the educator, has made a profound impact upon those who studied under him. Canadian history provides the bed-rock for Canadian nationalism and, therefore, Canadian existence. There could be "A Bright Future for a Dull Subject" (Essay #27) if it was made as relevant to young Canadians as it was to him. In "The Canadian University" (Essay #28), he continued on the theme — this time with the relevance of education in general. Primarily for the élite, the Canadian university at the same time was required to serve the nation by building a bridge between the enduring values of Western civilization and the newer Canadian way of life.

27 | *A Bright Future for a Dull Subject**

The historian is the custodian of human memory. On him falls the responsibility not only of securing and caring for whatever records of the past survive but also of interpreting them. His task is hard for he has to come to some sort of judgment upon the causes and sequences of events; he has to pass life in review and in some measure attempt to explain it. The advocate's duty is to make out a case against his opponent before the court, but the judge upon the bench has a harder duty, for with him rests decision. The historian must constitute himself a judge over men and events that he has never seen and must examine witnesses, long since dead, whose testimony invariably overwhelms him by its sheer bulk. Small wonder that many have thrown up their hands and have claimed that it is not the function of the historian to interpret but merely to "set out the facts."

This so-called scientific school of historians, under the impetus of German scholarship, flourished in the nineteenth century, but of late years we have come to realize that, because of the element of selection involved,

*Manitoba Arts Review 3 (Fall 1943): 10-21

"setting out the facts" is also a form of interpreting. In any historical situation there is no end to the "facts"; you cannot use them all. Who, for example, could "set out" the interminable series of facts connected with the career of Napoleon? Once selection is allowed, discretion, choice, judgment must also be allowed. Hence every historian sits in judgment upon the men and events that he writes about.

His judgments are not unimportant. How many times we hear the phrase "before the bar of history"! "It is the 'judgment of history' that has been his [Trotsky's] undeviating standard of right and wrong. On the day after the October Revolution he thundered to the Mensheviks, 'Go to the place where you belong from now on — the dustbin of history!'"[1] Today his tragic burden is that he too has been thrust into the "dustbin of history."

The historian cannot study men and women in a vacuum. He must, even if his interest be some specialized kind of biography, study his fellow-men in relation to the group to which they belong, that is, in relation to the society or community in which they live, for man is a social animal. Hence the historian must study society; and from society to the state, it is an easy step. Hence the necessary preoccupation of the average historian with some phase of the state. There is no hard and fast line between the past of the state and the present of the state. But the issues which involve the conduct of the state, political issues, are of all issues the most controversial and those that arouse greatest prejudice. Especially in Canada. Unfortunately, in so far as ideas go, we are among the most conservative of peoples, and matters which could be commonplaces of discussion in Great Britain or the United States can hardly be mentioned here. Hence the difficulty the Canadian historian finds in keeping from burning his fingers. But the scholar whose thought takes him squarely up to a given issue and who then refuses to face it is like the priest who compromises with sin. The historian of Canada must be a man of high convictions and with the courage to be true to them.

Any English-speaking historian will necessarily be concerned with the state in its form as a nation, and for this simple reason, that every English-speaking state being a self-governing community of *free men* is by that very fact a nation. It is therefore no accident that English history, American history, and to some extent Canadian history, is written in terms of the so-called nation-state, which may be defined as a community ordering its own life and holding together by some principle of inner cohesion.

There is today, thanks to the misbehaviour of certain individuals and of certain peoples, a disposition to criticize "nationalism." If these peoples

[1]Malcolm Cowley review of Leon Trotsky, *My Life* in *New Republic* 86, April 8, 1936, p. 254.

go in for an exaggerated expression of their own ego, then they are to be criticized, but the fact that they are peoples is not a subject for criticism. The nation is a perfectly natural expression of certain inevitabilities in the modern world and is no more to be deplored than is the rain or the snow.

There was a time in the remote past when the overgrown family was the unit of society. But as civilization grew, especially as knowledge of the written word grew and as communications improved, the overgrown family expanded into a more formal political entity. In ancient Greece it was the city, the *polis,* around which clustered all the associations which invariably bind men to each other. Later on, when the Germanic peoples had settled down and when the kings had succeeded in bringing some order out of feudal chaos, the nation-state developed. Some strong man such as Henry II of England or Philip Augustus of France succeeded in imposing his will and the formal expression of his will — laws and institutions — over a considerable area. If that area had a certain natural unity about it, there grew up a corporate tradition; men, whether they were Yorkshire-men or from Devonshire, learned to work together, shared each others' points of view, found they had certain things in common — such as language, a certain outlook on life, a certain way of regulating life, through laws and courts. Added to these formal matters, there were the thousand and one natural associations which spring from intimacy: family life, friendships, beliefs, stories, and songs. In the course of time, men such as Chaucer made their appearance and, drawing their inspiration from the life about them, embodied it in poetry or some other form of art. Through common memories of great tasks accomplished together, such as the Scottish tradition of the repulse of the English invader or the English memories of the Armada, a sense of unity arose. Those communities which managed to get these things first and which in troublous times could keep out the invader became the first nation-states, Scotland, England, France, Holland.

Not all the peoples of Western Europe were so fortunate. The German kings for centuries dissipated their efforts in the hopeless task of trying to incorporate Italy within their realm. The result was that their realm disappeared, the "Empire" became a shadow, and no German nation emerged from the innumerable fragments of medieval feudalism. Italy had much the same story. So did the Balkan peoples who fell under the sway of the Turk. Only in the nineteenth century was the historical process completed for these countries; because it was delayed so long and because men knew the suffering and shame that the delay entailed — the physical invasions and the invidious comparisons with the more fortunate foreigner — when its completion did come, it came with a violence that has disrupted our modern world. It is quite possible that had a German nation emerged at the same time as a French nation, we would not now be witnessing what seems to us the insanity of German nationalism, in which arrested development has produced a pathological condition.

The sentimental internationalist, if such still exists, who thinks that any people can jump over the stage of national life into international, needs reminding of two things: the first, that the progression towards an international order has taken the form for a thousand years of the making of small groups into larger ones; and the second, that if an international régime is to emerge, it will be based on the nations. It is foolish to think that the world will reach a point where German, Russian, Italian, and all the rest will be no more, all merged into universal men: they may learn to live in peace with one another, but they will not be one another, and the world would be infinitely poorer if they could be.

Clear historical thinking imposes upon us the necessity of nationalism as a stage — not necessarily the last stage, not necessarily the sum of human effort — but a stage in a community's development. Nationalism is simply that spirit of inner cohesion which holds together a large community of people, at peace with each other, and the nation-state is its expression.

Is there any need to apologize for such an aspiration? Is there any need to apologize for any social device which gives security to the individual, maintains law and order, enables men to believe that their children after them shall have the same rights and privileges as they themselves and which, by bringing to bear all the thousand familiar associations dear to the ordinary human, begets a tradition and a spirit that enriches life and adds to it a spiritual quality?

It is perhaps impossible to say just exactly what keeps a society going, what are the springs of its spiritual health: no doubt there are many. Among them, and not the least significant, is history. More than most of us realize, any society that amounts to anything lives on its past, on its history, and on its traditions. Is it necessary to illustrate that? Take English literature: Does one need to quote "This royal throne of kings, this sceptred isle ... this other Eden, demi-Paradise...." All Shakespeare's historical plays are a testimony of the living force of the English tradition. Or Wordsworth with his "We must be free or die who speak the tongue that Shakespeare spoke ...." Or Tennyson with his "Love thou thy land with love far brought from out the storied past." Or, among moderns, Masefield. Or among the historians themselves, such men as G. M. Trevelyan. The list could be extended indefinitely. The whole great structure of English literature is a testimony to the living force of the English tradition. As is English life, Englishmen talk familiarly still of Nelson or "The Duke" as if they were still among them.

In like manner Frenchmen look back to the great days of the "Sun King," Louis XIV (a true national king, whatever one may think of him), or Joan of Arc or Saint Louis, or those more distant ages of the Franks, and the saying goes echoing on, even in our own country among our French Canadians, with inspiration in it, "Gesta Dei per Francos."

We Canadians do not generally realize that our American neighbours also have their living traditions and that to them their history is a constant source of aid and comfort. Washington, Jefferson, Lincoln, these are not empty names: they are symbols of the ideas and qualities at the source of American life. The Americans have their own native, indigenous traditions peculiarly applicable to their own life; they also have their English inheritance, and the English traditions which had accumulated up to the Revolution have been built into their national structure just as they have into ours.

Every nation turns to its history as the continuing inspiration of its communal life, and those without a history sometimes find it necessary to invent one. The Serbians, for example, used to make a great point of the half-legendary Serbian empire which existed before the day of the Turk, back in the thirteenth century. In fact, the temptation to invent a suitable history for a new nation is as strong as the temptation for a *nouveau riche* to find an ancestral coat of arms. On both forms of forgery the historian must frown. But rightly understood and used, our history provides us with the assurance that our roots are commendable and honourable, with the conviction that having had a past, we shall also have a future, an honourable place among mankind, wherein our common concern shall mean something and accomplish something.

To take an example near home: what do our fellow Canadians, the French, draw from history? They look back to the indomitable courage and audacity of the explorers, to their Champlains, La Salles, and La Verendryes, to the devotion of their martyrs, men who were only slightly less French than they were Christian. They think of the dark days that followed the English Conquest when it seemed as if their institutions might be overturned and their race become submerged; they contrast those days with the steady progress they have made and the present place they hold within the Canadian Confederation, and they find that they are a people which by persistence and patience has known how to turn defeat into victory. Today they have the reward of their devotion to their historic ideals, and their history and traditions are an unfailing support to them. English Canadians will be wise if they allow them to bring it as their contribution to our common Confederation.

What have we other Canadians to put alongside this dynamic French-Canadian tradition? Can our history furnish us with a sustenance for national life of equal vitality with theirs? We possess, of course, just as did the Americans when they started national life, the inheritance of the English tradition. It has meant much to us: it has given us our institutions, our faith and morals, and most, if not all, of our sense of racial superiority.

From it we have drawn our love of freedom and our desire to govern ourselves. Not our democratic society; that is a product of a frontier environment. But we do not possess the pure English tradition here in Canada. What we have, rather, is British traditions — in the plural. We are a mixture, those of us whose mother tongue is English, and we inherit not only the tradition of England, but also, and perhaps in greater measure, two very different traditions, those of Ireland and Scotland. Ireland has an unhappy tradition, and that part of Ireland from which most of our people of Irish descent have come, Northern Ireland, notwithstanding the many excellences of its people, has a tradition of intolerance and bigotry, a fierce, fighting tradition that is almost unknown in England. It adds to those a hard common sense and an austere materialism. It stresses efficiency, success, and the unyielding passion of a beleaguered minority rather than the tolerant complaisance of the Englishman.

The Scots have given us, along with the collection of commendable qualities with which that admirable people have not been slow to acquaint us, an exaggerated caution and conservatism. There is not enough generous daring, reckless abandon, about the Scot. He is too fond of betting on a sure thing. His reach does not exceed his grasp. In public life, Scotland does not share the English tradition of compromise, and Scottish history, at least until the seventeenth century, was a tradition of violence; the best tradition of Scotland, and fortunately those by which we in Canada have been most influenced, lie in the state within the state constituted by the Presbyterian Church and expressed in the General Assembly. But it is the peculiar value of the English tradition that it has somehow come to embody such typical virtues as tolerance, a spirit of fair play, the love of free speech, equality before the law, parliamentary government — in other words, all the great fundamentals upon which rest the freedom of our modern English-speaking states.

Here in Canada our common English-speaking tradition is a mixture of all of these and is thus in some respects a new thing. Still it is inherited; it is not the tradition of the new land, though it will always lie at its foundations. But from the day the first English-speaking people came here a new tradition began to form. What is it?

In a country so large as this and so scattered, there has necessarily been much local diversity. Thus in one small province alone, and that one of the oldest, Nova Scotia, some ten or a dozen different groups can be distinguished, each with its own interests and still, after a century and three-quarters of common self-government, somewhat separate. The rest of the country presents a picture of the same kind, and as one advances westward the different groups, because settlement is more recent, become more and more distinct. When one reaches the Prairies he has — or had until recently — some difficulty retaining a sense of unity. He can hardly speak of a community at all, but only of groups of English Canadians, French Canadians, Germans, Ukrainians, Hungarians, Poles, etc. *ad infinitum*. It has been inevitable that these groups should fail to understand each other and that there should have been little trust or sympathy between them. The result has been a formless chaos which only the constraint exercised by Anglo-Saxon predominance has prevented from becoming anarchy. One of the most amazing of recent social spectacles has been the rapidity with which these various groups have been shaking down together since mass immigration was stopped in 1930, coming to find a common life under the single Canadian roof.

On top of racial groups stand the provinces and some of our provinces have strong traditions of their own, notably Nova Scotia and Quebec. Is there at the point of the pyramid any common element which could be called a Canadian tradition?

> The European who enters Canada from the United States is keenly conscious of a distinctly Canadian atmosphere. A certain repose and mellowness hover over Canada which is seldom found in the United States. Not only in French Canada but even in the Canadian west, one does feel a certain affinity with Europe.[2]

The European observer from whom these words are quoted apparently senses a certain identity of atmosphere throughout Canada. Observers tend to agree that there is less difference between Canadians from different parts of the country, however far apart, than between Canadians in general and Americans. Our accent for example, from Halifax to Vancouver is singularly uniform, far more so than American speech from Boston to San Francisco. That must mean something. There must be some common ground for all of us, some moulding force, which can hardly be merely climatic and geographic (which, in fact, differ considerably from region to region within the country).

M. André Siegfried in his brilliant book on Canada comes to somewhat the same conclusion as Herr Bonn.[3] In this country the atmosphere of the Old World has not been entirely sloughed off: our life is a compromise between our history and the stark forces of the continent. He builds up his thesis of Canada being the result of two lines of forces, a north-south axis and an east-west axis. He seems somewhat reluctant to admit that we are much more than a resultant. So many of our people, he thinks, have been unable to take the plunge and commit themselves irrevocably to this country. They have been unable to decide, he says, whether they

[2]M. J. Bonn, *The American Experiment, A Study of Bourgeois Civilization* (London: Allen and Unwin, 1933).
[3]André Siegfried, *Canada* (London: J. Cape, 1937).

wish to give to the new land that undivided allegiance through which alone it will be able to acquire a personality of its own.

The result is a depth of colonialism which is hard for the outsider to appreciate. Much of this is inevitable: the Dominion is not eighty years old, its population is not dense, and its economic problems are pressing and paramount. Much of it proceeds from that false philosophy of individualism which interprets everything in terms of the main chance, the vulgar get-rich-quick philosophy, essentially Philistine in its nature, which can find no room for any standards that are not materialistic, which refuses to see that we are members one of another and to sacrifice its own individual interests in the general interest. Much of it, perhaps most, comes from the confusion of loyalties which exists for every Canadian.

It may appear sentimental to talk about loyalties, but people cannot live without them, for they represent some enduring principle that is larger and more permanent than ourselves. There could be no society if every man were interested primarily in himself and did not have some sort of social ideal to which he could give adhesion, some sort of conviction that the life he lives is a worthy life, that it is approved by his fellows, who after he is gone will go on standing for much the same sort of thing as he stands for. The Canadian's loyalties are hopelessly divided. An Englishman's loyalties are to England, and these abstractions give him a strength and a faith almost as great as his religious faith. But are ours to Canada, to our province, or to the Empire? About one-third of our people are loyal first of all to the French tongue and the institutions of the French race. Most of us who are of English descent have never decided whether our primary loyalty is to our country or to the Empire, a choice which presents no difficulty to an Englishman who is for England first and for the Empire very secondarily. That curious symbol, the Union Jack, quite beclouds us.

If our primary allegiance is to be here, what is going to hold it? Our Canadian hearts glow with a mild degree of satisfaction when they learn that this country is the first nickel-producing country in the world, makes more newsprint paper than any other, and is the largest average exporter of wheat, that in short "Canada has vast natural resources." But a man cannot be "loyal" to a bushel of wheat nor even to five hundred million bushels of wheat. He needs something more than that. Even we Canadians, so submerged in our wheat, need something that will stand for as much to us as "la belle France" stands for the Frenchman.

As a former Governor General, to the great dissatisfaction of the die-hards, tried to tell us, this country will be an unsatisfactory country as long as the division of loyalties and the lack of content in the term "Canadian" exists. There will be no real spirit of inner cohesion. The railways have bound us together with bands of steel, but we still require to be bound together by other and stronger bands, those of a common loyalty. Looking over this country to discover some firm social cement, one finds differences in economic interest, racial differences, linguistic differences, religious differences, cultural differences. Heretofore some identity of race, religion, language, culture has been the bed-rock of society everywhere, but it is not possible in Canada to build a new society upon their identity. What social dynamic is there, then, powerful enough to weld our heterogeneity together? There seems to be no other than nationalism, that is, simply, a common lot and a common concern for it, a common citizenship and a common love for a common land.

Can we not find for all Canada, as our French friends have found for French Canada, some support for our new society in its history? As Canadian history has been treated heretofore one would have to say no. It has acquired the reputation for being the dullest of dull subjects, and schoolboys shun it. It has been treated with little deference in our universities, where it has been overshadowed by the more majestic structures of England and Europe. It has been the Cinderella among studies. That is partly because it has not the glamour and complexity of the histories of older countries, but more because it has not yet been properly understood. Canadian history has been written from various points of view. There have been those who have written about the "romance" of Canadian history, "The High History of the Hudson's Bay Company," the romantic voyageurs and so on. This kind of writing, distorting facts, magnifying the heroic, slapping on the colours, is essentially false history. Its counterpart is to be found in those misleading pictures of the Canadian scene with which our government and other agencies used to lure the unsuspecting immigrant to this country. Let us have truthfulness, whatever we have.

Then there have been the constitutionalists, under whose tyranny we have lived for over a generation. Solid fellows these, with their unceasing disquisitions on the exact nature of responsible government and their endless digging up of letters from Grey to Elgin and Elgin to Grey. They are men who in their way have done a service by their meticulous establishment of the process by which the shell of our life, its constitutional trappings, has evolved — but dull, horribly dull, and more responsible than anyone else for stifling interest. As schoolboys we have all suffered under them. "State the terms of the Quebec Act." "Give the causes of the Constitutional Act." Fancy feeding schoolchildren on those dry bones. No wonder they rebel and come to believe that a country with such a dull history must be a very dull country. Since it is next to impossible to get adults to appreciate constitutional niceties, the children surely might well be spared them.

Then we have our antiquarians, men who spend their lives trying to establish the exact site of some Hudson's Bay post, tracing down the genealogy of some obscure worthy, trying to find the name of the first settler at Smith's Corners, or working out the exact height of the Red

River flood of 1826. The antiquarian, too, is a worthy fellow, and the points that he establishes often have some value, but he is a small fellow and also rather a potterer, and, consequently, the word of the spirit can never be uttered by him.

Then, like every other country, we have had our jingoes, the writers who have wrung the changes upon the Heights of Queenston and the Plains of Abraham and have seen in the history of this country merely an extension of militant British imperialism. They have not lacked blood and fire, but it is not in our military tradition that the secret of our history is to be found, for while we are a fighting breed, we are not a military people.

Of late years there has been a great deal of history written in Canada: in fact it is hardly an overstatement to say that since the last war, especially since the *Canadian Historical Review* began publication in 1920, Canadian history has been almost completely rewritten. Many new fields have been explored, and many valuable points of view have been put forward. The economic historians in particular have done much work in bringing to light the true nature of the country. Thus the thesis has been convincingly developed that the Dominion of Canada, contrary to the general impression, has strong elements about it of natural geographic and economic unity and a challenge made to the too-frequent statement that our "natural lines of communication run north and south." The influence of the vast mass of the "Canadian Shield," the illimitable wilderness of rock and forest that lies between West and East, has been put in its true proportion. There have been evaluations of the place in our life that the great staple products have played.

We are even beginning to turn out an occasional fairly good biography, the most difficult of the historian's tasks. Our biographies used to be merely monuments to "a great and good man," fulsome in their eulogy, completely uncritical in their appraisal. They were epitaphs, "tombstone" biographies. But a biography of Joseph Howe, written a few years ago, shows a change for the better, painting its subject "warts and all." That indicates a maturity that we had not attained a generation ago when, for fear of paining descendants, it was still impossible to publish a biography which was anything but a work of pious memory. It is to the new consciousness of nationhood, a new and vital interest in the common concern, that we owe much, perhaps the greatest part, of this new mass of writing.

From all this work the true nature of this country's experience is gradually emerging. It is sufficiently remarkable. If 180 years ago, when first this country came into English hands, the conventional observer from another planet had flown over the earth looking for a site on which to build a nation, the very last patch he would have selected would have been the northern half of North America. If one looks at the map, it appears imposing, but when the actual surface is examined a tenth part of it at most is found to be habitable. Its climatic limitations need not be expanded on. A broad belt of mountains between the Maritimes and Quebec, a quite small strip of good land along the St. Lawrence River and the Great Lakes, and then the illimitable wilderness to the north — that is eastern Canada.

In the West, there is a scanty rainfall and again to the north the rocky wilderness. A gigantic wall of mountains separates the Prairies from the Pacific coast and breaks up the Province of British Columbia into a collection of mountain valley communities. Our chief access to the sea, through the St. Lawrence, is closed for several months each year, and one of the main railway lines to the Maritimes passes through American territory. Who, the observer might ask, can be lunatic enough to believe that territory such as this can come to be the home of millions of men inspired by a sufficiency of common purpose to keep together and provide for themselves the conditions of a reasonably good life. Yet here we are today, a going concern and the apparent act of lunacy has justified itself.

Perhaps because England kept Canada, the American Revolution occurred. At any rate, the Revolution gave Canada its first large body of English-speaking people, all of them strong in their determination to nourish their wrath and keep it warm. The Loyalists of Upper Canada found themselves nearly a thousand miles inland, isolated and cut off from markets for their produce, under the constant threat from the late enemy to the south and regarded with hostility by the French lower down the river into whose country they had come. It seemed impossible that a new British colony could survive under such conditions. Yet within a generation or two the Province of Ontario had grown up, had been put into communication with the outside world, and had begun to prosper.

In the same way, those people who regretfully left the old colonies to go and starve in "Nova Scarcity" within twenty-five years had wrung from that hard soil and from the seas a living sufficiently good to base a provincial patriotism upon, a provincial society which could produce its educated men, its statesmen, and its authors.

Again, when in 1791 the Province of Quebec was divided into Upper and Lower Canada, the French went their way and the English theirs. The provinces were chronically misgoverned, friction developed, and rebellion came. After the experiment of uniting them had been tried, it was found that, in Durham's famous phrase, they were still two nations warring in the bosom of a single state. Roughly concurrent with the political impasse the supply of good land, about 1860, came to an end. Population ceased to grow: the Americans once more closed their markets. The experiment seemed to have failed.

But a way out was found in one of the most remarkable achievements of statesmanship that the nineteenth century witnessed, Confederation. Had it not been for a most fortunate and favourable conjunction of circumstances

— the threat from the south, the loss of the Reciprocity Treaty, the Fenian raids, the manipulations of London and Montreal financiers to expand the credit base on which they had made loans by securing the Hudson's Bay territories and thus preventing the United States from eventually getting them, the persistence of Tupper in Nova Scotia, the momentary truce in the troubled political world of the Province of Canada and above all the extraordinary skill, versatility, and adroitness of John A. Macdonald — Confederation could never have occurred. But it did occur, and within it English Protestants and French Roman Catholics have managed to live on tolerably good terms. Logically, the rather miserable, scattered provinces should all have been absorbed into the United States. But they were not. Instead they caught a glimpse of a greater destiny — an experiment of national life.

Once again they ran into fog. Goldwin Smith spent years telling them what fools they were and how they must inevitably end their experiment in failure. So, possibly they would have, had it not been for the occurrence of another miracle. Nominally the Dominion had been extended to the Pacific by the inclusion of the Hudson's Bay territories in 1869 and of British Columbia in 1871, but the extension represented only a paper structure. Had it not been for the courage and vision — or the damn foolishness — of Sir John and the men who built the Canadian Pacific Railway, the paper nation could never have endured, for, for a poor country of 4,000,000 people even to think of trying to bridge the enormous gap between Ontario and the West and cross the mountains with a railroad seemed in 1871 another act of lunacy. Given the conditions of the time, it probably was, and the powerful intellects of the period, the Blakes and Goldwin Smiths, were absolutely correct in denouncing the hair-brained scheme. But the job was done. The damn fools won. The railway was built, the West was united to the East, and the Dominion as we know it was achieved.

Here we have, in these few facts, the real significance of Canadian history: our history embodies a determination to make good a lost cause; it is a continuous illustration of the possibility of achieving the impossible. It is a sublime act of faith.

Can we not believe that a country which has faced such difficulties, which has had the courage to defy "common sense," which has lived on faith and has literally moved mountains, is one for which some further destiny is reserved? Can we not feel that we, too, have our historic mission, a mission which shall justify our nationhood? Will not our history afford us aid and comfort as we march forward towards that destiny?

28 | *The Canadian University**

Universities are peculiar places filled with peculiar people. They — both the institutions and the people — stand for all the virtues of the intellect — freedom, clarity, tolerance, and so on — yet they are the guardians of conservatism. Universities resist change with great determination, yet constantly change. In Canada, the institutions — and some of their occupants — are marked by a superficial cosmopolitanism, yet they bear upon them the deep imprint of national circumstances. They prepare youth for the future but are themselves survivals of the Middle Ages.

The universities of the Western world have some eight centuries behind them. Despite the diversities which have arisen over this long period, they are still of a type, and students and teachers soon feel at home in almost any one of them, whether it be in Italy or in Iceland. Our Canadian universities have as clear a medieval descent as the oldest in Europe.

From the great universities of Italy and from the still greater University of Paris, the mother fount of learning, have sprung all the later institutions. The marks of their origins are upon each of them. The cap and gown, the hood, are medieval garments not much changed over the centuries. The principal "degrees" are the same as centuries ago. Teaching methods are not much altered: it is still mainly a matter of talking, listening, and arguing. Who of us would not find himself at home with fellow academic monks of the thirteenth century, eagerly complicating the abstraction of the day, discussing the excellence, or more probably, the shortcomings of students?

With the break in European history, the Reformation, the English universities began to go off in their own direction. Scottish universities seem to have remained more of the Continental type. When universities were begun in the American colonies, they reflected the English universities at a stage when divergence from the Continental model was less marked than it afterward became. Harvard was founded by Cambridge men, and Yale reflected Harvard. But seventeenth-century Cambridge was more like a French, Dutch, or Scottish university than Cambridge was later to be. If New England has influenced us, as it has, it in turn does not reflect

*Delivered to the Royal Society of Canada and published in the *Proceedings and Transactions, 3rd Series, 47 (1953): Section 2, 1-16.

the same English influence as has played on us in the last century or so from Oxford.

In England, the separation from the Continent and the substitution of Anglicanism for Catholicism seem to have strengthened the claims of the ruling classes upon the good things of life, education included. Medieval grammar schools housed sons of poor and rich alike, as did medieval Oxford colleges. After the Reformation, but still more after the Restoration, which represented the triumph of reaction, the wealthier classes secured the privileges of the grammar schools, and the poor boy began to be conspicuous at Oxford by his absence, or, if present, by his hard lot. One unlooked-for effect of the English Reformation was intensification of the class structure in English society.

In medieval times, the universities had been thronged with students, most of them poor, all of them on the same footing under the shelter of the universal church. The old Catholic world could therefore be, in a sense, democratic. The new Anglican world, devoted to the maintenance in power of a new ruling class, could not. "Free schools diverted those whom Nature or Fortune had determined to the Plough, the Oar, or other Handicrafts, from their proper design, to the study of the Liberal Arts, and even Divinity itself."[1]

In Scotland, which has also profoundly influenced higher education, class differences were not as conspicuous as in England. Scotland was poorer than England; Scotland was Presbyterian. Presbyterianism intensified religious debate. Higher education in Scotland consequently took a different form from that in England. English education in the course of the two or three centuries after the Reformation came to be dominated by "the Classics." In Scotland, the old medieval absorption in philosophy continued to hold the stage. In England, rich youths could buy books. In Scotland, poor youths still had to copy down the words of wisdom read out from the professor's chair. This practice was brought over to Canada, where it is possibly not yet quite extinct, for in Canada, too, the purchase of books is a heroic act.

In one group of Canadian universities, the survival of medievalism is particularly conspicuous — the universities of French Canada. Anyone who has sat in the older lecture rooms at Laval must have noticed the elaborate, imposing edifice at the front which serves as "the chair." To get into these sumptuous pieces of furniture, the professor ascends a few steps, and once there, fortified behind his mahogany barricade, sitting down, his books spread out before him, he is very literally speaking *ex cathedra*.

---

[1]Christopher Wise in his *Considerations Concerning Free Schools,* 1678, as quoted in S. E. Morison, *The Puritan Pronaos: Studies in the Intellectual Life of New England in the Seventeenth Century* (London: Oxford University Press, 1936).

(This same medieval tag survives in American university custom: although a declining habit, it is still good form to *sit* at your desk while lecturing.)

More important, until yesterday the curricula of our French universities were largely medieval also. Philosophy remained the core of higher learning and Latin its medium. This attitude towards Latin as a real language was very different from the English study of the Classics.

Our French universities, from several points of view, are less complex than our English. They represent a uniform culture transferred to Canadian soil and preserved here with singular fidelity, though with the desiccation which time inevitably brings to things preserved. Today, as they feel their way forward into the currents of modern life, they are being exposed to some of the storms English Canada encountered decades ago. The impact of science and of the scientific attitude fell on our English universities in the late nineteenth and early twentieth centuries. By now they have more or less accommodated themselves to it. This accommodation has yet to be made in French Canada, for the impact itself is just beginning to be felt.

The differences between our French universities arise, not from diversity of tradition, but from geographical location. Quebec, Montreal, Ottawa, St. Boniface College, and the Maritime institutions, each represent different phases in the relationships of French and English, based on the geographical distribution of the two races. Laval has the assurance of a community that has lived down the conquest and is once more almost entirely French. To this it adds its three centuries of history, a length of experience which the sensitive can *feel* just as they can feel *time* at Harvard. In Montreal, by contrast, the racial struggle still goes on: there is a tension in the atmosphere not felt in Quebec. Parenthetically, surely it is regrettable that this great city, a huge sociological laboratory where two historic cultures meet, has as yet produced from neither side, French or English, a social scientist to make some recording of the scene. The novelists have begun to explore the phenomenon, but some years ago when a sociological analysis was made, the sociologists to make it had to be imported from Chicago.

In Ottawa, the rapidly rising third centre of French education in Canada, there is a tone which differs from that of both Montreal and Quebec: a frank acceptance of biculturalism, an accommodation to it, a measure of fusion, even, of French and English approaches to education.

St. Boniface in Manitoba and the French institutions of the Maritimes resemble each other at least in this, that they are citadels of French culture within dominantly English areas. The French colleges of North Bay and Sudbury are, I suppose, similar. St. Boniface fights a rear-guard action against the omnipresent English and tends to fortify itself within the ancient walls of the Latin philosophy. The others, of which I know little personally, are situated in areas where the French language is advancing, not retreating, and thus probably have some of the buoyancy of an expanding culture.

In sum, French higher education in Canada would appear to be highly influenced by its relationship to the vast surrounding English world. Where this has been pushed back a bit, a sense of security allows of modernization: where it still presses, it causes the ancient ways to be tightly clung to.

No one would maintain that our English universities have the unity of the French: they represent a perplexing diversity of tradition. Even today, when some of them are going into their second century, the variety of their origins is reflected in internal stresses and strains. The variety of origin within staffs often gives rise to equally sharp tensions.

It would be tedious to go over the list of diversities in detail since everyone knows a good many items on it: the struggle between professional groups and the scholars, the division of scholarship between "sciences" and the rest, and many other such. Some institutions have consciously sought to preserve the English tradition, others the Scottish. There must be over a dozen founded to act as intellectual citadels for the various denominations. Within nearly all, the faculty itself has represented a variety of origins and, therefore, of competing traditions. Virtually every Canadian university staff has been a kind of melting pot, like the country itself, in which homogeneity has emerged but slowly, if at all. Add to all these fundamental differences between different individuals and groups on what constitutes the most desirable way of life.

To illustrate, we have church universities; federations of universities; more or less Gaelic universities; universities which are aspects of metropolitan commercial societies; private universities once resting on a church foundation, now floating free, as it were; municipal colleges; provincial universities with and without monopoly of the degree-granting power, and various others. We have institutions which still aim at turning out members of a governing class — leaders in church and state, in the old phrase — and institutions only too ready to respond to the demands of the commercial way of life. We have institutions of democratic and of aristocratic tone. There are, in fact, hardly two strictly comparable institutions in the whole of Canada. Of course, individual differences are all contained within the general framework of Western civilization.

In other words, the university must necessarily reflect its foundation and its surroundings. To some this may be heresy, for universities, wherever we find them, are sometimes thought of as mere segments of the universal *respublica literaria,* as consisting in collections of single-minded scholars untouched by race, clime, nation, and original sin.

On this give me leave to be sceptical. Waiving the question of original sin, something of the sort possibly was true when one culture prevailed throughout Europe. But after the great age of the thirteenth century, as new institutions were founded in Bohemia, Germany, Scotland, and other frontier regions, each tended to take on local characteristics. With the rise of the national state and the Reformation, breaking up the old medieval culture, the university began to reflect the society in which it was contained. Universities became aspects of nationalism, which, to a major degree, they remain.

There is nothing surprising in this. All education is, in essence, an aspect of politics, that is, it is a reflection of the hypotheses of the particular society. In fact, it is mostly plain simple indoctrination in those hypotheses, as the ringing platitudes in course of being delivered from a thousand convocation platforms now testify. We in Canada are still among those fortunate mortals whose society assumes that no artificial fetters should be placed on the working of the free mind, though how long we shall remain so depends on how far the present hysteria carries among our neighbours. The fact that we are free to pursue the truth as we see it does not, however, mean that we are pursuing universal truth: few of us are big enough for that. For a time, the civilized world did seem to boast a universal attitude towards the search for truth, in some disciplines at any rate. The scientist used to think of himself as a universal man. But now we have had Nazi science, and we still have Soviet science, just as we have Soviet art, as distinguished from bourgeois — or degenerate — art. So far has this gone, that today even the educated within the one society have little common cultural background. It is no longer possible to quote a verse of Scripture, still less a line of Horace, and expect it to be recognized.

The "isms" are but extreme examples of the fragmentation to which truth has always been subject. Oswald Spengler maintains that every civilization produces its own characteristic form of the most universal of all disciplines, mathematics. That may or may not be so, but it is not much more than might be expected, given the differences in men's environments, their interests, and points of view. Presuming society is "open," that is, that it allows of free inquiry, various disciplines are almost certain to go off in various directions, dependent upon local circumstances, though they can still remain on speaking terms, because the bond of free inquiry is there. Given a closed, authoritarian society, of course, the pursuit of truth, in the sense in which we understand it, stops. There can be little in common between the learned men the two conceptions produce, whether "scholars" or not. It is just possible that a mathematician might be equally at home at the universities of Harvard, Moscow, and Cairo: certainly an historian would not.

History as a subject illustrates very well the fragmentation of truth to which I have just referred. Outside our own Western society, our canons of historical study do not apply. Within it, time and the capacity of men's minds both being limited, most history tends to be national history. Naturally there are distinguished exceptions, but in general terms Englishmen write English history and for Englishmen; Frenchmen, French, for Frenchmen, and so on. Even when the historian attempts a theme drawn from outside his own society, his product bears unmistakable marks upon it of its place of origin. Gibbon wrote about Rome and Byzantium, but his book was unmistakably that of an eighteenth-century Englishman. Taine wrote a history of English literature which certainly could never have been written by any Englishman. There is hardly an area of culture, scholarly or artistic, which does not carry such marks of origin upon it. In music, for example, few would mistake the label "made in Germany" for the label "made in Italy."

It seems to me, therefore, that the university is an aspect of the society which harbours it. Today the university is national: tomorrow, it may be supernational. If, for example, NATO should turn into something like a state, there would evolve a NATO community, with its NATO universities indoctrinating their youth into love for NATO: *dulce et decorum erit pro NATO mori.*

There is another reason why the university is at present mainly a national institution, not an international, and that is that it has, as an institution, no power to stand up to the state. The German universities crumpled at the first blow, as had the Russian before them. And now the American universities seem to be following suit. The prevailing moods and passions of American life are quickly being reflected in American universities, bringing them into line. It is possible that the prestige of the greatest may enable them to resist, at least for a time, but for the majority, how could it well be otherwise? Despite fine words, universities as institutions are invariably timid and invariably conservative. Even if they were not, they would have little power of resistance to the state, for they represent only a small group, the intelligentsia: they are not like churches, which can summon moral fervour and mass support.

If conquering orthodoxies in their processes of *Gleichschaltung* are to be resisted, the fight will not be made by institutions but by the occasional individuals in those institutions who become martyrs to a cause.

Now the bearing of all this on Canadian universities is simply that, whereas in origin they are diverse, at their present stage and at the present stage of our development, they are, like the institutions of older lands, national. Not national without qualification — Canadian institutions representing a religious denomination may link up with similar institutions in other lands; Canadian schools of commerce are aspects of the general North American civilization — but nevertheless national, serving the Canadian people, French or English, as it demands to be served. Canadian institutions are not international; they are not cosmopolitan: they are national. Efforts to make them cosmopolitan in the midst of a local and rather parochial society are foolish and bound to fail.

It may be objected that institutions sponsored by a branch of a universal church cannot be dubbed "national." The words "national" and "of the state" are not to be confused. Our institutions are not like those of Germany, "of the state," for our North American pattern is one of considerable liberty for every group to follow its own way of life. Nevertheless, our institutions are now national in that they reflect the same, or very similar, attitudes towards all the large aspects of university life.

One indication that the humblest of colleges is now "national," in the sense in which I am using that word, lies in the almost universal form of government, which consists in a board endowed with supreme powers. The constitution of this board is provided for in some fundamental piece of legislation, and on the surface it often appears liberal and democratic. In practice university boards seem to be close to self-perpetuating. They represent various classes of interest in the community, with one or two conspicuous omissions, and in so far as they do this effectively, that is to the good. A class they do *not* represent is that class which constitutes the university, instructors and students. Another is *labour*.

We cannot too often remind ourselves that the essential corpus of any institution of higher learning is not governors, nor alumni, nor administrators, but scholars. Scholars come, ideally at any rate, before students. The scholar, frightened mouse that he often is, is the man who most often gets kicked around. In an ideal world, he would be running his own affairs. As it is, he is an employee, and sometimes made to feel the weight of that not too glorious status. He is carefully selected on the basis of his intellectual capacities and, more often than not, in the system of rating familiar to all of us, is an "A" man. As an "A" man, he is compelled to pass his life governed by the second-rate, successful fellows to whom when they were in his classes he had to award B's. There is no use complaining overly bitterly about that: the world over, I suspect, it is the "B" who gets to the top in the power struggle.

Nevertheless, it is not right that the company of scholars, which every university should be, should simply be "employees." They should be, in fact, a company — a corporation, with a voice in their own government. British visitors are commonly surprised that this is not so in North American university constitutions. In Great Britain, I understand, it is the ordinary thing for the governing body to contain a fair representation from the professoriate. The ancient universities have been self-governing for centuries, but the principle has also been carefully cherished in the newer institutions.

For the loss by academics of the right of self-government there are many explanations. Many academics themselves do not seem to want it.

They seem to be in favour of democratic processes in the abstract but against them in the concrete. They speak of the lobbying that would take place, the personal ambitions that would be unloosed, were the elective principle to be introduced into university government. This, it seems to me, is just a kind of finickiness that is dismayed by the rough-and-tumble of the power struggle. University men should practise what they preach. Democracy and freedom are not to be won and kept without fighting, and fighting means blows and blood.

The underlying explanation for the North American situation, Canadian included, probably lies in the nature of our society. English Canada has little respect, we all know, for the intellectual as such. This is partly because of the stark, hell-fire religious heritage lying behind so many of its people and more because of the hard fight they have had against physical nature. We have learned to use our hands, with tools in them, in fighting these millions of mostly barren square miles of ours and to use our minds as extensions of our hands — hence the prestige of "science," especially of applied science — but we have not yet learned to use our minds as minds, as the highest manifestation of humanity, as organs of pure reflection. Hence the instinctive opposition of the ordinary man to what he would call "the theorist." Hence his ready appreciation of people "who can do things." Canadian life has been one long eulogy of the practical man, whether he be farmer, businessman, engineer, politician, or, nowadays, soldier. It is executive action that we understand and admire.

How that works out in institutions of higher learning, I hardly need to say. Has there even been a professor, I wonder, who when presented with the opportunity to abandon the life of contemplation for the life of action has not jumped at the chance to become head of this, director of that, dean of the other thing? Has there ever been registrar or bursar whose stature, by one means or another, has not been made to seem a little larger than that of the mere "teacher"? Open any calendar and you are confronted with a list of "Officers of Administration," followed later by "Teaching Staff." The names of officers of administration should be printed in small type at the back of the book. I always have a feeling of regret when a man who could be a good scholar becomes an administrator. Surely the intellectual life, representing the ideal freedom of the mind, must be the best — and the foremost — of all lives. Without wishing in any way to offend my numerous good friends who are administrators, I must nevertheless maintain that the administrator, as such, is at best a necessary evil.

Only as the teaching staff turns itself into what I have called a company of scholars will Canadian universities really justify their existence. And that will not be until members of such staffs are seized with a sense of vocation as deep as the call to the religious life, of which, indeed, in a wide way of thinking, they represent a sphere. Our minds to us kingdoms are; let it be as dangerous to interfere with them as with our souls. But that will mean carrying an unaccustomed gospel to the Canadian people. Religion, they understand: intellectualism, scarcely at all.

It follows that the persons to carry such a gospel must be carefully chosen and fully aware of the nature of their tasks.

Our English-Canadian universities began as offshoots of metropolitan culture: they were little islands of British civilization transferred across the ocean. In some of them, American influence was also strong from the beginning, and as time has gone on, it has tended to strengthen. Direct European influence has always been slight. This despite a period when there were many professors with German doctorates and despite departments of modern languages. There has been no such impact made upon Canadian higher learning as was made by Germany in the nineteenth century upon American higher learning, though through this American channel a certain amount of German influence has come in indirectly. Everything considered, English-Canadian culture remains islanded within the Anglo-Saxon world. In the *Report* of the Council of this Society, you will find a suggestion that visiting scholars, "especially from France and the British Commonwealth," be invited to address branches. Could the parochial tone of the Canadian learned world be more sharply reflected?

Unlike good Americans, good Canadians, when they die, do not go to Paris.

The reflections of what might be called Anglo-Saxon parochialism are evident in every university circle. In every university in the country we have a few language masters. Their influence as such upon the spirit and outlook of our universities is nil. They have never succeeded in bringing to life even the second official language of the country in which they earn their living, let alone other languages. One of the best testimonies to the failure of the language master to make any impression upon the Canadian student would be the embarrassment of the average Fellow in Section II if he were put down in the middle of a group of Fellows from Section I, none of whom spoke English! The highly insular culture of Great Britain has normally produced a class of person who could speak French fairly well and who had some reasonable familiarity with French culture. Here, in this bilingual country, we, the English-speaking intelligensia, are, with few exceptions, prisoners of one language and one culture.

In this respect, we compare badly with the Americans. Our young men, attempting to go down to American graduate schools, are immediately confronted with the terrors of French and German. A student of mine recently was awarded a fellowship at a great New England university. He could not take it because, within two months of his arrival, he would have had to take a reading examination in German! He was horrified at the unreasonableness of the Yankees! Was his case exceptional?

My argument here is one of two aspects. I have sketched out one of them: it consists in a charge of parochialism in culture, our English-Canadian parochialism lying in our submergence in the English-speaking world. The other aspect might at first sight appear to lead in precisely this direction, but on fuller examination, I do not think it does. To put my position briefly, I feel that we can best escape from parochialism in culture by a more complete understanding of the local scene, a more complete, more sympathetic identification with it. For us, English Canadians, to continue to be merely lookers-on at the great plays staged in London and New York is to continue to be parochial, imitative, provincial, uncreative.

There is the element that vitiates so much academic work, cultural colonialism! It is all very well to talk about eclecticism, about internationalism or cosmopolitanism. The words do not apply, for in English-Canadian universities there is neither electicism, nor internationalism, nor cosmopolitanism: there is just submergence in the senior cultures of the race. Prolonged submergence, do not forget, means drowning. Many of us are already drowned. I can think of nothing more fatal to that creative spirit with which genuine scholarship must be infused than our normal over-respectful, virtually submissive, attitude to these two senior cultures and their exponents, especially the British.

So much filial piety is there in English Canada that it is difficult to make dispassionate analysis of any problem, cultural or otherwise, which involves our relationship to the British world, without immediately evoking hostile emotions. Such emotions are in themselves evidence enough of the condition I am attempting to describe, for they indicate that those in whose breasts they stir are not in their heart of hearts citizens of this new country, but persons whose sentiments still hark back across the seas.

In this place and at this time I do not intend to go into this old subject which I have discussed elsewhere *ad nauseam*. I must content myself with the family parallel — men must grow up, marry, found families of their own. It is the way of nature, for societies, as for individuals. What sadder sight than those men who, long after they have become adults, continue at their mother's knee!

This condition of submergence in itself goes a long way to explaining the relative sterility of the Canadian academic. As some one has said, there seems to be within us some "psychological block." Does submergence explain it? The best things, it may be believed, have already been said, the great thoughts thought elsewhere. Canadian scholarship, with exceptions, is not distinguished and it is not wide. In vain do we look for, among many others, the large, massive accomplishment of a Lawrence J. Gipson in *The British Empire before the American Revolution* or to the unconventional, iconoclastic, and encyclopaedic learning of a Herbert J. Muller, a man whose book *The Uses of the Past* comes from no more conspicious a place than Purdue. (Where is Purdue?) The average Canadian scholar would be afraid to be as "cheeky" as a Muller, setting himself up against all the great names of the past. The average Canadian scholar, that is, is provincial.

Canadian culture — or, if you like it better, culture in Canada — will never rise to manhood until it resolutely takes to standing on its own feet. Heretofore so many of the exponents of our learning have been like Lot's wife — constantly looking backward and as effectively turned to sterile salt.

How does a culture "stand on its own feet"? Well, in general terms, by drawing its vital forces from the life around it. Infinite illustrations could be given. I have already referred to that unexploited sociological laboratory, Montreal. I am inclined to think that, for citizens of Canada, it would be more genuinely a matter of culture to seek to understand the ins-and-outs of the racial situation in Montreal than to occupy themselves with intensive study of the Year III of the French Revolution. I have also referred to the situation of language teaching. I hope I will not be interpreted as making an attack on a particular discipline if I refer once more to French studies. My justification is that, in a country like this, these go far beyond the status of an academic "subject" and become issues of the highest national importance. They are open to examination by every citizen. Here we have in Canada a bilingual country, two rich cultures meeting — and what fascinating depths of history, sociology, law, philosophy, and theology the culture of French Canada offers to English Canadians only those know who have tried to examine it — yet this situation finds the minimum of reflection in our universities. I know there are honourable exceptions, but in general terms little or no advantage is taken by departments of French of the presence of a living French culture in the country. The result is only too often the reduction of French to the status of a dead language. If the situation is not quite that bad in the universities, it certainly is in the schools. Instead of a vital cultural area under study, more often than not we do not move beyond barren linguistics.

If I may be so impertinent, I would suggest to the language disciplines that they could greatly enrich and revive their fields if they interpreted them as studies not merely of language and literature but of every aspect of the culture concerned. German music, German philosophy, the whole vast range of German scholarship, German historiography, to all of these should the attention of the student be drawn. Such an undertaking would be ambitious, but in the end the study of a living culture, I am sure, would "pay off" — and it might help to redeem Canadian institutions from their confining English-language provincialism.

Incidentally, this Society includes at least one gentleman in German studies whose work has won international recognition. Under his leadership, I would guess that some such attitude as I have suggested has already been adopted. Indeed it may be that the cultural approach has already gone farther than I am aware of. In that case, my apologies!

The best testimony to scholarship, like charity, beginning at home is to be found in the existence and condition of the older social sciences, history, economics, and political science. It was in 1896 that the late Professor Wrong and Mr. H. H. Langton began to publish their *Review of Historical Publications Relating to Canada.* In 1920, this changed into the present *Canadian Historical Review.* To the University of Toronto, which has during all these fifty-seven years carried the annual deficits, Canadian historical studies owe an immeasurable debt. Canadian historians have tried to repay that debt by their labours. In 1923, they formed the Canadian Historical Association, whose annual meetings, following those of this Society, have provided cohesion and the stimulus which comes from friendly contacts. As a result of all this, Canadian historical writing can take its place honourably beside that of any other land.

Historical and social studies in Canada which have not related to Canada have not been outstanding.

Our "political economy," as it was originally called, from the first had a strong historical bent, so that it is perhaps not invidious to think of it as an aspect of our historical studies. At any rate, one would have difficulty in deciding whether historian or economist was the more correct term for Shortt, Skelton, Mackintosh, and our late dear colleague Innis. The same assertion can be made of political science, and now, as it slowly develops, of sociology. Our sociology is weak as yet, but so far it has not been marred by the excessive exercises in the virtuosity of technique which seem to characterize the subject in the United States. Canadian sociology, if we may judge by the Mackintosh and Joerg series of some twenty years ago or by the more recent Clark series now in publication, is seeing life not on the flat surface of "the present" (whatever "the present" is) but in the cube, under the impulsion not only of space, but also of time.

The latest recruit to these Canadian studies, one that should have joined the ranks long ago, is geography. Of course, its mother discipline, geology, has been established among us for a century. That science, it seems to me, is itself partly a social science. I count myself fortunate in having had a little taste of geological knowledge under such men as Coleman and Parks. The little I had has been of immense service. Like geology, Canadian geography will, from its very nature, be concerned with the world immediately around it, Canada. Already we have had some distinguished works clarifying the nature of the Canadian environment.

Now the reason that such studies are vital in a way that some others, I am afraid, are not, is simply that they begin with the here and the now, the familiar, the local environment, learn to understand it as well as possible — and, perhaps, to love it — and then work out from it to wider horizons. This is the point to which I have been trying to lead up. To begin with the local in studies is to end up with the universal. To begin with the universal is to end up with the parochial. It is a case of "Flower in the crannied wall ...."

Hence I suggest that if we are to get further towards the universal in scholarship and culture, we shall have to begin by becoming more local. Please do not misunderstand me: I am advocating no restriction of horizons. My observations are not motivated by the desire, found in some of the lesser nationalisms, to retire into a narrow, self-hypnotic realm of misty tribalism. Quite the reverse: I should like to rescue this country and its scholarship from provincialism. Only those can avoid provincialism who belong directly to some creative nucleus. They are inevitably provincials who, living in one community, continue to dream about a bigger and brighter existence in another. It is this kind of provincialism, stemming directly from our long colonial status, which today seems to me to be the greatest blemish on academic culture in Canada. In order to remove the blemish, we shall have first to become more local, more interested in what is going on under our noses. There is just as much culture to be distilled out of trying to understand the microcosm as the macrocosm. Before advancing we must get this firm foundation within ourselves, *reculer pour mieux sauter.*

Most of you are probably not primarily interested in Canadian studies — though your own work, whatever your field, will suffer if you are not. To those of you who are, I suggest that it would not only be an interesting experiment, but educationally and nationally valuable, if we could establish within our faculties of arts some kind of school of Canadian studies which would have for its object to do for this country just the same job as I suggested might be done for the linguistic disciplines. I think I could give a student a pretty good education if I could train him in the two Canadian languages, in Canadian history, economics, politics, law, and so on.

The objection will at once be raised that here we lack models of greatness: the supreme achievements lie elsewhere. It cannot surely be contended that it would be just as good to present students with the poetry of Bliss Carman as with Shakespeare!

Few would be so foolish as to exclude the great models of human accomplishment just because of their national origin: that is not the point. I am suggesting that we could find a good education in the study of a social group of some significance, such as our own, and its way of life. If we could approach things on that level, we might have less difficulty with "the great." At present, the innocent Canadian student is projected into the presence of "the great" in so determined a fashion as often to make him thoroughly frightened by them and them distasteful to him. You have all entertained students, I suppose, in your homes, and you all know how embarrassed they are for fear they should do the wrong thing, how impossible they find it even to find the formula that will enable them to take their leave! They are frightened on being dragged up into the rarefied and unfamiliar professorial atmosphere. It is much the same when they are dragged into the presence of the historical and literary "great." Not understanding such people, the student is apt to preserve his self-respect by refusing to take them seriously. I imagine that they would be less ill at ease with some of their own domestic half-greats. Old Sir John Macdonald, for example, is a figure whom they understand. That product of sophisticated aristocratic culture, Matthew Arnold, beloved of "Eng. Lit.," must appear to the average young Canadian philistine, if not to the exceptional student, as merely remote and peculiar.

In this rather rambling paper, I have just tried to start some hares, for, obviously, systematic discussion of such a large topic as "The Canadian University" is here impossible. My major concern is how the university can be preserved for the elect and not at the same time cut itself off from the mass. We live in an increasingly chaotic, nomadic society, which today is literally on wheels, whose culture never gets a chance to consolidate itself before it is shattered by new knowledge and new inventions. At the period of Confederation, there was a cultured, if sharply limited, group which apparently had the respect of the society it led. Today such a group, which, in any case, cannot have a common corpus of knowledge and common standards of taste, tends to be shoved off into corners by the great democratic public that storms against "culture-vultures" who like to have symphonic concerts on Sunday afternoons. This great public, coming up from below, its head full of sad American slave music and its belly full of Coca-Cola, has little respect for the academic "culture" of the classroom. What has got to be done is to create a new culture — a native culture, built upon the remains of the old, and let us hope, incorporating a good deal of it. It is sometimes as sad a business to hear Canadian academics gnawing over the meatless bones of Old World culture as it is to listen to Canadian academic music. A valid, vital culture will have to come out of the current scene, despite its crudities. In its formation, the academic must play a lead, not titter nervously as he hears the new harsh strains coming out of the rough-and-tumble dance hall.

The job of the Canadian university, particularly of its representatives in faculties of arts, is to build a bridge between the new ways of life, repellent though so many of their manifestations may be, and the enduring elements of the historic culture of the West. While keeping strong all possible links with other branches of the traditional Republic of Letters, it is to reflect, enlarge, dignify, and make healthy Canadian society.

IX.

External Relations

Having come to maturity, a nation moves to establish its new relationship with the outside world and to define the base upon which participation in international affairs will occur. For Lower, Canada reached psychological maturity in the decades between the two World Wars. Achievement of such a status required Canadians to re-evaluate their relationship with Britain. Quite early in his career he argued, in "The Evolution of the Sentimental Idea of Empire: A Canadian View" (Essay #29), that affection for the mother country by the colonists was the key element that had permitted the founding of the British Empire and that had maintained it over the years. Sentiment permitted a continuing relationship between Britain and the colony while allowing each to base its domestic and external policies upon self-interest, the only base with any semblance of reality. Lower's basic position in the great debate of the 1930's on Canada's identity and what its basis for action should be was set out in "Foreign Policy and Canadian Nationalism" (Essay #30). Rejecting both the imperialist and internationalist position, he argued that Canada had to understand itself and then act in accordance with its own self-interest. Only in this fashion could Canada control its destiny.

He wrote widely, making clear his position on specific issues. Through these essays he attempted to educate his fellow countrymen concerning Canada's situation in international affairs and to arouse them to thought and action. "The Maritimes as a Strategic Point in North America" (Essay #31) illustrated Canada's key position during World War II. (Tangentially, this essay is a good sample of his deep love of the sea and his understanding of its role in Canada's history.)

29 | The Evolution of the Sentimental Idea of Empire: A Canadian View*

The spectacular physical growth of the British Empire is apt to obscure

*History, n.s. 11 (January 1927): 289-303.

the no less important evolution of a few dominant and fairly simple ideas which from Elizabethan days until our own have never ceased to exert a profound influence upon its development. Imaginative glimpses of a greater Britain beyond the seas have, for example, been credited to Sir Walter Raleigh, and to them we probably owe the colonization of Virginia. The views on government, religion, and morals carried out to New England contained in themselves the seeds of the American Revolution. The administrative imperialism arising from the Seven Years' War led by another path to the same goal. Most important of all, as it was most extended in its scope, was the body of ideas comprised in the term the "mercantile system." "For nearly two hundred years, until the triumph of the free trade idea," says Mr. G. L. Beer, "the Empire developed, was dismembered and grew anew under this system."[1] After the dismemberment, the old idea was challenged and conflicting opinions struggled for supremacy. Gradually there emerged what, for want of a better name, may be called the sentimental view of empire, the idea that the Empire is similar to a family, held together merely by ties of affection. The origin and evolution of this idea, which the writer believes to have been the distinctive contribution of the colonies towards the building of the present organization, should be of interest.

The eighteenth century, it is often said, was an age of realism. It was singularly lacking in imaginative concepts. Its motives were practical, not sentimental. Among realists, the commercial type was probably the most thoroughgoing. It had reduced the founding of an empire to a problem in book-keeping. The desirability of a colony was in direct proportion to the amount of its trade with England. Illustrations of this point of view abound. For instance, in the pamphlet *An Examination of the Commercial Principles of the Late Negotiations between Great Britain and France in MDCCLXI,* the author, debating the relative values to Great Britain of Guadeloupe and Canada, clinches his arguments in favour of the former as follows: "The precise state of its [Canada's] commerce has fallen below my own mean opinion of its value; it is even below the income of many private estates.... The entire produce of this province might be imported hither in one single ship; and this is the whole existing value of *Canada* to the commerce and navigation of *Great Britain,* 14,000 l. to the former; a ship or two to the latter." Then follows a charmingly simple formula for deciding upon the respective merits of territorial accessions:

The following table will show in one view, the value of the acquisitions we were to have made by that treaty, and the price we were to have

---

[1]George Louis Beer, *The Origins of the British Colonial System, 1578-1660* (New York: Macmillan, 1922), p. 424.

paid for them; and whether all these acquisitions put together could be considered as an equivalent for the loss we should have sustained in the surrender of Guadeloupe. By the late treaty

We should have acquired	Ł	s.	d.		We should have lost.			
Canada, worth annually	14,015	17	1		*Guadeloupe*, worth			
Minorca, ditto	500	0	0			Ł	s.	d.
Senegal and *Goree*	37,000	0	0		annually	603,269	3	9
Total acquisition *per Ann.*	51,515	17	1					
Net loss *per Ann.*	551,753	6	8					
	603,269	3	9			603,269	3	9

After commenting upon the commercial advantages France would have obtained in the restoration of Guadeloupe, he adds: "The English, giving up a great part of this very trade out of their hands [would] acquire only a barren expense, without one single even possible advantage to our commerce; without any other consolation than the liberty of parading in boundless and fruitless forests, and amusing ourselves with idle speculations upon the importance of Canada."[2] This is hard-headed commercialism at its best, an extreme exposition of the book-keeping view of empire.

Although the findings of this "Examiner" were not allowed to go unchallenged, it is noteworthy that those who answered him did not assail his principles but merely his deductions. The *Thoughts on Trade in General,* etc. of "Ignotus," for instance, takes the book-keeping basis of empire for granted, but points out that "the plain design of the *Examiner* is to secure *Guadeloupe* ... to lessen the value of *Canada* [and] to insist upon the importance of his favourite isles,"[3] and that "*Canada* will admit of much greater improvements than *Guadeloupe,* and may in time furnish us with materials amounting to more than the whole imports from the latter."[4] In other words, as a businessman, "Ignotus" believed that Canada was the better speculation.

As with Canada, so in regard to the other provinces, opinion in the motherland held fast to the book-keeping view. There was practically no deviation from it. One who looked at the question from any other angle would have been considered, to put it mildly, peculiar. This was clearly seen by "Cato" in his *Thoughts on a Question of Importance, Whether it is probable that the Immence Extent of Territory acquired by this Nation at the late Peace will operate towards the Prosperity or Ruin of the Island*

---

[2]Attributed to William Burke, a cousin of Edmund Burke and a placeman on the establishment of Guadeloupe, (London, 1762), pp. 50-51.
[3](London, 1763), p. 3.
[4]Ibid., p. 60.

of Great Britain. "Cato" was against trade restrictions and his views bordered on free trade.

On page 36 of his work he says:

> Perhaps if all the laws on the subject [of trade regulations] were enumerated, it might be shown that the greater part are prejudicial. All the exclusive rights of corporations and monopolies of private companies, if these were necessary or useful at the beginning, have long ceased to be so, and yet many of them still continue. They must probably continue for ages yet to come, such is the spirit of the people: he would be a bold minister, nay, it would be a bold parliament that should attempt to lay them open. There is nothing that appears to me more clear, than that the restrictions we have laid our sister Kingdom of Ireland under are prejudicial to ourselves; and yet I would not be the man who should propose to take them off in an English House of Commons.[5]

There were very few "Catos" in the 1760's, and instead of an understanding of the colonies or any liberality towards them, there runs through the controversial literature of the pre-Revolutionary years merely a note of jealousy,[6] an inability, universal in the second stage of mercantilism, to regard them as aught else but markets, the fear that independence would be the worst of evils because it would terminate trade. The more thoroughly one becomes acquainted with the spirit of eighteenth-century England, with its grubbing commercialism and the arrogant ignorance of its ruling caste, the more intensely does the conviction come home to him that the break-up of the first Empire was inevitable.

In the prevailing darkness there were, it is true, honourable points of light. It is often said that had Chatham retained his health and continued in office, the Revolution might never have occurred. The fierce worship of liberty which characterized that imperious soul brooked no limitation in the sphere of its deity. His was no tribal God. "Surely we cannot in reason deny that portion of liberty, so hardly and honourably obtained, to our own brethren — brethren by the same common parent, and who are unquestionable heirs of the same glorious inheritance."[7] Nor was he

---

[5](London, 1765), p. 36. Two phases of mercantilism are usually distinguished. In the earlier period, until about 1750, colonies were valued for the raw material they supplied; hence tropical colonies were most useful. Later, with the development of the industrial revolution, their main function was to serve as markets for British manufactures. This, for the later mercantilists, was the chief purpose of the colonies of the second Empire. Its theories still live in projects for imperial perferences.

[6]One motive for this jealousy was the definitely expressed apprehension that, owing to their rapid expansion, the colonies might ultimately become the senior partners in the firm.

[7]Speech of 20 January 1775, quoted in Basil Williams, *The Life of William Pitt, Earl of Chatham*, 2 vols. (London: Longmans, Green, 1915), 2: 309.

alone. He counted on his side men such as Camden and Conway. All that was best in the Whig party, ineffectual and dissipated as its force had been during the dark days of the sixties when the foundation of the separation was being well and truly laid, at last rallied to the colonial cause; and the very forces which were attempting to extinguish freedom in America, by reaction kindled its fire afresh in Great Britain. All these men, had they had the opportunity, would have built on sure ground, and the framework of empire which might have sprung from their labours would doubtless have approximated very closely to that which has since developed. But they had not crossed the gulf between local liberty and imperial unity. Chatham would have bound the colonies by ties "of Wisdom and Moderation in this Great Nation, famed for humanity as for Valour, and of Fidelity and Grateful Affection from Brave and Loyal Colonies to their Parent Kingdom."[8] To none of them, with one great exception, not even to Chatham, does there appear to have come the vision of a great world-wide system of commonwealths in which Great Britain was only *primus inter pares*.

The exception was Edmund Burke. Burke, owing to his birth and circumstances, brought a certain detachment to his consideration of imperial problems and, as an Irishman, shared to no small extent the colonial viewpoint.[9] It is therefore no matter for surprise to find the typically colonial imaginative and sentimental concept of empire, which nowhere receives nobler expression than in his utterances, constituting the core of his doctrine. Almost every page of the great speech on conciliation emphasizes it, as the following quotations illustrate: "My idea of it [an Empire] is the aggregate of many States, under one common head." "The advantage to be derived from the communion and fellowship of a great empire." "Ireland has ever had from the beginning a separate, but not an independent legislature; which, far from distracting, promoted the union of the whole. Everything was sweetly and harmoniously disposed through both islands for the conservation of English dominion and the communication of English liberties. I do not see that the same principles might not be carried into twenty islands and with the same good effect. This is my model with regard to America." And, lastly, those famous phrases: "My hold of the Colonies is in the close affection which grows from common names, from kindred blood, from similar privileges and equal protection. These are ties, which, though light as air, are strong as links of iron."

Had Burke founded a school, the claim of the colonies to the origination of the present sentimental idea of empire would not be valid. But he did

[8] Provisional Act for settling the Troubles in America, 1775.
[9] The name of Colonel Barré may be recalled as another, but much less distinguished, example of the link between the Irish and the colonial points of view.

not. He and those who shared his opinions left no followers. His career is an episode in imperial history, not the beginning of an evolution. And, after the American war, he and his contemporaries looked on the great cause for which he had fought as an incident ended. The Empire was gone. What remained was of little consequence. Even his soaring imagination could not divine a new growth that would go far to compensate for the branches lopped away.

The Revolution, then, came and passed. "The result of the American war had, in truth, to use a vulgar expression, 'knocked the bottom' out of the much-vaunted mercantile system," says Mr. H. E. Egerton.[10] However, the pot was so large that, despite its defective bottom, its contents did not empty for many years. After Pitt's failure of 1783 in the attempt to base British-American relations on friendship and reciprocity,[11] the exponents of the accounting view of empire were once more able to determine the policy of the government. In the legislature of the next ten years, regulating colonial (especially West Indian) trade and trade with the United States, this opinion, inspired now by greater jealousy than before, found stricter application than ever.[12] Later, the great wars silenced controversy and delayed the advance of the new doctrines of free trade and *laissez faire*. Trade rose to great heights, and, as usual, little complaint against the existing order was heard so long as prosperity lasted. But after the peace came sharp commercial depression. Differences of opinion arose as to its cause and the remedy. Thoroughgoing mercantilists continued to stand out for the principles of their school (the eighteenth-century phraseology remained in current use almost unchanged until the 1840's) but, as the years went by, became less and less identified with imperial policy, and more and more linked with a purely selfish trade party, seeking protection for particular interests. Solomon Atkinson, in that partisan pamphlet of his, the *Letter to the Right Hon. W. Huskisson*,[13] has little to say about

[10] *A Short History of Colonial Policy* (London: Methuen, 1897), p. 256.

[11] See the Proclamation of 14 May 1783, to be found in George Chalmers, *Opinions on Interesting Subjects of Public Law and Commercial Policy* (London, 1784).

[12] For this period see, Lord Sheffield, *Observations on the Commerce of the American States* (London, 1784); Chalmers, *Opinions;* Richard Champion, *Considerations on the Present State of Great Britain and the United States of America, with a View of their Future Commercial Connections* (London, 1784) – a voice of liberality crying in the wilderness; Bryan Edwards, *Thoughts on the late Proceedings of Government respecting the Trade of the West India Islands with the United States of North America* (London, 1784); William Knox, *Extra-Official State Papers* (London, 1789); *A Collection of Interesting and Important Reports and Papers on the Navigation and Trade of Great Britain, Ireland and the British Colonies in the West Indies and America* (London, 1807); Alfred Thayer Mahan, *Sea Power in Its Relations to the War of 1812* (Boston: Little, Brown and Co., 1905); S.F. Bemis, *Jay's Treaty: A Study in Commerce and Diplomacy* (New York: Macmillan, 1923); S. E. Morison, *A Maritime History of Massachusetts, 1783-1850* (Boston: Houghton Mifflin, 1921).

[13] (London, 1827).

a self-contained empire, but a great deal to say about the shipping interest. The shipowners were, indeed, the very heart and soul of the post-Revolutionary mercantilism; they fought the battle of self-interest vigorously and persistently. There was no doubt that shipping had been very hard hit after 1815;[14] but long after the depression had passed, the shipowners continued to be the centre of resistance to every liberal trade measure. They succeeded in thwarting a reduction of the foreign timber duties for twenty-two years, on account of the carrying trade provided by colonial timber.[15] They resisted Huskisson in 1825 and Peel in 1842 and 1846. Public opinion having gradually outgrown their doctrines, these were given their death-blow by the repeal of the Navigation Acts and seem to have made their last appearance in the lobbyings of the firm of Pollock, Gilmour and Co., the Glasgow and Quebec shipowners, against the reduction in the duty on foreign timber contemplated in the budget of 1851.[16]

Direct reaction from mercantilism to its opposite extreme was responsible for the existence of a group representing what may be termed the intelligentsia of Great Britain, followers of Adam Smith, economic theorists, and, in general, men who had learned something from the history of the last half-century. Their views as to colonies are well known. Two lessons they had taken to heart: one was that trade, to increase and be profitable, did not need the colonial relation, trade with the United States being vastly greater than in colonial days and quite as profitable; the other was that famous dictum of Turgot's that colonies were like fruit which, when ripe, falls off. They had grasped the simple fact that colonization does not pay cash dividends. Hence they were for casting adrift all the remaining colonies and saving the expense attached to them. They looked at the problem from a purely commercial viewpoint. In this respect they also may be said to have been adherents of the book-keeping theory of empire. There would have been nothing inconsistent in an Edinburgh Reviewer holding strict mercantilist views; he need merely say, "We thought we were going to make money from colonies, but time has proved that we cannot; therefore let us abandon our undertakings." Of course, the school of the Reviewers did not hold mercantilist views; for one reason, because the logic of events showed that mercantilism had "blown up." In this sense, these early exponents of *laissez faire* may be regarded as products of the reaction from mercantilism. They were very fond of complimenting themselves on their

---

[14]See, specifically, *Hansard Parliamentary Debates,* 2d ser., 2 June 1820. But *Hansard* abounds with expositions of the shipowners' case.

[15]As in the cases of the attempted reductions of these duties by Althorp and Thomson in 1830 and 1835.

[16]See *Hansard Parliamentary Debates,* 3d ser., 7 June 1851, and the London *Morning Herald* during April, 1851.

enlightenment, but it is at least debatable if they were much nearer the truth than the party of trade interest. The modern Empire could not have been built on the principles of either group.[17]

Between these two very unlike products of the same system — hopeless mercantilists who had learned nothing and persons of the *laissez faire* beliefs who thought they had learned everything — stood at least two intermediate groups who shared certain tenets of both extremes. There was the rather illogical type of man such as Huskisson or Poulett Thompson, afterward Lord Sydenham, who, while in general agreement with the new economic teaching, believed that the colonies should "pay," that is, that they should return to the mother country certain direct commercial benefits such as a monopoly of the direct carrying trade (Huskisson)[18] or the privilege of regulating colonial trade for the benefit of Great Britain (Thompson).[19] Despite their intellectual relationship with *laissez faire,* such men as these two had no desire to break up the Empire. They were probably very good representatives of the average man, whose instincts would undoubtedly be for keeping what he had got. As Adam Smith says, no nation willingly abandons dominion over territory, no matter how worthless.

More constructive in attitude was the school of Wakefield, Durham, and Buller. While all three were of that liberal cast of intellect to which the doctrines of *laissez faire* made a natural appeal, their colonial creed had little in common with that dissolving force. Each was for much greater imperial activity rather than for much less. Nevertheless, it is questionable if their interest in colonization did not exceed their interest in the colonies; that is, they found their inspiration in the social and economic benefits which, as they believed, Great Britain derived from colonizing, rather than in any imaginative vision of the future of the colonies.

In any case, despite a small but noisy faction, there is little doubt that the Empire was not in serious danger of being broken up from the centre. National pride could hardly have sunk that low. Still less did dissolution threaten from the circumference. The essence of this article is the contention that it was in the colonies, not in the motherland, that there originated and developed that apparently secure basis for a permanent structure which may be called the sentimental view of empire. The evidence

---

[17]For expositions of their views see Bentham, *Emancipate Your Colonies* [1793] (London: R. Heward, 1830), a volume republished in 1838 with a long introduction, the author of which (Effingham Wilson) is unable to see any alternative between "Emancipation" and the "slavery" of mercantilism; see also the *Edinburgh Review* 40 (January 1825): 483 and 42 (August 1825): 271.

[18]See his speeches of 21 and 25 March 1825 and the Act of 1825 (6 Geo. 4, cap. 114).

[19]See his dispatch as Governor General of Canada to Russell, 26 May 1840: "The power of regulating colonial trade is one of the principal advantages derived from colonial possessions...."

for this, so far as England is concerned, is, as would be expected, mainly negative[20] One does not find among English sources evidences of imaginations captured by the concept of a great world-wide unity of the race, of a sort of British solar system, with Great Britain as the sun and her offspring in distant lands as attendant planets. British statesmen who believed in the Empire could always lay down good, solid reasons for its continued existence. In early days, as has been said, it was because overseas dominions provided either necessary raw materials or markets. Later on, vacant lands were an outlet for Britain's surplus population.[21] It was not until nearly a generation after responsible government had been achieved in Canada that British public men began to show a measured enthusiasm for the development of the overseas Empire.[22] Until late in the sixties, eventual separation was rather generally believed to be inevitable. Even after the discredit of the "Little Englanders," there were several stages to be worked through before the concept of a voluntary association of equal partnerships was reached, though this latter statement is equally true of the colonies, in which the idea of natural subordination to the centre has been particularly persistent. The vainglorious jingoism of the seventies was more dangerous and almost as objectionable as the weak-kneed defeatism which it succeeded. Salisburian imperialism, with its Colonial and Imperial Conferences and the spectacular ceremonial of its jubilees, stood on firmer ground and had the great merit of providing a common rallying point for all the self-governing Empire. That was its legacy to the present generation, and the splendid evidences of loyalty displayed in 1914 were its finest flowers. Loyalty rather than unity, be it noted, since the mainspring of colonial action in 1914 was still devotion to the motherland rather than to a larger whole of which each commonwealth was but a small part. The latest stage and problem is the achievement of unity, the substitution of loyalty towards the whole for loyalty merely towards the centre, and that in the face of the rapid growth of local nationalism.

Little blame can attach to the imperial statesman of the past for his

[20]For an excellent account of nineteenth-century British thought on the colonies see Bodelson, *Studies in Mid-Victorian Imperialism* (New York: A. A. Knopf, 1925).

[21]See, for instance, Durham, John George Lambton, 1st Earl of, *Lord Durham's Report on the Affairs of British North America,* edited with an introduction by C. P. Lucas (Oxford: Clarendon Press, 1912), 2:331, "I cannot participate in the notion that it is the part either of prudence or honour to abandon our countrymen when our government of them has plunged them into disorder.... The experiment of keeping colonies ... ought at least to have a trial, ere we abandon for ever the vast dominion which might supply the wants of our surplus population, and raise up millions of fresh consumers of our manufactures...."

[22]"All claims and interests must be subordinate to that policy which is to be found in the peopling and the opening up of the new country, with the intention of consolidating it, as an integral and an important part in the British Empire."Sir Edward Bulwer Lytton, 1858, with reference to British Columbia, quoted by Egerton, *Colonial Policy,* p. 311.

matter-of-fact attitude towards the outlying Empire. Two generations ago the colonies were mere pioneer settlements, largely unknown, involving direct annual charges on the British treasury, giving little in return but liable at any time to cause political complications with foreign powers. Those who went out to them, as a general rule, never returned, but simply faded from the memory of their native place. They contributed negligibly or not at all to disseminating in the motherland a knowledge of their new abodes. It required a very considerable degree of prophetic insight to discern in these struggling backwoods settlements strong young nations still attached to the parent system and sources of strength rather than weakness. Imaginative views of empire on the part of British public men, such as were revealed by Mr. Lloyd George in his reference to the dominions as "these young giants,"[23] have, in the typical British way, come when the facts warranted them and are evidences of hopes realized.

Not so in the colonies themselves. The settler carried out with him memories of the motherland, the glamour of her civilization, and pride in her strength. Naturally, his pleasurable recollections did not lose anything with the lapse of years. He passed many of them on to his children, who added to their imaginative fancies of the distant and omnipotent *alma mater,* their hopes and ambitions for their native land. The resulting amalgam, if the term may be used, was a rather dazzling conception of a world-wide British unity, growing ever larger and more powerful.

Nor was such a state of mind true merely of the later Empire. Although, unfortunately, it was lost on the "hard-headed," commonsense men of the eighteenth century, there was no lack of imaginative sentiment in pre-revolutionary days.

> With respect to the colonies, the surest method they can take to preserve inviolate their union with Britain is, upon every occasion, to demonstrate their loyalty to the best of kings, and their subordination to the government of Great Britain, by exorting their united efforts in the support and defence of the dignity of the British crown and of the rights of the British parliament; and by cheerfully and constantly submitting to the just determination of the grand council of the realm. A conduct opposite to this would make them forfeit the right of sons, and justly bring upon them the indignation and chastisement of the mother-country, ...

writes an essayist from Philadelphia in 1766.[24] The quotation could be duplicated many times. The Stamp Act decade abounded with language

---

[23]House of Commons, 2 December 1921.
[24]*Dissertations on the Reciprocal Advantages of a Perpetual Union between Great Britain and her American Colonies.*

that might have been used by the most extravagant of later Imperlialists. It is, however, unnecessary to labour the point. Up to the very eve of the Revolution, colonial writings are full of a spirit of respect and dutifulness towards the mother country. Had there been in England any approach to the same consciousness of the filial nature of the relation between the two countries as existed in America, the Revolution might have been indefinitely averted.

The new Empire in America was, of course, founded on the bed-rock of devotion to Great Britain. Among the Loyalists, passion for things British amounted almost to a religion. It hardly seems necessary to support this statement by documentary proofs: the spirit of the Loyalists still runs strong; it is to this day a part of the general body of ideas, beliefs, and sentiments of the average Canadian. There is an excellent exhibition of it in the pamphlet entitled *Observations upon the Importance of the North American Colonies to Great Britain,* written in 1825 by Chief Justice Sir Brenton Halliburton of Nova Scotia. His general thesis is that the maritime supremacy of Great Britain is threatened in only one direction — by the United States — that the United States can never successfully challenge that supremacy so long as her people are attracted away from the sea-coast westward to unoccupied farm-lands, but that the abandonment of the colonies by Great Britain would throw them into the arms of America, and that the accession of Nova Scotia, New Brunswick, and Newfoundland would supply her with just that permanent maritime population which she lacks. Discounting a certain local pride in the possibilities of Nova Scotia, we may admit some force in the contention. At any rate it is typical that this solicitude for the Empire should be actuated in part by jealousy of the United States. There is no doubt that the mere existence of the American Republic has always tended in Canada to increase the fervency of loyalty to the Crown. After emphasizing their maritime importance, he proceeds to picture the various excellences of the colonies, their capabilities of improvement, recent progress, and so on, the whole forming a plea for their retention based undisguisedly on sentimental attachment to the British connection. His head marshals his arguments, but his heart drives his pen.

> The inhabitants of British America have no desire to change their national character, and will feel disposed to cling to the Mother Country as long as she fosters and protects them. Does not sound policy then require that she should do so? Should a Country which will be capable of adding so much to her own maritime strength, be voluntarily abandoned by Great Britain? ... The preceding observations have been directed against those writers who have assumed as a general proposition — "that no colony is worth retaining unless the Mother Country obtains from it a revenue equal to her expenditure on it," and an

humble attempt has been made to induce His Majesty's Ministers to think that the North American Colonies are valuable appendages to the British Crown, independently of all considerations of pecuniary profit and loss .... Let us remember the declaration of the greatest Politician and Warrior that France has produced for ages; that all he required to render that country powerful upon the ocean, was *Ships, Colonies* and *Commerce*; and as the result of his observations upon the wants of France is confirmed by the experiences of the advantages which have resulted to Great Britain from such possessions, let us support and cherish them with the utmost care.[25]

Or take the exposition of the colonial system given in a pamphlet of 1833 by a Nova Scotian, Henry Bliss. This is much too long to summarize, but its atmosphere may be indicated by such passages as the following:

Let ministers then elevate and enlarge their views to the great circumstances in which they are placed. Let them endeavour to comprehend the whole dominions of Great Britain as one society, and the colonies for its integral parts, as much as if they adjoined Valentia or the Land's End, and then enact the laws of trade. Let but the Imperial government be like the dominions and equal to the means they have undertaken to administer; let them have the fortitude, the prudence and the justice, to say to the economists, dispute ye, and to the fanatics, exhort ye; but for neither the cant of philosophy, nor the cant of religion, will we betray the grand confederacy of islands and provinces beyond the seas, which, with these kingdoms, compose such an empire as the world never saw, such as, by your principles, could never have been founded, and such as your counsels would soon dissolve and destroy .... The Colonial System is so eminently prescribed by nature and society, that the history of the commerce, industry, and propagation of the human race has in all ages and countries exhibited but some modification of that economy, which it was reserved for the glory of England so to develope and improve, as in a comparatively short time to have become the mother of many peoples and the arbiter of all, and to have filled the vacant regions of the earth with cultivation and happiness, and received back into her own bosom the abundant harvest of their labours and increase.[26]

---

[25] pp. 17, 20, 34.

[26] Henry Bliss, *The Colonial System: Statistics of the Trade, Industry and Resources of Canada, etc.* (London: Richardson, 1833), p. 164. Quotations might be multiplied. See *inter alia* the Quebec *Gazette,* 26 October and 13 November 1820; St. John, N.B. *Courier,* 8 March 1828. One might contrast with the exact above, he matter-of-fact style of the English author of the tract entitled *The Colonies and Great Britain must be incorporated and form One Universal and Indivisible Empire* (London, 1839).

This is the language of pure emotion. The same sort of thing, more measured in tone, is to be found in George R. Young's series of letters on the colonial system.[27] All these Nova Scotians marshal pages of statistics to show the cash value of the colonies to Great Britain; they speak in the old, familiar accents of mercantilism, nor does the existence of an empire not bound together by trade relations appear possible to them; yet when they have exhausted their statistics and their testimonies drawn from the regions of commercial benefits, they both turn to rhetoric, and, as in the case of Judge Halliburton, one can see that the motive power behind their arguments is that sentimental attachment to what Bliss calls "a vast confederacy of Kingdoms, and islands and provinces spread through every quarter of the earth." Enlightened as the school of the *Edinburgh Review* may have been in the sphere of economics, there is no question but that the sentimentalists were right in maintaining that "such an Empire as the world never before saw, could never have been founded upon their doctrines." Cold-hearted *laissez faire* would have dried up the roots of the colonizing spirit; there is something spiritual and lasting in the rather vainglorious imperialistic temperament; it may be dangerous but it is constructive.

The hard business attitude assumed by the Reviewers the colonists were unable to understand. They knew themselves the most loyal of subjects. They were fully persuaded that the greatness of Britain depended upon her colonies, and, at the same time, they were dazzled by that greatness. Separation they could not conceive of. In short, the rim of the Empire in the early nineteenth century, as in the later, was much more conscious of the organization as a whole than was the centre. It would be no hard matter to compile quotations year by year down to the present century couched in the same sentimental and emotional language as those already given. Far from "cutting the painter," every English-speaking colony has continually insisted upon the painter's being frequently hauled inboard, inspected, and given an extra turn. England could hardly have got rid of any of her colonies, no matter how much she might have wished it. In the old Empire the sentimental or imaginative imperialism accepted defence and accorded trade regulation. In the new, it has accepted defence — often, indeed, clamoured for it — and also accorded trade regulation, which, so long as it was practised, operated very much in its favour. It never had anything to offer in return for defence except trade regulation, and when this was voluntarily abandoned, it had nothing to offer. Still it clung blindly to the Empire, in part because of the need for defence, in part because of the imaginative appeal made by that diversified and

---

[27]George R. Young, *Letters ... E. G. S. Stanley, M.P. upon the existing treaties with France and America, as regards their "Rights of Fishery" upon the coasts of Nova Scotia, Labrador and Newfoundland... With a general view of the Colonial Policy* (London, 1834).

ubiquitous entity. It was mainly a sentimental attitude — well illustrated by that oft-quoted phrase of Sir John Macdonald, "A British subject I was born, a British subject I will die." It did not worry about the future. It was essentially the attitude of a youth to his parent. A great deal of trust was demanded of the father; he might hope that the young man would turn out well, but in the meantime he was rather expensive. Not until the South African war did he become quite sure that his money had been well spent. From that time on, the parent has been displaying some of the children's enthusiasm for the common, as distinguished from the merely imperialistic, concern. The last war widened and deepened that enthusiasm. The children, on the other hand, are developing rather complex affairs of their own. Will they, now grown to maturity,[28] continue in the future to be as much interested in the family partnership as they have been in the past?

The role of the prophet is always dangerous.[29] Where there are so many elements to be considered as there are in the self-governing Empire of today, prediction is likely to be particularly futile. In reconnoitring the future, one may perhaps venture so far as to set down a few broad influences, but he would indeed be a bold man who would do more. First among forces of a centrifugal nature stands the developing nationalism of the dominions. There are many evidences of this, and it is not necessary to specify them. The invidious example of protective tariffs may be noted in passing. And there is the economic or social attraction exerted by other large political bodies, chiefly illustrated in the relations of Canada and the United States. There are the more general, but not less potent, forces of mere distance (a decreasing force) and of long periods of peace. A strong case could be made out for the line of evolution culminating in daughter states similar to Greek colonies; but, for that matter, the world would probably be no worse off if it had never attempted to improve on the classical type.

On the other side, there is the constant factor of British immigration, certainly not an agency that would turn the scale in a crisis, but yet a link of importance. There is the certain knowledge on the part of the dominions that they are of more importance as parts of a larger whole than they would be as separate entities and the no less certain realization that as separate entities they would be exposed to a multitude of political threats from which the power of the Empire now shields them — the old

[28]"He did not see that we could go any further without becoming independent": report of an address by Senator Belcourt to the Toronto Canadian Club, 11 November 1924. Since this opinion was given, we *have* gone further, and yet independence in the sense of separation is no nearer.
[29]With these concluding paragraphs compare the views of Messrs. A. F. Pollard, Ramsay Muir, and D. O. Malcolm, as published in volume 1 of this journal, 1916-1917.

desire for defence, that is, but with the defender now not merely Britain but the family of British nations. And as there are general forces making for separation, so there are corresponding general forces of cohesion: institutions and laws of very similar if not identical nature, the mere absence of irritants preventing any accumulation of ill-feeling, education based on ingrained sentiment, the slow growth of tradition. There is no good reason for expecting a change in sentiment, simply because there is little likelihood of acute differences of opinion. Of all sources of lawsuits, "line fences" are probably the most prolific, but there are no "line fences" in the Empire. Moreover, the average Anglo-Saxon agrees best with those of his relatives who live at a distance.

If, in conclusion, one tentative forecast may be risked, it is that the constitutional irrationalities which often bulk so large in contemporary eyes will have little importance either in making or marring the future: they will probably be solved in the thoroughly illogical, makeshift, yet satisfactory manner peculiar to the race. Further than this it is not wise to go. Whatever the future may have in store, the world is already the richer for the experience of the British league of nations in its regulation of the relations of its members otherwise than by the sword.

30 | *Foreign Policy and Canadian Nationalism**

Out of the welter of discussion in respect to the nature of Canada's international position, a certain clarity is at last beginning to emerge: we are rapidly passing through that period of adolescence in which a country, like a youth, has very cloudy ideas as to its own essential nature, and while we have not yet attained any marked degree of self-knowledge, we have at least arrived at certain broad generalizations. Most thoughtful people will probably agree that in respect to the conduct of our own political affairs, if not in respect to our cultural life, we have got beyond the stage of colonialism; that is, we have taken our fate into our own hands and do not look for our decisions to be made for us beyond our own borders. The implications of our geographical position are also gradually becoming clear. A writer in this periodical can take the view that a foreign policy for us is, like a professional career to a young lady of means, an agreeable adventure, not a necessity; in other words, that we are remote from danger and need have no particular concern as to how things go in the outer

**Dalhousie Review* 15 (April 1935): 29-36.

world. Our comfortable state of geographical security has existed for some time, but it is just being realized.

We have not got very far beyond these primary facts. We are an insular people and do not know very much of the great world. We have only recently established our own diplomatic service, and its rudimentary state is sufficient evidence of our paucity of interest in all but a few very obvious regions. We have belonged to the League of Nations since its beginning, but we are not very sure why we belong. Being a people steeped in the morality of good behaviour, we have been inclined to think of the League as a giant "up-lift" society and have supported it because it has been a good cause. Remote from the realities which gave it birth, during the entire period of our membership we have developed no positive policy in respect to it or indeed in respect to our place in the world, save the rather nebulous assumption that as a matter of course we are on the side of right.

Our relationships with the outside world, save in such aspects as the above, have continued in the realm of tradition: we grew up in the Empire, we have taken the Empire as a matter of course, and our present thinking is still largely confined within that framework. So near to a child is he still, that the youth, Canada, has hardly yet worn out his first pair of long pants.

This pleasant period of life will pass, is passing. Presently we shall have to face reality. But what is reality?

That the country has an option as to whether it shall have a foreign policy or not implies, it seems to me, some misconception of reality. Two peaceful neighbours need have no written code of behaviour *vis-à-vis* each other, but they must have some sort of relationship, if it is only one in which each agrees to ignore the other. Such mutual exclusiveness will be suddenly ended if, for example, the dog belonging to one of them walks across the lawn belonging to the other. Relationships of some sort with the rest of the world we must have, and the mode of conducting these relationships constitutes our foreign policy.

So far, Canadians who think about these things have hardly got beyond discussing great general ideas. This discussion, however, has elucidated the basic principles of our association with other countries. Canadian opinion seems to be falling into three schools of thought. One of these believes that tradition is good enough, that we can drift along as we have been drifting and leave our foreign relations to the mother country. A variant of this school of opinion would associate us more closely with England and the Empire, and seek to work out a rounded imperial foreign policy, the expression of a cohesive Empire, a British *bloc*.

The second school of thought clings to the League of Nations as the hope of the future. It is apprehensive of war in the near future, sees clearly enough that war would be the end of the Empire as it exists today and possibly the end of Western civilization. It believes that Canada cannot keep out of the coming war and that the international organization of mankind, together with its correlative, the abrogation of national sovereignty, is the only way to prevent war. Hence it is ready to cast in its lot with the generality of humanity as represented by Geneva, giving up to some sort of international body control of such things as materials likely to be used as munitions of war, vacant lands, immigration, and so on. It would, if carried to its logical end, make Canada into a kind of province of a world-wide state.

The third view may be described as nationalist. Those who hold it believe that nationalism for Canada means something very different from the fervent lunacies of the Europeans; they believe that for Canada it marks simply the emergence of a new social group, a new community come to self-knowledge and self-consciousness. They cannot see that it carries any suggestion of hostility to others, any more than the attainment of his majority does for the individual. Looking over the Dominion for some strong social cement, this group perceives racial differences, linguistic differences, religious differences, cultural differences so wide as to produce cultural — and even social — anarchy. No new community can be reared on a basis of language, culture, religion, or race, heretofore the bed-rock of societies everywhere. What social dynamic is there, then, powerful enough to weld our heterogeneous masses together? There seems to be no other than nationalism, that is, a common fate and a common concern for it, a common citizenship, a common love for the common land. If this country is to be welded together, if it is ever to be more than a string of provinces, more than a collection of English, French, and "Bohunks," ever to be a homogeneous community, then the only solvent strong enough to resolve these things must be a national spirit.

The nationalists go further: a true nation cannot be content with a partial life, having control over one aspect of its affairs and not over another. Canada is in some respects in this latter position. It has not yet taken into its own hands power to amend its own constitution, or to decide once and for all its lawsuits. In particular, on this all important question of war and peace, it may be committed by decisions made elsewhere. It may be committed because it is a member of the League of Nations and of the British Empire. As a member of the League, it could be projected into at least passive belligerency, conceivably (if it were true to its engagements) against even its own mother country. Few Canadians will worry about this latter contingency, and but few more will worry about the danger of our having to take part in League wars. League wars will probably be waged, if waged, at a safe distance from Canadian shores; and as Canadian enthusiasm is not likely to mount very high over a piece of mechanism, which is what the League is at present, there will be little likelihood of Canadians doing anything very active in a war to enforce the law. An occasional police expedition might occur, but that would be neither here nor there.

The commitment represented by membership in the Empire is much more serious. There is scarcely a stirring of humanity anywhere which does not impinge upon the Empire in some way or another. The Empire as a whole is in every possible relationship with every possible state. Opportunities for friction are endless. It is often said that the Empire is a power for peace; but we ought to be frank enough to face the unpleasant fact that it is so because, by fair means or foul, it has acquired such a huge proportion of the world's wealth that there is little left for it to desire. The Empire has only recently begun to stand for peace, and it might have a relapse.

There is one partner in the Empire which of all others is likely to get into trouble, Great Britain. She is too close to Europe to keep out of Europe's quarrels, and she has world-wide interests which she has not shown much hesitation about protecting. The interests of the white dominions do not extend far beyond their own territory; at least their interests of that type which gets a country into trouble, territorial interests; but those of Britain are everywhere. An Italian nationalistic movement makes trouble in Malta; a native tribe goes on the war path in Burma: in both cases, widely separated, Britain is involved. This huge, vulnerable rag-bag of possessions is no longer the matter for simple pride that it once was. It has been very profitable, but it is now becoming dangerous, both to its possessor and to the peace of the world.

Canadians of British descent now, thanks to the immigration policy of the last generation, unhappily a bare majority of Canadians, are attached rather to the mother country than to the Empire, and with the commendable loyalty of children to their parent, many of them are ready to accept unreservedly all the chances of the family connection. They take the attitude of the dog in the story, who when his master was sold out of his old home was asked by him if he would go on with him to another and unknown one. "Oh, yes, I'll go," said the dog. The French Canadian on the other hand is more like the cat of the same man. "Will there be a nice fire there and food?" asked the cat before consenting to go. That is, French-Canadian attachment to the Empire is not, and cannot be expected to be, a disinterested attachment. It is a sincere attachment, but it is so because the French Canadian thinks he can see value for him in the Empire.

There is a third group, growing large nowadays, which has the attachment neither of self-interest nor of sentiment, the so-called "New Canadians." To many a Slav on the western prairie, King George must be as obscure a figure as the Shah of Persia. To such a one the British North America Act holds out no special privilege. He is uprooted, traditionless, local. If he is ever to enter our communal life — and he is entering it—it is scarcely conceivable that he will come into the old imperial tradition. He will be a Canadian.

Now can these three groups be confined within the simple old imperial faith? What would happen to this incipient Canadian nation if another war such as the last should occur? Is it not reasonable to assume that the stresses and strains which were so painfully evident over the conscription issue, and whose evil heritage is still with us, would be reproduced on a larger scale? In 1914, this country was just like an unthinking schoolboy; it heard the call of the blood, and off its young men rushed, most of them knowing little and caring less about the real issues at stake. There was a great deal of talk about Prussianism and fighting for democracy and for stricken Belgium, but anyone who looks back to his own war experience knows very well that he did not enlist on matters of high principle so much as on an emotional impulse. The point is that it is very unlikely that the country will ever be in such an unanimous and chivalric state of mind on any future occasion. After all, we must have learned something from the Great War. The majority of those of us who fought — a not inconsiderable body — sum up their experiences in two words, "Never again." Most of the rest of us know that another crusade of the same sort would at least bankrupt the country, and those who think about the situation very acutely are aware that the racial factors just outlined would complete the damage. There would not be an unanimous response; there would be racial friction; those of British descent would be the first to go, they would be decimated as they were before, those of them who came back would find their places in many cases taken by the non-Anglo-Saxon, and the result of the whole affair would be racial division, internal dissension, and, in the western provinces at least, the eclipse of the people of British descent. A Communist said to the writer not long ago that he had not much hope of revolution as long as we were at peace, but with another upset of the magnitude of the last it was incredible to him that revolution would not occur. He would, of course, at once set to work to capitalize on all the types of dissension just referred to.

The chance of making a strong and homogeneous community out of our present heterogeneous elements would thus probably be thrown away if we were induced to go into another war waged in a distant theatre, a war in which our own immediate interests were not at stake. The nationalist here points out that it is practically impossible for our own immediate interests to be at stake in a war not on this North American continent, for the simple reason that we have no immediate interests outside this continent. We have our overseas trade, but we would not be sufficiently foolish to fight a war because some nation or other refused to trade with us. Apart from trade, from our sentimental connection with the people of Great Britain, and from the persons of a few citizens living abroad, we have nothing beyond the seas that would involve us in a quarrel with anyone. We are a peaceful nation, wanting no one else's territory (the great cause of war), and having no reason for not living on good terms with everyone. Why then should we ever again take a chance of dealing a suicidal blow to ourselves by taking part in some quarrel in which we had no concern?

Again, there is no possibility of any foreigner in the wickedness of his heart doing any harm to us. On both coasts we have thousands of miles of water, the best defence against invasion that can be conceived of and, even with the possibilities of the aeroplane reckoned in, a sufficient defence against any aggression from overseas except a mere raid. With the United States, we enjoy on this North American continent a private world of our own. We are not part of Europe, and European turmoil need not reach out and embrace us unless we deliberately go out to embrace it. No foeman will appear for us to drive back from our soil (though if he did, there is no reason to think that any one of the different elements would hang back when the matter was the defence of their own land); any war in which we engage will be one we enter of ourselves, not because our hand has been forced by local circumstances. For as long a period as can be reasonably foreseen, this country can have peace if it wants it.

The nationalist thus can see no good reasons for associating this country with other countries which are likely to get it into trouble, but many good reasons for attempting to keep his country out of trouble which does not concern it. He sees that in so far as the physical factors of geography and circumstances go, it is absurdly easy to keep this country out of such trouble, and he sees no sufficient reason for not taking advantage of the favourable position with which nature has endowed us. He is, however, not blind to the fact that irrationalism is stronger than rationalism and that matters of peace and war have to do primarily with the emotions. He recognizes quite frankly that the sentimental attachment of the people of British descent to the motherland is so strong as very likely to sweep this country in the future as in the past into a war which does not concern it. He believes such a thing would probably destroy this country as we know it. Recognizing that, whether we like it or not, we are living in Canada and not elsewhere and that we and our descendants are likely to go on living in this particular geographical area, he believes that the only thing to do is for the citizens of what after all seems to be a going concern of some permanence, the Dominion of Canada, to give to that concern, which happens to be their own country, their undivided loyalty. Regretfully, he admits that this may mean, if another cataclysm should occur, that they will have to withdraw that part of their loyalty which has hitherto been concentrated across the sea and bring it home, leaving there only the affectionate sentiments of a child who has moved out of the parental house into his own, some distance away.

The nationalist hopes the day of sharp decision may never need to come. It is possible that peace may be maintained for a long while. Still, he has not much faith in a Europe which fights the same battles over again century after century and never seems able to solve its own problems. He is willing to give what incidental aid he can to help such a continent to drag itself out of the mire, but it is apparent to him that Canada is too far away, too unconcerned with the issues, to do much more than give good will. In other words, the Canadian nationalist values the concept implied in the League of Nations as an instrument for keeping the world's powder magazine — Europe — from exploding, but he has not too much faith in its ability to do so or in the likelihood of its success in looking after the affairs of other continents. In particular, he is not anxious to have the same sets of people, those in control of the League, who seem so unable to resolve their own affairs, given any commission for resolving his.

The nationalist school of Canadian foreign policy thus takes an independent and to many people an unpopular attitude. It bases itself squarely on the necessity of creating a strong and reasonably homogeneous social group within the territory at present known as the Dominion of Canada, in other words, of completing the process begun in 1867. It believes that the process can be completed only if there is an assurance of a long, peaceful period for different elements to settle down together. It looks on a war in which this country is only indirectly interested, that is, any war not an actual invasion of Canadian territory, as one of the most powerful deterrents to this process of fusion and one likely to end the present experiment. It refuses to believe that any of the people living within this territory can have a duty superior to the duty owed to this community, whether it be to the land of their ancestors or to their race. It believes that room can be found in Canada for much variety of race, creed, and tongue, but that these things must be kept in their place, that the future can have no room for a Canadian who, let us say, considers himself primarily a Frenchman or, similarly, one who considers himself a British subject before a Canadian citizen.

Holding these views about the necessity of completing the social process, how can the nationalist in foreign policy do anything else than attempt to keep his skirts clear of the entanglements of the outer world? That is his foreign policy — quietly minding his own business, conscious that he has and need have no quarrel with anyone, giving this tender young plant, the Canadian nation, a chance to grow. That is the sort of foreign policy, albeit a negative and a sober foreign policy, that this country needs. It is a foreign policy which in defining our relationships with the outside world expects our citizens to conduct themselves, not as people of British descent or internationalists or French Canadians or free-traders or protectionists or provincials, but as Canadians.

31 | *The Maritimes as a Strategic Point in North America**

The Ogdensburg agreement of last August has for Canada the widest implications, both political and military. In its possible effects it directs the mind of the historian back to the middle of the eighteenth century, when another great war for world power was going on and the Atlantic coast of North America was playing a role somewhat similar to that of today. Then as now the English-speaking world was in harmony with itself, and its decisive connection with the sea was being demonstrated. Then the lands about the Gulf of St. Lawrence were the focus of the struggle: today, they may well prove the focus of a new age.

Much could be written on the varied aspects of the defence of this continent and of this Dominion. From the centre of the Pacific Ocean on through the silences of the Arctic, out through Greenland, Iceland, the British Isles, and further south, the eye of the strategist must range. He must think of Hawaii, and he must think of the Azores, of the Aleutians and of Trinidad. He must remember what history tells him about the command of the sea. He must fit into his puzzle the new element of air power. But however wide his glance, it is to be questioned whether it can light on anything more significant than these lands about the Gulf and between it and the Atlantic, sites of some of the classic campaigns of history.

From the days of the discoveries down to the present, two paths have led from the Old World to the New — the southern route towards the West Indies and the northern route towards Newfoundland and the mainland. Halifax and Bermuda are two points on the western arc of a naval circle or ellipse which in the old days ran round from England through them and on to New York. After the American Revolution, Halifax and Bermuda remained as the broken ends of the arch. A still larger ellipse went through the Azores to the Windward Islands and thence north along the American coast and back to England. Along it a vessel could sail with fair winds nearly all the way.

*Public Affairs 4 (December 1940): 57-60.

Of these two routes the northern one in its turn divides in two, the approaches to the St. Lawrence and the Atlantic coast from Nova Scotia westward. Whatever the other variants in the picture, whether in peace or war, from one age to another these two geographical constants remain — the long west-south-west sweep of the coast from Cape Breton to New York and the extraordinary channel into the interior constituted by the Gulf and River St. Lawrence.[1]

In the series of wars between England and France for the mastery of the outer world, Canada was safely French until the problem of the St. Lawrence approaches was solved. Newfoundland was surrendered by France under the Treaty of Utrecht in 1713 and the first great obstacle removed to an English advance into the St. Lawrence. But the French countered with Louisbourg, almost neutralizing the English advantage, for from it they were still able to command the approaches to the Gulf. Louisbourg, standing near the point at which Gulf and Atlantic merge, represents the essential oneness of the two aspects of the strategy of the region. This comes out plainly in the English reply to Louisbourg, the building of Halifax in 1749: the Atlantic coast of Nova Scotia was being used to gain command of the entrance to the Gulf and thence to the continent. With the taking of Louisbourg in 1758, the way lay open to Quebec and the next year Saunders's and Wolfe's army did the rest.

In the American Revolution, British naval power, based on the recent acquisitions, was adequate to prevent any threat to the St. Lawrence developing from seaward. Halifax therefore found its place as a base for operations, not to the east and the north but to the west and the south, against the Atlantic coast-line of the thirteen colonies. Since the British held New York for most of the war, it was not an advanced but a supporting base.

The last series of wars with the French, in the course of which a second was fought with the Americans, saw the fundamental elements disposed in somewhat different fashion still. As long as the United States was neutral, Halifax could be used as an assembly point, as the natural point of convergence for supplies going over from the Republic to Great Britain. In fact, except for the mechanical changes wrought by a hundred years, its role was exactly the same as during the last war. When, however, the War of 1812 began, the circumstances creating the point of convergence disappeared, and the Atlantic coast of Nova Scotia to some extent altered its functions. Halifax was still, of course, the northern base for the British fleet in North American waters, but the function of that fleet changed

---

[1] For further consideration of this see the author's "Geographical Determinants in Canadian History," in *Essays in Canadian History Presented to G. M. Wrong,* ed., R. Flenley (Toronto: Macmillan, 1938), pp. 229-52.

from commerce protection to the duties of a containing navy: in other words, it had to blockade the Atlantic coast of the United States. The remainder of the Atlantic coast of Nova Scotia and of the other Atlantic colonies fell into place as an area from which the enemy's trade and communications could be harassed by privateers.

The world war brought no new set of considerations to the surface: the approaches to the St. Lawrence were never threatened, and Halifax ended the war as it began it, a point of convergence for convoys, an extremely convenient point of departure for the shipping thronging over to British ports. Even the entrance of the United States, this time as an ally, made no essential change in the picture, though for the time being it once more restored the symmetry of the eighteenth century Atlantic ellipse.

In this second German war, the situation does not remain unchanged; new factors have potentially, if not actually, emerged. Halifax at once slips into its historic role, convoys once more enter and leave its harbour, but now owing to the victories of the Germans in Europe, thought must go beyond this relatively simple function. As long as the British barricade across the Atlantic holds, the position will be much as before. If that were to break, we would at once be precipitated into a position something like that which obtained while France still held Canada, with the important difference that instead of the English seeking to penetrate up the St. Lawrence, it might be the Germans. Defence thinking therefore goes back to the French position before the surrender of Newfoundland, 1713. France lost Canada in 1760 because from 1713 on she lost the approaches to the St. Lawrence. Canada today, the powerful Dominion, will not make that mistake a second time. Hence, not to mention our efforts to maintain our first, or trans-Atlantic line of defence, our advanced bases, the British Isles and Iceland, we have underwritten the defences of Newfoundland. No doubt, too, the old Louisbourg position, and the small islands lying just within the entrance to the Gulf, (Saint Paul Island, the Bird Rocks, Bryon Island, and the Magdalens) are not being lost sight of. It may even prove wise — though further knowledge is needed — to complement the great air base at Botwood, Newfoundland, with a patrol station on Sable Island, some 300 miles to the west-south-westward. Sable Island is 100 miles off the coast of Nova Scotia, and a flying base on it would appear to give facilities for good observation of both the length of the Nova Scotia coast and the outer approaches to the Gulf.

Another new factor lies in the Canadian-American Defence Committee and in the British grant to the United States of a base in Newfoundland. For the first time since the Seven Years' War, the whole coast of the continent is under what may rapidly become a single direction, and this time there is not the key-hole through to the interior that the French in that war had in Cabot and Belle-Isle Straits. Even supposing that Germany somehow got command of the sea, it would surely prove difficult for that country to penetrate this unbroken front.

Not even superior air power would enable her to do it, for if air power can dominate sea power in narrow waters — something not yet completely proved — it is of little avail when the scene of action is far from its bases, as a comparison of the present war in the Straits of Dover and the Mediterranean illustrates. The only way in which the Germans, or any trans-oceanic power, could get much advantage out of air power on this side of the water would be through seizing and holding a base. This base would have to be strongly held and of considerable area if it were going to be more than an annoyance — as Louisbourg once was.

If a sea campaign were ever to be fought from this side of the Atlantic, once again Halifax, while superficially altering its role, would really play the same part. It would be the main northern advanced base for American naval effort radiating out of New York, Boston, and other northern ports. An American battle squadron lying in Halifax harbour might then become a familar sight. It is only slowly that Americans, even New Englanders, are realizing the full significance of the "way down east" and discovering that "the east" does not end with Maine but stretches out another 800 miles or so into the Atlantic, to terminate at St. Johns. But American thoughts have recently gone forward with a bound, as the large amount of space devoted to Canada in American newspapers indicates, and the logic of geography is slowly making itself heard.

In the three centuries that have elapsed since they first came into the path of history, the geographical elements of the North Atlantic coast and its funnel-like opening into the interior have moulded the events that have been superimposed upon them. Sometimes the set of human action has been in one direction, sometimes in another. In this ebb and flow it is easy to see the essential nature of the great port that for two centuries has stood out so prominently in every war. Halifax is a kind of pivot from which armed action may be swung in any direction. The British first swung it up, across and into the Gulf, against the French, then down, across the routes to Boston and New York against the Americans. They bound it, as a principal centre of distribution, into the routes centring on their own islands. Today it is this again, and more; for potentially it is the centre of an arc lying both to east and west, not so much containing as excluding. Once more the Atlantic circle is complete, or virtually complete, leading from London through Newfoundland and Nova Scotia to New York and southward back again through the Bermudas. Only the Azores provide a conspicuous gap. If this circle remains complete, that will have important consequences for mankind.

It is too early yet to speculate upon those consequences, but surely the events of the last few months justify some optimism. The Ogdensburg agreement, the fifty destroyers, the American naval bases on British territory, the Canadian defence programme, at last conceived in a spirit other than that of colonial subordination, all these portend a new kind of Anglo-Saxon world. It will be a world in which Canada, the keystone of the Atlantic arch, can play a great part if she manifests the qualities that should be hers. These qualities do not consist only in manufacturing supplies or even in forming armies: they do not consist merely in industry or martial courage. Important as these things are, statesmanship, wide views, and moral courage in high places are more important. Without these our country may find itself in as uncomfortable a position as a small boy dragged along between two hurrying adults. On the other hand, with boldness, initiative, and imagination, this Dominion, though small numerically, may, thanks to its position and the energy of its people, find a proud place in world affairs.

Bibliography

The books, articles, and reviews in this bibliography are arranged in chronological order. The articles have been divided into the same categories as the essays in this volume. The bibliography has been prepared with the assistance of Mrs. Anne McDermaid, Assistant Archivist, Queen's University, Kingston, Ontario.

Books

_____ and Smith, W., trans. *Documents Relating to Canadian Currency, Exchange and Finance during the French Period.* Edited by Adam Shortt, 2 vols. Ottawa: King's Printer, 1925.

_____ and Innis, H. A., eds. *Select Documents in Canadian Economic History, 1783-1885.* Toronto: University of Toronto Press, 1933.

Settlement and the Forest Frontier in Eastern Canada. Canadian Frontiers of Settlement Series, vol. 9. Toronto: Macmillan, 1936.

_____; Coyne, J. B.; and MacFarlane, R.O. *Brief submitted to Royal Commission on Dominion Provincial Relations by the Native Sons of Canada,* December 8, 1937. Winnipeg: Albion Press, 1937.

The North American Assault on the Canadian Forest: A History of the Lumber Trade between Canada and the United States. Toronto: Ryerson Press; New Haven: Yale University Press; London: Humphrey Milford, Oxford University Press, 1938.

Canada and the Far East — 1940. I.P.R. Inquiry Series. New York: Institute of Pacific Relations, 1940. Reprint. Westport, Conn.: Greenwood Press, 1973.

Colony to Nation: A History of Canada. Toronto: Longmans, Green, 1946. 2nd and 3rd editions, 1949, 1957. 4th revised edition, 1964.

_____ and Chafe, J. W. *Canada. A Nation and How It Came to Be.* Toronto: Longmans, Green, 1948.

Canada: Nation and Neighbour. Toronto: Ryerson Press, 1952.

Unconventional Voyages. Toronto: Ryerson Press, 1953.

This Most Famous Stream: The Liberal Democratic Way of Life. Toronto: Ryerson Press, 1954. Paperback edition, 1967.

Canadians in the Making: A Social History of Canada. Toronto: Longmans, Green, 1958. "Toronto in the 1880's," excerpt from chapter 20, reprinted in *Our Century in Prose,* edited by E. H. Winter, pp. 133-38. Toronto: Macmillan, 1966.

_____ and Scott, F. R., et al. *Evolving Canadian Federalism.* Duke University Commonwealth-Studies Center Publication, no. 9. Durham, N.C.: Duke University Press; London: Cambridge University Press, 1958.

My First Seventy-Five Years. Toronto: Macmillan, 1967.
Great Britain's Woodyard: British America and the Timber Trade, 1763-1867. Montreal: McGill-Queen's Press, 1973.

Articles

HISTORICAL PAPERS — SPECULATIVE

"Determinism in Politics." *Canadian Historical Review* 27 (September 1946): 233-48.
"Why Men Fight." *Queen's Quarterly* 54 (Summer 1947): 187-200.
"Taking the Fairies out of the Woods: A Dialogue." *University of Toronto Quarterly* 16 (July 1947): 349-56.
"Time, Myth and Fact: The Historian's Commodities." *Queen's Quarterly* 64 (Summer 1957): 241-49.
"The Future of Man." *Queen's Quarterly* 68 (Winter 1962): 539-44.
"The Metropolitan and the Provincial." *Queen's Quarterly* 76 (Winter 1969): 577-90.
"Historical Perspective: Interview by Welf H. Heick." *Queen's Quarterly* 78 (Winter 1971): 518-35.
"That Humble Fellow, The Historian — Some Reflections On Writing History." *Journal of Canadian Studies* 7 (February 1972): 45-50.
"An Interview with A. R. M. Lower." In *The Craft of History,* edited by Eleanor Cook, pp. 1-43. [Toronto]: Canadian Broadcasting Corporation, 1973.

HISTORICAL PAPERS — PROFESSIONAL

"A Sketch of the History of the Canadian Lumber Trade." In *Canada Year Book,* pp. 318-23. Ottawa: King's Printer, 1925. Reprinted in Dominion Bureau of Statistics, *Forestry in Canada,* pp. 32-37. Ottawa: King's Printer, 1926.
"Credit and The Constitutional Act." *Canadian Historical Review* 6 (June 1925): 123-41.
"The Forest in New France." Canadian Historical Association. *Report* (1928): 78-90.
"Some Neglected Aspects of Canadian History." Canadian Historical Association. *Report* (1929): 65-71.
"Assault on the Laurentian Barrier 1850-70." *Canadian Historical Review* 10 (December 1929): 294-307.
"The Origins of Democracy in Canada." Canadian Historical Association. *Report* (1930): 65-70.
"The Trade in Square Timber." Toronto: Royal Canadian Institute Publications, 1932. Reprinted in *Contributions to Canadian Economics,* vol. 6, pp. 40-61. Toronto: University of Toronto Press, 1933, and in *Approaches to Canadian Economic History,* edited by W. T. Easterbrook and M. H. Watkins, Carleton Library Series, no. 31, pp. 28-48. Toronto: University of Toronto Press, 1967.
———— ed. "Edward Gibbon Wakefield and the Beauharnois Canal." *Canadian Historical Review* 13 (March 1932): 37-44.
"Three Centuries of Empire Trade." *Queen's Quarterly* 39 (May 1932): 307-25.

"Lumbering." In *Encyclopedia of Canada,* edited by W. S. Wallace, vol. 4, pp. 142-48. Toronto: University Associates of Canada, 1936.

"From Huskisson to Peel: A Study in Mercantilism." Royal Society of Canada. *Proceedings and Transactions,* 3rd series 31 (1937): section 2, 51-68 Reprinted in *Essays in Modern English History in Honour of Wilbur Cortez Abbott,* pp. 381-404. Cambridge, Mass.: Harvard University Press, 1941.

"The Product of Revolutions: Basic Factors in English History." Canadian Historical Association. *Report* (1938): 31-40.

"Geographical Determinants in Canadian History." In *Essays in Canadian History Presented to George Mackinnon Wrong,* edited by R. Flenley, pp. 229-52. Toronto: Macmillan, 1938.

The Development of Canadian Economic Ideas. A Supplement to J. F. Normano. *The Spirit of American Economics: A Study in the History of Economic Ideas in the United States prior to the Great Depression.* Committee on the Study of Economic Thought. Studies in the History of Economic Thought, vol. 1. Toronto: Longmans, Green, 1943.

"Two Ways of Life: The Primary Antithesis in Canadian History." Canadian Historical Association. *Report* (1943): 5-18. Also published in *University of Toronto Medical Journal* 22 (October 1944): 28-38. Reprinted in *Approaches to Canadian History,* pp. 15-28. Toronto: University of Toronto Press, 1967.

"Religion and Religious Institutions." In *Canada,* edited by G. W. Brown, pp. 457-83. Berkeley and Los Angeles: University of California Press; Toronto: University of Toronto Press, 1950. Reprinted, 1953.

"Political 'Partyism' in Canada." Canadian Historical Association. *Report* (1955): 88-95.

"Professor Webb and 'The Great Frontier' Thesis." In *The New World Looks at Its History,* edited by A. R. Lewis and T. F. McGann, pp. 142-54. Austin: University of Texas Press, 1963.

"Loring Christie and the Genesis of the Washington Conference of 1921-1922." *Canadian Historical Review* 47 (March 1966): 38-48.

"Metropolis and Hinterland." *South Atlantic Quarterly* 70 (Summer 1971): 386-403.

VALUES

"Calling Our Souls Our Own." *Listening Post,* May 1925, pp. 9-10, 24.

"Our Present Discontents." *Dalhousie Review* 13 (April 1933): 97-108.

"Colonialism and Culture." *Canadian Forum* 14 (April 1934): 264-65.

"Democracy and Parliament." *Dalhousie Review* 14 (April 1934): 5-15.

"Our Shoddy Ideals." *Maclean's,* 1 November 1937, pp. 24, 39-40.

"The Social Sciences in the Post-War World." *Canadian Historical Review* 22 (March 1941): 1-13.

"Canada and a Free Society: Liberalism, Its Nature and Prospects." Ontario Educational Association. *Annual Report* (1948): 68-75.

"Liberalism in Canada." In *Canada Looks Ahead: A Series of Addresses and Papers...,* pp. 151-71. Ottawa: Tower Books, 1948.

"The Essence of Liberalism." *Winnipeg Free Press,* 11 June 1948. Reprinted in *Winnipeg Free Press* pamphlet no. 20, May-July 1948, pp. 11-13.

"Our 'Target' for Population." *Financial Post,* 25 November 1950.

"The Time for Decision." *Country Guide,* March 1951, pp. 7, 91.

"I Came Back and I Am Content; editorial." *Maclean's,* 1 July 1951, pp. 2, 47-48.

"No Class in Canada?" *Saturday Night,* 12 July 1952, pp. 9, 18-19.

"The Massey Report." *Canadian Banker* 59 (Winter 1952): 22-32.

"This Question of Canadian Culture." *Queen's Commerceman,* Winter 1952, pp. 11-12.

"Conservatism: The Canadian Variety." *Confluence* 2 (December 1953): 72-82.

"Is Distrust of Ability Formula for Success?" *Saturday Night,* 23 April 1955, pp. 7-8.

"Canada and the Future." *Saturday Night,* 21 January 1956, pp. 9-10.

"Speaking to Each Other." Royal Society of Canada. *Proceedings and Transactions,* 3rd series, 56 (1962): 69-80.

"Canadian Values and Canadian Writing." *Mosaic* 1 (October 1967): 79-93.

NATIONALISM

"Nationalism and Peace." *The School* 3 (May 1915): 613-16.

"Canada — A Motherland." *Dalhousie Review* 6 (January 1927): 440-50.

"A Five-Year Plan for Canada." *Winnipeg Free Press,* 10 December 1932, magazine section, p. 1.

"In Unknown Quebec." *University of Toronto Quarterly* 6 (October 1936): 89-102.

"A Canadian Perspective." *Manitoban,* 10 November 1936, p. 1.

"The King and the Crown." In *Manitoba Essays,* edited by R. C. Lodge, pp. 122-41. Toronto: Macmillan, 1937.

"Canadian Unity and Its Conditions." Introduction to *Problems in Canadian Unity,* edited by Violet Anderson, pp. 1-21. Toronto: Nelson's, 1938.

"Bonnie Chairlie's Gone Awa'." *Canadian Forum* 19 (April 1939): 6. Reprinted in *Our Sense of Identity,* edited by Malcolm Ross, pp. 161-63. Toronto: Ryerson Press, 1954.

"Pitfalls for Canadian Freedom." *Events,* April 1939, pp. 263-68.

"French Canada and the World of Business." In *Réalizations canadiennes françaises,* pp. 20-23. Winnipeg: University of Manitoba published broadcasts, 1941, Also published in *La Liberté,* Winnipeg, 1 January 1941, p. 7.

"Our Democratic Institutions." *Dalhousie Gazette,* 10 January 1941.

"Towards a Canadian National Spirit." *The Native Son,* 31 March 1941, p. 7.

"The World Tomorrow." *Winnipeg Free Press,* 3 April 1941.

"Introduction: The Problem of Reconstruction." In *War and Reconstruction: Some Canadian Issues,* edited by A. R. M. Lower and J. F. Parkinson, pp. v-viii. Toronto: Ryerson Press, 1942.

"Why Canada Fights." *The Native Son,* January 1942, p. 1.

"What Ought to Be Done with Our Japanese ... (a) Native-born, (b) Others?" *Financial Post,* 21 March 1942.

"National Policy ... Revised Version." *Manitoba Arts Review* 3 (Spring 1943): 5-14.

"A New Community of Mankind." *Country Guide,* May 1946, pp. 5, 49-50.

Foreword to *The Land and the People of Canada,* by Frances A. Ross, pp. v-vi. Portraits of the Nation Series. Toronto: Longmans, Green, 1947.

"July First, 1867: The First Dominion Day." *Saturday Night,* 28 June 1947, pp. 28-29.

"If We Joined the U.S.A." *Maclean's,* 15 June 1948, pp. 7-8, 71-74.

"What This Country Needs Is Ten New Provinces." *Maclean's,* 15 October 1948, pp. 7, 77-79.

[Upper, L. E. G., pseud.] "Let's Move Our Mountains." *Saturday Night,* 27 December 1949, p. 25.

"Canada, 1925-1950." *United Church Observer,* 1 June 1950, pp. 9, 33.

"Mr. King." *Canadian Banker* 57 (Autumn 1950): 46-55.

"What is Democracy?" and "How to Maintain Democracy." *Winnipeg Free Press,* 7, 13 November 1950.

"Are There Canadians?" *Saturday Night,* 28 June 1952, pp. 1, 17-18.

"The Crown in Canada." *Canadian National Magazine,* June 1953, pp. 4-5, 13. Reprinted in *Queen's Review,* January 1954, pp. 3-10, 18.

"The Question of Private T. V." *Queen's Quarterly* 60 (Summer 1953): 170-80.

"She's Our Queen, Too!" *New Liberty,* June 1953, p. 33.

"The Survival Value of a Soft Nation." *Saturday Night,* 31 October 1953, pp. 7-8.

"Canadians,; 'Good Second Bests,'" *New Liberty,* November 1953, pp. 25, 63, 65-66, 68.

"The Question of National Television." *Canadian Forum* 34 (March 1955): 274-75.

"Arguments Against Going to the Dogs." *Saturday Night,* 1 October 1955, pp. 7-8.

"The Forest: Heart of a Nation." *Canada Month,* November 1963, pp. 21-23. Reprinted in *Canadian Reflections,* edited by P. G. Penner and J. McGechaen, pp. 260-66. Toronto: Macmillan, 1964.

"The Flag Issue Sums Up Our Whole Historical Experience." *Montreal Star,* 11 July 1964.

"Canada at the Turn of the Century, 1900." *Canadian Geographical Journal* 71 (July 1965): 2-13.

"Public Parks before Private Property on Canada's Lakeshores." *Commentator,* October 1966, pp. 24-25.

"'British North America' in the 1860's." In *Canada One Hundred, 1867-1967,* pp. 6-14. Ottawa: Queen's Printer, 1967.

"Factors in Confederation." In *Canada One Hundred, 1867-1967,* pp. 15-19. Ottawa: Queen's Printer, 1967.

"Centennial Ends: Centennial Begins." *Queen's Quarterly* 74 (Summer 1967): 236-47.

"Canada 100: A New Nation Fighting for Survival 1870-1900." *Winnipeg Free Press,* Centennial Edition, 1 July 1967.

"Agitation: The Struggle for Self-Rule." *Imperial Oil Review,* July 1967, pp. 24-63.

"Ontario — Does it Exist?" *Ontario History* 60 (June 1968): 65-69.

BICULTURALISM

"Two Nations or Two Nationalities?" *Culture* 4 (December 1943): 470-81.

"Bilingualism in Canada's History." *Ottawa Citizen,* 19, 20, 21 February 1963.

"How to Make the New Canada: Extend Canadians' Rights to Be French across Canada." *Maclean's,* 8 February 1964, pp. 26, 36.

"Bilingualism: A Mystification." Kingston *Whig Standard,* 14 March 1964.
"Would Canada Be Better Off without Quebec?" *Maclean's,* 14 December 1964, pp. 27, 51-52.

CIVIL LIBERTIES

"Wartime Democracy in Canada." *New Republic* 102 (15 April 1940): 503.
————; Lapp, J. A. S.; and Wirth, L. "Civil Liberties and the Fifth Column." *The University of Chicago Round Table* 121 (7 July 1940).
"Some Reflections on a Bill of Rights." *The Fortnightly Law Journal* 16 (15 February and 1 March 1947): 216-18; 234-37.
"Two Ways of Life: The Spirit of Our Institutions." *Canadian Historical Review* 28 (December 1947): 383-400.
"The French Origins of English Civil Liberty." *Culture* 9 (March 1948): 18-28. Reprinted in *As a Man Thinks,* edited by E. Morrison and W. Robbins, pp. 131-43. Toronto: Gage, 1953.
"Brief to the Committee of the Senate on Human Rights." In Canada, Parliament, Senate, *Proceedings of the Special Committee on Human Rights and Fundamental Freedoms,* pp. 311-25. Ottawa: King's Printer, 1950.
"Whence Cometh Our Freedom." *Food for Thought* 11 (February 1951): 5-12.
"So This Is a Free Country, Is It?" *New Liberty,* May 1953, pp. 15, 92-95.
"Our Heritage of Liberty." Broadcast on C.B.C., 28, 29, 31 March and 1 April 1955.
"Is the RCMP a Threat to Our Liberty?" *Maclean's,* 6 July 1957, pp. 8, 57-58.
"The Bill of Rights: The War Measures Act 'an inquitous piece of legislation.'" *Canadian Commentator,* March 1959, pp. 2-3.
"Testimony." In Canada, Parliament, House of Commons, Special Committee on Human Rights and Fundamental Freedoms, *Proceedings,* pp. 312-37. Ottawa: Queen's Printer, 1960.
Letter to Editor re RCMP on Campus. Kingston *Whig Standard,* 18 December 1962.
"Lower on Liberty." *Canada Month,* June 1963, p. 26.

IMMIGRATION AND POPULATION

"Immigration and Settlement in Canada, 1812-1820." *Canadian Historical Review* 3 (March 1922): 37-47.
"The Exodus to the United States: Is It Real or Imaginary?" Toronto *Globe,* 22 May 1924.
"New France in New England." *New England Quarterly* 2 (April 1929): 278-95.
"The Growth of the French Population of Canada." Canadian Political Science Association. *Proceedings* (1930): 35-47.
"The Case Against Immigration." *Queen's Quarterly* 37 (Summer 1930): 557-74.
"Can Canada Do Without the Immigrant?" *Maclean's,* 1 June 1930, pp. 3-4, 70-71.
"The Growth of Canada's Population in Recent Years." *Canadian Historical Review* 13 (December 1932): 431-35.

"Why Immigration Plans Fail." *Country Guide,* September 1937, pp. 7, 45-46.
[Attributed to A. R. M. Lower.] "Canada: I. Immigration: A Negative View. II. Another View of Immigration." *Round Table* 29 (March 1939): 398-411.
"Myth of Mass Immigration." *Maclean's,* 15 May 1949, pp. 16, 69-71.
"How Large a Population for 1975?" *Financial Post,* 25 November 1950.
"The Growth of Population in Canada." In *Canadian Population and Northern Colonization,* edited by V. W. Bladen, *Studia Varia* of the Royal Society of Canada, no. 7, pp. 43-68. Toronto: University of Toronto Press, 1962.

EDUCATION

"Paying for Higher Education." *Winnipeg Free Press,* 31 October 1931.
"Why Write Essays?" *Manitoban,* 25 September 1936, p. 2, 6.
"Social Sciences in Canada." *Culture* 3 (December 1942): 433-40.
"Reconstruction in the Light of the Last Twenty-five Years." Manitoba Educational Association Convention. *Report* (July 1943): 69-71.
"A Bright Future for a Dull Subject." *Manitoba Arts Review* 3 (Fall 1943): 10-21.
_____ contributor. *Rapport du Comité des manuels d'histoire du Canada.* Montreal: La Société canadienne d'éducation, 1946.
"In Quest of Social Science Material." Canadian Library Association. *Bulletin* (February 1947): 57-58.
"Does Our Education Educate?" *Maclean's,* 15 November 1948, pp. 9, 72-76.
Contribution to "Opinions d'historiens anglo-canadiens 'Pour ou contre le manuel d'histoire unique?'" *L'Action Nationale,* May 1950, pp. 354-58.
"The Importance of History." *Canadian School Journal,* August-September 1952, p. 262.
"The Canadian University." Royal Society of Canada, *Proceedings and Transactions,* 3rd series, 47 (1953): section 2, 1-16.
"Uses and Abuses of Universities." *Saturday Night,* 25 April 1953, pp. 7-8.
"High School Weak Link in Educational System." *Saturday Night,* 11 September 1954, pp. 7-8.
"Canadian University: Time for a New Deal." *Queen's Quarterly* 62 (Summer 1955): 243-56.
"Education in a Growing Canada." In *Canadian Education Today,* edited by Joseph Katz, pp. 1-13. Toronto: McGraw-Hill, 1956.
"How Good Are Canadian Universities?" Canadian Association of University Teachers. *Bulletin* 11 (November 1962): 4-11.
"Queen's, Yesterday and Today." *Queen's Quarterly* 70 (Spring 1963): 69-75.
"Administrators and Scholars." *Queen's Quarterly* 71 (Summer 1964): 203-13.
"The Uncomfortable Lecturn." *Commentator,* February 1969, pp. 14-15.
"Once Again: The Uncomfortable Lecturn." *Commentator,* July-August 1969, pp. 15-16.

EXTERNAL RELATIONS

"The Evolution of the Sentimental Idea of Empire: A Canadian View." *History* n.s. 11 (January 1927): 289-303.

"Foreign Policy and the Empire: A Canadian View." *The Nineteenth Century and After* 114 (September 1933): 257-64.

"Europe, War and Canada." *'Toba'* 1 (March 1934): 16-17.

"Is There an Empire Foreign Policy?" *International Affairs* 13 (September 1934): 746-47.

"Says Canada's Foreign Policy Should Keep Her Free of Entanglements." *The Native Son,* December 1934, p. 1.

"Foreign Policy and Canadian Nationalism." *Dalhousie Review* 15 (April 1935): 29-36.

"The Social and Economic Bases of Canadian Foreign Policy." In *Canada, The Empire and the League,* pp. 100-111. Toronto: Nelson's, 1936.

"General and Specific Aspects of Canadian Foreign Policy." In *Canada, the Empire and the League,* pp. 145-54. Toronto: Nelson's, 1936.

"Foreign Policy in the Far East." Conference on Canadian-American Affairs. *Proceedings,* pp. 212-14. Boston: Ginn and Co., 1936.

"Canada and War in the Pacific." In Canadian Papers, Yosemite Conference, 1936, vol. 4, paper 14, pp. 96-120. Toronto: Canadian Institute of International Affairs, [1936].

————, with Frank, Solomon; McWilliams, R. F.; and Tarr, E. J. "A Policy of Isolation for Canada: Is it Practicable? Is it Desirable?" *Interdependence* 13 (1936): 13-31. Also published by the League of Nations Society in Canada in their National Study Project, 1935-36, of Radio Broadcasts.

Address to the 14th Annual Conference of the League of Nations Society in Canada. *Interdependence* 13 (1936): 191-95.

"Canada and the League: How Far Should Canada Go?" *Country Guide,* January 1936, pp. 10, 26-27.

"Canada and the Americas." *Dalhousie Review* 17 (April 1937): 17-21.

"External Policy and Internal Problems." *University of Toronto Quarterly* 6 (April 1937): 326-37.

"This Island Nation." *Canadian Defence Quarterly* 14 (April 1937): 306-10.

"Canada Can Defend Herself." *Canadian Forum* 17 (January 1938): 341-44.

"America and the Pacific." *Dalhousie Review* 18 (April, 1938): 45-49.

[Marsden, A. R., pseud.] "The European Minuet." *Winnipeg Free Press,* 10 May 1938.

"Motherlands." *Dalhousie Review* 18 (July 1938): 143-48.

"The Defence of the West Coast." *Canadian Defence Quarterly* 16 (October 1938): 32-38.

"National Interests in the Pacific: American and Canadian." Conference on Canadian-American Affairs. *Proceedings,* pp. 105-26. Boston: Ginn and Co., 1939.

"Canada and the New World Order." *Canadian Forum* 19 (May 1939): 44-46.

"The United States through Canadian Eyes." *Quarterly Journal of InterAmerican Relations* 1 (July 1939): 104-11.

"Canada and Foreign Policy." *Queen's Quarterly* 47 (Winter 1940): 418-27.

"Canada Now Centre of U.S. — Empire Defence." *Financial Post,* 31 August 1940.

"The Maritimes as a Strategic Point in North America." *Public Affairs* 4 (December 1940): 57-60.

"Canada's New American Relationships." *The Native Son,* January 1941, p. 9.

"The Canadian-American Defence Agreement and Its Significance." *Round Table* 31 (March 1941): 347-57.

"Rampart of the East: Newfoundland Today and Tomorrow." *Winnipeg Free Press,* 18, 20 October 1941.

"Canada's Foreign Policy." *New Commonwealth Quarterly* 7 (April 1942): 271-80.

"Newfoundland in North Atlantic Strategy." *Foreign Affairs* 20 (July 1942): 767-70.

"Commonwealth Policy." *The Native Son,* January 1944, p. 10.

Canada as a Pacific Power. Canadian Wartime Information Board. Canadian Affairs Pamphlets, 1, no. 13 (November 1943). Canadian edition also published as 1, no. 4 (March 1944).

"The Commonwealth in the Post-War World." *Country Guide,* April 1944, pp. 9, 50-52.

"Canada and the Pacific after the War." Ninth Conference of the Institute of Pacific Relations. Canadian Papers, no. 2. Toronto: Canadian Council, Institute of Pacific Relations (Canadian Institute of International Affairs), 1945.

"Transition to Atlantic Bastion." In *Newfoundland,* edited by R. A. MacKay, pp. 484-508. Toronto: Oxford University Press, 1946.

"Canada, the Second Great War, and the Future." *International Journal* 1 (April 1946): 97-111.

"World Organization or Else!" *Manitoba School Journal* 8 (May 1946): 6-7.

"Canada — Next Belgium?" *Maclean's,* 15 December 1947, pp. 9, 51-53.

"Canada in the New, Non-British World." *International Journal* 3 (Summer 1948): 208-21.

"U.S. Revisited: Some New Comparisons." *Saturday Night,* 24 December 1955, p. 9.

"Some Angry Home Thoughts from Abroad." *Maclean's,* 13 February 1960, pp. 10, 51-52.

"Canada in World Affairs." In *The Decisive Years,* edited by S. M. Philip, pp. 4-8. Toronto: Barker Publishing Company, 1965.

"Canada and the United States." *Contemporary Review,* May 1970, pp. 242-45.

MISCELLANEOUS

_____, with Melvill, C. D.; and Comeau, N. A. "Reports on Fisheries Investigations in Hudson and James Bay and Tributary Waters in 1914." Department of the Naval Service. *Annual Report* for the fiscal year ending March 13, 1914, Appendix. Ottawa: King's Printer, 1915.

"Extracts from the log of...." *The Sailor,* November 1919, p. 12.

"Two Christmas Nights Afloat." *The Sailor,* December 1919, p. 22.

_____ ed. *Bulletin,* nos. 1-6. Cambridge, Mass.: Business Historical Society, June 1926 to March-April 1927.

"The Business Historical Society." *Industry,* 25 December 1926, p. 5.

"Paddling Your Own Canoe." *The New Outlook,* n.s., 18 May 1932, p. 469.

"How to Win the Election." *Winnipeg Free Press,* 12 October 1935.

"Quebec City Today." *Saturday Night,* 8 August 1936, p. 5.

[Marsden, A. R., pseud.] "The British Whirligig." *Canadian Forum* 18 (September 1938): 171-73.

"Sir John A. Macdonald." *Dalhousie Review* 19 (April 1939): 85-90.

"A Half-Forgotten Builder of Canada (William Hamilton Merritt)." *Queen's Quarterly* 46 (Summer 1939): 191-97. Reprinted in *Canadian Portraits,* edited by R. G. Riddell. Toronto: Oxford, 1940.

————— ed. "An Unpublished Letter of Daniel Webster." *New England Quarterly* 12 (June 1939): 360-64.

"Conscription of Wealth." *Country Guide,* November 1939, pp. 12, 60-61.

"Sir John Macdonald in Caricature." Canadian Historical Association. *Report* (1940): 56-62.

"Light." *Saturday Night,* 10 February 1940, pp. 6, 9.

"Lohengrin and the Conservative Party." *Canadian Forum* 22 (February 1943): 327-28.

"The First and Second Empires: A Comparison." *The Native Son,* October 1943, p. 2.

"By River to Albany." *The Beaver,* Outfit 275 (June 1944): 16-19.

"The Forest Industry and Lumbering in Nova Scotia about 1840." *Halifax Chronicle,* 18 October 1944.

"Canadian Equation" *Canadian Forum* 24 (February 1945): 257.

"Premier King Out — Then What?" *Financial Post,* 31 January 1948.

[Upper, L. E. G., pseud.] "Animals and the Class War." *Saturday Night,* 28 February 1948, p. 29.

"Historian Sees History Made: Here's Some Advice for Political Conventions." *Financial Post,* 14 August 1948.

"Imperialism or Metropolitanism?" In *Nehru Adhimdan Granth: A Birthday Book,* pp. 403-6. Calcutta: 1949.

[Upper, L. E. G., pseud.] "Square on the Hypotenuse." *Saturday Night,* 4 January 1949, p. 19.

"Europe Is Still Alive." *Queen's Quarterly* 57 (Spring 1950): 1-20.

"Germany Revisited." *International Journal* 5 (Spring 1950): 141-62.

"Reginald George Trotter." Royal Society of Canada. *Proceedings and Transactions,* 3rd series, 45 (1951): 119-20.

"Germany Looks to the West." *Saturday Night,* 3 April 1951, pp. 9, 11.

"The Mariposa Belle." *Queen's Quarterly* 58 (Summer 1951): 220-26.

"On the Hope Report." *United Church Observer,* 1 August 1951, p. 9.

"The West and Western Germany." *International Journal* 6 (Autumn 1951): 300-307.

"Trans-Canada Crossing." *The Native Son,* October 1951, pp. 1, 12-15.

"Lake Freighter." *Queen's Quarterly* 58 (Winter 1951-52): 508-14. Reprinted in *Saturday Night,* 17 May 1952, pp. 12, 30-31, and in *Unconventional Voyages,* pp. 123-29. Toronto: Ryerson Press, 1953.

"How I Heard the News: Two Wars and a Peace." *Queen's Quarterly* 59 (Spring 1952): 32-38.

"People of the Prairies: Seeing the Pacific from Winnipeg." *Saturday Night,* 5 July 1952, pp. 11, 20.

"The Adam Shortt Notebooks in the Douglas Library." *Queen's Review,* October 1952, pp. 182-85.

"Harold Adams Innis, 1894-1952." Royal Society of Canada. *Proceedings and Transactions,* 3rd series, 47 (1953): 89-90.

"Lumberjack's River." *Queen's Quarterly* 60 (Spring 1953): 24-40.

"Keep the Farmers off the Farms." *Saturday Night,* 26 March 1955, p. 13.

"Our Elderly Adolescents." *Saturday Night,* 28 May 1955, pp. 31-32.

"The Simple Men." *The Beaver,* Outfit 286 (Autumn 1955): 16-19.

[Fly, G. D., pseud.] "One View of Progress." Kingston *Whig Standard,* 1 May 1956.

"Collins Bay United Church Found Too Small for Growing Population of Neighbourhood." Kingston *Whig Standard,* 2 June 1956.

"Present Collins Bay Church Built by Volunteer Labour." Kingston *Whig Standard,* 8 June 1956.

"Some Reflections on Kingston's Architecture." *Historic Kingston,* 1957, pp. 3-12.

"Pearson and the Mantle of Laurier." *Canadian Commentator,* February 1958, p 3.

"Beginning of a New Political Era." *Canadian Commentator,* May 1958, pp. 3-4.

"A New Book That Challenges Our Myths [Excerpts from *Canadians in the Making*]." *Maclean's,* 2 August 1958, pp. 12-13, 35-39.

"The Gods Canadians Worship." *Maclean's,* 25 October 1958, pp. 22-23, 66-74.

"'Udawah's Stream': The Ottawa River." *Queen's Quarterly* 66 (Summer 1959): 203-16.

"Canadian Historian A. R. M. Lower Introduces South African Historian Arthur Keppel-Jones." *Maclean's,* 8 October 1960, p. 19.

"The Social Responsibilities of the Business Man." *The Business Quarterly,* University of Western Ontario, Winter 1962, pp. 11-16.

Letter on Roman Catholicism. *United Church Observer,* 1 March 1963, p. 2.

"Do Citizens Want a Parkway?" Kingston *Whig Standard,* 23 May 1963.

"Mr. Lesage's Eye Is on the Goose." Kingston *Whig Standard,* 4 April 1964.

"The Quinte Parkway." *Park News,* November 1965, pp. 14-16.

_____ ed. "Three Letters of William Osgoode, First Chief Justice of Upper Canada." *Ontario History* 57 (December 1965): 181-87.

"Loyalist Cities: Saint John, New Brunswick and Kingston, Ontario." *Queen's Quarterly* 72 (Winter 1965-1966): 657-64.

"Is Canada a Christian Country?" *United Church Observer,* January 1967, p. 5.

"Great Britain Today." *Queen's Quarterly* 75 (Summer 1968): 208-21.

"Three Ojibway Folk Tales." As told by Paul Michel of the Lake Nipigon Ojibways. *Queen's Quarterly* 75 (Winter 1968): 584-91.

"Adam Shortt, Founder." *Historic Kingston,* January 1969, pp. 3-15.

"The United Empire Loyalists." *Loyalist Gazette,* Spring 1969, pp. 9-12.

"My Recollections of the West [1925-1945]." Canadian Historical Association. *Historical Papers* (1970): 19-29.

"Townsman and Countryman." *Dalhousie Review* 50 (Winter 1970-71): 480-87.

"Arthur Leonard Phelps, 1887-1970." Royal Society of Canada. *Proceedings and Transactions,* 4th series, 9 (1971): 93-96.

Introduction to *History of the Settlement of Upper Canada,* by W. Caniff. Canadiana Reprint Series of Rare Books. Belleville: Mika Studio, 1971.

"History As Pageant." *Dalhousie Review* 54 (Spring 1974): 1-15.

Reviews

Toombs, Lawrence C. *The Port of Montreal.* In *Canadian Historical Review* 8 (September 1927): 266-67.

Cowan, Helen I. *British Emigration to British North America, 1783-1837.* In *Canadian Historical Review* 9 (March 1928): 70-72.

Wrong, G. M. *The Rise and Fall of New France.* In *The Nation* 128 (6 March 1929): 288, 290.

"Canada and the Problems of the World's Population and Migration Movements." Review article in *Canadian Historical Review* 12 (March 1931): 55-59.

Hutchins, Fred H. *The Colonial Land and Emigration Commission.* In *Canadian Historical Review* 13 (March 1932): 64-65.

Wade, Mason. *The Overlanders of '62.* In *North Dakota Historical Quarterly* 7 (January and April 1933): 179-80.

Wittke, Carl. *A History of Canada.* In *The Annals of the American Academy of Political and Social Science* 172 (March 1934): 183.

Davis, B. P. and C. L. Davis. *The Davis Family and the Leather Industry.* In *Canadian Historical Review* 16 (June 1935): 210.

Woods, R. G. *A History of Lumbering in Maine, 1820-61.* In *New England Quarterly* 9 (March 1936): 157-58.

Wood, Richard. *A History of Lumbering in Maine, 1820-61,* and A. G. Hempstead. *The Penobscot Boom and the Development of the West Branch of the Penobscot River for Log Driving.* In *Canadian Historical Review* 17 (June 1936): 209-10.

Jessup, P. and F. Deak, eds. *Neutrality: Its History, Economics and Law.* In *International Affairs* 16 (May 1937): 447-49.

Kuczynski, Robert. *Population Movements*; A. M. Carr-Saunders. *World Population: Past Growth and Present Trends*; M. C. Maclean. *Analysis of the Stages in the Growth of Population in Canada*; M. R. Davie. *World Immigration, with Special Reference to the United States*; and D. R. Taft. *Human Migration: A Study of International Movements.* In *Canadian Historical Review* 18 (December 1937): 428-39.

Schott, Carl. *Landnahme und Kolonisation in Kanada am Beispiel Südontarios.* In *Canadian Journal of Economics and Political Science* 3 (November 1937): 584-85.

Brebner, J. B. *The Neutral Yankees of Nova Scotia: A Marginal Colony during the Revolutionary Years.* In *New England Quarterly* 10 (December 1937): 798-99.

Creighton, D. G. *The Commercial Empire of the St. Lawrence, 1760-1850.* In *Canadian Historical Review* 19 (June 1938): 207-10.

Young, Charles H. and Helen R. Y. Reid. *The Japanese Canadians*; L. E. Law; J. A. Corey; F. A. Knox: A. E. Prince; and C. A. Curtis. *Live and Learn: 5 Political Creeds*; F. H. Soward. *Moulders of National Destiny*; and Harold Macmillan. *Economic Aspects of Defence.* In *Dalhousie Review* 19 (July 1939): 261-63.

"Robert Laird Borden: His Memoirs." In *Public Affairs* 2 (June 1939): 180-84.

Eliot, G. F. *The Ramparts We Watch.* In *Pacific Affairs* 12 (September 1939): 318-20.

Saunders, S. A. *Studies in the Economy of the Maritime Provinces.* In *Canadian Historical Review* 20 (December 1939): 437-38.

Fraser, I. F. *The Spirit of French Canada; A Study of the Literature.* In *New England Quarterly* 13 (September 1940): 571-72.

Macdonald, N. *Canada, 1763-1841, Immigration and Settlement*; J. Hedges. *Building the Canadian West*; and G. Britnell. *The Wheat Economy.* In *Political Science Quarterly* 55 (September 1940): 463-66.

"The Defence of Canada." Review of C. P. Stacey. *The Military Problems of Canada: A Survey of Defence Policies and Strategic Conditions, Past and Present.* In *University of Toronto Quarterly* 10 (January 1941): 239-41.

Smith, R. A. *Our Future in Asia,* and W. C. Johnson. *The United States and Japan's New Order.* In *Pacific Affairs* 14 (March 1941): 122-24.

Poole, T. *A Sketch of the Early Settlement and Subsequent Progress of the Town of Peterborough* .... In *Canadian Journal of Economics and Political Science* 8 (February 1942): 137.

Burt, A. L. *A Short History of Canada for Americans.* In *Canadian Historical Review* 23 (September 1942): 327-28.

Coyne, F. B. *Cooperage Industry: The Development of The Cooperage Industry in The United States.* In *Journal of Economic History* 2 (1942): 110.

Hutchins, J. G. B. *The American Maritime Industries and Public Policy, 1789-1914: An Economic History.* In *Canadian Journal of Economics and Political Science* 8 (November 1942): 612-15.

Klingberg, F. J. *The Morning of America.* In *North Dakota Historical Quarterly* 10 (January 1943): 53-54.

Pritchett, J. P. *The Red River Valley, 1811-49.* In *The Beaver,* Outfit 274 (June 1943): 50.

Long, M. H. *A History of the Canadian People. I. New France.* In *Canadian Historical Review* 24 (September 1943): 304-6.

Albion, Robert G. and J. B. Pope. *Sea Lanes in Wartime: The American Experience, 1775-1942.* In *Canadian Historical Review* 24 (September 1943): 421-22.

Hughes, E. C. *French Canada in Transition.* In *Canadian Journal of Economics and Political Science* 10 (February 1944): 99-101.

Soward. F. H. *Twenty-Five Troubled Years, 1918-1943.* In *International Affairs* 20 (July 1944): 412-14.

Brynes, A. *Revolution Comes of Age.* In *Canadian Forum* 24 (September 1944): 142.

"The Little Emperor." Review of A. S. Morton. *Sir George Simpson: Overseas Governor of the Hudson's Bay Company.* In *The Beaver,* Outfit 275 (September 1944): 48-49.

Ryerson, S. B. *French Canada: A Study in Canadian Democracy.* In *Canadian Journal of Economics and Political Science* 10 (November 1944): 529.

Johnsen, Julia. *Canada and the Western Hemisphere.* In *Canadian Forum* 24 (December 1944): 219.

Williamson, H. F., ed. *Growth of the American Economy.* In *Journal of Economic History* 4 (November 1944): 240-41.

Tansill, Charles C. *Canadian-American Relations, 1875-1911.* In *Canadian Historical Review* 25 (December 1944): 449-51.

Graham, Gwethalyn. *Earth and High Heaven,* and Hugh MacLennan. *Two Solitudes.* In *Canadian Historical Review* 26 (September 1945): 326-28.

Chow, S. R. *Winning the Peace in the Pacific: A Chinese View of Far Eastern Postwar Plans* .... In *Canadian Journal of Economics and Political Science* 11 (November 1945): 646-47.

Calvin, D. D. *A Saga of the St. Lawrence: Timber and Shipping Through Three Generations.* In *Journal of Economic History* 6 (November 1946): 225.

Lingard, C. *Territorial Government in Canada.* In Toronto *Globe and Mail,* 28 October 1946.

Fahrni, Margaret Morton and W. L. Morton. *Third Crossing: A History of the First Quarter Century of the Town and District of Gladstone in the Province of Manitoba.* In *Canadian Historical Review* 27 (December 1946): 440.

Innis, H. A. *Political Economy in the Modern State.* In Toronto *Globe and Mail,* 4 January 1947, p. 8.

McInnis, E. *The War: Sixth Year.* In *Canadian Forum* 27 (October 1947): 165-66.

Liberman, S. *Building Lenin's Russia.* In *Journal of Economic History* 7 (November 1947): 258-59.

Allen, J. G. *Editorial Opinion in the Contemporary British Commonwealth and Empire.* In *American Historical Review* 53 (January 1948): 379-80.

Masters, D. C. *Rise of Toronto, 1850-1890.* In *Queen's Quarterly* 55 (Spring 1948): 90-91.

Taylor, G. *Our Evolving Civilization: An Introduction to Geo-Pacifics*; D. L. Sturzo. *Nationalism and Internationalism*; F. S. Northrop. *The Meeting of East and West: An Inquiry Concerning World Understanding*; B. Russell. *Philosophy and Politics*; and W. C. Graham, ed. *Education and the New Age.* In *International Journal* 3 (Spring 1948): 261-63.

Davidson, W. H. *William Davidson, 1740-1790: An Account of the Life of William Davidson, Otherwise John Godsman of Banffshire and Aberdeenshire in Scotland and Miramichi in British North America.* In *Canadian Historical Review* 29 (September 1948): 311-12.

Neff, E. *The Poetry of History: The Contribution of Literature and Literary History to the Writing of History since Voltaire.* In *Queen's Quarterly* 55 (Autumn 1948): 350-51.

Kennedy, Howard, commissioner. *Report of the Ontario Royal Commission on Forestry.* In *Canadian Journal of Economics and Political Science* 14 (November 1948): 507-10.

Wade, Mason, ed. *The Journals of Francis Parkman.* In *Queen's Quarterly* 55 (Winter 1948): 495-98.

Jones, R. L. *History of Agriculture in Ontario, 1613-1880.* In *American Historical Review* 54 (January 1949): 418-19.

Bishop, M. *Champlain: The Life of Fortitude.* In *Queen's Quarterly* 56 (Autumn 1949): 435-36.

McIlwraith, T. F. *The Bella Coola Indians.* In *Queen's Quarterly* 56 (Autumn 1949): 439-40.

McInnis, E. and J. H. S. Reid. *The English-Speaking Peoples: A Modern History.* In *Queen's Quarterly* 56 (Autumn 1949): 464.

Rich, E. E., ed. *Part of Dispatch from George Simpson ...*; H. A. Innis, ed. *The Diary of Simeon Parkins, 1766-1780*; E. E. Rich, ed. *Minutes of the Hudson's Bay Company, 1679-1684*; and E. E. Rich, ed. *Copy Book of Letters Outward,*

May 29, 1680-July 5, 1687. In *Queen's Quarterly* 56 (Autumn 1949): 432-34.

Hardy, H. R. *Mackenzie King of Canada: A Biography,* and A. Meighen. *Unrevised and Unrepented: Debating Speeches and Others.* In *Canadian Historical Review* 31 (September 1950): 309-11.

Meinecke, F. *The German Catastrophe: Reflections and Recollections,* and L. B. Namier. *Europe in Decay: A Study in Disintegration, 1936-1940.* In *Queen's Quarterly* 57 (Autumn 1950): 399-402.

Sanderson, C. R., ed. *The Arthur Papers ... Papers Mainly Confidential, Private and Semi-official. ... Part II.* In *Queen's Quarterly* 57 (Autumn 1950): 404-5.

MacLeod, M. A., ed. *The Letters of Letitia Hargrave.* In *Queen's Quarterly* 57 (Autumn 1950): 405-6.

Spitz, D. *Patterns of Anti-Democratic Thought: An Analysis and a Criticism, with Special Reference to the American Mind in Recent Times.* In *Queen's Quarterly* 57 (Autumn 1950): 410-11.

Ramsey, R. W. *Henry Ireton.* In *Queen's Quarterly* 57 (Winter 1950-51): 570-71.

Mitchell, R. J. and M. D. R. Leys. *A History of the English People.* In *American Historical Review* 56 (April 1951): 639-40.

Hutchison, Bruce. *The Fraser.* In *Queen's Quarterly* 58 (Spring 1951): 113-14.

Carrington, C. E. *The British Overseas: Exploits of a Nation of Shopkeepers.* In *International Journal* 6 (Summer 1951): 244-46.

LeBourdais, D. M. *Canada's Century.* In *Canadian Forum* 31 (September 1951): 136.

Glazebrooke, G. P. de T. *A Short History of Canada.* In *Canadian Forum* 31 (October 1951): 162.

Royal Commission Studies: A Selection of Essays Prepared for the Royal Commission on National Development in the Arts, Letters, and Sciences. In *Canadian Historical Review* 32 (December 1951): 381-83.

Gillis, D. H. *Democracy in the Canadas, 1759-1867.* In *Canadian Journal of Economics and Political Science* 18 (February 1952): 114.

Timlin, M. F. *Does Canada Need More People?* In *Queen's Quarterly* 59 (Summer 1952): 236-38.

Rich, E. E., ed. *James Isham's Observations on Hudson's Bay, 1743,* and *Notes and Observations on a Book Entitled a Voyage to Hudson's Bay in the Dobbs Galley, 1749.* In *Queen's Quarterly* 59 (Autumn 1952): 412-13.

Putnam, D. F. (ed.), B. Brouillette, D. P. Kerr, and J. L. Robinson. *Canadian Regions: A Geography of Canada.* In *Queen's Quarterly* 59 (Winter 1952-1953): 519-20.

Hutchison, Bruce. *The Incredible Canadian: A Candid Portrait of Mackenzie King: His Works, His Times, and His Nation.* In *Queen's Quarterly* 59 (Winter 1952-1953): 560-63.

Chapman, L. J. and D. F. Putnam. *The Physiography of Southern Ontario.* In *Queen's Quarterly* 59 (Winter 1952-1953): 520-22.

Brunet, M. *Histoire du Canada par les textes.* In *Canadian Historical Review* 34 (March 1953): 58.

Angus, H. F. *Canada and the Far East, 1940-53.* In *Canadian Historical Review* 35 (June 1954): 154-55.

Canada: Nation on the March. In *Canadian Historical Review* 35 (December 1954): 352-53.

Gilmour, G. P., ed. *Canada's Tomorrow: Papers and Discussions*.... In *International Journal* 9 (Autumn 1954): 314-15.

Toynbee, A. J. *The World and the West.* In *International Journal* 9 (Winter 1954): 54-55.

The Colonial and Imperial Conferences from 1887 to 1937. In *Canadian Bar Review* 33 (May 1955): 619-21.

"A Critique of Toynbee's *Study of History*" [vols. VII-X]. In *Canadian Forum* 35 (August 1955): 103-5.

Farr, D. M. L. *The Colonial Office and Canada 1867-1887.* In *Canadian Bar Review* 34 (March 1956): 353-55.

Rich, E. E., ed. *John Rae's Correspondence with the Hudson's Bay Company on Arctic Exploration, 1844-55.* In *Queen's Quarterly* 63 (Autumn 1956): 452-53.

Innis, H. A. *The Codfisheries: The History of an International Economy.* In *Queen's Quarterly* 63 (Spring 1956): 156-57.

Mann, W. E. *Sect, Cult, and Church in Canada.* In *Canadian Historical Review* 37 (June 1956): 185-86.

Sharp, P. F. *Whoop-up Country: The Canadian-American West, 1865-1885.* In *World Affairs Quarterly* 27 (October 1956): 300-301.

Barraclough, Geoffrey. *History in a Changing World.* In *Queen's Quarterly* 64 (Winter 1957-1958): 612-13.

Banks, M. A. *Edward Blake, Irish Nationalist: A Canadian Statesman in Irish Politics, 1892-1907.* In *Canadian Journal of Economics and Political Science* 24 (May 1958): 285-86.

Kohr, L. *The Breakdown of Nations.* In *Queen's Quarterly* 65 (Spring 1958): 134-35.

Soward, F. H. and E. McInnis. *Canada and the United Nations.* In *Canadian Historical Review* 39 (June 1958): 157-58.

Walsh, H. H. *The Christian Church in Canada.* In *Canadian Historical Review* 39 (September 1958): 251-52.

"Monument amid the Tombstones." Review article on R. MacGregor Dawson. *William Lyon Mackenzie King: A Political Biography, 1874-1923.* In *Queen's Quarterly* 66 (Spring 1959): 146-50.

Gowans, A. *Looking at Architecture in Canada.* In *Queen's Quarterly* 66 (Spring 1959): 152-53.

McGovern, W. M. *Radicals and Conservatives.* In *Canadian Journal of Economics and Political Science* 25 (August 1959): 379-80.

Rich, E. E., ed. *The History of the Hudson's Bay Company, 1670-1870. Volume 1, 1670-1763.* In *Queen's Quarterly* 66 (Autumn 1959): 483.

Brunet, M. *La Presence anglaise et les Canadiens: Études sur l'histoire et la pensée des deux Canadas.* In *Queen's Quarterly* 66 (Winter 1959-1960): 681-82.

Talman, J. J., ed. *Basic Documents in Canadian History.* In *Canadian Forum* 39 (August 1959): 117.

Bertrand, J. P. *Highway of Destiny.* In *Queen's Quarterly* 66 (Winter 1959-1960): 682.

"Sound of Battles Long Ago." Review of F. H. Underhill. *In Search of Canadian Liberalism.* In *Saturday Night,* 10 December 1960, pp. 56-58.

"Mackenzie King through his Diaries." Review article on J. W. Pickersgill. *The*

Mackenzie King Record, Vol. I, 1939-44. In *Queen's Quarterly* 68 (Spring 1961): 169-73.

Cowan, H. I. *British Emigration to British North America: The First Hundred Years.* In *Canadian Journal of Economics and Political Science* 28 (August 1962): 444-45.

McDougall, R. L., ed. *Our Living Tradition.* In *Canadian Historical Review* 44 (March 1963): 48-49.

McGregor, F. A. *The Fall and Rise of Mackenzie King: 1911-1919.* In *Queen's Quarterly* 70 (Summer 1963): 298-99.

"Lawrence H. Gipson and the First British Empire: An Evaluation." Review article in *Journal of British Studies* 3 (November 1963): 57-78.

Beal, John R. *The Pearson Phenomenon.* In *Winnipeg Free Press,* 4 April 1974.

"An Emigrant Looks Back." Review of J. K. Galbraith. *The Scotch.* In *Tamarack Review* 33 (Autumn 1964): 98-102.

Schmeiser, D. A. *Civil Liberties in Canada.* In *Canadian Historical Review* 46 (March 1965): 51-52.

Porter, J. *The Vertical Mosaic: An Analysis of Social Class and Power in Canada.* In *Canadian Historical Review* 47 (June 1966): 158-61.

Gilbert, H. *Awakening Continent: The Life of Lord Mount Stephen. Volume I, 1829-91.* In *American Historical Review* 71 (July 1966): 1474-75.

Preston, R. A. *Canada and "Imperial Defense": A Study of the Origins of the British Commonwealth's Defense Organization, 1867-1919.* In *Queen's Quarterly* 74 (Autumn 1967): 555-56.

Pickersgill, J. W. and D. F. Foster. *The Mackenzie King Record. Vol. II. 1944-45.* In *Queen's Quarterly* 76 (Summer 1969): 346-49.

Clark, S. D. *The Developing Canadian Community.* In *Queen's Quarterly* 76 (Autumn 1969): 549-50.

Lumsden, Ian. *Canadian and U.S. Relations.* In *Globe Magazine,* 4 April 1970.

"Andy McNaughton: Crusading Canadian." Review article on John Swettenham. *McNaughton.* In *Queen's Quarterly* 77 (Winter 1970): 681-23.

Speaight, Robert. *Vanier, Soldier, Diplomat and Governor General: A Biography.* In *Queen's Quarterly* 77 (Winter 1970): 637.

Index